Gluten-Free
ALL-IN-ONE
FOR DUMMIES®
A Wiley Brand

by Ian Blumer, MD, FRCPC,
Sheila Crowe, MD, FRCPC, FACP, FACG, AGAF,
Danna Korn, Linda Larsen,
Dr. Jean McFadden Layton, Nancy McEachern,
Connie Sarros

FOR DUMMIES®
A Wiley Brand

Gluten-Free All-in-One For Dummies®

Published by: **John Wiley & Sons, Inc.,** 111 River Street, Hoboken, NJ 07030-5774, www.wiley.com

Copyright © 2015 by John Wiley & Sons, Inc., Hoboken, New Jersey

Published simultaneously in Canada

For general information on our other products and services, please contact our Customer Care Department within the U.S. at 877-762-2974, outside the U.S. at 317-572-3993, or fax 317-572-4002. For technical support, please visit www.wiley.com/techsupport.

Wiley publishes in a variety of print and electronic formats and by print-on-demand. Some material included with standard print versions of this book may not be included in e-books or in print-on-demand. If this book refers to media such as a CD or DVD that is not included in the version you purchased, you may download this material at http://booksupport.wiley.com. For more information about Wiley products, visit www.wiley.com.

Library of Congress Control Number: 2015937167

ISBN: 978-1-119-05244-9

ISBN 978-1-119-05244-9 (pbk); ISBN 978-1-119-05251-7 (ebk); ISBN 978-1-119-05253-1 (ebk)

Manufactured in the United States of America

10 9 8 7 6 5 4 3 2 1

Contents at a Glance

Recipes at a Glance

Pies and Cakes 461

Table of Contents

· ·

Introduction

· ·

Not so many years ago, the gluten-free lifestyle was reserved for an obscure cluster of people who were forced to settle for wannabe foods that resembled sawdust but didn't taste as good.

Today, the gluten-free lifestyle is sweeping the world with the force of a really big blowtorch, and the ramifications are enormous. Gluten-free products abound (and are a far cry from the foods people used to choke down), labels are far less ambiguous, and people no longer look at you like you have four heads when you ask for a burger without the bun.

Being gluten-free isn't about being on a diet. It's about living a lifestyle. Whether you've been gluten-free for decades or are only considering the idea of giving up gluten, this book is loaded with information that can affect every aspect of your life, from the obvious — your health and how you shop, cook, and eat — to more subtle facets, like minimizing expenses, socializing, dealing with friends and family, and managing various emotional ups and downs. This book is the reference guide you need to help you with all those aspects. It's your reference for living — and loving — a gluten-free lifestyle.

About This Book

Gluten-Free All-in-One For Dummies, like all *For Dummies* books, is divided up so you don't have to read it all at once, or even front to back, if you don't want to. You can skip from B to R to A and even reread B if you want. You can read it sideways and standing on your head, if you'd like; all you have to do is find a section you're interested in and dig in (how's *that* for liberating?).

Peruse the table of contents and see which chapter or subject really floats your boat, and start there. Or you can flip through the book and see which of the headings catches your interest.

If you're new to the gluten-free lifestyle and have tons of questions, you're probably best off starting at Book I, Chapter 1 and working your way through most of the book in order. But do what you feel. Really.

Finally, one important note: It should go without saying that you'll want to make sure to choose gluten-free ingredients when making the recipes in this book. So, for example, when we call for bread, we mean the gluten-free kind, and when we call for nonstick cooking spray, make sure to find a gluten-free version (because cooking spray can, believe it or not, contain gluten).

Icons Used in This Book

To make this book easier to navigate, the following icons help you find key information about the gluten-free lifestyle and gluten-free cooking.

This icon indicates practical information that can help you in your quest for improving health and fitness, adopting a gluten-free diet, or making one of the recipes.

When you see this icon, you know that the information that follows is important enough to read twice!

This icon highlights information that may be detrimental to your success or physical well-being if you ignore it.

This icon gives you a heads-up that what you're reading is more in-depth or technical than what you need to get a basic grasp on the main topic at hand.

Beyond the Book

In addition to all the material and recipes you can find in the book you're reading right now, this product also comes with some access-anywhere goodies on the web. Check out the eCheat Sheet at www.dummies.com/cheatsheet/glutenfreeaio for helpful insights and pointers on satisfying your sweet tooth for gluten-free success, the lowdown on converting any recipe to gluten-free, and some advice on testing for celiac disease. Get even more info about the gluten-free lifestyle at www.dummies.com/extras/glutenfreeaio.

Where to Go from Here

This book is organized so you can read it in the way that makes the most sense to you; feel free to jump around to the information that's most relevant to you right now. You can use the table of contents to find the broad categories of subjects or use the index to look up specific information.

Do you want to know more about the great reasons to go gluten-free? Start with Chapter 2 of Book I. Want information about how to get through the grocery store without going astray from your lifestyle? Head over to Book II, Chapter 3. Feeling hungry and want to get started on the recipes? Feel free to jump right into the recipes in Books III through V.

And if you're not sure where to begin, read Book I. It gives you the basic information you need to understand why and how eating and living gluten-free can help you improve your health and quality of life.

Book I

Getting Started with Going without Gluten

getting started
with

Going
without
Gluten

Visit www.dummies.com for free access to great Dummies content online.

Contents at a Glance

Chapter 1

Gluten-Free from A to Z: The Basics of Being Gluten-Free

In This Chapter

▶ Getting a grip on gluten

▶ Discovering the advantages of a gluten-free lifestyle

▶ Making the most of meals

▶ Losing the gluten and loving the lifestyle

▶ Taking your gluten-free self out into the world without cheating

*Y*ou may not be feeling it, but you're lucky to be looking into the gluten-free lifestyle now, when you're much less likely to receive a quizzical look when you ask questions about food. It wasn't long ago that people hearing about gluten would ask whether you meant glucose and finding gluten-free products on typical grocery shelves was the stuff of science fiction.

These days, gluten-free-ness is one of the fastest-growing nutritional movements in the world — and for a lot of good reasons. People everywhere are feeling healthier, more energetic, and finding relief from a range of illnesses and discomforts, like celiac disease and even menopausal symptoms. This chapter gives you a basic rundown of what living gluten-free is all about.

What Is Gluten, Anyway, and Where Is It?

Gluten has a couple definitions; one is technically correct but not commonly used, and the other is commonly used but not technically correct. For the purposes of most of this book, here's the common definition: *Gluten* is a mixture of proteins in wheat, rye, and barley. Oats don't have gluten but may be contaminated by having been processed on the same equipment as gluten-containing grains, so they're forbidden on a strict gluten-free diet, too.

You can find lots of information about what you can and can't eat in Chapter 4 of Book I, as well as a detailed listing of safe and forbidden ingredients at www.celiac.com or other websites. But you need to have a general idea of what kinds of foods have gluten in them so you know what to avoid. Foods with flour in them (white or wheat) are the most common culprits when you're avoiding gluten. The following are obvious gluten-glomming foods:

- ✔ Bagels
- ✔ Beer
- ✔ Bread
- ✔ Cookies, cakes, and most other baked goods
- ✔ Crackers
- ✔ Pasta
- ✔ Pizza
- ✔ Pretzels

But along with these culprits come not-so-obvious suspects, too, like licorice, most cereals, and some natural flavorings. When you're gluten-free, you get used to reading labels, calling manufacturers, and digging a little deeper to know for sure what you can and can't eat.

You have to do without those foods, but you really don't have to do *without*. There's a subtle but encouraging difference. Food manufacturers make delicious gluten-free versions of just about every food imaginable these days. You find out more about those options and where to buy them in Book II, Chapter 3.

You may see lots of labels proudly declaring a product to be wheat-free (some of which, like spelt and kamut, aren't really wheat-free at all). When something says it's wheat-free, it doesn't mean the food is gluten-free.

Gluten is in wheat, but it's also in rye and barley — and most people don't eat oats on the gluten-free diet, either. So something can be wheat-free but still have other gluten-containing ingredients, like malt, which is usually derived from barley. In that case, the product is wheat-free but not gluten-free.

Anyone who's spent more than a day on planet Earth has been barraged with messages hailing the virtues of wheat — especially in its whole form. Wheat and other grains hog most of the food pyramid(s), suggesting you should eat gobs of it, and it's touted as a good source of fiber and nutrients. Wheat does provide some health benefits, but you can find those benefits in other food sources, too. So how can wheat be at the root of so many health problems?

For three reasons, wheat may not be the key to perfect dietary health:

- ✔ **Wheat was invented yesterday.** Wheat wasn't introduced until the Agricultural Revolution, about 10,000 years ago — that's yesterday, evolutionarily speaking. Before that, people ate lean meats, fish, seafood, nonstarchy vegetables, berries, and fruits. When wheat came on the scene, it was completely foreign.

- ✔ **Humans don't fully digest wheat.** Human bodies have to adapt in order to tolerate wheat, and lots of people don't tolerate it well at all. Most humans have only one stomach — and one just isn't enough to digest wheat. Cows have four stomachs (actually, four chambers within one stomach). That's why Bessie the Bovine does okay with wheat. The wheat goes from one stomach to another and another and — well, you get the picture. By the time it reaches tummy number four, it's fully digested and Bessie's feeling fine.

- ✔ **Wheat contributes to leaky gut (Z is for *zonulin*).** When people eat wheat, they produce extra amounts of a protein called *zonulin.* The lining of the small intestine is basically a solid wall of cells that most materials can't pass through on their own. On the lining of the small intestine, zonulin waits for nutrients to come along. When important vitamins and minerals are present, zonulin tells the passageways in the intestinal wall to open so those nutrients can pass into the bloodstream. The blood then carries the nutrients to other parts of the body.

  When some people eat wheat, they produce too much zonulin and the gates open too wide. All sorts of stuff gets into the bloodstream, some of which, like toxins, shouldn't be there. This increased permeability of the lining of the small intestine, or *leaky gut syndrome,* can cause lots of different health issues.

Discovering the Benefits of a Gluten-Free Lifestyle

The gluten-free lifestyle isn't about your diet. Sure, this book talks about food, but the diet itself takes up only a few pages. Being gluten-free involves a lot more than just cutting gluten out of your diet. It affects every aspect of your life, from how you communicate and with whom, to how you handle ordering at restaurants, attending social functions, and dealing with emotional challenges.

It's important to take control of your diet — or, if it's your kids who are gluten-free, help them gain and retain control. Going gluten-free also gives you an opportunity to reach out and help others who may be embarking upon the wonderful world of gluten freedom, as well as a chance to discover more about nutrition and what you're actually putting into your body on a daily basis. If that sounds like a lot of work, relax. You hold in your very hands the book that guides you through it. And not only can you feel better, but you also can feel better about yourself!

You have lots of company. The gluten-free movement is sweeping the nation for plenty of reasons, but the one that stands out is that when people give up gluten, they often feel better. This section tells you what the gluten-free diet can do for your body — the benefits you can enjoy in addition to all the emotional perks of the lifestyle.

People today live in a quick-fix, panacea-pursuing, pill-popping, make-me-better-fast society, and if they see promise of a quick way to fix what's ailin' them, they're buyin' it. Changing both your diet and your lifestyle is neither quick nor easy, but the benefits of going gluten-free can be fantastic — no surgery or medication required!

Eating isn't supposed to hurt

Food is fuel — it's supposed to give you energy and make you feel good, not make you hurt. But when you eat things that your body doesn't like for some reason, it has a sometimes not-so-subtle way of telling you to knock it off. Food that your body objects to can cause gas, bloating, diarrhea, constipation, and nausea — and even symptoms that don't seem to be associated with the gastrointestinal tract, like headaches, fatigue, depression, joint pain, and respiratory distress.

Luckily, when you figure out which foods your body doesn't approve of, you can stop eating them, and then your body stops being so pouty. In fact, if you feed it right, your body can make you feel great in lots of different ways.

Abstinence makes the gut grow stronger

When gluten is making you sick, nasty battles are going on inside your gut. Hairlike structures called *villi* line your small intestine. The job of the villi

Book I

Getting
Started
with Going
without
Gluten

is to increase the surface area of the small intestine so it can absorb more nutrients. Villi protrude (picture fingers sticking up) so that they have more surface area to absorb important nutrients.

For people who have gluten intolerance, the body sees gluten as a toxin and attacks the gluten molecule. In doing so, it also inadvertently attacks the villi, and those villi get blunted and shortened, sometimes to the extreme of becoming completely flat. This attack can reduce their ability to absorb nutrients — sometimes dramatically.

Blunted and flat villi can't absorb stuff so well, so those good-for-ya nutrients just slide right by and you don't get enough of the important vitamins, minerals, and other nutrients that are vital for good physical and emotional health. You may develop what's called *malabsorption* and become poorly nourished.

Don't worry! This story has a happy ending. Your villi are tenacious little things, and when you quit eating gluten, they begin to heal right away. Before you know it, your villi grow back and absorb nutrients again, and your health is fully restored. In other words, abstinence makes the gut grow stronger.

By the way, *lactase,* which is the enzyme that breaks down the sugar lactose, is produced in the tip of the villi. When the villi get blunted, sometimes your ability to digest lactose decreases and you become lactose intolerant. When you quit eating gluten and the villi heal, you may be able to tolerate dairy foods again.

Making nutrition your mission: Head-to-toe health benefits

Twelfth-century physician Maimonides said, "Man should strive to have his intestines relaxed all the days of his life." No doubt! When your intestines aren't relaxed — or when they're downright edgy or uptight — they affect all your other parts, too. It's kind of like when you're in a really good mood and your best friend is grumpy — the situation can make you grumpy, too; one cantankerous intestine can be a buzz-kill for the entire body.

In a way, the body's reaction to gluten doesn't compute. For some people, eating gluten can cause headaches, fatigue, joint pain, depression, or infertility; at first, those types of symptoms may seem unrelated to something going on in your gut, much less something you eat — much less something as common in your diet as wheat.

But those problems — and about 250 others — are symptoms of celiac disease and gluten sensitivity. People with celiac disease or gluten sensitivity do sometimes have gastrointestinal symptoms, but more often the symptoms are *extraintestinal,* meaning they take place outside the intestinal tract.

If your body has problems with gluten, the gluten-free diet may help relieve lots of symptoms, such as these:

- Fatigue
- Gastrointestinal distress (gas, bloating, diarrhea, constipation, vomiting, heartburn, and acid reflux)
- Headaches (including migraines)
- Inability to concentrate
- Weight gain or weight loss
- Infertility
- Joint, bone, or muscle pain
- Depression and anxiety
- Respiratory problems

The list's impressive, isn't it? The idea that eliminating one thing from your diet — gluten — could improve so many different conditions is almost hard to believe. Yet it's true — and it really makes sense when you realize that if the food you're eating is toxic to your body, your body's going to scream in lots of different ways.

In people with gluten intolerance, eating gluten may make the symptoms of some psychiatric conditions worse. Some of the most fascinating findings recently indicate that removing gluten from the diet can improve behaviors of people with these conditions:

- Autism
- Schizophrenia and other mood disorders
- Attention-deficit (hyperactivity) disorder (ADD/ADHD)

Millions of people have wheat *allergies,* which are different from gluten sensitivity or celiac disease — and they, too, improve dramatically on a wheat-free/gluten-free diet.

But beyond the obvious improvement you enjoy if you have an intolerance, other conditions and symptoms can improve on a wheat-free diet, such as PMS and menopausal symptoms. Eliminating wheat may even slow or reverse the signs of aging, reducing wrinkles and improving the tone and texture of skin.

Deciding Whether You Should Be Gluten-Free

Many people who go gluten-free do so not because they have any of the conditions listed in this section, but because they're striving for a healthier lifestyle.

The authors of this book believe gluten isn't good for anyone (more on that in Chapter 2 of Book I), especially in the highly refined form that most people know, like bread, bagels, and pasta. Cutting wheat and other gluten-containing grains out of your diet certainly isn't a bad thing and can have significant health benefits if you eat a wholesome, diverse diet. Heck, it can even be the key to maintaining your weight!

Maybe you'll find it compelling to adopt a gluten-free lifestyle when you realize that the gluten-free diet may relieve or even completely alleviate certain health problems. (The earlier section "Making nutrition your mission: Head-to-toe health benefits" lists the conditions exacerbated by gluten.)

This isn't a diet du jour. We realize that new diets pop up faster than celebrity babies with odd names, and that the diets last about as long as the celebrity marriages do. This is a lifestyle. It's a lifestyle that's perfectly in sync with the way our bodies were designed to eat — and that's why it's so effective in improving our health.

Our bodies weren't designed to eat that junk listed in the "Common foods that contain gluten" section. Bagels? Cereal? Pasta? We don't *think* so! Our bodies can rebel against those foods in ways that can sometimes severely compromise our health, and for many people, the gluten-free diet is the best — sometimes the only — treatment.

Chapter 2 of Book I explains more about gluten's effect on the body. For extensive, detailed information about the many medical conditions that benefit from a gluten-free diet, see the companion book to this one, *Living Gluten-Free For Dummies* (Wiley).

Mastering the Meals

This book is about a lifestyle, not a diet. But no matter where that lifestyle takes you — eating in, eating out, attending social events, choosing, planning, shopping, preparing — being gluten-free all comes down to one thing: food.

If you're a culinary hacker and you're afraid you'll have to wake up at 4 a.m. to bake gluten-free bread and make pasta from scratch, turn off the alarm and go back to sleep. Plenty of gluten-free specialty foods are available to take the place of all your old favorites. Better yet (from a health standpoint), you're likely to find that those foods become less important to you. And considering that they're really not very good for you, that's a good thing.

Whether you're a kitchenphobe or a foodie, living a gluten-free lifestyle offers you an enormous selection of foods and ingredients to choose from.

Planning and preparing

Putting together smart and healthful gluten-free meals is a lot easier if you plan ahead. Walking through a store, perusing restaurant menus, or (gasp!) sitting in a bakery with a growling tummy isn't exactly conducive to making good food choices.

Give yourself a healthy advantage by planning and even preparing meals in advance, especially if your busy schedule has you eating away from home frequently. If you know you'll be pressed for time at breakfast or lunch, make your meals the night before, and bring healthful gluten-free snacks in resealable plastic bags.

One of the coolest things about adopting a new dietary lifestyle is exploring new and sometimes unusual or unique foods. You may never have heard of lots of gluten-free foods and ingredients, many of which not only are gluten-free and delicious but also are nutritional powerhouses. With the new perspective on food that the gluten-free lifestyle can offer you, you may find yourself inspired to think outside the typical menu plan, exploring unique and nutritious alternatives.

Shopping shrewdly

The healthiest way to enjoy a gluten-free lifestyle is to eat things you can find at any grocery store or even a farmer's market: meat, fish, seafood, fruits, and nonstarchy vegetables (see Book II, Chapter 3 for more tips on shopping). If you want to add canned, processed, and even junk foods to your shopping list, you can still do most of your shopping at a regular grocery store, and you can even buy generics.

If you hope to enjoy the delicious gluten-free specialty products that are available these days, you can find them in health food aisles or at health food stores or specialty shops. Or you can shop in your jammies on one of the many Internet sites specializing in gluten-free products.

Considering your kitchen

For the most part, a gluten-free kitchen looks the same as any other kitchen — without the gluten, of course. You don't need to go out and buy special gadgets and tools, and with only a couple exceptions, which we cover in Book II, Chapter 2, you don't need two sets of pots, pans, utensils, or storage containers, either.

If you're sharing a kitchen with gluten, you need to be aware of some contamination issues so you don't inadvertently *glutenate* (contaminate with gluten) a perfectly good gluten-free meal. Keeping your crumbs to yourself isn't just a matter of hygiene, but it can mean the difference between a meal you can eat and one you can't.

Some people find having separate areas in the pantry or cupboards for their gluten-free products helpful. This idea is especially good if you have gluten-free kids in the house, because they can see that you always have on hand lots of things for them to eat, and they can quickly grab their favorite gluten-free goodies from their special area.

Cooking outside the recipe box

Give someone a recipe, you feed 'em for a meal. Show them how to make *anything* gluten-free, and you feed 'em for a lifetime. The point is, you can make anything gluten-free, and you're not constrained by recipes or the fact that you can't use regular flour or breadcrumbs. All you need is a little creativity and some basic guidelines for using gluten-free substitutions, which you can find in Chapter 4 of Book II.

If you're a die-hard recipe fan, never fear — you find all kinds of recipes in Books III through V. Most of them are super simple to follow but leave your guests with the impression that you spent all day in the kitchen (and being thus indebted, they may volunteer to do the dishes).

Getting Excited about the Gluten-Free Lifestyle

Most people who embark on a gluten-free lifestyle are doing so because of health issues — and that means they have little or no choice in the matter. When people are forced to make changes in their routine, especially changes that affect what they can and can't eat, they're not always so quick to see the joy in the adjustments.

If you're a little gloomy about going gluten-free, you aren't alone. But prepare yourself to read about the scores of reasons to be excited about the gluten-free lifestyle (for you impatient types, feel free to skip to Chapter 6 of this Book for a jump-start on the "Kumbaya" side of being gluten-free).

"A" is for adapting your perspective on food

If you've been eating gluten for a long time — say, for most of your life — then giving up foods as you know them may seem like a tough transition at first. Besides the obvious practical challenges of learning to ferret out gluten where it may be hidden, you have to deal with emotional, physical, social, and even financial challenges.

You have to do only one thing to learn to love the gluten-free lifestyle, and that's to adjust your perspective on food just a tinge. You really don't have to give up anything; you just have to make some modifications. The foods that used to be your favorites can still be your favorites if you want them to be, just in a slightly different form.

Or you may want to consider what may be a new and super-healthful approach for you: eating lean meats, fresh fruits, and nonstarchy vegetables. Again, you may have to tweak your perspective a bit before the diet feels natural to you, but it is, in fact, natural, nutritious, and naturally nutritious.

Savoring gluten-free flavors

People who are new to the concept of being gluten-free sometimes comment that the diet is boring. When we ask what they're eating, their cuisine routine usually centers on carrots and rice cakes. Who wouldn't be bored with that? That type of a diet is appalling, not appealing.

A healthful, gluten-free diet doesn't have to be boring or restrictive. You're not constrained to eating 32 individual portions of fruits and vegetables each day, like a rabbit nibbling nervously on carrots. If you enjoy bland foods, snaps for you. But if you think gluten-free has to be flavor-free, you're in for a pleasant surprise.

Getting out and about

You don't have to let the gluten-free lifestyle hold you back from doing anything you want to do. Well, okay, there are some things you can't do — like eat a pizza from the place around the corner or devour a stack of gluten-laden donuts. But as far as your activities and lifestyle are concerned, you can — and should — get out and about as you always have.

For the most part, ordering out isn't as easy as walking into a restaurant and asking for a gluten-free menu. But eating at restaurants is definitely doable, and getting easier every day; you just need to learn to special order, tune in to contamination concerns, and ask — chances are getting better all the time that they may actually have a gluten-free menu. Traveling is a breeze when you master eating at restaurants (and get a handle on language considerations, if you're traveling abroad). Going to social events just requires a little advance planning, and holidays may barely faze you after you get the hang of going out in gluten-free style. Chapter 6 of Book I gives you more information on being gluten-free when you're out and about.

Raising kids to love the lifestyle

Lots of ideas are key in raising happy, healthy, gluten-free kids. Some of the highlights include giving them control of their diet from day one, always having yummy gluten-free treats on hand, reinforcing the benefits of the gluten-free lifestyle (if you need some crib notes, see Chapter 6 of Book I), and remembering that they're learning how to feel about the lifestyle from *you*. Promoting an optimistic outlook can instill a positive approach in them.

By the time your kids are teens, they should be in full control of the diet. The most you can do is help them understand the diet and, just as important, the implications if they choose not to follow it. Young adults away from home at college have a huge advantage these days, as many colleges and universities now feature and highlight gluten-free menu options.

Kids are flexible and resilient. Adopting a new lifestyle is usually harder for the parents than for the child.

Setting realistic expectations

Setting reasonable expectations for what life will be like after you adopt a gluten-free lifestyle is important because you *will* encounter challenges and you need to prepare to handle them well. Friends, family, and loved ones may not understand. They may not accommodate your diet when you hope or expect they will. You may find social events to be overwhelming at first, or you may get confused or frustrated and feel like giving up on the diet. You can overcome these trials and emerge stronger for them.

This book is the resource you need — wade your way through it, and dog-ear the pages you want to come back to when you need some practical or emotional reminders for how to deal with difficult issues. If you have an optimistic but realistic approach, you'll encounter fewer obstacles along the way.

Arming yourself with good information

The good news is that because the gluten-free diet is exploding in popularity, you can find lots of information about it. The bad news is that not all of that information is accurate.

Be leery of what you hear and read, and check the reliability of the source on everything. If you find conflicting information — and you will — dig deeper until you find out which source is right. Just remember to keep a skeptical eye out for the good, the bad, and the completely ludicrous.

Surviving Social Situations

Eating away from home and entertaining guests at your place can be intimidating when you're on a restricted diet, but you really can do it successfully! All it takes is a few supplies and an adventurous attitude. And with some easy food-preparation techniques, whipping up a delicious and satisfying meal — even for people who can eat anything — is no trouble at all.

Fortunately, gluten-free eating is popular. Most people have heard of the gluten-free diet, and many restaurants are prepared to accommodate you. So surviving social situations on a gluten-free diet may not be as tough as you fear.

Informing family and friends

Book I

Getting
Started
with Going
without
Gluten

You probably know how annoying it is to hang out with people who never do what you want to do or eat where you want to eat and constantly try to change the plans of the group. But that doesn't need to describe you just because you need to avoid gluten.

One of the first ways for you to set the stage for social survival is to tell your family and friends about the limitations of your gluten-free diet. Be specific but brief about what you can and can't eat. If someone asks for information about gluten or your new diet, feel free to share the basics in a positive light. No need for tons of detail on personal health issues or a lecture on the evils of gluten. If no one asks, assume people aren't interested in making it a topic of discussion.

 Some people may feel you're judging them when you decide not to eat something they do, so try not to dwell on things you've read that led you to trying a gluten-free diet or on the ills of wheat in the modern diet. And don't expect your friends and family to adopt your new gluten-free lifestyle or even remember what you can eat. You may be lucky enough to have people around who want to go the extra mile for you, but that has to be their choice, not your demand.

Use these tips to be an upbeat gluten-free diner:

- ✔ Asking if something contains gluten is very important because you can't tell by looking. Ask, "Can you tell me if this contains gluten?" If it does, just skip it. No need for a big explanation. If the person you're talking to doesn't know what gluten is, your best bet might be to talk with the manager.

- ✔ Avoid saying, "I can't eat that." Just say, "No thanks," when offered a gluten-containing item.

- ✔ Don't pout or complain if there's nothing you can eat at that moment. You can always eat before or after an event.

- ✔ Always be prepared with a protein bar or snack in your car or backpack.

- ✔ Avoid discussing diet or digestion issues during a meal!

- ✔ Don't generalize why everyone should go gluten-free.

Successfully cohabitating with people who don't share your gluten-free lifestyle requires a bit of organization and communication. Here are a few simple ideas to help you keep your environment safe and your roommate relations strong:

- ✔ Be kind and specific about your expectations of cooking and cleaning procedures. Reassure roomies that you're not limiting what they can prepare, just asking that they keep things clean.

✔ Keep your foods and preparation items as separate from others' as possible.

✔ Clean your kitchen well daily.

✔ If you find your frustration level rising because of lack of cooperation on the part of your roommates, take on kitchen duty yourself.

If you're gluten-free because of celiac disease, gluten sensitivity, or serious allergies, avoiding cross-contamination with gluten-containing foods and kitchen gadgets is critical. Keep a chart of who's supposed to clean the kitchen each day if necessary, but make sure it actually gets done — every day. See Chapter 2 of Book II for tips on organizing and setting up a shared kitchen and details on avoiding cross-contamination.

Going out on the town

Venturing out of the house on a gluten-free diet doesn't need to be daunting. Gluten-free eating is much more popular and understood now than it was even a couple of years ago. A little preparation goes a long way toward triumphant gluten-free dining and travel. This section offers tips on ordering at a restaurant and finding gluten-free food when traveling.

Eating at restaurants

Every day it seems like a new chain or local eatery is announcing a gluten-free menu. But menu or not, you can find great gluten-free food choices almost anywhere.

When dining out, ask questions every time. Does the server know what gluten is? Does the restaurant have a gluten-free menu? Will the chef come out to speak with you about how to prepare your meal? If you feel uncomfortable with the answers you receive, then take your business elsewhere. Making sure your meal is gluten-free takes some effort, but you can enjoy eating at restaurants that accommodate your needs.

Another bonus: When you ask questions, you help increase awareness of gluten intolerance! And hopefully this results in more food choices for everyone in the future.

Here are some suggestions for making your restaurant experience a little easier:

✔ **Check out the menu ahead of time.** If you know where you're dining, check the restaurant's website. Restaurants often have menus online; if not, then call and ask before you go.

Book I

Getting
Started
with Going
without
Gluten

- ✔ **Narrow down your choices.** At the restaurant, find two or three dishes that look good to you and that seem "safe" (no obvious gluten) and ask the server for details. Don't expect the server to spend time going over the entire menu with you. It's easier and safer to have him check on just a few dishes than, say, all the salads offered by the place.

- ✔ **Get the server's attention.** Try to spend a few minutes talking with the server about your gluten-free diet and food ingredients before everyone else orders. A good time may be when he comes to take drink orders or to tell you about the specials.

- ✔ **Communicate.** Explain your dietary needs before you order and always ask the server to ask the chef whether something contains gluten or how it's prepared. See the nearby sidebar for a restaurant card you can share.

- ✔ **Speak to the manager.** If your server doesn't seem to get it, talk with the restaurant manager before you order. We've had many restaurant managers approach us during a meal and say, "Feel free to ask for me when you get here next time, and I'll make sure you're taken care of."

- ✔ **Substitute.** Don't be afraid to ask for modifications to your selections. For example, request rice, polenta, potatoes, or a vegetable instead of pasta. (Check out Chapter 4 of Book I for the lowdown on savvy food substitutions.)

- ✔ **Check your food.** When your food comes, check everything — twice; mistakes happen! If your salad has croutons on it or your hamburger comes with a bun, *don't* actually send it back. Keep it at the table and alert your server that you need another order. Don't let them take the contaminated plate away, as sometimes kitchen staff simply remove croutons or a bun (not good enough!) and return the contaminated dish to you.

- ✔ **Enjoy!** When you're confident that your food is safe, eat up and enjoy!

Even when you take precautions, risk of cross-contamination and mistakes exists. Everyone has a different level of tolerance, but the goal is always zero tolerance — no gluten! Over time, you'll compile a list of places you know can accommodate you safely, and your gluten-free life will become easier because you'll be ready with suggestions when your friends want to order late-night pizza, go celebrate at a restaurant, or order carryout for dinner.

When dining out with a group of friends, splitting the bill may not always be equitable if you didn't share that pitcher of beer or bruschetta appetizer. Just kindly mention that you'll give a smaller portion since you didn't partake. Asking for your own check at the beginning of the night may be an easier solution to avoiding an awkward situation when the bill arrives.

Attending parties and potlucks

You don't have to avoid your gluten-eating friends or starve when enjoying your college party scene. Here are some simple ideas for surviving social gatherings:

- ✔ Eat before you go. You can look for veggies and other safe foods to munch on at the gathering, but you won't be famished if you can't find safe options.
- ✔ Keep your expectations low if you aren't bringing any food.
- ✔ Check with the host to make sure it's okay to bring a dish. Find easy and delicious recipe ideas in Books III through V. You never need to mention you're gluten-free!
- ✔ For potlucks, bring two dishes — a main dish and a side or dessert that you and others can enjoy — to give yourself more choices.

Considering catered events

Don't let your gluten-free restrictions keep you away from weddings and other celebrations! A few minutes of prep work can make it easy for you to enjoy festive meals with your friends and family.

One of our best suggestions for setting yourself up for a great night out is to ask the host who's catering the party. Ask him whether he minds if you call the caterer and arrange for a gluten-free meal. Most caterers are well aware of what this entails, but a quick conversation can ensure you get safe fare. This special request usually doesn't cost the host extra money because it's often just a matter of leaving off sauces and making sure that side dishes are free of croutons, breadcrumbs, and sauces.

On the night of the event, find the catering event manager when you arrive and alert her that you ordered a gluten-free version of the meal. You probably won't get a gluten-free version of the dessert, but maybe you can snag some after-dinner fruit or a cup of coffee.

Overcoming the trials of traveling

Planes, trains, and automobiles can all offer successful travel fare — even for the gluten-free! In fact, most cruise lines have great gluten-free choices now. So do some research before a trip and find out what (if anything) you need to do to keep your travel drama-free and nourishing. If you're wondering which foods to pack for a trip, how to find gluten-free meals along the way, and how to manage your diet in an airport, read on.

Book I

Getting
Started
with Going
without
Gluten

Packing for road trips

Road trips are the easiest kind of travel to manage in terms of avoiding gluten. Just stock your car with your favorite snacks and bring a cooler for perishables. You're in control of what you have available and where you stop, and that makes gluten-free car travel a breeze!

Here are some good road-trip snacks that are easy to pack in a bag or cooler:

- ✔ Sandwiches on gluten-free bread
- ✔ Fresh fruit and veggies
- ✔ Dried fruit
- ✔ String cheese and yogurt
- ✔ Nuts and seeds
- ✔ Homemade or store-bought gluten-free trail mix
- ✔ Gluten-free cereals and granola bars
- ✔ Chips and gluten-free crackers and pretzels
- ✔ Gluten-free cookies or brownies

Before you pull out of town, check online for gluten-free restaurants along your route. Most fast food restaurants have gluten-free/allergen menus.

You can also load smartphone apps to help you find restaurants in the cities and towns you'll pass through. One favorite app is Find Me Gluten Free. It lists links to gluten-free menus of popular chains and also shows you where to eat gluten-free near where you are at any given moment. Easy!

If you're visiting a theme park or resort, a list of the gluten-free offerings is likely available online. Most places have a guest services phone number to call for gluten-free information as well.

Enjoying gluten-free airport fare

Are you flying any time soon? If so, chances are that you plan to depart from a major airport and may even stop at one or two along the way. If you find yourself searching for something to eat, rest assured that you can find good gluten-free food — from grab-and-go fare to gourmet cuisine — at most airports. You just need to know what to look for.

When you're in the mood for a snack, keep your eyes peeled for fresh fruit, frozen yogurt (watch the toppings, though), nuts, some candy, dried fruit, many bagged chips, cheese, salads (no croutons, and choose oil and vinegar dressing), and coffee, including some coffee specialty drinks. Always check labels before you buy.

Corn chips and potato chips are generally gluten-free unless they have wheat in the spices, like a taco flavor or sometimes barbecue flavor. It's pretty safe to stick with salted chips, but check the labels. Some cool chip versions may be available at the airport as well; sweet potato chips, rice chips, bean chips, or veggie chips. On candy, watch out especially for malt and wheat in the ingredient list. Steer clear of anything with a cookie crunch or licorice. Did you know one of the main ingredients in Twizzlers is wheat flour? Find out what exactly to look for on food labels in Chapter 5 of this Book.

When you need a bit more substance, look for national chain restaurants that have gluten-free menus. Most airports have their restaurants and stores listed on their websites, so you can make a plan before you take off. But in every setting involving food, stay vigilant about asking questions and using good judgment based on how you see employees handling things.

A couple of airlines offer a gluten-free meal for a fee if you call at least 72 hours in advance, but it's safer to bring food on board. Mistakes happen, and you could end up with nothing to eat on a long flight if you're not prepared with your own gluten-free stash. Often, there's nothing gluten-free on airplanes, but hopefully that will change as more travelers stop consuming gluten.

All U.S. airports allow you to bring food through security unless it's in liquid form. You must purchase drinks inside the airport after you pass security. Anything from leftovers to trail mix should make it through security, although international flight security may restrict you from carrying fruits and vegetables. Check the latest rules and regulations online before planning what to pack if overseas travel is in your plans.

Chapter 2

Glimpsing Good Reasons to Go Gluten-Free

*M*aybe you're new to the gluten-free lifestyle and you want to know what you can safely eat and how to turn it into a gluten-free gastronomic delight. Or maybe you've been gluten-free and are looking for some spice in your life and some giddyap in your gluten-free.

Maybe you suspect you have some type of gluten sensitivity, and you're trying the gluten-free diet to see if you feel better; or you're trying the gluten-free diet to help manage your weight. Or maybe someone you love and cook for (or cook for and love) is going gluten-free and you're doing your best to support, encourage, and nourish your hungry guy or gal.

Why you're cooking gluten-free doesn't really matter, because you *are*. And that's awesome. Because the gluten-free diet can be the healthiest diet on the planet, it may dramatically improve your health, both physical and emotional.

For those of you who really want to dig into the details about the health benefits of a gluten-free diet, you may want to consider buying the companion to this book, *Living Gluten-Free For Dummies*. It contains everything you need to know about the medical conditions as well as practical and emotional guidelines for living (and *loving*) a gluten-free lifestyle.

For now, here are the basics so you know why your health may dramatically improve when you go gluten-free. Too good to be true? Read on, friends, read on.

Looking Into the Downsides of Wheat

You've probably been raised to believe that wheat — especially whole wheat — is really good for you. Although wheat does offer some health benefits, the same benefits can easily be found in other foods without the unpleasant side effects that many, if not most, people experience. But here's the bottom line: Wheat's not good for anyone, whether you have gluten sensitivity or celiac disease or not. Here are ten big problems with wheat.

Humans don't fully digest wheat

The human stomach may not fully digest wheat. Cows, sheep, and other ruminant animals do just fine with wheat because they have more than one stomach to complete the digestion process. When the partially digested wheat leaves their stomach, it goes to another stomach where it is further broken down, then to another and another until the process is complete.

Unlike our bovine buddies, we humans have only one stomach. When the wheat leaves our tummies, it's not fully digested. Those undigested portions begin to ferment, and do you know what the byproduct of fermentation is? Gas. Icky, belchable, fart-forming gas. For many people, this accounts for the gas and bloating they feel after they eat wheat, whether they have gluten sensitivity or not.

Wheat is a pro-inflammatory agent

Recently, lots of books and articles have been written on the subject of *pro-inflammatory foods*. These foods are rapidly converted to sugar, causing a rise in the body's insulin levels (read more about this in the later section, "Wheat can mess up your blood sugar levels"), causing a burst of inflammation at the cellular level. Almost everyone knows that blood sugar rises from eating sweets (cakes, cookies, and candy). But lots of foods not considered sweets have pro-inflammatory effects — foods that have wheat in them, like cereal, pasta, breads, and bagels. These foods can be high in simple starches; when these are broken down, they act the same as sweet foods, raising blood sugar levels, releasing insulin, and causing inflammation. Bear in mind that the inflammation occurs in all people, not just those with wheat or gluten sensitivities.

It turns out that inflammation, once thought to be limited to "-itis" conditions like arthritis, may actually be at the root of a number of serious conditions, including heart disease, Alzheimer's, and some types of cancer. And if vanity is the only way to prove a point, consider this: Dr. Nicholas Perricone, renowned author of *The Wrinkle Cure,* considers inflammation to be the "single most powerful cause of the signs of aging."

One great tool for identifying pro-inflammatory foods is the *glycemic index.* The glycemic index measures how fast your blood sugar rises after you eat a food that contains carbohydrates (like pasta, potatoes, and bread). It rates foods on a scale from 0 to 100, where water is 0 and table sugar is 100. The lower the glycemic index rating, the less likely the food is to be pro-inflammatory. Foods made from wheat, especially refined wheat, have a glycemic index in the 50 to 80-plus range, putting them on the high side and classifying them as pro-inflammatory.

Book I

Getting
Started
with Going
without
Gluten

Wheat can cause leaky gut syndrome

So what is leaky gut syndrome? Good question. The simple-and-not-perfectly-correct-but-close-enough answer is that *leaky gut syndrome* is a condition whereby stuff is leaking from your gut into your bloodstream — stuff that shouldn't be there, like toxins (and large molecules like gluten!).

So how does it happen? When people eat wheat, their bodies produce extra amounts of a protein called *zonulin.*

The lining of the small intestine is basically a wall of cells that most materials can't pass through on their own. When important vitamins and minerals are present, zonulin tells the passageways in the intestinal wall to open so those nutrients can pass into the bloodstream. The blood then carries the nutrients to other parts of the body, where they can be used to nourish the body.

But when people eat wheat — not just people with celiac disease, but all people — their zonulin levels rise too high, and the passageways open too much and let things into the bloodstream that shouldn't be there. This increased permeability of the lining of the small intestine, known as leaky gut syndrome, can cause a variety of problems health-wise.

For people with celiac disease, leaky gut syndrome starts the cascade of events that lead to health problems. Gluten is a large molecule that really shouldn't be able to get into the bloodstream, but it does because zonulin levels are too high, and the body allows it in. After it's in the bloodstream, the body sees the gluten molecule as an invader — a toxin — so it launches an attack, and in doing so, it damages the area around the gluten molecule, which includes the lining of the small intestine. The *villi,* which are short hair-like structures that are designed to increase the surface area of the small intestine so it can absorb more nutrients, are damaged in the attack. That's why people with celiac disease who continue to eat gluten often have serious nutritional deficiencies.

Refined wheat has little nutritional value

Most of the wheat people eat is *refined,* which means manufacturers take perfectly good wheat — which has some nutritional value, especially in the bran and germ — and they take the good stuff away. You can read "refined" as "little nutritional value" wheat. Sadly, that's the form that most of our wheat-based products use — refined wheat nearly void of nutritional value, making it a high–glycemic index food that just makes you fat and messes with your insulin production.

Did you know that manufacturers actually have to *enrich* refined wheat because they've taken out all the nutrients? And even then, the wheat's not that valuable, nutritionally speaking. Whole wheat provides more nutritional value than non-whole wheat, but it's still wheat, and there are more than just a few reasons that wheat may not be good for anyone.

Wheat may cause wrinkles

Aha! Now *that* got your attention! Okay, so you can live with the gas, bloating, and leaky gut syndrome, but wrinkles? I think *not!* Well then, put down that bagel, or buy stock in Botox, because according to some experts, the inflammatory effect of wheat — especially refined wheat — can cause wrinkles (see the earlier section "Wheat is a pro-inflammatory agent" for more on pro-inflammatory foods).

The most famous of these experts is Dr. Nicholas Perricone, a dermatologist and adjunct professor of medicine at Michigan State University, who maintains that inflammation contributes to accelerated aging and that through diet (and supplements and creams), you can erase scars and wrinkles, increase the production of collagen and elastin, enjoy radiance and glow, and develop a dewy, supple appearance to your skin.

Of course, this wouldn't be relevant unless the "diet" he refers to has something to do with being gluten-free. Although Dr. Perricone doesn't pinpoint gluten as a culprit per se, he does say that the pro-inflammatory response caused by wheat causes the skin to age more quickly, and he maintains that avoiding foods like wheat may help reverse the aging process.

Wheat may contribute to menopausal symptoms

Menopause, the time in a woman's life between about ages 45 and 55 marking the completion of her childbearing years and the end of her menstrual cycles, is often a time of marked hormonal changes. Depression, anxiety, headaches, leg cramps, varicose veins, irritability, and the famous "hot flashes" that occur are some of the more common symptoms.

Book I

Getting
Started
with Going
without
Gluten

But many doctors believe that lifestyle changes can minimize these symptoms, and one of those lifestyle changes is diet. Although there is some debate over wheat's role in these lifestyle changes, many experts, including Christiane Northrup, MD, author of *The Wisdom of Menopause,* believe that eliminating wheat from the diet — especially refined wheat — can help relieve menopausal symptoms.

Wheat is one of the top-eight allergens

Millions of people are allergic to wheat — so many, in fact, that it has made it onto the top-eight allergen list. Keep in mind that an allergy to wheat is different from celiac disease or other forms of gluten sensitivity — we talk more on that later in this chapter.

Allergic reactions to wheat can include gastrointestinal distress (stomach upset), eczema, hay fever, hives, asthma, and even *anaphylaxis* (a severe, whole-body allergic reaction), which is life-threatening.

Other than the anaphylaxis, these symptoms sound a lot like gluten sensitivity or celiac disease, don't they? That's why sometimes it's hard to tell the difference. That's also why sometimes people get allergy testing and find out they're *not* allergic to wheat — so they're told to go back to a normal diet of pizza, bread, and bagels. Not necessarily good advice, because they could actually have gluten sensitivity or celiac disease. So it's important to be properly tested.

Wheat can mess up your blood sugar levels

Some foods cause your blood sugar levels to spike, which causes your body to produce insulin. That, in turn, causes your blood sugar to fall dramatically. Basically, your blood sugar levels go from the even keel they should be on, to being the best roller coaster ride in the park. Easy, Evil Knievel. That's not a good thing in this case.

Our bodies are designed to work with stable blood sugar levels. When they're up, then down, and all around, it causes a domino effect of not-so-healthy things to occur. Lots of people talk about *hypoglycemia* — a weak, shaky feeling that usually goes away after eating, especially after eating sweet foods.

Although most people don't have "true" hypoglycemia, they may feel hypoglycemic when their blood sugar drops too much. The problem with the idea of "fixing" this feeling with sugary foods is that it just continues this roller coaster of blood sugar levels that are too high, and then too low. One of the most serious conditions that can result from blood sugar whiplash is insulin resistance and diabetes.

Wheat can make you fat

You know the kind of fat that sneaks up on you when you think you're doing everything right, but those getting-tighter-every-day jeans say otherwise?

It could just be the wheat — especially refined wheat. That's because of what it does to your blood sugar — yeah, you can cheat and look back at the section before this one if you didn't read it well enough the first time — but again, it's not that complicated. Refined wheat is a high–glycemic index food that causes your blood sugar to spike. That makes your body produce insulin, which, by the way, is often referred to as the "fat-storing hormone."

Yikes. Just when you thought you were being so good by leaving the cream cheese off the bagel — you should probably ditch the bagel altogether.

Many people have gluten sensitivity or celiac disease and don't know it

Maybe you've heard (or even said) things like, "I think I'm allergic to dairy because the cheese on my pizza makes me bloat." Oh, really? What makes you think it's the *cheese?* Because more people have heard of lactose intolerance than gluten intolerance, they figure that must be what's making them feel icky.

Most people have no idea that they have a gluten sensitivity or celiac disease, so they usually start pointing to all the wrong culprits: cheese (dairy), tomato sauce (acids), or soy. But they're blaming the wrong foods. These people have no idea that the typical American diet comprised of bagels, pasta, pizza, cakes, cookies, and pretzels could be wreaking havoc on nearly every system in their bodies, so they continue to eat them and wonder why they don't feel good.

So how many people fall into this category? No one knows for sure. We do know that 1 in 100 people has celiac disease — but most don't know it. No one knows how many people have gluten sensitivity, but estimates are that it may be as high as 50 percent, or even 70 percent, of the population. Top that with those who have a wheat allergy, and — here, let us get our calculator out — tons of people + gobs more = an astoundingly high percentage of the population!

Recognizing Different Types of Gluten-Related Problems

Book I

Getting
Started
with Going
without
Gluten

Lots of people — maybe even *most* people — have some form of gluten sensitivity. But is it sensitivity, allergy, or celiac disease? Sometimes it's tough to tell. These sections delve deeper into the types of gluten-related issues.

Allergies to gluten-containing foods

There's really no such thing as an allergy to gluten. If you happen to be allergic to all three gluten-containing grains (wheat, rye, and barley), then you might have reason to say that you were allergic to gluten — even though you're really allergic to the three grains that fall under the gluten umbrella. But most people misuse the term and say they're allergic to gluten when what they really mean to say is that they have an intolerance or sensitivity to gluten, or they have full-blown celiac disease.

Allergies to gluten-containing foods are just like other food allergies. They're all responses to a food allergen, and the reaction that someone has to those foods varies from person to person and from one food to another.

Allergic symptoms can be respiratory, causing coughing, nasal congestion, sneezing, throat tightness, and even asthma. Acute allergic reactions to food usually start in the mouth, with tingling, itching, a metallic taste, and swelling of the tongue and throat. Sometimes symptoms are farther down the intestinal tract, causing abdominal pain, muscle spasms, vomiting, and diarrhea.

Any severe and acute allergic reaction also has the potential to cause anaphylaxis, or anaphylactic shock. This life-threatening condition affects different organs, and symptoms can include a feeling of agitation, hives, breathing problems, a drop in blood pressure, and fainting. In some cases, an anaphylactic response to an allergen can be fatal unless the person having the allergic reaction receives an epinephrine (adrenaline) injection.

Distinguishing between gluten sensitivity and celiac disease

Gluten sensitivity can mean a lot of different things, and that label is often misused; it's a very fuzzy term. Basically, it's a sensitivity to gluten — hence the clever term. Often used interchangeably, the terms sensitivity and intolerance mean that your body doesn't react well to a particular food and you should avoid it. Symptoms of gluten sensitivity are usually the same as those of celiac disease, and as with celiac disease, they usually go away on a gluten-free diet.

Unlike gluten sensitivity, *celiac disease* is well-defined. It's a common, yet often misdiagnosed, genetic intolerance to gluten that can develop at any age, in people of any ethnicity. When people with celiac disease eat gluten, their immune systems respond by attacking the gluten molecule, and in so doing, the immune system also attacks the body itself. This is called an *auto-immune response,* and it results in damage to the small intestine, which can cause poor absorption of nutrients.

Although the damage occurs in the gastrointestinal tract (specifically in the small intestine), not all symptoms are gastrointestinal in nature. That's because celiac disease is multisystemic — the symptoms show up in many different ways and can occur in just about every organ of the body. In fact, symptoms are vast and varied, and they sometimes come and go, which makes diagnosis difficult.

Does someone who has gluten sensitivity also have celiac disease? Not necessarily. Or maybe. How's that for ambiguity? The upcoming sections clarify.

You're told you have gluten sensitivity, but you actually have celiac disease

Some people who are told by a healthcare professional that they have "gluten sensitivity" actually have celiac disease, but their testing was done improperly or was insufficient to yield conclusive results.

Say, for instance, that someone is IgA deficient (*IgA* is a special type of protein that the body produces to fight infections), and many people are. Most of the time it doesn't cause a problem. But it makes testing for celiac disease difficult, because most of the celiac tests are based on starting with a normal level of IgA. If a person doesn't have enough IgA in his body, that would make some of the celiac tests appear to be normal when actually the person's levels should have been elevated (indicating celiac disease) if he weren't IgA deficient. In other words, the person has celiac disease, but because testing was incomplete (the doctors didn't test to determine if he was IgA deficient), the results were interpreted incorrectly.

Another reason you may have celiac disease but be told you have gluten sensitivity is if the *type* of testing you undergo is specific to gluten sensitivity, not celiac disease. For instance, a stool test and a few types of saliva tests check for gluten sensitivity, but if you have celiac disease, they'll be positive. So you would, in fact, have celiac disease — but the only test you're taking in this case is for gluten sensitivity, so that's what you'll be "diagnosed" with.

Book I

Getting
Started
with Going
without
Gluten

If you're diagnosed as having gluten sensitivity, you may want to ask if any specific tests were done to test for celiac disease. Some antibody tests are more specific for celiac disease as well as genetic tests. If those tests weren't performed, you may want to get them done so you have a more definitive diagnosis. Be sure that you don't avoid gluten before you test. Doing so can give you a false result.

You don't have celiac disease — yet

Sometimes in the very earliest stages of celiac disease, testing for celiac disease will be negative, but the tests for gluten sensitivity may be positive. In this case, the person has celiac disease, but it's too early to show on tests. If that person continues to eat gluten, the testing will eventually be positive (and damage will be done!).

As far as celiac testing goes, "once tested" doesn't mean "forever tested." In other words, if you're negative today, it doesn't mean you're negative forever. There's no timeline to follow in terms of how often you should have a specific test for celiac disease, but it's important to be aware that it can develop at any time.

You have gluten sensitivity, not celiac disease

Some people do, in fact, have gluten sensitivity that is not celiac disease. Symptoms are generally the same as those for celiac disease (see the very next section), and, as with the disease, health improves on a gluten-free diet.

Sorting Out the Symptoms of Gluten Intolerance

Ask most people what the most common symptom of celiac disease or gluten sensitivity is and, if they know anything about either one (and don't look at you and say, "Huh?"), they'll most likely erupt in a loud, unabashed, confident chorus of "diarrhea, diarrhea, diarrhea!"

Yet most people with celiac disease or gluten sensitivity don't have diarrhea. In fact, they don't have any gastrointestinal symptoms at all! And if they do have gastrointestinal symptoms, they're often constipated, or they suffer reflux or gas and bloating.

Gluten sensitivity and celiac disease have hundreds of symptoms. The following sections list some of the more common ones, starting with the symptoms that are gastrointestinal in nature.

Pinpointing gastrointestinal symptoms

The gastrointestinal symptoms of gluten sensitivity and celiac disease are vast. Although most people think diarrhea is the most common symptom, gastrointestinal symptoms can include constipation, gas, bloating, reflux, and even vomiting.

These are some of the "classic" — though not the most common — symptoms of celiac disease:

- Abdominal pain and distension
- Acid reflux
- Bloating
- Constipation
- Diarrhea
- Gas and flatulence
- Greasy, foul-smelling, floating stools
- Nausea
- Vomiting
- Weight loss or weight gain

Checking out non-gastrointestinal symptoms

Celiac disease and gluten sensitivity are gastrointestinal conditions because the damage is done to the small intestine. But people more commonly have what are called *extraintestinal* (outside the intestine) symptoms. These make up an extensive list of more than 250 symptoms, including the following:

- Fatigue and weakness (due to iron-deficiency anemia)
- Vitamin and/or mineral deficiencies
- Headaches (including migraines)
- Joint or bone pain
- Depression, irritability, listlessness, and mood disorders
- "Fuzzy brain" or an inability to concentrate

- Infertility
- Abnormal menstrual cycles
- Dental enamel deficiencies and irregularities
- Seizures
- Ataxia (bad balance)
- Nerve damage (peripheral neuropathy)
- Respiratory problems
- Canker sores (aphthous ulcers)
- Lactose intolerance
- Eczema/psoriasis
- Rosacea (a skin disorder)
- Acne
- Hashimoto's disease, Sjögren's syndrome, lupus erythematosus, and other autoimmune disorders
- Early onset osteoporosis
- Hair loss (alopecia)
- Bruising easily
- Low blood sugar (hypoglycemia)
- Muscle cramping
- Nosebleeds
- Swelling and inflammation
- Night blindness

Watching for symptoms in kids

Kids who have celiac disease tend to have the "classic" gastrointestinal symptoms of diarrhea or constipation. They may also have some of the following symptoms that aren't gastrointestinal in nature:

- Inability to concentrate
- Irritability
- ADD/ADHD or autistic-type behaviors
- Failure to thrive (in infants and toddlers)

- ✔ Short stature or delayed growth
- ✔ Delayed onset of puberty
- ✔ Weak bones or bone pain
- ✔ Abdominal pain and distension
- ✔ Nosebleeds

Considering Your Options for Testing

With such an overwhelming assortment of symptoms, it's no wonder people are often misdiagnosed before finding out that they have celiac disease or gluten sensitivity. It's also no wonder so many people go undiagnosed.

A *Reader's Digest* article titled "10 Diseases Doctors Miss" cited celiac disease as one of the top-ten misdiagnosed diseases. In all fairness to the medical community, it can be tough to diagnose celiac disease when you think of the myriad symptoms. Headaches, fatigue, infertility, depression — if you go to your doctor for any of those things, it's unlikely that he or she is going to say, "Hmm, you're depressed. Let's test you for celiac disease." No, it's far more likely that you'll be given an antidepressant and sent on your way.

Don't despair. Plenty of doctors are extremely knowledgeable about these conditions and will do proper testing. If yours isn't one of those, keep looking until you find one who is. There are even some tests that you can order yourself without a doctor's intervention.

Looking into tests

It seems like there should be one single test you can take that would definitively determine whether you have gluten sensitivity, celiac disease, or none of the above. But alas, it's not that simple.

For one thing, there are different types of tests: blood, stool, saliva, and intestinal biopsy. In most cases, one type of test may determine whether you have celiac disease or gluten sensitivity — but most tests don't discern between the two or test for both. In other words, one test looks for gluten sensitivity but not celiac disease; another looks for celiac disease but not gluten sensitivity. And most people only get one (maybe two) of those tests, so they're rarely tested for both conditions.

So which test is best? Sounds like a simple question, but there's no simple answer. The gold standard for testing for celiac disease is a blood test followed by an intestinal biopsy. If both tests are positive, you're deemed to be confirmed as having celiac disease.

What *can* be said for certain — or close to it — is that if you test positive for celiac disease, you have celiac disease. That's because the tests for celiac disease are very specific, highly sensitive, and extremely reliable — especially when they indicate a positive outcome (diagnosis of celiac disease).

However, if the test is negative and your symptoms go away on a gluten-free diet, then you probably have some form of gluten sensitivity.

Unfortunately, there are false negatives and occasional false positives. Some people test negative yet find that they don't feel right when they eat gluten. Perhaps it was a false negative — or maybe gluten just doesn't sit right with you.

Bottom line: If it makes you feel bad, don't eat it!

Sadly, because the protocol for defining and diagnosing gluten sensitivity isn't well established and there's some disagreement about definitions of gluten sensitivity in the medical community, patients are often told to ignore inconclusive or confusing test results and to go back to eating their bagels and pizza. If you aren't sure you can trust your test results, you may want to be tested again at a later time.

Going gluten-free without testing

You may be tempted to skip the testing and jump right into a gluten-free diet. If, for instance, you highly suspect you have celiac disease or gluten sensitivity, it makes sense — going gluten-free can help you start healing the minute you start the diet. Most people begin feeling better right away, some take months to improve, but in the long run, you can look forward to improved health — sometimes dramatically improved.

But — and this is a great big caution flag here — if you plan to be tested, don't give up your gluten just yet. You have to be eating gluten for an extended length of time before getting the blood test or the intestinal biopsy.

If you don't eat gluten, or haven't eaten it for long enough, your body may not produce enough antibodies to show up on the tests, and the results *will* come back negative for gluten sensitivity or celiac disease — even if you *do* have the condition.

In other words, the gluten-free diet will "heal" you. Your body will no longer think it has celiac disease or gluten sensitivity. It will stop producing antibodies, and your intestines will heal — so the tests that determine whether you have the conditions will tell you that you don't, even if you do.

After you've gone gluten-free, you can't be properly tested for celiac disease.

No one knows for sure exactly how much gluten you need to eat to be properly tested, but if you eat the equivalent of one or two pieces of gluten-containing bread a day for at least three months, you should have enough gluten in your system to provide a measurable response.

Keep in mind, though, that you may be causing damage to your body by continuing to eat gluten! It's a conundrum, for sure!

If you decide to continue to eat gluten before testing and you have severe symptoms, talk with your doctor to decide whether you should continue to eat gluten.

Realizing the Consequences of Cheating

If you actually have gluten sensitivity and not celiac disease, you may be able to get away with eating gluten from time to time. Just make sure you remember those pesky false negatives and misdiagnoses, and make *sure* you don't have celiac disease if you're going to indulge.

Some people are told they're gluten sensitive when they really do have celiac disease. If that scenario applies to you and you continue to eat gluten, even if it's just every once in a while, you could do some serious unseen damage, not to mention you may continue to suffer unpleasant symptoms.

On the other hand, if you do have celiac disease and you want to improve your health by following a gluten-free diet, you're going to have to do it 100 percent. A "gluten-free lite" diet won't get rid of your symptoms, and it will continue to damage your body. The next few sections explain why.

Compromising your health

If you have gluten sensitivity or celiac disease and you continue to eat gluten, you *are* compromising your health, even if you don't feel any symptoms. Even the tiniest amount of gluten will cause you problems because you're still setting off autoimmune responses and your body is being robbed of important nutrients that it needs to function properly and stay strong.

When you have celiac disease, every bit of gluten you eat affects your intestinal tract adversely and keeps you from making healthy progress. That means you'll need to be extremely careful about reading labels, choosing ingredients, and avoiding contamination while cooking.

Developing associated conditions

Certain conditions are associated with celiac disease. It's usually tough to tell which one developed first, but because awareness of *other* conditions is higher than that of celiac disease, people are usually diagnosed with the other one first.

It's important to understand the association between conditions for a few reasons:

- ✓ Someone who has one condition is more likely to have the other.
- ✓ If you don't give up gluten, your chances of developing an associated condition may increase.
- ✓ An associated condition is a red flag that you may also have gluten sensitivity or celiac disease. If you have one of these conditions, you should be tested for gluten sensitivity or celiac disease.
- ✓ If people in your family have an associated condition, you may want to consider urging them to be tested — and being tested yourself.

Autoimmune diseases

Several autoimmune diseases are associated with celiac disease, including

- ✓ Addison's disease (hypoadrenocorticism)
- ✓ Autoimmune chronic active hepatitis
- ✓ Crohn's disease
- ✓ Insulin-dependent diabetes mellitus (type 1 diabetes)

   About 6 percent of people with type 1 diabetes have celiac disease, but many don't know it. They often find managing blood sugar levels much easier on a gluten-free diet!

- ✓ Myasthenia gravis
- ✓ Raynaud's phenomenon
- ✓ Scleroderma
- ✓ Sjögren's syndrome

✔ Systemic lupus erythematosus

✔ Thyroid disease (Graves' disease and Hashimoto's disease)

✔ Ulcerative colitis

Studies have shown that if you have celiac disease, the earlier in life you go on a gluten-free diet, the lower your risk of developing associated autoimmune diseases. And sometimes symptoms of other autoimmune diseases, like multiple sclerosis, improve on a gluten-free diet.

Mood disorders

Some of the mood disorders associated with gluten sensitivity and celiac disease include

✔ ADD (attention deficit disorder) or ADHD (attention deficit hyperactivity disorder)

✔ Autism

✔ Bipolar disease

✔ Depression

Nutritional deficiencies

Because gluten sensitivity and celiac disease affect the small intestine, nutritional deficiencies usually develop. These can include

✔ Specific vitamin and mineral deficiencies

✔ Anemia

✔ Osteoporosis

✔ Osteopenia (low bone mineral density)

✔ Osteomalacia (soft bones)

Neurological conditions

Some neurological conditions are associated with gluten sensitivity and celiac disease, including

✔ Epilepsy and cerebral calcifications

✔ Brain and spinal cord defects (in newborns born to mothers with celiac disease who are eating gluten)

✔ Neurological problems, such as ataxia, neuropathy, tingling, seizures, and optic myopathy

Other conditions

Several other conditions are commonly associated with celiac disease, including

Book I

Getting
Started
with Going
without
Gluten

- ✔ Cancer (such as non-Hodgkin's lymphoma)
- ✔ Down syndrome
- ✔ Internal hemorrhaging
- ✔ Organ disorders (of the gallbladder, liver, spleen, or pancreas)
- ✔ Tooth enamel defects
- ✔ Cystic fibrosis

Understanding How Gluten Affects Behavior

You're probably not going to get too far in a court of law pleading, "The wheat bread made me do it!" But gluten is sometimes guilty when it comes to affecting behavior and moods.

Gluten can affect your behavior in many ways. Some behavioral manifestations of gluten sensitivity and celiac disease can include

- ✔ Inability to concentrate or focus
- ✔ Attention deficit disorder (ADD) and attention deficit hyperactivity disorder (ADHD) type behaviors
- ✔ Autism
- ✔ Depression, bipolar disorder, schizophrenia, and mood disorders
- ✔ Irritability
- ✔ Lack of motivation

Connecting gluten and autism

Dietary interventions for developmental and behavioral disabilities have been the topic of many heated discussions for decades. One of the most remarkable things about the gluten-free diet is that it seems to play a role in reversing autistic behaviors — at least in some cases.

Several credible double-blind, placebo-controlled studies are underway at reputable universities to study the relationship between gluten and autism. The results of these studies are eagerly anticipated and will most likely have a dramatic affect on the way pediatricians view the disorder.

Gastrointestinal problems seem to be more prevalent in people with autism than in the general public — do they have a higher incidence of celiac disease? No one has studied that. Is there a connection? Maybe. The scientific community believes that there's a genetic basis for autism. But interestingly, there seems to be a nutritional component.

The most popular diet promoted as a "cure" for autism is a gluten-free, casein-free diet (*casein* is the protein found in milk). No one claims that this works in all cases; nor do they say it's truly a cure. But *if* a dietary intervention protocol could actually improve autistic behaviors, wouldn't that be amazing? Some say it can. Just a short time ago, the evidence was largely anecdotal, but now the "Defeat Autism Now!" protocol recommends that every autistic child be placed on a gluten-free, casein-free diet for at least three months.

In some autistic children, gluten and casein are turned into a sort of drug that the brain makes, much like morphine. Essentially, many autistic children are "drugged" on wheat and milk products, as if they were on a morphine drip.

Basically, when people with autism eat gluten and casein, they get a high off of the foods, and they become addicted. This "high" is similar to the one experienced by opiate users, and it may account for some of the typical traits found in autistic kids, such as repetitive movements like head banging and spinning, being withdrawn, and having a fascination with parts of objects (like fixating on one part of a toy rather than the toy itself).

Results on the gluten-free, casein-free diet vary. Some see improvement within a week, some within a year, and others see no improvement at all. Even in those who report behavioral changes, the changes themselves vary. Some people with autism are able to sleep through the night, others become more verbal and interactive, and some are completely "normalized" on the diet.

The gluten-free diet can be *especially* difficult for a person with autism, because these folks tend to develop food preferences, and these usually include gluten-containing foods.

Delving into depression and other mood disorders

People with celiac disease have a higher incidence of mania, seizures, and other neurological problems. In addition, clinical depression, bipolar disorder, schizophrenia, and a variety of mood disorders can sometimes be associated with or exacerbated by gluten sensitivity and celiac disease. Some journal articles even list these disorders as symptoms of celiac disease, and these conditions sometimes improve on a gluten-free diet.

Schizophrenia has been associated with celiac disease since the 1960s, when it was first noted that restricting gluten and dairy led to improvement in some institutionalized patients. Interestingly, the same opiate-like chemicals found in the urine of autistic people are often found in schizophrenics.

Some investigators have noted that the incidence of schizophrenia is higher in places where wheat is the staple grain than where people normally eat non-gluten-containing grains. In one study done in the highlands of Papua, New Guinea, where little or no grain is consumed, only two people out of 65,000 adults could be identified as chronic schizophrenics. In the coastal area, where wheat is consumed more, the prevalence of schizophrenia was about three times higher.

Book I

Getting
Started
with Going
without
Gluten

Chapter 3

Taking a Closer Look at Celiac Disease

Gluten sensitivity and celiac disease are similar in many ways: symptoms, treatment, and maybe even some of the testing methods. But because gluten sensitivity hasn't been well defined and celiac disease has, this chapter focuses on celiac disease.

Celiac disease has a bunch of names that all mean the same thing, including *sprue, celiac sprue, nontropical sprue* (not to be confused with tropical sprue), *gluten-sensitive enteropathy, Gee-Herter disease,* and *coeliac disease* (the European spelling).

Exposing One of the Most Common Genetic Diseases of Mankind

Three aspects of celiac disease make it uniquely contradictory and intriguing. These factors interrelate, inviting a closer look at this complex condition:

✔ Celiac disease is extremely common but remarkably underdiagnosed.

✔ If undiagnosed, it can severely compromise your health.

✔ It's fully treatable by diet alone.

So just how common is it? Well, since you asked . . . .

Occurring in nearly 1 percent of the population, celiac disease is one of the most common genetic diseases of mankind. According to the Center for Celiac Research, the numbers break down like this:

✔ As many as 1 in 133 people has celiac disease (most don't know it). (Remember, this number doesn't take into account those who have nonceliac gluten sensitivity.)

✔ For people with "classic" symptoms, the incidence is 1 in 40.

✔ For people with parents or siblings with celiac disease, the incidence is 1 in 20.

✔ For people who have an aunt, uncle, grandparent, or first cousin with celiac disease, the incidence is 1 in 40.

To put these numbers in perspective, celiac disease is more common than Crohn's disease, ulcerative colitis, multiple sclerosis, Parkinson's disease, and cystic fibrosis combined. Check out Table 3-1 to see how celiac disease measures up.

Table 3-1	Incidence of Common Genetic Diseases in the U.S.
Disease	*Estimated Number of People*
Celiac disease	3 million (www.celiaccenter.org)
Epilepsy	2.7 million (www.epilepsyfoundation.org)
Parkinson's disease	1 million (Parkinson's Disease Foundation)
Alzheimer's disease	4.5 million (Alzheimer's Association)
Ulcerative colitis	500,000 (Crohn's and Colitis Foundation of America)
Crohn's disease	500,000 (Crohn's and Colitis Foundation of America)
Multiple sclerosis	300,000 (National Center for Health Statistics)
Cystic fibrosis	30,000 (National Institute of Diabetes & Digestive & Kidney Diseases)

Celiac disease is obviously extremely common. But gluten sensitivity (which is not celiac disease) is thought to be even more so. No good prevalence studies have been done for nonceliac gluten sensitivity, but some experts estimate that the majority of people have some form of gluten sensitivity.

People often wonder, if celiac disease is so common, why don't more people have it? They do! They just don't know it yet (and may never know it).

Pinpointing Who Develops Celiac Disease and Why

Book I

Getting
Started
with Going
without
Gluten

Doctors have no way to identify who will develop celiac disease. What they *do* know is that you need at least three parts of the puzzle to develop the condition:

- ✔ The genetic predisposition
- ✔ A diet that includes gluten
- ✔ An environmental trigger

Even if you have all three, you may never develop celiac disease. You *can* say, though, that if you're missing one of these three pieces, you won't develop celiac disease (but you may still have gluten sensitivity).

Celiac disease is a nondiscriminatory condition, found in all races and nationalities. It's commonly thought to be more prevalent in people with Northern European ancestry, but that distinction is diminishing as people are becoming more diverse and intermingled.

Prevalence studies do show differences in the incidence of celiac disease in different ethnicities. But those figures are skewed by the fact that some nations test more than others. Northern Europe, for instance, has been way ahead of the United States in its awareness of celiac disease for decades. Testing has been far more comprehensive, which may explain why that region reports more people with the disease. Northern Europe doesn't necessarily have more affected people — just more people have been diagnosed.

Some people think that civilizations that developed between the Tigris and Euphrates rivers in the Middle East, where grain was first cultivated, have had longer to evolve to cope successfully with gluten-containing grains; that's why the prevalence of gluten sensitivity among these people is lower. Other groups, like the Germans, the Scandinavians, and the Celts of England, Scotland, and Ireland, began cultivating wheat only in limited amounts in the post-Roman era. They were mostly hunter-gatherers until the Middle Ages, so those populations have had less time to adjust to gluten-containing grains.

It's in the genes

No one knows all the genes that are involved in developing celiac disease, but researchers do know of two key players: HLA DQ2 and HLA DQ8. You don't need to have both — just one will do — and DQ2 is the one seen most often in people with celiac disease.

The DQ gene comes in different types, called *alleles*. Researchers have identified the combination of these alleles that results in the highest risk of developing celiac disease.

But about one-third of the general population has these genes and doesn't develop celiac disease, so knowing whether you have them is valuable if you want to rule out celiac disease. In other words, if you have the genes, you may or may not develop celiac disease. But if you don't have either gene, there's a 99 percent chance that you won't develop celiac disease (which may leave you wondering about that 1 percent!). Keep in mind also that if you don't have these genes, you can still have nonceliac gluten sensitivity.

Celiac disease isn't dominant or recessive — it's *multifactorial* or *multigenic*, meaning that several different types of genes play a part in the development of the condition.

Triggering celiac disease: What turns it on

People use the word *trigger* in two ways when they talk about celiac disease. The first refers to gluten being the "trigger" for initiating a response of the body's immune system (you can delve into that topic more deeply in the next section). The other meaning is an environmental trigger that "flips a switch," so to speak, launching celiac disease into an active mode.

Most people have a pretty clear idea of when their celiac disease was triggered, because in many cases they're relatively healthy, and then *boom!* Their symptoms appear "out of the blue," and they have no idea why.

Common triggers include the following:

✔ Pregnancy

✔ Surgery

✔ Car accident or other physical injury

✔ Divorce, job loss, death in the family, or emotional trauma

✔ Illness

Understanding Celiac Disease and What It Does to the Body

Celiac disease is an *autoimmune disease* (a disease in which the immune system attacks the body) that gets activated when someone eats gluten. To help you understand exactly what damage is being done, this section gives you just a taste of basic human anatomy, specifically focusing on the gastrointestinal tract.

Some people think that because celiac disease is an autoimmune disease, someone with celiac disease has a compromised immune system. Not at all! In fact, the opposite is true — the immune system in people with celiac disease is working overtime to fight what it perceives to be bad guys — like gluten.

How your guts are supposed to work

You've got guts, but do you know how they work? Help is here. When food gets to the upper part of your small intestine, it has already been chewed, swallowed, passed through the stomach, and broken down by enzymes into nutrients that the body can use to nourish itself.

The small intestine is lined with hairlike projections called *villi*. The purpose of the villi, shown in Figure 3-1, is to increase the surface area of the intestine so they have more room to absorb important nutrients.

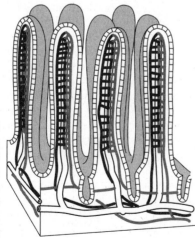

Figure 3-1: The villi of the small intestine absorb nutrients.

The lining of the small intestine is basically a solid wall. All the cells on the lining are joined by *tight junctions*. When the body is ready to absorb the nutrients, these tight junctions open the space between cells and let the good stuff in — but keep the bigger bad stuff, like toxins, out.

How do the tight junctions know how far to open? They have a comrade-in-arms named *zonulin*. Zonulin is a protein — its job is to be a gatekeeper, opening the tight junctions just enough to let in the good stuff but keep out the bad stuff.

How your guts work with celiac disease

When someone with celiac disease eats gluten, everything's going along just fine until the gluten reaches the small intestine.

The first thing that goes wrong at this point is that wheat causes the body — in all humans, not just celiacs — to produce too much of the protein *zonulin*. This excess of zonulin causes the junctions between cells in the small intestine to open too much, and next thing you know, there's a party in the bloodstream and all sorts of things can get into the bloodstream that shouldn't be there — things like toxins and gluten fragments.

When stuff leaks through the intestinal wall that normally shouldn't be able to, it results in a condition called *leaky gut syndrome.*

So now, thanks to the excess of zonulin that was released because the person ate gluten, the gluten fragment has made its way into the bloodstream. In people with celiac disease, the body sees gluten fragments as invaders — toxins that shouldn't be there. So it launches an all-out attack against these invaders, but — and here's why celiac disease is called an *autoimmune response* — the body also attacks itself.

An *autoimmune disease* is one in which the body's immune system produces antibodies that react against normal, healthy tissue (rather than against bacteria or viruses), causing inflammation and damage. Celiac disease is unique in that it's the only autoimmune disease for which people know the trigger that sets off the response. A survey from the American Autoimmune Related Diseases Association found that 45 percent of people eventually diagnosed with an autoimmune disease were initially labeled as hypochondriacs because doctors thought they were imagining their symptoms.

Specifically, the body attacks the villi on the lining of the small intestine. As the villi get chopped down — *blunted* is the technical term — they can no longer be as effective in absorbing nutrients. That's why you see *malabsorption* (poor nutrient absorption) and nutritional deficiencies in people with celiac disease who still eat gluten.

Book I

Getting
Started
with Going
without
Gluten

Because the food is just passing through without being absorbed the way it's supposed to be, you sometimes see diarrhea. But think about this: The small intestine is nearly 22 feet long, and damage from celiac disease starts at the upper part — so there's *lots* of small intestine to compensate for the damaged part that's not able to do its job. By the time you have diarrhea, you're usually a very sick puppy.

And now for the pop quiz. Kidding! Really, that little lesson wasn't so bad, now, was it? And just think of what a hit you'll be at cocktail parties now that you can enrapture your friends with discussions of your villi, zonulin, and leaky gut syndrome.

Gut Feelings: Gastrointestinal Symptoms

If you've been experiencing gastrointestinal symptoms, but, out of embarrassment, have been hesitant to see your doctor about them, you're certainly not alone. Indeed, lots of people find themselves in this same boat. Doctors, however, are *never* embarrassed discussing GI symptoms, and your doctor's comfort with this will soon put you at ease, too. (In fact, GI specialists have been known to say: "It may be poop to you, but it's bread and butter to me!" Well, actually, they word it somewhat less, ahem, tastefully.)

The gut stops here: Diarrhea, celiac disease, and you

Diarrhea is the frequent passage of watery or semi-formed stools. Pretty much everyone — whether having celiac disease or not — gets diarrhea from time to time, often from relatively harmless (but decidedly unpleasant) conditions such as viral gastroenteritis ("stomach flu").

Loosely speaking: Diarrhea due to celiac disease

Diarrhea is the symptom of celiac disease that is best known to the world at large and it comes as a surprise to most people — including many doctors, by the way — to learn that, in fact, upwards of 50 percent of people with celiac disease *have no diarrhea at all;* indeed, for some people living with celiac disease, the main bowel problem is that of constipation! Contrary to popular belief, diarrhea should no longer be considered a hallmark of this disease.

Of those people with celiac disease who do get diarrhea, its nature can vary to a great extent; both between people and even for a given person. If you have diarrhea, it could be that you've noticed that you have some days where you feel that you're spending the entire day on the toilet and other days where you could be a hundred miles from the nearest bathroom and care not a whit (well, passing urine aside).

If you have not been diagnosed with celiac disease and you see your doctor to report that you are having alternating constipation and diarrhea, the odds are high that your doctor will not have celiac disease high up on his radar as a possible cause for your problem and instead will be more likely to consider irritable bowel syndrome (IBS). This is perfectly understandable because IBS is a very common cause of these kinds of symptoms. Nonetheless, it can't hurt for you to mention — especially if you're not responding sufficiently well to treatment for IBS — that you've read (here) that celiac disease can also cause these symptoms. Who knows; perhaps you will end up being responsible for figuring out your own diagnosis?

Celiac disease does *not* cause blood to appear in or on the stool. If you see blood with your stool, you should let your doctor know. It may be that there's nothing going on beyond some minor problems with hemorrhoids, but much more serious causes exist, including bowel cancer. Blood in the stool is not a symptom to be ignored.

An absorbing discussion about malabsorption

Some people, especially those with the classical form of celiac disease, have severe, unremitting diarrhea. This can be evidence of *malabsorption.* Malabsorption is a condition in which one is unable to properly absorb nutrients from food. If you malabsorb fat, the fat you eat stays in your intestine and — it's got to go somewhere — becomes part of your stool. Having stool that contains fat is called *steatorrhea.* If you have steatorrhea, your family will know you have this problem almost as quickly as you do. Why? Well, everyone's stool smells, shall we delicately say, *unpleasant,* but steatorrhea smells dreadful. Horrible, "Call in the fumigators" awful. Also, these fatty stools tend to stick to the bowl so you may find yourself needing to get a brush to scrape off the remnants of your trip to the bathroom, lest the next visitor have an eyeful. Other features of steatorrhea are that the stools are bulky and tend to float.

Eating when you're suffering from severe malabsorption is like filling your car's gas tank only to find the fuel gauge showing you're nearly empty because you've got a hole in your tank. The gas goes in, but gets drained out without being used; your food goes in but also does not get used, the nutrients instead being passed out of your body with your stool.

Malabsorption isn't an "all or none" phenomenon. Some people with celiac disease — especially children with the classic form — have severe malabsorption and, as a result, lose a great deal of ingested nutrients from the body. This can result in loss of muscle mass, fat stores, fatigue, lethargy, and weight loss. Much more commonly, however, malabsorption is selective, with only a limited variety and amount of nutrients (particularly iron) being lost from the body and with virtually no symptoms being present. This is seen in many people with the atypical form of celiac disease and, because of the frequent absence of symptoms, it's often only after a routine blood test done at an annual check-up or for some other, coincidental reason comes back abnormal that the diagnosis of celiac disease eventually gets made.

Treating diarrhea due to celiac disease

The mainstay of treating diarrhea (and other bowel complaints) due to celiac disease is to follow a gluten-free diet. Within a few weeks of getting on track with your diet, you will likely notice an improvement in your bowel troubles. It may, however, take months before things are back to normal. If your symptoms don't settle, then you and your healthcare providers will need to determine whether some other problem is going on. Considerations include

- ✔ Having some other, coexisting intestinal problem (such as irritable bowel syndrome)
- ✔ Having a complication from your celiac disease (such as lactose intolerance)
- ✔ An incorrect diagnosis of celiac disease
- ✔ Ongoing, typically inadvertent, ingestion of gluten

Olfactory challenges: Sniffing out the importance of flatulence

Here's another cocktail-party tidbit for you: The average adult farts 13 times per day. Although everyone routinely passes gas, people with celiac disease can be particularly prone to flatulence.

Celiac disease doesn't present a classical or typical pattern of flatulence. Indeed, passing more wind than the last Nor'easter means you likely have a problem with your gut (celiac disease or otherwise), but the absence of lots of flatus doesn't necessarily mean that all is well and, in particular, doesn't rule out the possibility you've got celiac disease.

Flatus is caused by bacteria in the large intestine acting on undigested or incompletely digested food (specifically, carbohydrates) that's made its way down to the colon after having not been absorbed into the body by the small intestine. As the large intestinal bacteria munch on the nutrients that have come their way, they produce gasses, including the infamous hydrogen sulphide, which is the main cause of flatus's malodour.

If you have steatorrhea (see the preceding section), your gas may be particularly malodorous. This can be an important clue for your doctor, so share this — so to speak — with him or her, and don't feel embarrassed.

Abdominal symptoms: Belly pain, bloating, and beyond

As with flatus (see the preceding section), every person on the planet experiences abdominal symptoms of one sort or another from time to time. With celiac disease, however, abdominal symptoms are often much more of a problem and, indeed, may be part and parcel of one's existence.

In addition to well-known and well-understood terms (like cramps), there are a few other, sometimes-misconstrued terms worth looking at when talking about abdominal symptoms:

- **Abdomen:** The part of your body between your chest and your pelvis — not just your stomach, which is, of course, the organ connecting the esophagus and the (small) intestine.

  Why mention this at all? If you were to mention to a healthcare provider that you are having "stomach pain," how your words are interpreted may be very different than if you were to mention you were having "abdominal pain." Many people use these two terms interchangeably and most healthcare providers recognize this. Nonetheless, to avoid confusion, it's best to just use the word "abdomen" unless you are very certain your symptom really is coming specifically from your stomach (which, by the way, is often exceptionally difficult to know).

- **Bloating:** The symptom of feeling that one's abdomen is overly full. Typically, if someone says they feel bloated, they are referring to a feeling of fullness, as if they have too much gas in the intestine, but the term is also used by people to describe a similar feeling due to other causes such as feeling overly full with food, or even feeling constipated.

- **Abdominal distension:** The physical equivalent to the symptom of bloating. In other words, it's something that a doctor observes when she examines you. Having said that, the word *distension* is also often (and perfectly legitimately) used synonymously and interchangeably with the term *bloating*.

Bloating (and, therefore, abdominal distension) due to celiac disease is typically most bothersome after a meal, but it can also be present even if you haven't recently eaten. Although bloating isn't a serious or life-threatening symptom, it can be very unpleasant. Marked and persistent abdominal distension used to be seen quite often in very young children affected by severe celiac disease, but thankfully this seldom happens nowadays as children with celiac disease are typically diagnosed (and treated) much earlier in the process than used to be the case.

Abdominal cramps are sharp, often piercing, pains that can be felt in a variety of places. They are typically fleeting, lasting from seconds to minutes. Cramps are usually caused by contractions of the intestine, and as the contraction relaxes the discomfort eases. Passing flatus sometimes also helps ease a cramp, which you probably know from personal experience.

Abdominal symptoms from celiac disease don't have features that are specific to this particular illness, which is part of the reason that celiac disease so often gets overlooked. Perhaps you had the experience, before your celiac disease was diagnosed, of telling your healthcare provider that you were having abdominal discomfort, bloating, and so on, and you were then misdiagnosed with some other ailment like, for example, irritable bowel syndrome (IBS). If so, you're in good company; this happens all the time. As healthcare providers become more aware that celiac disease is so common, and how often celiac disease presents with atypical features, they'll no doubt have a heightened level of alertness to look out for this condition, and the condition will be more quickly diagnosed.

Reflux and heartburn

Reflux is a condition in which acid from within the stomach passes back up into the esophagus — the swallowing tube that connects the mouth to the stomach — giving rise to a burning feeling behind the breastbone (sternum).

Reflux is the short form for *gastroesophageal reflux*. If someone has chronic problems with reflux, the condition is called *gastroesophageal reflux disease* (or GERD).

The stomach produces acid, which helps to digest food. How much acid is in the stomach? Well, the stomach produces so much hydrochloric acid that stomach fluid is, brace for this fact, 1 million times more acidic than water.

The stomach has special protective mechanisms so that all this acid doesn't normally damage the stomach lining. (When this mechanism fails, people are susceptible to stomach ulcers.) The esophagus, however, doesn't have these same protective features and as a result is susceptible to damage from acid. To protect the esophagus from being exposed to the stomach's acid, the part of the esophagus that attaches to the stomach has a valve-like feature (called the *lower esophageal sphincter*) that blocks the stomach acid from entering. When this valve is weak, acid travels up from the stomach into the esophagus and damages it, giving rise to the symptom of heartburn.

Most people, whether or not they have celiac disease, experience reflux and heartburn from time to time — particularly after a large meal or drinking more than their fair share of coffee. Heartburn is more likely to be a problem as a person enters middle age. Heartburn is also particularly common during pregnancy and, especially, labor.

Non-drug therapy

If you have celiac disease, you may be more prone to reflux and, therefore, heartburn. The reflux (and heartburn) may be present both more often and more persistently. Following a gluten-free diet can help lessen your reflux but often is insufficient. Here are some non-drug therapies that may help ease your symptoms:

- Avoid ingesting — or, at the least, limit the consumption of — those things (such as coffee, tea, and spicy foods) that trigger your symptoms.

- Avoid overeating — especially in the late evening before going to bed. (When you are lying down, you are especially prone to reflux because you don't have gravity helping to keep acid in the stomach and out of your esophagus.)

- Avoid excessive liquid intake for a few hours before going to bed.

- Try to lose weight if you are overweight. (Being overweight is a contributory factor leading to reflux.)

Drug therapy

Despite the measures discussed in the preceding section, many people still have problematic symptoms. In this case, a variety of medications are available to help you, including:

- **Antacids:** Include Maalox, Mylanta, and many others. Antacids can be obtained without a prescription and are often an excellent treatment choice if you get heartburn just occasionally.

- **H_2 blockers:** Go by a variety of names, including, in alphabetical order, cimetidine (Tagamet), famotidine (Pepcid), nizatidine (Axid), and ranitidine (Zantac). Many H_2 blockers are available over-the-counter and have various other trade names. These drugs can be used on an "as needed basis" to treat an episode of heartburn or, under a doctor's supervision, on a routine basis to prevent heartburn.

- **Proton pump inhibitors:** Go by a variety of names, including, in alphabetical order, dexlansoprazole (Kapidex), esomeprazole (Nexium), lansoprazole (Prevacid), omeprazole (Losec, Prilosec, Zegerid), pantoprazole (Pariet, Protonix), and rabeprazole (Aciphex). Proton pump inhibitors are especially potent at suppressing acid production from the stomach and have become very popular therapies.

If you get just occasional heartburn, simply take an antacid or an H$_2$ blocker when you need to. If your problem is occurring regularly, follow the non-drug preventative strategies outlined previously. If, however, your heartburn is occurring frequently or is particularly bothersome for you, speak to your doctor about whether you might benefit from taking a proton pump inhibitor.

Rarely, celiac disease causes such severe and intractable reflux that the recurring presence of stomach acid in your esophagus leads to scarring and, eventually, narrowing of the esophagus (a *stricture*). If you develop a stricture, you will have difficulty swallowing solid foods such as bread or steak, with the food getting stuck in your esophagus. This difficulty is typically felt as a sudden pain behind the lower part of your sternum that comes on as you are eating and eventually eases as the food finally passes through the obstruction. If you are experiencing this symptom, be sure to mention it to your doctor so that he or she can determine if you have a stricture.

Indigestion

Indigestion (*dyspepsia*) is a common gastrointestinal symptom of celiac disease. Though indigestion can be defined in many different ways, most commonly it refers to an aching, uncomfortably full, or burning discomfort that typically occurs after eating and is felt in the upper part of the abdomen (as opposed to GERD, where the main symptom is a burning behind the breastbone).

Almost everyone, whether having celiac disease or not, experiences indigestion from time to time (think third helping of Thanksgiving turkey, or beer and pizza when out with "the boys"). If you have celiac disease, however, you are more prone to indigestion, and it may occur without any obvious food overindulgence.

Many people with celiac disease have put up with years of bothersome indigestion only to have it nearly vanish within a few months of starting a gluten-free diet. Indeed, eliminating gluten from your diet will likely be the only therapy you require (apart, that is, from possibly needing to avoid that third helping of turkey, but, hey, if it's Thanksgiving, what the heck . . .).

Weight Loss Related to Celiac Disease

Until recent years, when much has been learned about celiac disease, it had been thought that celiac disease was primarily a childhood ailment and was pretty well always associated with weight loss. Although this is true of what is called *classical celiac disease,* it is, in fact, not true of the majority of people with celiac disease, most of whom have *atypical celiac disease* and do not experience weight loss. Having said all of this, weight loss in adults with celiac disease can and does occur, and, if it happens to you, it's important that you are aware of the possible causes.

When you lose weight due to celiac disease, you typically lose no more than a few pounds and have no cause for alarm. If, however, you are losing substantial amounts of weight, you should seek very prompt medical attention.

Looking at the issue of weight loss in four different settings is helpful. Weight loss can be caused by

- Active celiac disease
- Dietary change after a person starts following a gluten-free diet
- A co-existing condition
- Complications from celiac disease

The next few sections look at each of these scenarios.

Weight loss due to active celiac disease

Having active celiac disease — that is, ongoing damage to the small intestine — can lead to weight loss from two main causes.

- **Loss of appetite:** Celiac disease can make you feel generally crummy, and if you feel that way, you may not have much of an appetite, which, in turn, leads you to eat less. This reduced intake of calories results in loss of weight.
- **Malabsorption:** As you can read earlier in this chapter in the section "An absorbing discussion about malabsorption," celiac disease damages the small intestine, which is the place where nutrients are absorbed into the body. If you have a reduced ability to absorb these nutrients *into* your body, they — and the calories they contain — are then lost *from* the body with your stool. This is called *malabsorption.* Lost calories cause lost weight.

Weight loss due to the gluten-free diet

People with celiac disease may find that they lose some weight once they start on a gluten-free diet. Following a gluten-free diet entails giving up certain calorie-rich gluten-containing foods such as are found in junk foods or restaurant buffets. As a result of ingesting fewer calories, you may find yourself losing weight after you've started your gluten-free diet.

Weight loss due to a coexisting condition

A number of different diseases are not caused by celiac disease but occur with greater frequency if you have celiac disease. Several of these conditions can result in weight loss *unrelated* to your celiac disease.

If you have celiac disease, have gotten on track with your gluten-free diet, and are ingesting sufficient calories but are still losing weight, then you and your doctor should consider the possibility that you have one of these coexisting conditions:

- **Addison's disease:** The adrenal glands are under-functioning.
- **Depression:** People who feel depressed often lose their appetite.
- **Diabetes:** Having high blood glucose levels (a hallmark feature of diabetes) causes weight loss.
- **Hyperthyroidism:** The thyroid is over-functioning.

Weight loss due to a complication of celiac disease

Celiac disease can cause complications that, in turn, can cause weight loss. These are *not* common occurrences, but if other causes of weight loss have not been found, they should be considered. Here are the most important ones to be aware of:

- **Pancreatic insufficiency:** This is a condition in which the pancreas is unable to make sufficient quantities of digestive enzymes, and as a result, you get malabsorption.
- **Small intestinal bacterial overgrowth (SIBO):** This is a condition in which there are excess numbers of bacteria in the small intestine; these excess bacteria consume some ingested dietary nutrients and also damage the small bowel, and as a result, digestion is impaired and malabsorption develops.
- **Intestinal cancer:** Cancer of the small intestine is a rare complication of celiac disease and is most likely to develop if you've had many years of severe, uncontrolled celiac disease.

Save yourself untold grief: Before you and your healthcare providers start an extensive search for one or more of the conditions in the preceding list, make sure you have eliminated all gluten from your diet. What a shame it would be if you went through all sorts of tests to look for why you were unexpectedly losing weight if, in fact, the cause was nothing more than the fact that you were still (inadvertently) ingesting gluten.

Non-Gastrointestinal Symptoms and Celiac Disease

When most people think "celiac disease" — when they think of it at all — they think "gut." And indeed, the gut is the root of the condition and the place where many people experience symptoms. Nonetheless, if you have celiac disease, you are at increased risk of other organs malfunctioning.

Your other organs may malfunction

- ✔ **As a *direct result* of your celiac disease:** An example of direct effect would be celiac disease damaging your intestine and, as a result, impairing your ability to absorb vitamin D into your body, leading to osteoporosis.

- ✔ ***In association* with celiac disease:** If you have blond hair, you are more likely to have blue eyes, but, of course, your blond hair did not cause you to have blue eyes. This is an *association*, not cause and effect. In the same vein, celiac disease affecting the gut may be associated with other bodily ailments without directly causing them. Sometimes, this is because if you have one type of immune disorder (like celiac disease), you are at increased risk of having other immune disorders (like Type 1 diabetes). More often, however, the reason for this association is either only partly known or is simply obscure.

In the following sections, you find out about non-gastrointestinal symptoms that you may experience if you have celiac disease. Depending on the symptom in question, it may be present as a direct result of your celiac disease or, alternatively, because you have an associated condition.

As you read in this section of the many ailments that are associated with celiac disease, bear in mind that most people with celiac disease *never* experience *any* of the problems discussed here. Having said that, they can, and so it's important that you be aware of them.

With some important exceptions (such as the skin rash called *dermatitis herpetiformis,* described in a moment), each of the conditions in this section requires its own specific treatment. In other words, the gluten-free diet you need to follow to help control your celiac disease does not generally help you manage these other ailments.

Rash decisions

If you have celiac disease, you are at increased risk of having one of several different types of skin rash. The following are visual changes that come with some of the skin diseases most commonly linked to celiac disease.

- ✔ **Dermatitis herpetiformis:** If you develop small, intensely itchy, pinkish blisters on the elbows, knees, or buttocks (less often on the shoulders, scalp, face, and back), you may have dermatitis herpetiformis (DH). The link between DH and celiac disease is so strong that DH is sometimes referred to as "celiac disease of the skin." Both conditions are triggered by exposure to gluten, have the same antibodies present, and respond to the elimination of gluten from the diet.

- ✔ **Psoriasis:** Red, scaly sores affecting your skin — particularly the scalp, elbows, knees, and back — may indicate you have psoriasis.

- ✔ **Vitiligo:** If you develop patches of pale (to the point of being white) skin, you may have vitiligo.

Mulling over mood, thinking, and neurological issues

People with celiac disease are at increased risk of having certain mood, thinking, and neurological disorders. It is far from clear why this association exists, and it is always worth bearing in mind that an association isn't the same thing as cause and effect. These are the related conditions to be aware of:

- ✔ **Ataxia** is a condition in which the balance is affected, causing one to walk unsteadily.

- ✔ **Epilepsy** ("seizures") is a condition in which episodes of abnormal electrical discharge occur in the brain leading, depending on the area involved, to abnormal movements or behaviors.

- ✔ **Migraine headaches** are intense, typically throbbing headaches, which are often preceded by visual warning symptoms.

- ✔ **Peripheral neuropathy** is a condition in which the nerves in the feet (far less often, the hands) are damaged, typically causing numbness.

- ✔ **Attention Deficit/Hyperactivity Disorder (ADHD)** is a condition in which the affected person has difficulty paying attention, tends to be overly active, and often acts impulsively.

- ✔ **Autism** is a condition in which the affected person has difficulties communicating and interacting socially.

- ✔ **Depression** and other psychiatric disorders.

Feeling fatigued

The previous section shows various mood, thinking, and neurological issues. But what if your problem is simply that you feel tired? Run down. Exhausted. Worn out. Could this feeling be due to your celiac disease? The quick answer is, well, there is no quick answer. In this section, you find out about the possibilities.

You might imagine that, if you have chronic abdominal pain, are getting recurring bouts of diarrhea, and are malnourished because you're not sufficiently absorbing important nutrients into your body, that you'd feel tired. You bet! So, yes, if you have these symptoms, it would likely be no surprise to you that fatigue is part and parcel of the process. Fortunately, soon after you start your gluten-free diet, these symptoms start to ease (though, if you're very malnourished, your tiredness may take longer to improve than the other symptoms just mentioned).

Some people with celiac disease, however, feel fatigued even in the absence of gastrointestinal symptoms (and most people with celiac disease have the so-called "atypical" type in which GI symptoms are minimal or nonexistent). Although the cause may be unrelated and coincidental (literally thousands of different ailments can cause fatigue), a few celiac-related/associated conditions can lead to fatigue and, therefore, should be considered by you and your doctor:

- ✔ **Anemia:** Several types of anemia may occur if you have celiac disease. Of these, the most common one, and also the one most likely to lead to tiredness, is *iron-deficiency anemia*. This is typically readily determined by performing a simple blood test.

- ✔ **Depression:** Tiredness is a common symptom experienced by people who are depressed. It is, however, not the only symptom seen with depression; rather, it occurs in the context of a number of other features, including difficulty sleeping and feeling helpless and hopeless.

- ✔ **Fibromyalgia:** Fibromyalgia is a musculoskeletal condition in which tiredness is a very common feature.

- ✔ **Thyroid disease:** The thyroid gland is a small hormone-secreting gland located in the front of the neck just above the breastbone (sternum). The thyroid helps regulate a great many different processes in the body. If the thyroid is under-functioning (a condition called *hypothyroidism*), fatigue commonly results. What is far less widely known is that if the thyroid is *over*-functioning (a condition called *hyperthyroidism*), fatigue is also very frequently experienced. If you have celiac disease and you have unexplained fatigue, be sure to ask your healthcare provider if your thyroid function has been checked. Your thyroid function is readily tested by performing a simple blood test. (The most commonly used test to screen for thyroid malfunction is called a TSH, which stands for *thyroid stimulating hormone*.)

If your celiac disease is well controlled yet you feel fatigued on an ongoing basis, you are doing yourself a disservice if you simply attribute your tiredness to your celiac disease. Instead, you should discuss your symptom with your doctor to determine what else might be causing it.

Hormonal (endocrine) problems

If you have celiac disease, you are at increased risk of certain hormonal (endocrine) conditions:

- **Addison's disease** is a disorder of the adrenal glands in which one loses weight and has low blood pressure and the skin darkens.
- **Type 1 diabetes** is a condition in which the body is unable to produce insulin, and as a result high blood glucose levels develop. Symptoms of elevated blood glucose include excessive thirst, frequent urination, and weight loss.
- **Thyroid over-functioning (hyperthyroidism),** which can cause weight loss, fatigue, tremor, palpitations, diarrhea, and other symptoms.
- **Thyroid under-functioning (hypothyroidism),** which can cause weight gain, fatigue, dry skin, brittle hair, muscle aches, and other symptoms.

Musculoskeletal problems

If you have celiac disease, you may be at increased risk of the following musculoskeletal disorders:

- **Rickets and osteoporosis** are conditions in which you have insufficient bone strength and mass.
- **Rheumatologic problems** including:
    - **Sjögren's syndrome** is a condition in which you have decreased ability to make saliva and tears.
    - **SLE** ("lupus" or, more fully, *systemic lupus erythematosis*) is a disorder in which the joints and other body tissues become inflamed and painful.
    - **Raynaud's phenomenon** is a condition in which blood flow to the fingers and toes is temporarily impaired upon exposure to cold temperatures leading to episodes of pallor of the digits.
    - **Fibromyalgia** is a condition in which one experiences a variety of aches and pains but without evidence of inflammation in the body.

Cancer

Fortunately, cancer related to celiac disease seldom occurs, but it can. Following are the most important types to be aware of:

- **Enteropathy-associated T cell lymphoma** is a form of lymph cell cancer.
- **Small intestine adenocarcinoma** is a form of cancer of the small intestine.

Gynecological and obstetrical problems

A variety of different but related gynecological and obstetrical problems may occur if a woman has celiac disease, including

- Irregular periods
- Infertility
- Miscarriages
- Early (premature) delivery

Other problems

Of the remaining, important disorders associated with celiac disease, the key ones to be aware of are the following:

- **Anemia:** Anemia can cause fatigue, shortness of breath, rapid heart beat, and other symptoms.
- **Mouth ailments:** Aphthous ulcers ("canker sores") are one example.
- **Dental problems:** These include the loss of the tooth's protective enamel coating.
- **Liver and bile duct disorders:** Liver disease can lead to jaundice, bleeding problems, and, potentially, many other problems.
- **IgA deficiency:** This is a *congenital* (meaning that one is born with it) inability to produce normal amounts of the IgA form of antibody.
- **Chromosome defects:** Turner syndrome and Down syndrome are conditions due to abnormalities in the chromosomes. (Chromosomes contain DNA, which is the genetic blueprint responsible for many of the traits of living organisms.)

Chapter 4

Grasping the Ground Rules of the Gluten-Free Diet

In This Chapter

▶ Understanding what gluten is

▶ Knowing what you generally can and can't eat

▶ Introducing superfoods and other stuff you may not have heard of

▶ Uncovering gluten in nonfood items

*W*hether you're brand-new to the wonderful world of gluten-freedom or an old pro who's been gluten-free for years, this chapter tells you facts about the gluten-free diet that may surprise you.

The diet seems like it should be so easy: Gluten is in wheat, rye, and barley — so just avoid those foods, right? If the diet was that simple, the book would be finished. No, the diet's not quite that straightforward, thanks to additives, flavorings, derivatives, fillers, binders, and other fancy terms that are really just euphemisms for "stuff that may have gluten in it."

The good news is that the list of foods you can eat is a lot longer than the list of foods you can't. Sure, you're going to have to kiss your pizza goodbye (but wipe the crumbs off your lips — those crumbs are loaded with gluten), along with your bagels, bread, cookies, brownies, cakes, and — yep — beer (at least, the kinds of those foods you're probably used to).

But you'll realize the amazing world of incredible gluten-free foods that can take the place of your old favorites — some of which you may never have heard of before, like *quinoa* (if you read the rest of this chapter, you may even know how to pronounce it). You'll know that *Job's Tears* are not a religious icon, but that they are gluten-free. And if you think *ragi* is a spaghetti sauce and *sorghum* is what you get when you have your teeth cleaned, now's the time to find out more about some of the unique grains and starches available to you on a gluten-free diet.

Don't be discouraged if you feel like the guidelines are a little overwhelming at first. For some people, accepting what's allowed and what isn't on a gluten-free diet requires an entirely different mindset. For others, it's less dramatic of a change. And for still others, it's a welcome skew from the everyday fare.

Whether you're a one or a ten on the I'm-overwhelmed-by-this-diet scale, this chapter is key because it establishes basic gluten-free guidelines. It outlines what is and isn't gluten-free and why you sometimes have to question a product. It introduces you to gluten-free alternatives that you may never have heard of. It also talks about nonfood items that you may or may not need to be concerned about, such as dental products, alcoholic beverages, medications, and external products like lotions and shampoos.

When in Doubt, Leave It Out

At some point, you will wonder whether a product is gluten-free: You're at a restaurant or party and you have no idea what's in the food, the labeling isn't clear, no labels are in sight, or you don't know half the words on the label. And if you don't have your handy-dandy copy of *Gluten-Free All-in-One For Dummies* nearby, you may be tempted to make assumptions that could get you in trouble.

Don't do it. If you need a reminder of what you're doing to your body when you eat gluten, take a look at Chapter 2, which talks about associated conditions and serious complications that can develop if you have gluten sensitivity or celiac disease and you eat gluten, even from time to time.

Even if your symptoms are mild or absent, the damage gluten causes — even small amounts of gluten — can be severe.

You're a lot better off being safe instead of sorry, so follow this common-sense commandment: When in doubt, leave it out.

Defining Gluten So You Can Avoid It

You have to know what gluten is — and not just so you can be the life of the party, sparking tantalizing conversations that begin with audacious lines like, "So which do you find harder to avoid? Gliadin, hordein, or secalin?" (Yeah, that'll get the party started, Smooth Talker.) No, you need to know about gluten so you can avoid it (gluten, not the pickup line). The definition of this term is so convoluted that it's hard to offer a technically correct definition of gluten at this point, but here goes.

Book I

Getting
Started
with Going
without
Gluten

Gluten is what scientists call a storage protein, what bakers call the dough-forming elastic ingredient in wheat, and what some newbies to the gluten-free diet pine away for. Gluten is a group of proteins that technically comes from wheat and only wheat.

At some point in the not-so-distant history, someone made the association between wheat (specifically, gluten) and celiac disease. People widely accepted that gluten makes celiacs sick, which is true. Soon physicians realized that barley and rye make celiacs sick, too, and people started saying, "Celiacs can't eat gluten. They can't eat wheat, barley, and rye, either; therefore, wheat, barley, and rye all have gluten." Right? Kind of, but not really. One of the types of proteins in gluten is also in barley and rye.

Prolamins are a class of proteins present in a variety of grains, and they're what cause problems for people who can't eat "gluten." Technically, gluten is made up of the proteins glutenin and *gliadin,* a specific type of prolamin in wheat. However, *gluten* has become a general term for any kind of potentially harmful prolamin. The prolamins that cause damage to people with gluten sensitivity and celiac disease include *gliadin* (in wheat), *secalin* (in rye), and *hordein* (in barley). Other grains have prolamins, too (corn's prolamin is called *zein,* and rice's prolamin is *orzenin*), but their prolamins aren't toxic to people with gluten sensitivity or celiac disease.

The "wheat, barley, and rye (and maybe oats) all have gluten" idea stuck, and even though it isn't technically correct, it *is* widely accepted today. For the purposes of simplicity, this book sticks with it, too.

Wheat-free doesn't mean *gluten-free.* Something can be wheat-free and still have, for instance, malt (derived from barley), so then it's not gluten-free.

Recognizing Gluten-Free Foods at a Glance

Keep in mind that you have to become familiar with lots of ingredients when you're learning the intricacies of the gluten-free diet.

The reason the gluten-free diet can seem cumbersome at first is that "derivatives" of gluten-containing grains may contain gluten. And, of course, processed foods — which contain seasonings, additives, and flavorings — can contain ingredients that raise questions, too.

But breaking foods down into those that usually have gluten and those that don't isn't too tough. Keep in mind that these lists vary and that they're only to get you started. You can find up-to-date lists of foods that are safe, forbidden, and questionable at www.celiac.com.

Forbidden grains

Don't think this section negative for starting with the forbidden grains — it's just that the list is a lot shorter than the list of grains you can eat. You need to avoid these grains on a gluten-free diet:

- ✔ Barley
- ✔ Oats (because of contamination issues)
- ✔ Triticale (a hybrid of wheat and rye)
- ✔ Rye
- ✔ Wheat

You need to avoid (or at least question) anything with the word *wheat* in it. This includes hydrolyzed wheat protein, wheat starch, wheat germ, and so on. Wheat grass, however, like all grasses, is gluten-free. Keep a few additional details in mind:

- ✔ Wheat starch is actually wheat that has had the gluten washed out. In some countries, a special type of wheat starch called Codex Alimentarius wheat starch is allowed on the gluten-free diet — but it's not allowed in North America, because some people question whether the washing process completely removes all residual gluten.

- ✔ Triticale is a made-up grain — a hybrid of wheat and rye. Inventors developed it to combine the productivity of wheat with the ruggedness of rye, not just to add another grain to your list of forbidden foods. And relatively speaking, it's fairly nutritious for people who can eat gluten (but wait till you hear about "alternative grains" in the next section!).

- ✔ Wheat has several names and varieties. Beware of aliases like *flour, bulgur, semolina, spelt, frumento, durum* (also spelled *duram*), *kamut, graham, einkorn, emmer, farina, couscous, seitan, matzoh, matzah, matzo,* and *cake flour*. Often marketed as a "wheat alternative," spelt is as much of a wheat alternative as you are a human alternative. It's not even remotely gluten-free. Einkorn and emmer are sometimes touted as being safe, but they, too, contain harmful prolamins and must be avoided on a gluten-free diet.

- ✔ Wheat just isn't what it used to be. In fact, in an effort to bring down the cost of commercial baked goods and make wheat slightly more nutritious for the countries the U.S. ships to, ambitious farmers are actually finding ways to hybridize wheat to make it have more gluten than ever.

- ✔ Derivatives of gluten-containing grains aren't allowed on the gluten-free diet, either. You can find a complete listing at www.celiac.com, but the most common derivative that you have to avoid is malt, which usually comes from barley. Avoid malt, malt flavoring, and malt vinegar. If malt is derived from another source, such as corn, that fact usually appears on the label. If it's not specified, though, don't eat it.

Grasses like wheat grass and barley grass, frequently sold in health food stores and at juice bars, are gluten-free. The grass hasn't yet formed the gluten-containing proteins that cause problems in people with gluten sensitivity and celiac disease. When you can watch someone cut the grass so you know it's fresh and hasn't sprouted yet, you're safe. Be careful, though, of grasses that are an ingredient in a product. These grasses could be contaminated with seeds, and because you don't know for sure, you could risk getting gluten.

You should avoid sprouted grains because you don't know where in the sprouting process the grain is. Eating the sprouts could be okay, but it may not be. Berries are the seed kernels and are definitely not safe. The jury's still out on bran, so until food scientists do more research, remember the common-sense commandment: *When in doubt, leave it out.*

Book I

Getting
Started
with Going
without
Gluten

Grains and starches you can safely eat

You have lots of choices for gluten-free grains and starches. Even if you're an old pro who's been gluten-free for years, we're guessing some of these may be new to you:

- Amaranth
- Arrowroot
- Beans
- Buckwheat/groats/ kasha
- Chickpeas (garbanzo beans, besan, cici, chana, or gram — not to be confused with graham, which does have gluten)
- Corn
- Garfava
- Job's Tears
- Mesquite (pinole)
- Millet

- Montina (Indian ricegrass)
- Oats (but they may be contaminated with wheat and other grains)
- Potato
- Quinoa (hie)
- Ragi
- Rice
- Sorghum
- Soy
- Tapioca (gari, cassava, casaba, manioc, yucca)
- Taro root
- Teff

Glutinous rice does not contain gluten! Manufacturers make glutinous rice, or *sweet rice* or *mochi,* by grinding high-starch, short-grain rice. Glutinous rice thickens sauces and desserts in Asian cooking and is often the rice used in sushi.

You may run across different names or forms of corn that are gluten-free in addition to plain ol' corn. They include grits, hominy, masa, masa harina, harinilla (blue corn), atole, maize, polenta, corn gluten, and, of course, cornstarch, corn flour, corn bran, and cornmeal.

Gums, such as xanthan and guar gum, contain no gluten. People use them frequently in gluten-free baked goods because gums help give the spongy, elastic texture that gluten-containing flours usually provide. For some people, gums — especially guar gum — may have a laxative effect.

Other foods that are usually gluten-free

In general, these foods are usually gluten-free (the list refers to plain, unseasoned foods without additives and processed products):

- ✔ Beans
- ✔ Dairy products
- ✔ Eggs
- ✔ Fish
- ✔ Fruit
- ✔ Legumes
- ✔ Meat
- ✔ Nuts
- ✔ Poultry
- ✔ Seafood
- ✔ Vegetables

The foods listed here are naturally gluten-free. You can buy specialty products such as cookies, cakes, brownies, breads, crackers, pretzels, and other products that have been made with gluten-free ingredients. Find out more about those products and where to buy them in Book II, Chapter 3, which covers shopping.

Foods that usually contain gluten

Companies offer special gluten-free varieties of some foods, and those gluten-free varieties obviously don't have gluten in them. But unless you're buying specialty products, you can assume that the following foods contain gluten:

- Beer
- Bread, breadcrumbs, biscuits
- Cereal
- Communion wafers
- Cookies, cakes, cupcakes, donuts, muffins, pastries, pie crusts, brownies, and other baked goods
- Cornbread
- Crackers
- Croutons

- Gravies, sauces, and roux
- Imitation seafood (for example, imitation crab)
- Licorice
- Marinades (such as teriyaki)
- Pasta
- Pizza crust
- Pretzels
- Soy sauce
- Stuffing

 Seitan, pronounced say-*tahn,* is a chewy food made from gluten that resembles meat in texture. Also called *wheat meat,* seitan is made by making dough out of wheat flour and water, kneading it to develop the gluten, and rinsing away the starch and bran, leaving only the gluten. They then simmer it in water or vegetable broth that's been seasoned with soy sauce, resulting in a chewy, firm, meatlike food . . . food that not only is *loaded* with gluten but *is* gluten. Loosely translated, the Japanese word seitan means "is protein"; it's called *kofu* in China (but don't confuse it with tofu, which — when unflavored — usually is gluten-free).

Exploring Alternative Grains and Superfoods

When it comes to grains beyond corn, wheat, and rice, most people don't know barley from bulgur. Actually, you've got a great big world of grains out there to be explored, many of which are gluten-free, delicious, and loaded with nutritional value.

They're called "alternative grains," yet many aren't grains at all. Instead, they're grasses, seeds, or flowers. People also call them *superfoods* because they're foods that are *super* nutritious. Take a look at some of these alternative grains and discover an entirely new world of gluten-free superfoods (where *is* that cape?).

For years, rumors have spread that some of these alternative grains aren't safe for people with gluten sensitivity or celiac disease. These foods are, in fact, gluten-free. Some people may have had reactions to these grains (as they would to corn, soy, or other allergens or foods to which they may have a sensitivity), but it's not a gluten reaction. But regardless of whether a food contains gluten, if it makes you sick, don't eat it!

Amaranth

Loaded with fiber, iron, calcium, and other vitamins and minerals, amaranth is also high in the amino acids lysine, methionine, and cysteine, and it's an excellent source of protein. A small beadlike grain, amaranth is not only nutritious but also delicious, with a pleasant peppery and hearty, nutty flavor.

Amaranth isn't a true cereal grain at all, but it's a relative of the pigweeds and ornamental flowers called *cockscomb*. People grow it not only for its seed but also for its leaves, which you can cook and eat as greens. Amaranth can be milled or toasted, which gives it extra flavor. You can even pop some varieties like popcorn, boil and eat them like cereal, or use them in soups and granolas or as a side dish. You should always cook amaranth before eating it, because like some other edible seeds, it contains compounds that can inhibit the proper absorption of certain nutrients.

For centuries, the Aztec culture depended on amaranth and believed it had mystical powers that could bring strength and power even to the weakest of men. The name means "not withering" or, more literally, "immortal." Amaranth may not make you immortal, but it is extremely nutritious — and gluten-free.

Arrowroot

Once revered by the ancient Mayans and other inhabitants of Central America as an antidote to poison arrows, arrowroot is now used as an herb thought to soothe the stomach and have antidiarrheal effects. People use it in cooking as a thickener for soups, sauces, and confections.

An easily digested and nutritious starch, arrowroot is a fine white powder with a look and texture similar to that of cornstarch. The translucent paste has no flavor and sets to an almost clear gel. You can use arrowroot in gluten-free cooking or as a thickening agent to replace cornstarch, although it thickens at a lower temperature than either cornstarch or wheat and its consistency doesn't hold as long after cooking. The superfine grains are easy to digest, making arrowroot a perfect "invalid" food. In fact, arrowroot biscuits are one of the first solid foods babies can safely eat (but beware — manufacturers usually add wheat flour to arrowroot biscuits, so they're not gluten-free).

Buckwheat (soba)

The fact that buckwheat is gluten-free often confuses people; after all, buckwheat has the word *wheat* right in the name. But buckwheat isn't even related to wheat; in fact, it's not even a true cereal grain. It's a fruit, a distant cousin of garden-variety rhubarb. The buckwheat seed has a three-cornered shell that contains a pale kernel known as a *groat.* In one form or another, groats have been around since the tenth century B.C.

High in lysine, which is an amino acid lacking in many traditional grains, buckwheat contains several other amino acids — in fact, this grain has a high proportion of all eight essential amino acids, which the body doesn't make but still needs to keep functioning. In that way, buckwheat is closer to being a complete protein than many other plant sources. It's also high in many of the B vitamins as well as the minerals phosphorus, magnesium, iron, copper, manganese, and zinc. And buckwheat is a good source of linoleic acid, an essential fatty acid.

Whole white buckwheat is naturally dried and has a delicate flavor that makes it a good stand-in for rice or pasta. When the hulled buckwheat kernels are roasted, they're called *kasha,* which has a deep tan color, a nutty flavor, and a slightly scorched smell. Cooks often use buckwheat in pancakes, biscuits, and muffins — but be aware that manufacturers often combine buckwheat with wheat in those products, so you have to read the labels carefully before buying buckwheat products. In Japan, people often make buckwheat into *soba,* or noodles, which sometimes — but not always — have wheat flour as well.

Mesquite (pinole)

Most people know of mesquite as an on-the-grill flavoring that makes foods taste smoky and sweet. But mesquite has been a staple for Native Americans for thousands of years. Its sweet, fragrant flowers make a honeylike substance, and the pod produces a ground meal called *pinole.* Mesquite flour is a low-glycemic-index flour (it's a 25 — see Chapter 1 of Book II for what that kind of rating means), making it helpful in controlling blood sugar levels. Furthermore, soluble fibers in the seeds and pods slow the absorption of nutrients, which also helps in managing blood sugar.

The sweet pods and seeds are a good source of fiber, calcium, manganese, iron, and zinc. They're also high in protein, and they contain the amino acid lysine, which isn't present in many traditional grains. Not only does mesquite flour stabilize blood sugar, but it tastes great, with a sweet, slightly nutty flavor that bears a hint of molasses.

Mixes that combine mesquite with other gluten-free flours are now available, making creating gluten-free goodies with this unique flour a snap.

Millet

Not a grain at all, millet is actually a grass with small, round, ivory and yellow kernels that swell when you cook them. Millet supplies more servings per pound than any other grain.

Millet is packed with vitamins, minerals, and other nutrients. High in iron, magnesium, phosphorus, and potassium, it's also loaded with fiber and protein, as well as the B-complex vitamins, including niacin, thiamin, and riboflavin. Millet is easier to digest than many traditional grains because it's more alkaline — it has a higher pH and therefore doesn't add to the acid already in your stomach.

Millet has been a staple food in Africa and India for thousands of years, and people grew it as early as 2,700 B.C. in China, where it was the prevalent grain before rice became the dominant staple. Today millet is still a significant part of the diet in northern China, Japan, Manchuria, and various areas of the former Soviet Union, Africa, India, and Egypt. Grown today in Western countries mostly for cattle and bird feed, millet is gaining popularity as a nutritious, delicious part of the human diet as well.

Montina (Indian ricegrass)

Montina is actually Amazing Grains's trademarked name for Indian ricegrass. Indian ricegrass was a dietary staple of Native American cultures from the Southwest United States to Canada more than 7,000 years ago. Extremely hearty, Indian ricegrass was a good substitute during years when maize crops failed or game was in short supply. It has a bold flavor and is loaded with fiber and protein.

Quinoa (hie)

Quinoa (pronounced *keen*-wa) — and also called *hie* (pronounced *he*-uh) — is yet another of the grains that isn't really a grain; it's actually a fruit and a relative of the common weed lambsquarter. The National Academy of Science describes quinoa as "the most nearly perfect source of protein from the vegetable kingdom."

Like other superfoods and alternative grains, quinoa is packed with lysine and other amino acids that make it a complete protein. It's also high in phosphorus, calcium, iron, vitamin E, and assorted B vitamins, as well as fiber. Quinoa is usually pale yellow in color, but it also comes in pink, orange, red, purple, and black.

Because the uncooked grains are coated with *saponins* — sticky, bitter-tasting stuff that acts as a natural insect repellent — you should rinse quinoa thoroughly before cooking. Most quinoa that you buy in the store has already been rinsed.

Although new to North Americans, people in the South American Andes have cultivated quinoa since at least 3,000 B.C. Ancient Incas called this annual plant "the mother grain" because it was self-perpetuating and ever-bearing. They honored it as a sacred food product, because a steady diet appeared to ensure a full, long life; the Inca ruler himself planted the first row of quinoa each season with a golden spade.

Sorghum (milo, jowar, jowari, cholam)

Sorghum is another of the oldest-known grains (that isn't a true cereal grain), and it has been a major source of nutrition in Africa and India for centuries. Now also grown in the United States, sorghum is generating excitement as a gluten-free insoluble fiber and is probably best known for the syrup that comes from one of its varieties.

Because sorghum's protein and starch are more slowly digested than that of other cereals, it may be beneficial to diabetics (and healthful for anyone). It's high in iron, calcium, and potassium, and doctors actually used to prescribe it as a supplement for people low in these nutrients.

Sorghum fans boast of its bland flavor and light color, which don't alter the taste or look of foods when you use sorghum in place of wheat flour. Many cooks suggest combining sorghum with soybean flour. Sorghum is also fermented and used in alcoholic beverages.

Sorghum and millet are both rich in a group of compounds called *nitrilosides*. Some people notice a correlation between high nitriloside intake and low cancer rates, leading some to speculate that nitrilosides may actually help fight or prevent cancer. For instance, in Africa, where as much as 80 percent of the diet consists of high-nitriloside-yielding foods, the cancer incidence is very low.

Teff (tef)

It's tiny, but teff is a nutritional powerhouse. Teff is the smallest of the grains that aren't true cereal grains; in fact, the name itself means "lost," because if you drop it on the ground, you probably won't find it. A staple grain in Ethiopia for nearly 5,000 years, teff packs a protein content of nearly 12 percent and is five times richer in calcium, iron, and potassium than any other grain. Teff, which has a sweet, nutty flavor, grows in many different varieties and colors, but the most common are ivory, brown, and reddish-tan varieties.

You can cook the whole grain and serve it with sliced fruit or as a breakfast cereal with butter and brown sugar on top. Or you can add teff flour to baked goods to add a unique flavor and beef up the nutritional value.

If you've heard of teff, it's probably in reference to *injera,* a traditional fermented bread with a spongy texture and yeasty taste. Treated as an edible utensil, injera is used to soak up juices and soups, and even to grab meat and eat it. Beware, though; traditional injera has wheat flour added to it.

Checking Up on Questionable Ingredients

The diet gets a little trickier when you don't know that a food is almost always gluten-free or gluten-loaded. In this section, you discover which items you need to question and some of the foods people used to question but now know are gluten-free.

Knowing which foods to research

Of course, to be safe, you need to question everything. Consider tea, for instance — read the label and you just might find barley malt.

Some ingredients aren't so clear, because sometimes these ingredients are gluten-free and sometimes they're not. For these ingredients, you have to look deeper into the question of "Is it or isn't it?" that is covered at length in Chapter 5 of Book I.

Ingredients you need to question include

- ✔ Brown rice syrup
- ✔ Fillers

Book I

**Getting
Started
with Going
without
Gluten**

✔ Flavors and natural flavorings

✔ Seasonings and spice blends

✔ Stabilizers

✔ Starch (in pharmaceuticals)

These ingredients don't always have gluten. In fact, they rarely do. But according to the U.S. Food and Drug Administration Code of Federal Regulations, they *can* contain gluten, so to be safe, you need to check.

Thanks to relatively new labeling laws, there are far fewer "questionable" ingredients. Now manufacturers have to clearly indicate whether a product has wheat in it. See Book I, Chapter 5 for more details on the new laws.

Putting an end to the controversy over certain foods

People used to question certain ingredients, and they were on the have-to-dig-deeper-to-make-sure-this-is-gluten-free list. These people questioned ingredients because of rumors, bad information, and misunderstandings. They questioned because of ambiguous labeling laws. But today, thanks to new labeling laws and more definitive research, the following ingredients are no longer in question:

✔ Alcohol (distilled)

✔ Caramel color

✔ Citric acid

✔ Dextrin

✔ Flavoring extracts

✔ Hydrolyzed plant protein (HPP)

✔ Hydrolyzed vegetable protein (HVP)

✔ Maltodextrin (except in pharmaceuticals)

✔ Modified food starch

✔ Mono- and diglycerides

✔ Starch (in food)

✔ Vanilla and vanilla extract

✔ Vinegar (except malt vinegar)

✔ Wheat grass

✔ Yeast (except brewer's yeast)

The gluten-free status of these ingredients applies to ingredients produced in the United States and Canada. Other countries may have different manufacturing processes.

Flavorings have been considered a questionable ingredient on the gluten-free diet for years. But according to Shelley Case, one of the leading authorities on the gluten-free diet, there's little or no need to question flavorings anymore. She points out that gluten can be used in flavorings in only two instances. One is in hydrolyzed proteins, but with current labeling laws, wheat has to be declared on the label if it is used. The other is in barley malt extract or syrup, but Case points out that it's almost always listed on the label as "barley malt," "barley malt extract," or "barley malt flavoring." She notes that some companies may list it as "flavor (contains barley malt)," but very rarely is it listed as only "flavor" or "natural flavor." So why leave it on the "to be questioned" list? Because "very rarely" leaves room for the possibility, however slight, that barley malt may have been used and listed only as a "flavoring."

The Buzz on Booze: Choosing Alcoholic Beverages

In any discussion of the gluten-free lifestyle, someone inevitably shoots his hand up Arnold Horshack–style, with a please-tell-me-it-ain't-so look on his face, and asks: "Beer doesn't have gluten in it . . . does it?" Yeah, it does.

But lots of alcoholic beverages are gluten-free — and if you try, you can even find gluten-free beer. What follows is the buzz on booze.

Booze you can use

The list of gluten-free alcoholic beverages is way longer than the list of bevies that are off-limits. Other forms of alcoholic beverages may be gluten-free in addition to these, but this list covers the basics of the booze you can use:

- ✔ Bourbon
- ✔ Brandy
- ✔ Cider (occasionally contains barley, so be careful)
- ✔ Cognac
- ✔ Gin

Book I

Getting
Started
with Going
without
Gluten

- ✔ Rum
- ✔ Schnapps
- ✔ Tequila
- ✔ Vodka
- ✔ Whiskey (such as Crown Royal and Jack Daniels)
- ✔ Wine (and sparkling wine or Champagne)

Knowing what kinds of liquor you can consume can be confusing, because some alcoholic beverages are distilled from gluten-containing grains. However, as long as the drinks are distilled and the grains aren't added back into the gluten-containing mash, the drinks remain gluten-free.

Step away from the bottle

Just a few types of alcoholic beverages aren't allowed on the gluten-free diet. They include (but may not be limited to)

- ✔ Beer (with a few exceptions)
- ✔ Distilled spirits that are added back to the mash
- ✔ Malt beverages

The distillation process completely eliminates any traces of gluten, which is why you can safely eat distilled vinegar, vanilla made with distilled extracts, and many alcoholic beverages made from distilled alcohol. If you're not sure whether your favorite bevy is gluten-free, check the gluten-free alcoholic beverages list in this chapter and confirm with the manufacturer.

Give three cheers for gluten-free beers! Several gluten-free beers are available commercially, including Redbridge by Budweiser.

Making Sure Your Medications and Supplements Are Safe

Remember, anything you ingest can cause problems if it's not gluten-free — even a tiny little pill. Be sure to check the label first, because some products actually say "gluten-free" right on the label.

Starch and modified food starch in pharmaceuticals may come from wheat. If you see either of these on the label, you need to call the manufacturer and find out more about where the starch is from.

If you're wondering about a prescription drug, ask the pharmacist if he or she knows whether the product is gluten-free. If the pharmacist doesn't know, ask for the package insert and use the pharmacy's *Physician's Desk Reference* (PDR) (the Canadian version is called the Compendium of Pharmaceutical Specialties [CPS]) to look up the name and phone number of the manufacturer. Then you can just call the manufacturer and find out.

Keep a few tips in mind:

- ✔ Have your pharmacist make a notation in the computer, either under your personal records or under the record for that drug, indicating whether the product is gluten-free. That way you'll know for the future, as will others who ask.

- ✔ If the product is over-the-counter, call the manufacturer to confirm the drug's gluten-free status. Usually, the drug company sends you a list of all the gluten-free products it makes, and you can keep the list on hand.

   Figure out now which of the over-the-counter products you commonly use are gluten-free. For instance, painkillers, fever reducers, cold medications, and anti-inflammatories are often gluten-free — but you sure don't want to be wondering about it at 1 a.m., when your child's earache is keeping him — and you — up at night.

- ✔ Write "GF" in permanent marker on the medication container. That way you don't have to wonder whether the drug is safe when you need to take it.

- ✔ See www.glutenfreedrugs.com for more information, or take a look at some of the product guides and downloadable databases commercially available.

Using Nonfood Products: What You Need to Know

You may get a lot of conflicting information about nonfood products and whether you need to be concerned. You may hear that you need to beware of plastic storage containers, pots and pans, lotions, shampoos, envelopes, stamps, glues . . . what's a gluten-freebie supposed to do?

The biggest question is, if you're not eating it, does it really matter? The answer is, sometimes yes and sometimes no. (What, you expected something more concrete?)

Play-Doh has gluten in it. Sure, you're not supposed to eat Play-Doh, but really — who can resist a nibble or two? Lots of recipes for gluten-free play-doughs are available from a quick search on the Internet.

You don't have to worry about plastic storage containers, pots and pans, envelopes, or stamps. The following sections let you know what to check out and what you can let slide.

Makeup matters

Well, sometimes it matters. And sometimes it doesn't. The makeup that matters most is makeup you're likely to get in your mouth (or someone else's), like lipstick, lip gloss, lip balm, and anything else that goes on or near your lips. Foundation, eye makeup, powder, and other makeup products shouldn't matter unless you get them close to your mouth and could possibly ingest them.

Lotions and potions

Experts assert that the gluten molecule is too large to pass through skin, so lotions, shampoos, conditioners, and other external products shouldn't be a problem unless you have open sores, rashes, or dermatitis herpetiformis, also know as DH.

Sometimes lotion from your hands or arms can get on the food you're eating or preparing, and that can cause a problem. Be sure to wash your hands well (along with any other area that may touch food) so you don't end up eating your lotion.

In spite of the scientific evidence suggesting that external products shouldn't pose a problem, many people insist that they do have a reaction to external products that contain gluten. Who's to argue? If it bothers you, don't use it.

Dental products

You're really not supposed to swallow your toothpaste, mouthwash, or other dental products — but you're undoubtedly going to get a swallow or two from time to time, and if it contains gluten, that can potentially cause a problem. You'll probably never find a toothpaste or mouthwash that does contain gluten, but remember to read labels just in case.

Most products used in the dental office, such as polish, fluoride, and other dental agents, are gluten-free. But call your dentist in advance and ask him or her to check for you.

Chapter 5

Making Sure It's Gluten-Free: Digging a Little Deeper

Aproduct is either gluten-free or it isn't, right? End of story? Well, no.

If you like things simple and straightforward, this is-it-gluten-free-and-why-isn't-there-a-simple-answer issue is no doubt driving you nuts. The good news is that there's a lot less ambiguity than there used to be, and clarity is improving all the time. The bad news is that sometimes you still have to take an extra step (or four) before you know for sure whether a product is truly gluten-free.

In this chapter, you discover how to do everything you can to ensure that the food you're eating is as gluten-free as it can be. You run through the art of reading labels, investigate why "100 percent gluten-free" may not really mean 100 percent gluten-free, and get a crash course in calling manufacturers.

Gluten-Free Ambiguously: Why It Isn't So Straightforward

You: Does your product contain gluten?

Polite Lady on Phone: We don't add any gluten to our products.

You: (heavy sigh of relief) Oh, terrific. Then it's gluten-free, right?

Polite Lady on Phone: Oh, no, I didn't say that. Thank you for calling!

You may feel like you're being toyed with. Customer service reps seem to specialize in obfuscation, euphemism, and other forms of double-speak when you ask the seemingly simple question, "Is it gluten-free?"

Truth is, they're not messing with you to get their jollies. Questions arise for a variety of reasons. The most common causes involve ambiguous labeling, uncertainty about the origin of ingredients, and contamination concerns.

Loose labeling terminology

It would be great if you could just read a label and know what ingredients are in a product. Isn't that the point of having ingredient listings? But unfortunately, labels aren't always telling the entire story, and some ingredients aren't consistent; sometimes they have gluten, and sometimes they don't.

A law called the Food Allergen Labeling and Consumer Protection Act (FALCPA) that took effect in 2006 has helped — a lot. This law requires clear labeling of all foods that contain any of the top eight allergens — wheat, milk, eggs, fish, shellfish, tree nuts, peanuts, and soybeans. This means manufacturers must clearly identify wheat and all of its derivatives on food labels. For more info on this law, see the upcoming section "What the labeling law does and doesn't do."

With the law in place, knowing which foods are definitely off-limits because they contain wheat is much easier. Reading labels and knowing what's in a product is much more definitive, because wheat is really the bulk of what you're avoiding on a gluten-free diet.

Although wheat and its derivatives are now called out on all labels, you still need to watch for other gluten-containing grains (barley, rye, and cross-contaminated oats) and their derivatives, and realize that they can be (but aren't often) hidden in flavorings and additives.

Malt usually comes from barley, and products that use malt as a flavoring don't necessarily call it out on the label. Natural flavorings, for instance, may contain barley malt but be listed as "natural flavorings" on a label.

What the labeling law does and doesn't do

Book I

Getting
Started
with Going
without
Gluten

The Food Allergen Labeling and Consumer Protection Act (FALCPA), which requires manufacturers to clearly identify wheat and its derivatives on ingredient labels, is amazing progress for people avoiding wheat. Getting this labeling law passed was huge, and the celiac community was super influential in getting it done. While the law is immensely useful in helping to identify foods that aren't safe on the gluten-free diet, it also causes a little bit of confusion from time to time. The biggest areas of concern include these two:

- ✔ **How much wheat must be in the product to be subject to labeling requirements:** "One hundred percent gluten-free" is not only unrealistic but untestable, though you can test for "100 percent wheat-free." The new law calls for "zero tolerance," meaning that a product must have absolutely no allergen (in this case, wheat) in it — so even ingredients with the offending protein gluten removed have to be labeled as being allergenic. However, any food with less than 20 parts per million of gluten can be labeled gluten-free.

- ✔ **Overlabeling:** Sometimes manufacturers label food as having wheat in it even if it doesn't. That's because some interpretations of the new law say that wheat should be on the label if an ingredient's original source was wheat — even if that wheat is completely gone by the time the product is processed.

Some foods from gluten-containing grains — like citric acid, glucose syrup, and distilled vinegar (not malt) — are so highly processed that what grain they were derived from doesn't matter. They are, and always have been, gluten-free after processing (most of the time these foods come from gluten-free sources, anyway). But some interpretations of the labeling law require companies to put wheat on the label if those products were made from wheat; this leads consumers to believe that the product contains gluten when it actually doesn't.

Manufacturers can ask for an exemption if they can prove that the ingredient doesn't cause a harmful allergenic response or if they can provide scientific evidence that the ingredient doesn't contain allergenic proteins. This may be a challenge, because proving that white bread causes damage for people with various forms of gluten sensitivity, autism, autoimmune diseases, and other conditions can be tough enough. Proving the opposite is even harder.

In other words, although FALCPA was supposed to have proposed a firm definition of "gluten-free" for labeling purposes by 2008, it didn't happen.

"Gluten-free" may not mean 100 percent

In reality, something that's gluten-free isn't necessarily 100 percent gluten-free. That food may actually have minute traces of gluten, but as long as those traces are truly small, the product may sometimes still be called gluten-free and be safe for everyone — regardless of sensitivities or disease.

For a variety of reasons usually concerning cross-contamination, even foods that are inherently gluten-free sometimes turn out to contain gluten. Of course, this does not mean you should cheat, figuring you're going to get glutenated anyway. Quite the opposite. You need to be even more diligent to make sure you're doing everything you can to be safely gluten-free — as gluten-free as you can be.

Contamination risks

One of the most common reasons a product that is technically gluten-free may have trace amounts of gluten is contamination. Even if a product is made without any gluten-containing ingredients, contamination can occur at several points during processing and preparation. (Contamination is a risk when you're preparing and cooking your own foods, and manufacturers are dealing with food on a much larger scale. You can see more about how to avoid contamination in the kitchen in Chapter 2 of Book II.)

Grain processing

Commercially grown grains can contain trace amounts of other grains, because preventing cross-contamination is nearly impossible. The cross-contamination starts at the farm, where crops are often rotated between fields each year, and volunteer crops from previous years can pop up where they're least expected. Contamination can also occur in grain storage, during transportation, and during milling.

So if the product you're eating contains a grain — even a non-gluten-containing grain — there's a risk of contamination. Usually, the amount of contamination is miniscule and doesn't pose a health threat. The only time you know there's no cross-contamination is when the grains come from suppliers who grow, harvest, mill, and package only one (gluten-free) grain.

Oats are a good example of a grain that often undergoes cross-contamination. Frequently rotated with fields where wheat is grown, oats — gluten-free in and of themselves — can be contaminated in the fields as well as in the transportation and milling processes. Oats are more likely to be contaminated (and at greater levels) than other grains, which is why oats land on the forbidden list but other grains are still considered safe.

Book I

Getting
Started
with Going
without
Gluten

Shared equipment or facilities

Many companies produce several different products on one production line. For instance, a company that produces several types of cereal may run them all on the same equipment. Although the United States and many other countries have strict laws about cleaning lines between products, sometimes traces of gluten remain on the lines — or in the facility — and contaminate the gluten-free products that are made there. Some people eat only products made in dedicated gluten-free facilities.

Mysterious ingredient sources

Sometimes the gluten-free status of a product is questionable because tracking the source of its ingredients is tough. Most product manufacturers get their ingredients from a variety of suppliers. Sometimes a supplier can't guarantee the gluten-free status of the ingredients it's supplying or an ingredient's source can't be traced.

Some suppliers may not really understand what gluten-free is and yet still may claim that their ingredient is safely gluten-free when, in fact, it may not be.

Defining Safe Amounts of Gluten

The term *safe amounts of gluten* may appear to be an oxymoron, given the vehemence about staying gluten-free you find throughout this book.

Yet the truth is that there's a threshold of gluten that's safe for everyone, even on a daily basis. The amount that's safe is equal to about a fraction of a crumb — a teensy-weensy fraction of a teensy-weensy crumb.

People measure gluten in *parts per million (ppm)*. The U.S. Food and Drug Administration has proposed a limit of 20 ppm for a food to be labeled "gluten-free." This threshold has yet to be formally adopted, but 20 ppm is becoming the standard for declaring a food to be gluten-free.

How much is a part per million, anyway? For easier math, take bread that contains 200 ppm of gluten as an example. Cut that slice of bread into 5,000 pieces, and you have 5,000 crumbs. One of those crumbs is equivalent to 200 out of a million parts — equal to the amount of gluten in that piece of bread. That fraction of the bread weighs about 0.006 grams, or about 0.0002 ounces.

A couple of relatively new certification programs with easy-to-recognize logos are making an impressive and helpful mark on the gluten-free community. Two support groups were behind the birth of the certification process. Gluten Intolerance Group (GIG) launched the first certification program in the United States with the Gluten-Free Certification Organization (GFCO) symbol. The *Certified Gluten-Free* logo indicates that a food contains less than 10 ppm of gluten. The GFCO checks ingredient lists, tests foods, and inspects manufacturing plants, giving shoppers the assurance that a product is gluten-free and the manufacturing facility is free of contaminants. Celiac Sprue Association (CSA) also has a seal indicating that products are gluten-free (and oat-free), testing to less than 5 ppm of gluten. When you see these symbols, you can trust that the foods you're eating are safe.

Testing for Gluten in Foods

With so many questions about what does and doesn't have gluten, you should have a test you can do to know for sure. And you do!

Several types of gluten tests are available; some are used commercially, and some are designed for consumer use. Some of the commercial tests are so sensitive they can detect as little as 5 ppm (parts per million); several manufacturers of gluten-free products use them to ensure the purity of their foods.

Gluten home tests usually work a lot like a home pregnancy test: A series of lines appear on a small wand to give you a reading. To dissolve the gluten, you mix the food with some fluid in a tube; you then use a small comb to place the liquid in the wand, which is about the size of a large, flat pen. The liquid flows through a test "window," and within about five minutes, lines appear to indicate whether the food contains gluten.

Home tests can be a great way to test foods you're not sure about. The most popular test is called EZ Gluten, which works on flours, mixes, or prepared foods. It tests to 10 ppm, so it's extremely sensitive. You can order it at www.ezgluten.com.

Deciphering Label Lingo

The good news — and the bad news — is that you don't have to look for "gluten-free" on the label. In other words, there's a big, bold world of gluten-free goodness that doesn't say "gluten-free" on it but is nonetheless gluten-free. The first step to finding out whether a food is gluten-free is reading labels.

Reading ingredient labels on food products can be informative, enlightening, question-provoking, emotion-evoking, confusing, frustrating, timesaving, and time-consuming — all in one. Sometimes seeing what's in the foods you eat is downright scary. But for people who are serious about being gluten-free, label reading is not optional.

Reading labels is almost an art, beginning with the label flip-scan. If you've been reading labels for a while, you know the score — you grab a product and, with a fancy twist of the wrist, you flip to the list of ingredients and scan for forbidden items. Spot one, and the product goes back on the shelf. This becomes such a habit that you may find yourself doing the label flip-scan with products you don't even eat.

Reading labels can be intimidating at first because many processed foods contain all sorts of multisyllabic ingredients that you've probably never heard of (most of those are chemicals, and many of them are on the safe ingredients list). But you get used to the many (sometimes scary) ingredients you actually eat, and before you know it, you've mastered the label flip-scan — all while you make mental calculations of how much you can save with your double coupons.

Reading Glutenese: Knowing what to look for

The key to efficient label reading is knowing what to look for. Of course, if you happen to spot the words "gluten-free" on the label, you may find yourself wanting to do a touchdown dance. Go ahead. Seeing "gluten-free" on a label is worthy of celebration.

But usually, label reading is far more complex than that, and you're relegated to poring over lengthy lists of ingredients.

For ingredients other than wheat, or to check ingredients you've never heard of, the safe and forbidden ingredients and additives lists at www.celiac.com are a good guide. (Click on Safe Gluten-Free Food List / Unsafe Foods & Ingredients to find the lists.) You might want to print a copy of the lists and take them with you when you shop. When you encounter ingredients you've never heard of, you can check your lists and decide whether the product goes back on the shelf or in the cart.

Check labels often. Ingredients change, and a product that may have been gluten-free at one time may not necessarily still be gluten-free.

Avoiding tempting marketing come-ons

Labels are cluttered with enticements touting tempting benefits like *organic, all-natural, no GMOs, healthy, nutritious,* and the forever-to-be-dreaded *new and improved.* Few of these claims are substantive, and none of them say anything about the gluten-free status of a product. In fact, "new and improved" is actually a euphemism for "now you definitely have to check ingredients — again — because we've changed our formula."

People sometimes make the erroneous assumption that if a product is healthful, it's more likely to be gluten-free. Not true. In fact, if you see the words *whole grain* emblazoned on a label, step away from the product. Chances are, it's not gluten-free.

Even if a product says *wheat-free* on the label, that doesn't mean it's gluten-free. You still need to watch for barley, rye, and oats — as well as their derivatives.

Checking with Food Manufacturers

After you've read the label and you've determined that the product doesn't include any obvious sources of gluten, you may want to check with the manufacturer to make sure your food doesn't have any hidden sources.

These days, checking is pretty easy. Most products have a toll-free phone number listed right on the package. When you call that number, you often get connected with someone who actually knows what you're talking about, and the company usually sends you a whole bunch of coupons for its products. In fact, the manufacturer will sometimes send you a long list of its gluten-free items.

Sometimes, though, you get the friendly customer service rep, the coupons, and the list but confusing answers to your questions.

Take a cellphone into the store with you. That way, when you find a food you have questions about, you can call right then and there.

For the most part, all you have to say when you call is, "I'd like to find out whether your product is gluten-free," and the friendly customer service reps know exactly what you're talking about. Occasionally, though, being specific is helpful and even necessary. Say, "I'm calling to see whether this product is gluten-free, which means it doesn't contain wheat, rye, barley, or oats." You may educate one more person about gluten.

Some manufacturers have voluntarily adopted a policy to declare all gluten-containing ingredients and their derivatives, so if you don't see anything on their labels, you don't have to contact the company. When you contact a company and find out that this is its policy, make note of it. Before long, you'll have a list of companies that declare their gluten-containing ingredients and you won't have to spend so much time checking the status of products.

Book I

Getting
Started
with Going
without
Gluten

Interpreting company responses

When you call a company to find out whether its product is gluten-free, you get one of a few responses. Interpreting these responses sometimes requires a little inference, deduction, and conjecture on your part. If you can't get a straight answer, play it safe and leave the product out of the cart. These are the most common responses you get and the possible interpretations.

"We can't guarantee our product is gluten-free."

This doesn't necessarily mean "Our product may not be gluten-free." It usually translates to "Yes, our product is gluten-free, but our legal department asks that we cover our tushies by telling you we can't guarantee it."

Aside from legal considerations, the "We can't guarantee our product is gluten-free" reply — the most common you'll hear — may be for other reasons as well:

- ✔ The product has ingredients that may be derived from a gluten-containing source.
- ✔ The company gets ingredients from other suppliers and doesn't know for sure that they're gluten-free.
- ✔ The company suspects that other products produced in the facility could cause contamination.
- ✔ The company doesn't test for gluten, so even though the company is certain the products are gluten-free, it doesn't want to guarantee that.
- ✔ The company suspects its products are gluten-free but doesn't completely understand the concept, so it defers to this reply.

If you're told "We can't guarantee our product is gluten-free," ask questions and find out why they won't vouch for the product's gluten-free status. With more information, you can decide for yourself whether the product is safe to eat.

"Our product is not gluten-free."

Sometimes the "No, our product is not gluten-free" response is really what the customer service rep means, and gluten that isn't clearly indicated on the label is in the product.

But don't make the mistake of interpreting this one as always being "Our product is not gluten-free." You need to probe a little deeper. A customer service rep who suggests that whey or — good grief — canola oil may be the source of gluten should raise red flags.

"Yes, our product is gluten-free."

You have to judge for yourself whether the person on the other end of the phone truly understands the concept. Did Sally Jo really understand what you were talking about? Or did she then say, "Of course we don't put gluten in our products — sugar isn't good for you, anyway"?

Sometimes the rep follows up the gluten-free claim with "There are no sources of wheat, rye, barley, or oats, and there are no questionable additives. Therefore, it's safe for someone with wheat allergies, gluten intolerance, or celiac disease." Feel the love, baby. Feel the love.

Other times when the rep gives this response, she gets a little squirmy if you push her. For instance, if you reply, "Terrific! Then I can assume the brown rice syrup is from a non-gluten-containing source, right?" she asks you to hold. For a really long time. You may want to probe a little more before trusting her final answer.

"We won't tell."

Hey, it's not like you're trying to steal the special sauce formula (ketchup and mayo — whoopdidoo). You just need to know whether the product is going to cause severe intestinal trauma.

Company representatives who won't tell you anything about the ingredients probably don't have a good idea of what's in the product themselves, so avoiding those foods is a good idea.

"Huh?"

Hey, at least you know where you stand with these people — no fakers or know-it-alls in this bunch. They don't have a clue what you're talking about, and that's okay!

Fortunately, this isn't a common response anymore, but it does happen. Politely try to explain what types of ingredients may be in the product you're calling about, and if it still doesn't click, ask to speak to a quality control supervisor or nutrition expert.

Getting the most out of your calls to manufacturers

Book I

Getting
Started
with Going
without
Gluten

If you're going to take the time to contact manufacturers to learn more about the products you're eating, you may as well get the most out of the calls. Here are a few things to keep in mind:

- **Tune in.** Really listen to the person on the other end of the phone. Does he get it, or is he faking it? Is he giving you conflicting information or taking wild guesses? Does he sound confident and knowledgeable? You need to assess these things before you know for sure that you can trust what he says.

- **Don't be afraid to take it up a notch.** Asking to speak to a supervisor is not offensive or rude. If you feel the person you're talking to isn't giving you credible answers, ask to speak with a supervisor or the director of quality control or nutritional services.

- **Learn from the answers.** If you see an ingredient on a package you've never heard of, call the manufacturer about it. If the customer service rep tells you that product is gluten-free, take note. That means the ingredient is gluten-free, too. Feel free to question the specific ingredient to make sure, and you may find that the customer service rep is especially knowledgeable and can tell you the exact source.

- **Acknowledge the rep's knowledge.** You need customer service reps, and the fact that they're becoming more knowledgeable about the gluten-free status of the company's products is immensely helpful. If they're friendly and knowledgeable, let them know how much you appreciate it. Maybe even take the time to write a letter to the company thanking it for supporting the gluten-free community by having knowledgeable customer service reps and gluten-free products.

- **Speak up.** Being a squeaky wheel is not only okay but important — you should call frequently. One reason to call often is that ingredients change and you need to continually verify that a product is still gluten-free. But calling is also beneficial for everyone, because it sends a message to the company that the gluten-free community is important. Calling encourages better labeling, and maybe company leaders will think twice before adding malt flavoring to their products!

- **Take note.** You may want to keep a folder of the products you use the most and make note of when you called the manufacturer and what response you got. You may even want to share your homemade product list with others.

Mark it up for safety! After you've called a manufacturer about a product you have in your pantry, use a permanent marker to write "GF" all over it so you remember that it's gluten-free.

Getting product listings from a company

Food manufacturers, restaurants, stores, and distributors are usually happy to send you lists of their gluten-free products, and sometimes they ice the (gluten-free) cake with a few coupons.

Keep in mind that if a product isn't on the list, that doesn't mean it's not gluten-free. Recently, someone on a chat site received a listing of gluten-free items from a fast-food chain. She quickly posted an announcement that the broiled chicken was not gluten-free, sending shockwaves through guilt-ridden mommies who had stuffed their kids full of the chicken patties for weeks. Making a few calls proved the chicken was, in fact, gluten-free but hadn't made the list due to publication deadlines.

Also remember that just because a product is on the list doesn't mean it's always gluten-free. An item could be gluten-free one day and make it onto the list, and next thing you know, cruel gluten-spiking chefs somewhere take a vote and decide to add malt flavoring.

If you want to buy product listings, you have a few choices. Product guides are available from some support groups, and they're very helpful, but realize that they may not include regional brands and that they're up-to-date only at the time of printing. Smartphone apps are a better option.

Searching for Information: The Good, the Bad, and the Completely Ludicrous

The good news is that tons of information on gluten, gluten sensitivity, celiac disease, related disorders, and the gluten-free diet is available. The bad news is that lots of it is garbage.

No matter what the source, always question the credibility of the authors, and remember that even seemingly credible sources can perpetuate bad information.

You may find that a lot of the information is conflicting. One source says vinegar is safe; another says it's forbidden. A few tips can help sort out the reality from the ridiculous:

Book I

Getting
Started
with Going
without
Gluten

- ✔ **Check the publication date.** Information on the Internet and in books and magazines can become outdated the minute it's published, so make sure what you're reading is current.

- ✔ **Look for credentials.** Are the authors knowledgeable, or are they just sharing personal experiences and opinions? Where do they get their information? Not all writers are reliable: You don't need a license to publish, nor do you have to let the facts get in the way of a good story.

- ✔ **Compare the information to what you find from other sources.** A lot of the information out there is conflicting, so compare all the sources and figure out which source stands up to closer scrutiny. The sources of information cited in this chapter are reputable and reliable.

The Internet, for better and for worse

The Internet is awfully convenient. You can be in your jammies, cup of coffee in hand, before the sun even rises and find out more about gluten than you ever knew you didn't know. The problem is that you can't always trust what you read online, and checking credibility is difficult. Furthermore, people publish information to the web and sometimes forget about it or don't take the time to update it. What you're looking at could be several years old — and lots has changed in the past several years.

A nonprofit group called Information Center for Online Resources and Services, Inc. (ICORS; www.icors.us/contact-us.html), runs a celiac *listserv,* which is a list specifically targeted to the celiac community. You subscribe to the list (make sure you do so from the e-mail you want to use each time), and then you receive postings from other people — questions, comments, product recommendations, recipes, and similar topics. You can post your questions and comments, too. You receive the posts as e-mail, and they also appear in a threaded discussion on a web page.

Keep in mind that this list is open to anyone and that you have to carefully scrutinize any information for accuracy. To subscribe, send an e-mail to listname-request@listserv.icors.org, substituting "listname" with the name of the mailing list you're interested in.

A quick Internet search should also turn up several chat sites for people living a gluten-free lifestyle.

Magazines and newsletters

Some outstanding magazines and newsletters are targeted to the gluten-free community. They're one of the best places to find current, accurate information about gluten-free products, guidelines, and the medical conditions that benefit from a gluten-free diet. In particular, try these resources:

- ✔ *Gluten-Free Living* (www.glutenfreeliving.com)
- ✔ *Living Without's Gluten Free & More* (www.glutenfreeandmore.com)
- ✔ *Journal of Gluten Sensitivity* (www.celiac.com)

The major support groups (discussed in the following section) have excellent newsletters as well.

Support groups

Australia, Ireland, Spain, the United Kingdom, Finland, and many other countries have their own support groups that meet the needs of the celiac and gluten-free communities. You can find them with a quick Internet search. The national support groups in the United States include

- ✔ Gluten Intolerance Group (www.gluten.net)
- ✔ Celiac Disease Foundation (www.celiac.org)
- ✔ Celiac Sprue Association (www.csaceliacs.org)
- ✔ Raising Our Celiac Kids (R.O.C.K.), available through www.celiac.com
- ✔ GFCF Diet Support Group Information website (www.gfcfdiet.com)
- ✔ Autism Network for Dietary Intervention (www.autismndi.com)

Check the websites to see which group most adequately meets your needs and has a chapter near you. These support groups meet regularly and offer a variety of programs.

Chapter 6

Loving the Gluten-Free Lifestyle

For some people, it isn't the gluten-free diet itself that presents the biggest challenge — it's getting out of the house. (Sure isn't much of a lifestyle if it all happens within the same four walls, is it?) Even people who've been gluten-free for years sometimes feel uncomfortable about venturing away from home.

Yet getting out is important. Life in a bubble is for oxygen molecules, not humans. Does venturing outside require extra effort on your part? Sure. Might you receive a meal contaminated with gluten? Yep. Are you going to pay $20 for a meal that would have cost $6 to make at home? Darned straight. Is it worth it? Absolutely.

This chapter has answers for jumping out into the world without shirking your lifestyle. You come away from it equipped to handle the people and dietary concerns that enable you to eat in restaurants, and you find out about some of the other major challenges to living gluten-free, like teaching your kids how to manage for themselves and combating the emotional struggles that commonly accompany the switch to gluten-free and the temptations that can seem unending.

You've got this — really. Read on.

The Golden Rules of Going Out Gluten-Free

You've just arrived at the social event of the year. You're energized, you look fabulous, and you're eager to spend a great evening with friends. And you're famished. You zero in on the buffet table, loaded with the most amazing spread you've seen in decades, and slowly you begin to realize that you can't eat anything within a 2.8-mile radius. Your mood plummets as fast as your panic rises, because you realize you're going to be there all night with nothing to eat.

What follows are some basic rules of going out gluten-free. These rules should prevent such a buzz-kill scenario, because there's no reason to let a little food (or lack thereof) ruin a good time. Armed with these practical and emotional guidelines, you can make your social experiences as spectacular as ever.

Don't expect others to accommodate your diet

You shouldn't *expect* anyone to accommodate your gluten-free diet — even the people you love the most are going to forget or make mistakes. But they don't make mistakes because they don't care — they (usually) do. Often the lack of gluten-free goodies is just an oversight. And sometimes people think they understand the diet, but they miss some of the intricacies and what they think is gluten-free is floating in teriyaki.

Ask what's for dinner

When you're gluten-free and attending a social function, asking what's for dinner won't earn you a spot on the social circuit blacklist. Of course, some ways of asking are ruder than others, but I assume that you have more tact than that and can simply say to the host or hostess, "I have a dietary restriction and was wondering if it would be okay to ask you about what you're serving so I can plan accordingly." Most of the time, people are receptive to sitting down with you, discussing the menu, even asking for your input, and accommodating your diet as best they can.

Fill 'er up before you go

Because you can't expect any gluten-free goodies at the party, filling up before you go is a good idea. That way you're not starved and fixated on food, and you can enjoy the party for what it's really all about: fun and friends.

The biggest problem with this rule is that if you get to the party and find lots of gluten-free goodies you can eat, you'll be so excited that you'll eat them all, even though you're not hungry. Beware of popping buttons.

BYOF: Bring your own food

Don't worry that bringing your own food may offend the host. First, you can always discuss this option with him in advance. But if you don't, you can discreetly explain to him that you have a dietary restriction and, rather than burden him with the details ("I know you've been busy getting ready for this party . . ."), you thought it would be easiest just to bring a few things for yourself to eat. Ask where you should put your things and whether serving yourself when you get hungry is appropriate. Of course, the setting does determines the type of food you bring and how you bring it.

Bite your tongue when they make a mistake

You sat down with the hostess, talked about her plans for the meal, and decided where she could make a few accommodations for you. You get to the party only to find croissants surrounded by phyllo-filled finger foods and breaded fried stuff. You:

(A) Pout and starve.

(B) Pout, starve, and yell at the hostess.

(C) Pout, starve, scream rude things at the hostess, and pick the innards out of the phyllo-stuffed thingies. (No! They're glutenated!)

(D) None of the above. You enjoy the party and relax. You weren't hungry anyway, because you filled up before you came.

The correct answer, of course, is D.

Enjoy the company

It doesn't matter whether you're at a nightclub, a festive party for 500, a restaurant enjoying an intimate dinner for two, a wedding, or a wake — social gatherings are not about the food. They're about the occasion, the atmosphere, the ambiance, the people you're with . . . oh, and did I mention that you don't have to clean up?

Most societies use food as a focal point to draw people close during times of socialization and celebration. But don't lose sight of the celebration itself and the reason people are gathering in the first place. (If you're invited to a bread-tasting party, ignore this paragraph — in that case, it is about the food.)

Dining Out: Restaurant Realities and Rewards

Being on a gluten-free diet shouldn't hold you back from going out. Sure, eating at restaurants involves some risk. You don't know for sure what ingredients are in your food, no matter how much you try to educate your server and chef. Kitchen and waiting staffs are busy and can (and do) make mistakes, and cross-contamination is always an issue.

But with just a little extra effort, you can help ensure that your meal is safely gluten-free, and you can enjoy gluten-free dining as one of life's more pleasurable social experiences.

Consider some tips for eating out that can help make your gluten-free dining experiences the best they can be:

- **Be pleasant and grateful.** If you're demanding, you'll put them on the defensive. When they accommodate your requests, be extremely grateful.

- **Give them just enough information.** Not too much, not too little. You may have to read the server to see whether she is really "getting" what you're saying.

- **Don't be afraid to ask for what you want.** You're paying for the meal, and you should be able to enjoy it, knowing it's safe for you to eat.

- **Make it clear to the server and chef that this is a serious condition.** If you have to sound alarming, do so. One of the best ways to get their attention is to say, "It's kind of like an allergy to peanuts." You know it's not *really* like an allergy to peanuts, but it will get their attention.

- **Call ahead, if you can.** Remember to avoid busy hours. See whether they can fax or e-mail you a menu. At the same time, you can fax or e-mail them a list of ingredients you can and can't have.

- **Know how foods are prepared.** The more you know about traditional preparation, the better decisions you can make when ordering.

Book I

Getting
Started
with Going
without
Gluten

✔ **Bring your own food.** Not only can you bring your own bread or crackers to snack on, but you can even bring food for them to cook for you. Remember to offer suggestions for how to keep your food from becoming contaminated by the rest of the food in the restaurant.

✔ **Send it back if it's not right.** If you end up with a salad with croutons on it, don't pick out the croutons and eat it. That's not safe! Nothing is wrong with politely saying, "Excuse me. I must have forgotten to mention that I can't have croutons on my salad. Do you mind bringing me a new one?" Everyone knows you mentioned it; you're just letting them off the hook.

Choosing the restaurant

Don't go to Sam's All We Serve Is Pizza and whine that you can't eat anything. You're setting yourself up for frustration and disappointment if you choose a restaurant that, by the very nature of its menu selections, isn't likely to have much (if anything) that's gluten-free.

Instead, go to restaurants that have large and diverse menu selections, or choose an ethnic restaurant that's likely to have more gluten-free foods. Happy gluten-free dining starts with choosing restaurants that are likely to have foods on the menu that are already gluten-free or that the kitchen staff can easily modify.

Finding eateries with gluten-free menus

Lots of restaurants have gluten-free menus these days — some even post them online so you can decide where you want to go and what you want to order before heading out the door. The Gluten Intolerance Group (www.gluten.net) hosts a terrific program called the Gluten-Free Restaurant Awareness Program (GFRAP). GFRAP works with restaurants to help them provide gluten-free meals, providing materials about gluten-free guidelines, access to dietitians with expertise in the gluten-free diet, tips on maintaining a safe kitchen, and staff education. You can find a restaurant by using Gluten Intolerance Group's search function on its website.

A gluten-free menu is ultra convenient and somewhat comforting, but remember that many items on a "regular" menu are naturally gluten-free or can easily be made without gluten. So if the restaurant you want to go to doesn't have a gluten-free menu, or if nothing on the gluten-free menu floats your boat, don't despair. You'll likely still find something you can safely eat.

Restaurants that are good gluten-free bets

As a general rule, these types of restaurants are a good bet:

- **All-you-can-eat soup and salad:** Not only do these restaurants usually offer lots of items that are gluten-free, but they often have their ingredients handy so you can check soups and salad dressings to be sure.

- **Barbecues:** Although you have to check the sauces, many barbecues are good bets because they do traditional fare such as ribs, chicken, pork, corn on the cob, mashed potatoes, and potato salad.

- **Breakfast houses:** Be careful here — some breakfast places make the scrambled eggs with a boxed egg that has wheat flour mixed in (ick!). So ask for fresh eggs. You may also be able to get hash browns, fruit, yogurt, and lots of other good breakfast stuff.

- **Fast food:** Fast-food joints offer fries, shakes, salads, chili, and other foods that are often gluten-free. If you order a burger, make sure it's without a bun — even if you pluck it off, the bun contaminates your dinner. Many fast-food places offer a lettuce bun, even if they don't advertise that they do so. Several restaurants even post their nutritional information and ingredients online.

  When you're getting fries, make sure they're not breaded or coated in anything, and ask what other foods are fried in the same oil. You don't want to order fries that have been swimming with onion rings or something else that contaminates the oil with gluten.

- **Indian:** Many of the ingredients in Indian cooking are inherently gluten-free.

- **Mexican:** Mexican cooking includes many naturally gluten-free foods. Restaurants often guard their cooking secrets, but most Mexican recipes call for spices such as cumin, epazote, garlic, oregano, salt, and pepper. *Carnitas,* a traditional simmered pork dish served with corn tortillas, shredded lettuce, tomatoes, rice, and beans, is an example of a Mexican dish that's usually a safe bet. But as is the case with any meal, you need to make sure the kitchen staff doesn't add flour to the sauce, and, of course, specify corn tortillas instead of flour if you get a choice.

- **Mongolian barbecue:** Mongolian barbecues are essentially choose-your-own stir-fry restaurants. Because you can make your own sauces and add your own ingredients, Mongolian barbecues tend to be a good bet for gluten-free dining. Be sure to have the cooks thoroughly clean the grill before cooking your meal. And tell them that you have food allergies so they can keep your food separate from your neighbor's teriyaki chicken.

Book I

Getting
Started
with Going
without
Gluten

✔ **Steak and seafood:** These restaurants are likely to have steaks or burgers, seafood, salads (hold the croutons), baked potatoes or rice, french fries, and ice cream for dessert.

✔ **Thai/Vietnamese:** What a treat to be able to go to a Thai or Vietnamese restaurant and eat noodles! Be careful — not all their noodles are gluten-free, but most of them are rice-based and are safe. For the most part, the sauces they use are gluten-free, too.

Calling ahead

Don't be afraid to call a restaurant ahead of time to talk about the menu and to figure out whether the chefs can accommodate your gluten-free diet. If possible, have someone fax or e-mail you a menu so you can see what the restaurant serves that's likely to be gluten-free, and then call back and discuss the ingredients with the head chef. You can also fax or e-mail the restaurant a list of safe and forbidden ingredients. Sometimes restaurants are so accommodating that if you give them enough notice, they'll get special ingredients for your meal.

Making smart menu choices

Set yourself up for success. Choose menu items that are likely to be gluten-free or that the kitchen staff can easily modify to be gluten-free. Obviously, breaded and fried items aren't going to be your best bets, although sometimes cooks can use the same meat, season it with spices, and grill it instead.

Ordering is a four-step process:

1. **Find the foods on the menu that are already likely to be gluten-free or could easily be modified to be gluten-free.**

2. **Choose the item(s) you want.**

3. **Ask about ingredients and food-preparation methods. We go into detail about this later in this chapter.**

4. **Make sure you've made your order clear and offered suggestions for how to season and prepare your meal.**

Talking with the staff: Ask and ye shall receive

Don't be afraid to ask for what you want. People ask for special considerations at restaurants all the time, even when they don't have dietary restrictions. If you feel that the server isn't getting it, ask to talk with the chef. Of course, be tactful about it. Asking for special considerations for your meal isn't rude — especially when your health depends on it.

Yes, you really do need to talk to the server and maybe even the chef . . . and, yes, you sometimes need to give them lots of detail. But for the most part, you should keep explanations as simple as possible and work your way into detail if you need to. You may be surprised at how little you need to say.

Having restaurants cook the food you bring

Many restaurants allow you to bring your own food into the restaurant, and they may warm it or even cook it for you. If you do this, be aware of how they normally cook their food, because you probably need to watch out for some contamination concerns.

For instance, most pizza places use convection ovens that blow the flour all around. If you bring a pizza crust and ask them to use their toppings and cook it, you have to be sure their toppings aren't contaminated (they often are), and then you have to make sure they wrap the pizza securely in aluminum foil before warming it in the oven — otherwise, your gluten-free pizza goes into a pizza oven that's blowing flour all over. Same goes for bringing a pre-made gluten-free pizza with you — make sure it's wrapped carefully before asking them to warm it in their ovens.

Pasta places often allow you to bring gluten-free pastas and cook them for you. Be sure to remind the workers to use a clean pot, clean water, clean utensils, and a clean colander before they make your gluten-free pasta.

Not to state the obvious, but you probably should ask the restaurant to prepare your food only if you're actually buying some of theirs. A group of four, each of whom has brought his own meal in, won't win any popularity contests. But if one person in a group of four brings his meal, it's not usually a problem. Restaurants don't usually charge extra to warm or prepare meals you bring yourself, but you should ask to be sure.

Remembering the art of healthy tipping

When people accommodate your gluten-free diet and give you the peace of mind that helps you enjoy the multidimensional, multisensational experience of dining out, you should express your gratitude. If they've done it with an eager-to-please attitude, showing your appreciation is even more important.

The number of people going gluten-free is skyrocketing. Every server you talk to, every chef you inform, and every tip you leave will better the future for everyone going gluten-free today, tomorrow, and beyond.

Raising Happy, Healthy, Gluten-Free Kids

It's one thing when adults need or choose to adopt a gluten-free lifestyle. It's an entirely different ballgame when your kids need to be gluten-free. This section is loaded with information to help you deal with your roller-coaster emotions, the practicalities of having kids on the gluten-free diet, and the psychological impact this situation may have on your family.

The most important message of all is this: Getting the diagnosis is *good* for your child's life and yours. If you're having trouble believing us, read on.

Talking to your kids about being gluten-free

Whether your child is 18 months or 18 years old, now's the time to talk, and the entire family needs to be included. How you do this depends on your style, your intrafamily relationships, and your child's ability to understand the intricacies of the subject matter. Talking to your kids is step one in making sure they develop healthy attitudes and habits.

Even if your entire family doesn't choose to go gluten-free, having a gluten-free kid in the house affects everyone. All the family members need to know about your child's condition, the diet, and how to handle a variety of situations that may arise.

Everyone you talk to about the gluten-free lifestyle — and the conditions that require it — finds out how to feel about the gluten-free lifestyle from you. Is being gluten-free bad? Scary? Good? How you talk about it has a far greater impact than you may know.

The most important person to stay upbeat around is your child. For the rest of her life, how she feels about being gluten-free depends on you and your attitudes. She doesn't know how to feel — this situation is all new to her (granted, it's new to you, too). Give her the advantage of starting off upbeat and optimistic. If she's like most kids, she'll take it from there and will provide amazing strength and inspiration.

The level of detail you get into depends on your child's age, maturity, and ability to understand this type of situation. In a nutshell, you want to give him the "why" he's gluten-free (to feel better), the "what" (what gluten-free means), and the "what now" (what he can eat now that he's gluten-free), which is really most important, because that's what matters most to him.

Chances are, your child has had health or behavioral issues that led to the need for a gluten-free diet, so start the discussion with something positive, like, "You're going to feel *so* much better now that you're going to be eating gluten-free foods!"

Kids think in specifics. Drive the point home to them with something they can personally relate to, like, "You know how much your tummy's been hurting lately?" or "You know how hard it is for you to focus in class?" — "You won't have that anymore now that you're gluten-free!" Specifics can help children understand exactly *what's* going to be better on the gluten-free diet.

Then a few weeks into the lifestyle, remember to point out to your kids how much better they feel, thanks to the yummy gluten-free foods they're eating.

Don't underestimate what your kids can grasp. When explaining the diet to your child, use the "big" words like *gluten* (spare them *carboxymethylcellulose,* though, okay?). Even if your child has developmental or learning disabilities, use the proper terminology so that he can better communicate what he can and can't eat to others.

Of course, he's not going to understand at first (did *you?*). Give him examples he can understand — explain that "gluten is in lots of the foods we used to eat, like bread, cookies, and crackers," and then quickly let him know that *lots* of yummy foods don't have gluten in them.

Always focusing on what your child *can* have is important. Anytime you or your child asks about or points out a food that's off-limits, try to point out something equally scrumptious that's gluten-free. A couple of simple sentences do the trick: "You're right, Trevor, you can't eat those cookies. But you *can* have this candy bar, because it's gluten-free!"

Help your child make the connection that gluten makes him feel bad. Whenever you talk about gluten, point this out: "You're right, you can't eat that. It has gluten, and gluten makes you feel icky." This way, he learns to associate gluten with feeling bad — and that's great.

Kids need to learn to talk to other people — both adults and other kids — about their gluten-free lifestyle. They'll be doing it for the rest of their lives, and there's no time to start like the present. Of course, exactly what they say and how they communicate it depends on their age, their personality and style, who they're talking to, and how comfortable they are talking about this type of situation.

Teach your child a phrase to use, even if he's too young to know what it means. Use something comprehensive that he can repeat to adults. For instance, teach him to say, "I can't eat gluten. That means I don't eat wheat, rye, barley, malt, and oats." That definition isn't technically correct (malt *is* from barley, and oats are gluten-free but sometimes contaminated), but it tells adults what they need to know.

Giving your child control of the diet

If your child doesn't take control of his diet, the diet will control him. No matter how young he is, he needs to learn from day one to make decisions about what he can and can't eat — and how important it is not to cheat, no matter how tempted he is.

From a psychological standpoint, it's important for the gluten-free diet not to take front-and-center-stage in your child's life — and that means he should be thinking of other things most of the time. But when it comes time to eat, he needs to realize how important it is that he makes good choices. He needs to pay close attention to food.

Giving your child control doesn't mean you let her make all the decisions by herself — as in everything else in life, children need a little guidance, especially at first. You can do a lot together to help kids learn how to make good food choices.

✔ **Read labels together.** Even if your child is too young to read, pretend. Hold the ingredients label where you can both see it, and go through the ingredients out loud, one by one (just like when you're tired and reading them bedtime stories, you can skip the superfluous stuff). Point to the words, and when you come to pertinent ones, like *wheat,* remind them, "Nope. This one has gluten in it." And then, because you're well conditioned to quickly point to the alternative, follow up with, "Let's try *this* one," and grab something you know is gluten-free.

✔ **Make a game out of it.** When you're reading labels or talking about foods, see who can decide which one is gluten-free (or not) first. (Note to you competitive types: Let 'em win a few.)

✔ **Have your child call manufacturers.** After she's seen you do it a few times, let your child make the calls. Sometimes being on another extension so you can take over is a good idea.

✔ **Have your child plan the menu.** Not only does this idea give him a chance to practice figuring out what's gluten-free and what isn't, but you know he'll actually eat everything he's served. So what if his menu consists of french fries, rice, candy bars, and gluten-free macaroni and cheese? Go with it. Remember, for that meal at least, he's in control.

✔ **Have your child pack her lunch.** If it's not perfectly nutritionally balanced, make some suggestions and see whether she'll add the nutritious stuff you want. If not, go with it. It won't kill her to have one bad meal — but it will let her know she can choose foods that are gluten-free (and yummy!).

✔ **Let your child cook.** Kids *love* to cook, even though it usually ends up being far more work than if they don't help. Figuring out how to cook at an early age is important for all kids, especially for kids who will be requiring some specially prepared foods for the rest of their lives.

Your children are going to make mistakes. Mistakes won't kill or permanently harm them, and with any luck, it'll cause some discomfort so they realize the importance of being more attentive.

Beating the Blues: Overcoming Emotional Obstacles

Live within this lifestyle for any length of time, and you're sure to encounter your share of emotional challenges, as most people do when they adopt a strict gluten-free lifestyle. The idea is to find out how to identify those challenges and obstacles and overcome them.

The key to remember is this: Deal with it; don't dwell on it. You can be mad, sad, uncomfortable, ticked off, and out-of-your-head ready to scream with frustration. That's okay. All those reactions and emotions are perfectly normal when someone has told you to change your entire life. But getting mired in the negativity and difficulty of it all is easy, in which case these feelings may begin to consume you. Allow yourself to experience the tough emotions, and then move on.

Recognizing common emotional struggles

Book I

Getting
Started
with Going
without
Gluten

When someone tells you that you have to do something (a situation so many people who go gluten-free face), you're likely to have a harder time with it. Toss in the unique social and practical challenges that arise when you're living a gluten-free lifestyle, and some people find themselves dealing with all sorts of complex emotional issues:

- **Social activities revolve around food.** Because you don't eat gluten, you may feel isolated, or you may be afraid to participate in these social functions because you think you won't be able to eat anything.

- **People you love don't get it.** Sometimes, no matter how much you say or don't say, some people, many of whom are your closest buddies, just don't get it.

- **People may think you're crazy.** When you try to explain this to some people, or when they watch you stumble through one of your first experiences ordering at a restaurant, they may think you're outlandishly high-maintenance, that you're picky, that you have an eating disorder, or that you're crazy.

- **They call it "comfort food" for a reason.** Weight-management lectures aside, for better or for worse, many people find eating to be a stress reliever. When your food options are limited, eating can be disconcerting and can create anxiety.

- **Some people don't do well with change of any type.** For those people, something that involves changing their entire lifestyle can be really disruptive.

- **You're losing control in your life.** You're hereby "sentenced" to a life of dietary restrictions. Wow. How's that for taking control away? You've been eating since you were a baby and choosing your own foods not long after that, and now someone's going to tell you what you can and can't eat? It's tough sometimes.

- **It seems so permanent.** Oh, wait. That's because it is. And that doesn't help someone feeling "put upon" by their restrictions.

- **You feel like you're on an island.** If you do, you'd better hope it's a big island, because millions of people are going gluten-free. But we digress. The gluten-free lifestyle seems isolating to some people; they even feel ostracized. If you're feeling like that, read on, because this part of the book should help you realize that you have control over those feelings and that you don't have to be isolated or feel like you're alone in this.

In the upcoming sections, you find out about some of the common emotions people experience when they hear they have to go gluten-free.

Sheer shock and panic

On one hand, it all seems so sudden. You're in the doctor's office talking about your bowel movements or lack thereof, and the next thing you know, you're branded with a condition that will change the way you eat for the rest of your life. Yet in some ways, it's not sudden at all. Chances are, you've been having health issues for years. And now it has a name. And a treatment. Both of which can stun you.

Have you ever had fingers that were so cold they were nearly frozen? But when they begin to thaw, they throb and feel like you've just run them through a wood chipper. That's kind of how you feel when sheer shock turns to pure panic. That's when the reality of the words "diet for life" begins to sink in, and you start to panic. What will you eat? How will you do it? Where will you find special foods? Can you do it?

Rest assured that these feelings are normal, and they do pass. You will figure out what you can eat, and your panic will subside as you become more comfortable with the diet, which begins on day one. The learning curve is steeper for some than others, but you *will* learn, and the panic will wear off.

Anger and frustration

The shock and panic have subsided, and you're beginning to feel more comfortable with what you can and can't eat. But something's eating at you. You realize you're miffed. Peeved. Fightin' mad and agonizingly frustrated!

Anger is a healthy emotion, and learning to deal with it is one of the most valuable lessons you can learn in life. Taking your anger out on the people closest to you is tempting, especially if they're adding to the frustration by being less than understanding about your new lifestyle. If you need help dealing with the anger, reach out. But don't lash out, especially at the people closest to you, because they're not to blame, and they can be immensely supportive when you need it most.

Grief and despair

Are you grieving? Do you feel like you've lost your best friend? In a way, you may have. Food, your control over what you eat, and even the simple act of putting food into your mouth can soothe you and bring you comfort. When you're forced to give up your favorite foods (if they weren't your favorites before, they will be after you give them up!), the change can make you feel sad and melancholy. Furthermore, some people feel they're the only ones who have this problem, which can intensify feelings of isolation or loneliness.

If your child is going gluten-free, those feelings of grief can magnify. You dream that your children's lives will be carefree and ideal; having to deal with dietary restrictions that prevent them from eating what seem to be staples in a child's diet isn't usually part of your plan.

Some people reach a point of desperation or despair. They find the diet to be cumbersome and difficult, and they keep making mistakes. Then they figure if they can't do this right, they may as well not do it at all, and they give up.

Grief and despair are normal emotions, but don't give in to them. You will get over your feelings of sadness and loneliness, and this lifestyle doesn't have to be the least bit isolating or depriving. As for doing it right, give it your very best effort — truly 100 percent — and you will get it. Dealing with a mistake from time to time is better than giving up and not trying at all.

Loss and deprivation

You may feel a couple kinds of loss when someone tells you that you have to go gluten-free. You obviously lose your favorite foods — and what about the social situations that seem to go hand-in-hand with them?

Many of your favorite foods, at least in the form you know them, are a thing of the past. At first, the social situations may not seem the same without them — and they aren't just the same. They're the same but different, and that's okay. Remember when you attend these events that they're not really about the food — they're about the socialization. Also remember to bring yourself foods that you love.

Another kind of loss people feel is a loss of convenience. These days, food is prewashed, precut, prepeeled, precooked, prepackaged, pre-resealed, and practically pre-eaten and premetabolized into tummy fat before you ever get it home from the store. Convenience foods come as a complete snack or meal, in various combinations to please any palate. Yes, these foods are convenient — and sometimes, when you pluck them from the aisles of the produce section, they're even good for you and gluten-free. But many of them, for you, are a thing of the past.

Okay, so giving up gluten isn't as convenient — and you miss your old faves. But look what you've gained. Your health! The gluten-free diet is your key to better health, and that's priceless.

Sadness and depression

Occasionally, people get so overwhelmed with the whole concept of their medical condition and the gluten-free diet that they feel an impending doom, and they experience depression to some degree.

Be aware that depression can be a symptom you experience if you eat gluten despite your intolerance. Could the depression be due to accidental (or intentional) gluten ingestion? Or is it a lingering emotional discomfort from the pre-diagnosis days? Some people, before they're diagnosed (and some even afterward), are accused of "making up" their problems, or they're told the symptoms are all in their head. The accusations themselves can be so hurtful and frustrating that they cause the person to go into a state of depression.

Unfortunately, depression caused by illness can result in a vicious cycle. The physical symptoms lead to suffering and depression, and then the depression makes the physical symptoms worse. If you're feeling depressed, make sure your diet is 100 percent gluten-free so you know that what you're feeling isn't a symptom of gluten ingestion. Also consider therapy of some type, whether it's confiding in friends or seeking professional help.

If you feel your case of the blues isn't serious and you want to try to work it out on your own, see whether these activities help:

- ✔ **Exercising:** When you exercise, your brain produces endorphins, and those chemicals create a natural high. Exercise also helps you get rid of stress hormones that build up in the body and wreak all sorts of physical and emotional havoc.

- ✔ **Eating well:** And that means, besides eating a healthy diet, staying strict about your gluten-free diet. Eating gluten exacerbates the physical and mental symptoms you may experience, and if you're gluten intolerant, gluten robs you of the important nutrients that are supposed to energize you and make you feel good. Stay away from high-glycemic-index foods, because they mess with your blood-sugar levels and affect your moods.

- ✔ **Avoiding alcohol:** Booze is bad news for people suffering from depression. Alcohol is a depressant, so by definition, it brings you down. It also interrupts your sleep patterns, which are important for feeling your best.

- ✔ **Relaxing (whether you want to or not):** It's hard sometimes, but relaxation (even if you force it) is important to maintaining your mental health. Sometimes you may forget to take care of yourself, but doing so is crucial — otherwise, you won't be able to help anyone.

- ✔ **Doing something nice for others:** You can find this next postulate under the Second Law of Happiness: The amount of happiness you feel is directly proportional to the happiness you bring to others. Seriously, have you ever been down and done something nice for someone? Not feeling better when you make someone's day is practically impossible.

Dealing with denial

When you hear you have to give up gluten for health reasons, deciding to run, not walk, to the nearest sand pit to start digging a hole for your head is quite common. It's called denial, and nearly everyone goes through it, to some extent. You'll pass through a few phases of denial, starting with the most immediate.

Right off the bat

Your doctor: You have (insert condition), and you need to eliminate all gluten from your diet beginning immediately.

You: Gluten? You mean like honey or sugar or something?

Your doctor: No, I mean like pizza, bread, and beer.

You: Surely you can't be serious.

Your doctor: I am serious, and don't call me Shirley.

Okay, so this is no time to joke, even if it is with classic jokes. But the initial reaction is a common one: I can't have that condition; I've never even heard of it. I'm too fat to have that. I'm too old to have it. I'm too (insert adjective that will support your denial) to have that.

You can deny till the cows come home (where *were* they, anyway?), but that doesn't help your health any. What does help is getting on track as fast as you can, because you have improved health to look forward to.

Denial down the road

Another type of denial settles in after you've been gluten-free for a while and you're feeling great. In fact, you feel so good that you start to think maybe nothing was really wrong with you, and you can't really remember ever feeling all that bad.

Of course, this is about the time the reality of going gluten-free for the rest of your life starts to set in, and you're tempted to cheat — but it's not cheating if you don't really need to be gluten-free, now, is it? So begins the battle in your brain, where good and evil don't see eye to eye.

The good half of your brain is telling you, "Mmmmm, this is the yummiest gluten-free cracker I've ever had!" But the demon-in-denial side is saying, "No way am I sittin' through another football game eating rice cakes and drinkin' white wine while the other guys are plowin' through pizza and belchin' their beer. Besides, I don't have an intolerance . . . come on, just one piece of pizza . . . ."

Step away from the pizza box. This is a period of ambivalence, in which you're hoping beyond hope that you don't really have to give up gluten and are "proving" it to yourself by ignoring red flags (and your conscience).

Acceptance

The biggest problem with denial is that it justifies eating gluten. When you have this epiphany, "realizing" that you don't need to be gluten-free, it's tempting to run, not walk, to the nearest donut shop.

Resist the temptation. If you've been gluten-free for a while, then yes, you feel great, but that's because of the diet, not in spite of it. The danger in testing your little theory is that you may not have any reaction when you do, and then you're likely to jump to the obvious (by which we mean "desired") conclusion that you never needed to eliminate gluten in the first place.

If you're still not sure that you really should be gluten-free, you can take these steps to clarify things for you a bit:

- **Get properly tested.** Denial is one of the most compelling arguments in favor of proper testing. Check out Chapter 2 in Book I for more information about testing.

- **Realize that "negative" tests don't always mean you're free to become a glutton for gluten.** Allergy tests don't pick up celiac disease; celiac tests don't always pick up sensitivities. The tests have changed over the years, and maybe your tests were done long ago. You can also get false negatives — and problems with gluten can develop at any point, so just because you were negative once doesn't mean you'll be negative again. And finally, some people are negative on all the tests, yet their health improves dramatically on a gluten-free diet. Go figure.

- **Get another opinion.** If you're particularly stubborn, you may even want to get a third. Kind of like if Dad says no, ask Mom — but if they both say no, you may want to admit defeat.

- **Talk to others who've been there, done that.** Most people have gone through denial in one form or another. Talk to people who've been diagnosed with a condition that requires them to be gluten-free. They'll probably give you that smug smile with the yep-you've-got-a-classic-case-of-denial look on their faces, because they've been there before. You won't really need to hear much more.

- **Take notes.** Write down your symptoms, how you feel when you eat certain foods, and the symptoms of gluten sensitivity, celiac disease, or whatever condition you may have. Do you see a correlation? When you eat certain foods, do you notice that some of the symptoms you have are similar to some of the symptoms of the condition? Hmmmm. . . .

Getting back on track when you're feeling derailed

If you don't take control of this diet, the diet will control you. Part of the reason you sometimes feel out of control when you're told to go gluten-free is that you're afraid. Afraid of messing up. Afraid of believing inaccurate information. Afraid of letting go of your habits and favorite foods. Afraid you'll feel deprived. Afraid of being different. Afraid of trying new foods. Afraid of an entirely new lifestyle.

The only way to get beyond the fear is to try new things. Be creative — explore new foods — tantalize your taste buds with all the gluten-free goodies you can think of. Arm yourself with accurate information. Be prepared when you're out and about. Taking control of the diet — and giving your kids control of theirs — is key to living and loving the gluten-free lifestyle.

If you're finding that all your favorite comfort foods are now off-limits, realize that those old comfort foods were probably *dis*comfort foods that actually made you feel bad because they have gluten in them. Choose new favorites, but try to avoid the pitfall of undermining weight-management efforts by turning to food for solace.

When the only food you can eat is gluten-free, every menu item begins to look like a croissant. Wanting what you can't have is the essence of human nature. Tell someone he can't juggle machetes, and he's likely to have a sudden urge to juggle machetes.

It's perfectly normal to feel like your selections are limited (they are limited but not limit*ing*) and to pine away for freshly baked sourdough. It's also normal to peruse a menu and feel like the only thing you can order is a side of fruit — or to stare at your pantry and see only saltines.

Focus on what you can eat rather than what you can't. The list of things you can eat is a heckuva lot longer than the list of things you can't, and if you don't believe it, start writing, friend. Make a list of all the things you can eat — and good luck getting to the end of it.

One of the fastest ways to make a particular food take center stage in your life is to ban it, because it's human nature to want what you can't have. For many people, putting gluten on the no-can-do list makes them want it even more. So if you're feeling deprived, indulge yourself! Not with gluten, of course, but with your favorite gluten-free treat. A splurge from time to time can remind you of lots of delicious things you can eat and can help take your mind off the things you can't.

When it comes to your dietary restrictions, you will most likely encounter people who appear unconcerned, uninterested, thoughtless, and sometimes even downright rude. From time to time you may have hurt feelings and may even feel ostracized. (How's that for sugarcoating it?) Other times you'll find that people do care but forget to make accommodations or just don't "get it" and serve foods you can't eat.

Don't be annoyed or offended. People are busy and sometimes so focused on their own fast-paced lives that they can't possibly remember to accommodate yours. Most of the time they're not being rude or thoughtless (okay, sometimes they are); they're just unaware. Be glad they asked you to dinner, and either bring something you can eat, order the salad, or suggest a different restaurant. Save the negative energy for something that really matters — like the kid next door who feels compelled to practice the drums at midnight.

Attitudes spread like germs through a preschool — and, like germs, you can't see them, but if you catch the bad kind, they can make you feel pretty nasty. Sometimes humans are like germs, silently spreading crummy attitudes to unwitting victims. If you're unhappy about having to adopt a gluten-free lifestyle and haven't used some of the tips in this chapter to help shake your anxiety, at least don't spread your misery around. Many people, if not most, aren't all that familiar with gluten, the gluten-free lifestyle, and the medical conditions that benefit from it. Chances are, you're the first person who's teaching them about it.

If you feel compelled to whine about the foods you miss or express excessive feelings of deprivation and despair, people will feel sad and sorry for your "misfortune." Do you really want their pity? Try instead to portray being gluten-free to others as a great lifestyle, a positive event in your life, and a healthful way to live so that others can feel that way, too.

Redefining Who You Are

If your doctor has diagnosed you with gluten sensitivity or celiac disease, you may feel different. You are different from other people — and that's okay. We're all different. Some have an interest in sports, others an aptitude for accounting. We readily acknowledge and accept that we're different in those types of things, but sometimes we don't like to be different with this diet. Your diet is different — but in the big picture, your restrictions are no different from those of people, such as vegans or people with peanut allergies, who have other diet restrictions.

Yes, you're different from other people — but you're not different from who you were before your diagnosis. Your lifestyle is different, but you're not.

Sometimes people let their condition define who they are. Try not to do this. Is having this condition a disappointment? Maybe — maybe not. But okay, maybe you're bummed about it, and that's okay.

What you're not is a victim, a martyr, or a sick person. In fact, you're on the road to recovery and amazing health. Lots of people have some kind of adversity in their lives, and they deal with it — you can, too.

Resisting the temptation to cheat

People are following approximately 4.2 gazillion diets out there: low-fat, high-protein, low-carb, low-calorie, low-glycemic, and everything in between. The thing they all have in common is that people cheat on them. It's a fact. People cheat on diets.

But you can't cheat on this one, especially if you have celiac disease. No, not even a little. "Everything in moderation" and "a little won't hurt you" do not apply if you have gluten sensitivity or celiac disease. Resisting the temptation to cheat starts with understanding why you want to cheat.

If you're spending a lot of time (or money on diet books) figuring out why you want to cheat on your diet, you're working too hard. A lot of factors may play a part, but it all boils down to one reason, really: You *want* to. You *want* that cookie, that pasta, or that bagel. After all, if you didn't want it, it wouldn't be a temptation.

You may want to eat the forbidden glutenous goods for a lot of reasons, and if you hope to resist the temptation, it's important to figure out what's driving your desire. Some of the more common triggers for temptation to cheat on the gluten-free diet include the following:

- ✔ **It's just too good to resist.** This statement isn't profound or worthy of pop psych talk shows, but most people who indulge in a food not on their diet do so because it's just too yummy to say no.

- ✔ **Just this once.** Not a good plan. There's a slippery slope between "just this once" and a diet that's long forgotten.

- ✔ **You want to fit in.** If everyone else were jumping off a cliff, would you? (Bungee jumpers aren't allowed to answer that.) Truthfully, other people probably aren't paying much attention to what you're eating, anyway. Social situations are about the company, the conversation, and the ambiance. Yeah, it's about the food, too, but people aren't paying attention to what *you're* eating.

✔ **It's a comfort food for you.** In difficult times, people sometimes have certain foods they turn to. If a gluten-containing goodie is your comfort food, a weak moment may send you straight to the food that you think will make you feel better — even though you know it won't.

✔ **It's a special occasion.** Try again. This excuse may work for other diets, but not this one. Eating even a little bit of gluten may turn your social affair into a dreaded nightmare. No occasion is worth compromising your health, and furthermore, special occasions are about the *occasion,* not the food.

✔ **You're bored by the diet.** If all you're eating is rice cakes and celery, of course you're bored. Live it up, get creative, and try new things. Use this book as a guide to figure out exactly what you *can* eat, and then challenge yourself to try something new. If you need a little inspiration, check out Book II, Chapter 4 which offers ideas for getting creative in the kitchen, and learning to make anything gluten-free.

✔ **A little won't hurt.** Yeah, it could. If you plan to use this excuse, you're assigned to read Chapter 2 of Book I.

✔ **The diet's too hard.** Hey, this is a *For Dummies* book, remember? This book is supposed to make it really easy to figure out what you can and can't eat, and how to live (and love!) the lifestyle. Sometimes it's not easy to change your perspective. But you *can* do it, and between your friends, family, and books like this, you've got plenty of support.

✔ **Someone's sabotaging your diet.** People do this! In fact, it's common. Usually they're not aware that they're doing it, and they do it for all different reasons. Sometimes they do it because they're jealous that you're getting healthier than they are. Sometimes they do it because they don't "believe" you need to be on the diet. Other times, people do it because they don't want to have to follow the clean-kitchen rules or don't want to have to put the effort into preparing gluten-free foods. Don't succumb to the sabotage efforts. Instead, try to find someone who seems particularly supportive of your gluten-free lifestyle, and ask for help. People *love* to help, and they get tremendous satisfaction out of lending a shoulder, an ear, or a hand.

✔ **I've already blown it so much, it doesn't matter anymore.** Not true. Today can be the first day of the rest of your gluten-free life.

Although these are powerful factors in enticing you to go for the gluten, overcoming the temptation is important. Sometimes the key to saying no is taking a look at the consequences.

You choose to cheat — or not — because you have full control over what you put in your mouth. When you cheat on the gluten-free diet, you're cheating yourself out of better health.

Book I

Getting
Started
with Going
without
Gluten

Keeping consequences in mind

One of the tough parts about looking at the consequences of your actions is that if they're not immediate and drastic, you sometimes feel that they don't matter. People who are dieting to lose weight often don't notice any consequences from a setback or two because they don't see the extra inches jump back onto their thighs when they eat a bowl of ice cream — and, for that matter, they may never gain the weight back, because for them, a high-calorie indulgence from time to time may be okay.

If you have gluten sensitivity or celiac disease, though, the consequences can have serious adverse affects on your health, and if you cheat chronically, those effects can be cumulative. In fact, you could be setting yourself up to develop conditions like osteoporosis, lupus, thyroid disease, and lots of other conditions that aren't worth that bagel.

After you realize why you want to cheat and you remind yourself of the consequences, you have to finalize the deal by just saying no. You can follow a few tips to make resisting a little easier:

- **Indulge in your favorite gluten-free goodie.** If you're craving a brownie, eat it — the gluten-free kind, of course. Just about anything that has gluten in it has a gluten-free counterpart these days. If you'd rather just grab a (gluten-free) candy bar, that's cool, too. If you're tempted to eat something with gluten, try to find something else that will satisfy at least as much but still keep you on track with your gluten-free lifestyle.

- **Reward yourself when you resist.** If you've been challenged by temptation and successfully overcome it, give yourself a treat. It doesn't have to be food — maybe you buy yourself something special or do something nice for yourself. Doing so can reinforce your strength and commitment to the lifestyle.

- **Simplify what you need to.** If the diet seems too cumbersome, maybe you're trying to do too much and you need to go back to the basics. If your menu plans are overwhelming, cut out something so you don't have so much to think about. If you don't understand the diet, read parts of this book again, particularly Chapter 4 in Book I.

- **Make your lifestyle a priority.** Going gluten-free is about you — your health and your future. If you find this lifestyle too difficult because of your work commitments, think about changing your schedule. If you have negative people in your life who seem to sabotage your efforts, avoid them if you can. If something's not working in your life, change it. Being gluten-free is about more than a diet; it's about a lifestyle, and it should be a high priority.

Book II

Making the Switch without Losing Your Mind

Glycemic Index Ranges

Classification	GI Range	Examples
Low GI	55 or less	Most fruit and vegetables (except potatoes), quinoa, and most other alternative grains
Medium GI	56–69	Orange juice, some pastas, some brown rices
High GI	70 or more	White bread, baked potato, most white rices, pizza, crackers, bagels, beer

The *glycemic index* (GI) is a way to measure how much effect a particular food will have on your blood sugar levels. The higher the glycemic index, the more quickly that food is broken down during the digestion process, and the more quickly blood glucose levels will rise.

Contents at a Glance

Chapter 1

Making Nutrition Your Mission When You're Cooking Gluten-Free

. . . .

. . . .

*I*t's not too tough to eat a healthier diet if you know what's nutritious and what isn't. The problem is, even people who think they know often don't.

Nutritious food is more underappreciated than the parent of a teen. But even teenagers appreciate parents more than most people appreciate food for the value it provides. Not the so-stuffed-you-can't-move feeling you get from pizza and beer. And for those of you who consider yourselves to be health food fanatics because you use skim milk on your frosted flakes, that's not quite getting there, either.

It's about the valuable things food offers — taste, fulfillment, satisfaction, and — oh yeah — *nutrients*.

In this chapter, you take a look at some foods you may have thought were nutritious but aren't — and explore some foods you may never have heard of that pack a powerful nutritional punch. You get tips for weight management and energy enhancement, and an overview of the optimal diet, which just happens to be entirely gluten-free.

Appreciating Your Food

Most of you definitely pay attention to what you eat, whether you want to or not — faithfully reading labels and scrutinizing the ingredients, acutely aware of where gluten could be lurking, and avoiding it like vampires avoiding garlic. But if you want to be healthy, you should really pay attention, tuning in to your food and what it offers, way beyond whether it's gluten-free.

People tend to think that *gluten-free* means *healthful.* After all, gluten-free foods are usually available only at "health food" stores, and they cost four times what "normal" foods cost. More importantly, they don't have the evil villain gluten in them, so they have to be nutritious, right? Nope.

The way most people approach the gluten-free diet really isn't all that nutritious, but it *is* gluten-free, so they get points for that.

Another way to approach the diet, though, is ultra-nutritious. It can fuel your body, help prevent disease, improve your skin's appearance, help you manage your weight, reverse the signs of aging, decrease symptoms of PMS and menopause, and increase longevity. It's gluten-free — nutritiously!

Food is obviously essential — without it, you'd starve. But the *type* of food you eat has powerful effects on preventing disease and on maintaining proper organ function, energy levels, moods, appearance, athleticism, and even your longevity and how you age. Almost everything about how you look and feel is directly related to the food you eat.

Feeling Optimal Requires Optimum Nutrition

Sure, you've heard the expression, "You are what you eat." But what does that mean, really? You may eat a lot of apples, but you're not an apple. Maybe it should be said that, "Your quality of health is dependent upon the quality of food you eat" — but that's not so catchy, and it's tough to grasp.

Few people would argue the fact that you need to eat a nutritious diet — the problem is that most people don't know what that means. And when you're eating gluten-free, you need to be aware of some special considerations when striving for optimal nutrition.

Fueling versus filling

Lots of people have used the car analogy to explain nutrition. They tell you that to get maximum performance from your vehicle, you have to use high-quality gas — and to get maximum performance from your body, you have to give it high-quality foods. However, you should eat to *fuel,* not to *fill.*

That analogy has a few problems: The first problem is that most people don't know what high-quality foods are. How can you put "good fuel" in your body when you don't really know what good fuel is? The second problem with the car-body analogy is that most people put crummy gas in their cars and their cars run just fine, so they figure they can get away with putting crummy gas in their bodies, and they'll run just fine, too — albeit a little gassy from time to time.

What they don't realize is that you can get away with putting crummy gas in an average car — but your bodies aren't your average car. The human body is a finely tuned, high-performance vehicle. You put crummy gas into a Ferrari, and you're going to find it knocks and pings (gas and bloating), doesn't start as easily (tough time getting out of bed?), doesn't go as fast (lethargic), the engine doesn't burn as cleanly (constipation), it shoots out more exhaust (fartola), and the engine wears out faster (uh-oh).

The last problem with the analogy revolves around individual sensitivities. Imagine now that you *do* know what good fuel is, and that you have pulled into an exclusive gas station that brags of having the highest-quality gasoline from one of the world's best refineries. It should be free of anything that might cause harm to your engine, right? Not necessarily. What if you're driving a diesel-powered car? Just a few minutes running with that "high-quality" gasoline, and your diesel car would be dead. In this case, the gas is good — it's just the wrong fuel type for your car.

Getting enough nutrients when you're gluten-free

Over the years, many people have claimed that the gluten-free diet is deficient in a variety of nutrients. Their reasoning comes from the fact that flour is generally enriched with vitamins. When you stop eating flour, you're missing that fortification and the supplemental nutrients it provides.

If you follow the "healthy" approach to the gluten-free diet as described in this chapter, you get a nutritionally sound diet.

If you go gluten-free the unhealthy way — simply substituting gluten-free goodies for the breads, bagels, pizzas, pastas, cookies, cakes, and pretzels that you were eating before — then there's some merit to the claim that the gluten-free diet may have some nutritional deficiencies, because you won't have the advantage of the enrichment found in most products made with flour.

Fiber

Getting enough fiber in your diet can be an issue in gluten-free diets. Gluten-free flours, such as rice and tapioca, don't offer much fiber and can cause associated problems.

The best source of fiber is fresh fruits and veggies. Broccoli, for instance, provides 25 percent of your daily fiber needs in just 1 cup. Not to mention it has 200 percent of the daily recommended dietary allowances (RDA) for vitamin C, 90 percent of the daily RDA for vitamin A in the form of beta carotene, and lots of niacin, calcium, thiamin, and phosphorus. All of this for only 45 calories!

Other nutrients

People who have gluten sensitivity or celiac disease often become sick and malnourished as a result. They usually have compromised digestion and absorption that may result in nutritional deficiencies, the most common of which are iron, essential fatty acids, vitamins D and K, calcium, magnesium, and folic acid. The good news is that when you go gluten-free, your body heals quickly and regains its ability to absorb nutrients. If you need help, seek the help of a professional to ensure adequate nutrition.

Some people believe that no matter how healthy your diet is, it's still important to take supplements. This reasoning is generally based on the fact that food isn't as nutritious as it used to be. Soils are becoming depleted of important nutrients, so the crops grown in them are less nutrient-dense than they once were. Furthermore, chemicals and genetically modified foods are changing the nutritional composition of even the most wholesome foods. For these reasons, many people believe that supplementation is key to getting all the nutrients you need, especially if you take part in athletic endeavors or exercise heavily.

Choosing a Healthier Approach to the Gluten-Free Diet

There are two ways to go on the gluten-free diet: one is ultra-healthy, and the other is — well, *not* — and not even close:

- ✔ **The unhealthy way:** This is the version of being gluten-free that could be called the "substitution diet." People continue to eat all the normal foods they ate before — breads, bagels, cookies, cakes, pizza, crackers, and pretzels — but they eat the gluten-free version. Sometimes people who do this actually end up eating more junk than they did when they were eating gluten because they use the gluten-free goodies to help them get over their "I'm feeling deprived and restricted" thoughts.

- ✔ **The healthier approach:** If man made it, don't eat it. In other words, stick to the natural foods that your body was designed to eat: lean meats, seafood and fish, fruits, veggies, nuts, and berries. These foods are healthiest because the human body was designed to eat them — it's not surprising that they're all naturally gluten-free, as well, because your body wasn't designed to eat gluten. Sticking to natural, healthy foods is a win-win!

Book II

Making the Switch without Losing Your Mind

A lot of information is available about the healthier approach, which is usually referred to as the *Paleolithic diet.* That's because this diet is based on eating the foods that our hunter-gatherer ancestors ate in Paleolithic times (before the Agricultural Revolution). They didn't eat wheat — there wasn't any. They didn't eat grains or dairy — those foods just didn't exist in their diet. Our bodies weren't designed to eat those things, which is why so many people have intolerances to them.

Dining with cavemen: The Paleolithic diet

It's most likely fair to say that rarely, if ever, did cavemen eat croissants. You know why? It's because early humans were hunter-gatherers, eating what they could hunt — and gather.

They ate what their bodies were designed to eat — lean meats, fresh fruits, and nonstarchy vegetables. There was no agriculture, so there were no farm animals or crops. That means no gluten.

You may be thinking that with some scary (and hairy) exceptions, today's humans don't really resemble cavemen, so this stuff isn't relevant — but you'd be mistaken. DNA evidence shows that, genetically, humans have hardly changed at all in the last 40,000 years.

Because the hunter-gatherers lived in the Paleolithic era, their diet is cleverly called the *Paleolithic diet,* which follows these basic guidelines:

- ✔ **Lean meat, fish, and seafood:** *Lean* meat is key in the Paleolithic diet. Back in the day, the slow, plump porkers that people eat today just weren't on the hunting grounds. Their animals were lean, mean, fighting machines — as were the hunters who ate them.

  A good wooly mammoth steak is hard to find these days. But lots of lean meats are available at any store — you may even want to experiment with lean game meat like alligator, buffalo, ostrich, kangaroo, and rattlesnake.

- ✔ **Fruits and nonstarchy vegetables:** There are lots of great fruits you can eat, including apples, figs, kiwis, mangos, cherries, and avocados. Just about any vegetable is a good bet (except for starchy ones like potatoes, yams, and sweet potatoes). Artichokes, cucumber, broccoli, cabbage, spinach, and mushrooms offer lots of nutritional value.

- ✔ **Nuts and seeds:** Not only are these accepted on the Paleolithic diet, but they're a great source of monounsaturated fats, which tend to lower cholesterol and decrease the risk of heart disease. Nuts and seeds include almonds, cashews, Macadamia nuts, pecans, pistachios, pumpkin seeds, sesame seeds, and sunflower seeds.

- ✔ **No cereal grains:** Grains weren't part of the diet until about 10,000 years ago. That's *yesterday,* evolutionarily speaking. Interestingly, when grains were introduced, health problems began to increase. While there's no scientific evidence to make a correlation, it's interesting to note that the average height of humans decreased, and people had more infectious diseases than their ancestors, more childhood mortality, and shorter life spans. They had more osteoporosis, rickets, and other bone-mineral disorders as well as vitamin and mineral deficiencies that caused diseases like scurvy, beriberi, pellagra, and iron-deficiency anemia.

- ✔ **No legumes:** Off-limit legumes include all beans, peas, peanuts, and soybeans.

- ✔ **No dairy:** If you're worried that you're not going to get enough calcium if you cut out dairy, load up on broccoli, cabbage, and celery. Some of the best sources of calcium come from greens, like beet greens, kale, and mustard greens.

- ✔ **No processed foods:** (Of course.)

As a general rule, you can probably simplify the Paleolithic approach to this guideline: If humans made it, don't eat it.

You have to choose a lifestyle that you're comfortable with and that satisfies *and* nourishes you — and the solution may be a modified version of this diet. But overall, this approach offers complete nutrition, it's comprised of foods that are low-glycemic load, and, best of all, it's gluten-free.

Find your own balance. Everyone is different — maybe you don't want or need that much protein. Maybe you're a vegetarian and choose to get your protein from other sources. The approach here is simply a starting point to give you an idea of a healthful way to be gluten-free. For more information, you can discuss the diet with your doctor or dietitian.

Comparing caveman-style to low-carb diets

Diet trends come and go faster than celebrity engagements. Within a matter of weeks, the absolutely-guaranteed-to-make-you-lose-20-pounds-in-20-minutes diet is replaced with an approach that doesn't even remotely resemble it. So how can they all be right? They can't.

And although the caveman approach outlined in this chapter can help you with weight management, the objective here isn't to talk about weight loss; it's to talk about achieving optimal health through nutrition — and that just happens to involve a gluten-free diet.

You're probably gathering by now (that's a pun, in case you missed it) that the hunter-gatherer approach is low-carb. But it's not like some of the other no-carb or low-carb diets. Here are the important distinctions:

- ✔ **This isn't a low-carb or no-carb lifestyle.** It's a *good*-carb lifestyle.

- ✔ **Eliminating carbs as some diets recommend cuts out foods like fruits and vegetables.** That means you're missing out on important vitamins, minerals, fiber, antioxidants, and other nutrients.

- ✔ **Some of the low-carb diets suggest eating high-fat foods like cheese, butter, and bacon.** These can cause cholesterol levels to skyrocket.

- ✔ **Most popular low-carb, high-fat diet plans don't make a distinction between good fats and bad fats.** Monounsaturated fats are good; saturated fats are mostly bad. Polyunsaturated fats are a little of each, depending on the ratio in which you eat them.

✔ **Most low-carb, high-fat diets don't talk about the dangers of salt.** People do need sodium in their diets to help regulate fluid balance, but if you get too much of it, sodium can cause high blood pressure, which can lead to heart disease and other health problems. It also messes with the body's ability to absorb calcium, which can eventually lead to bone loss and osteoporosis.

Even if you don't salt your food, you could be getting way too much salt in your diet. The sodium that's found naturally in foods like shellfish and some cheeses isn't usually a problem. But processed foods are often loaded with sodium in the form of flavor enhancers, thickeners, and preservatives. Even sodas often have sodium to help them maintain carbonation.

When you're counting carbs, you can easily see why you get more food for your carb count when you eat fruits and veggies than when you eat gluten. The average carbohydrate content of fruits is about 13 percent. For non-starchy vegetables, it's about 4 percent. And it's almost zero for lean meats, fish, and seafood. For contrast, the carbohydrate content of cereal grains like wheat averages a whopping 72 percent.

Reviewing the more healthful approach

This simple approach for a healthier gluten-free lifestyle gets you where you want to go — without stress or confusion:

✔ **Keep it gluten-free,** for sure. Don't get so lost in this approach that you forget the whole point!

✔ **Watch the carbs** — making sure the carbs you're eating are good carbs like fruits and vegetables.

✔ **Try to stick to low-glycemic-load foods,** which raise your blood-sugar levels gradually.

✔ **Make sure the foods you eat offer nutritional value.** Stay away from foods that are basically empty calories.

✔ **A Paleolithic approach — eating seafood, lean meats, fruits, and nonstarchy vegetables — is extremely healthful.** Modify the diet to meet your personal preferences and needs.

Good food is food that goes bad quickly. That means fresh produce and other foods without many preservatives.

Good Carbs, Bad Carbs: Tuning In to the Glycemic Index and Glycemic Load

Hey! Put down that remote control! You may be tempted to skip this section because this sounds complicated, tedious, boring, or all of the above. Please don't! It's a really important section, and it's the basis for a lot of what you find in this chapter, so hang in there.

To start, here's a pop quiz: True or false — a potato is worse for you than a candy bar. The answer is *true* — at least, if you're talking about how each food affects your blood-sugar levels. Now are you interested? Read on.

Perusing the glycemic index (GI)

All carbs are not created equal. When you eat carbohydrates, the digestive process breaks them down into the sugar, glucose, which is what gives your body the energy it needs to function. Because glucose is a sugar, it raises your blood-sugar levels when it enters your bloodstream.

The *glycemic index* (GI) is just a measurement of how much your blood sugar increases in the two hours after you eat. Foods high in fat and protein don't really affect your blood-sugar levels that much (if anything, they stabilize it), so the glycemic index really concerns only foods high in carbohydrates.

To measure the glycemic index of food, you need a reference point. To determine that reference point, someone had to find a food that had a super-high glycemic index — one of the nastiest foods you can eat in terms of turning to sugar the minute you eat it. And the winner was . . . white bread! The glycemic index of white bread was set at 100, and all foods are compared to it.

A food's glycemic index is how much that food increases your blood-sugar level compared to how much that same amount of white bread would increase it. (The amount of food is measured in grams of carbohydrates, not by the weight or volume of the food.)

Some charts use pure glucose as the reference point instead of white bread. In the white bread index, glucose has a glycemic index of 140, so different charts have different glycemic indices for a particular food, depending on whether they use the white bread or the glucose scale. To convert to a white bread scale, multiply the score on the glucose scale by 1.4.

The lower the glycemic index, the less effect that food has on blood-glucose levels. Obviously, the higher a food's glycemic index, the more it causes a spike in blood sugar.

The glycemic effect of foods depends on a bunch of things, including the type of starch that's in it, whether that starch is cooked, how much fat is present, and the acidity. For example, adding vinegar or lemon juice (acidic) to a food actually lowers the glycemic index. And fat or dietary fiber can help inhibit the absorption of the carbohydrates, which also lowers the glycemic index. That, by the way, is why a candy bar — which has fat in it — has a lower glycemic index than a potato. Processing affects the glycemic index of a food, too. The more highly processed a grain such as rice, corn, or wheat is, the higher its glycemic index and the more quickly your blood sugar rises.

People with diabetes used to think they had to avoid sugar — as in table sugar. But simple sugar (like table sugar) doesn't make your blood-glucose level rise any faster than complex carbohydrates do. That's why using the glycemic index is a more valuable tool in controlling blood-sugar levels than cutting down on sugar is.

The glycemic index value tells you how fast a carbohydrate turns into glucose, but it doesn't tell you how much of that carbohydrate is in a particular food. That's where the glycemic load comes in. And as luck would have it, that's what is discussed in the next section.

Take a look at the glycemic indices of some grains and starches. Remember, lower is "better," because a lower score means the food doesn't cause a rapid rise in your blood sugar. You may find variations from one chart to another. This glycemic index is based on the glucose scale, where glucose = 100.

Food	Average Glycemic Index
Rice (white)	88
Potato (baked)	85
Corn	75
Millet	75
White bread	73
Whole-wheat bread	72
Refined flour	70
Rice (brown)	57
Buckwheat	54
Quinoa	51
Whole-wheat flour	45

Hauling the glycemic load (GL)

Using the glycemic index alone can be misleading. Watermelon, for example, has a high glycemic index, but because watermelon is mostly water, you'd have to eat a lot of it to raise your blood sugar much. The glycemic load (GL) measurement is actually a little more valuable. *Glycemic load* looks at how many grams of available carbs a food provides. The *available carbohydrates* are the ones that provide energy, like starch and sugar but not fiber.

The key is that glycemic load is measured by serving size, which not only standardizes the numbers so you can compare one food to another but also allows you to add up your total glycemic load for each meal. Less than 80 glycemic load units per day is a low-glycemic-load diet; more than 120 is high.

The only hitch with glycemic load is that the portion size is subjective. So a small portion of white bread, for instance, may end up with a lower glycemic load than a large portion of buckwheat. Then you'd see a run on white bread, and the world would never be the same.

Here's an example of how serving size affects glycemic load. A baked Russet Burbank potato has a glycemic index of 85 (that's high!) and a glycemic load of 26 for a 150-gram serving. A 120-gram serving of banana has a glycemic index of 52 and a glycemic load of 12. The banana's better for you. But if you're mainly concerned about blood sugar and your choice is between eating that baked potato and eating two large bananas (130 grams each), you can splurge on the potato — your blood-sugar level rises about the same amount no matter which you eat.

To calculate the glycemic load, multiply the glycemic index percentage (glycemic index divided by 100) times the grams of *total carbohydrates* per serving. Of course, you also can go online and do a search for glycemic-load charts that use standard serving sizes.

For each food, glycemic index and glycemic load numbers are ranked this way:

	Glycemic Index	*Glycemic Load*
Low	Below 56	Below 11
Medium	56 to 69	11 to 19
High	70 and up	20 and up

Book II

Making the Switch without Losing Your Mind

What do blood-sugar levels have to do with anything?

Lots. Your blood-sugar levels can have profound effects on your health in many ways: disease cause and prevention, weight loss and weight gain, moods, energy levels, and even how quickly you age.

The underlying principle is simple: What goes up must come down. When you eat high-glycemic-load foods — such as bread, pasta, bagels, pizza, cookies, and cakes (gluten-free or not) — your blood sugar spikes. And chasing that spike in blood sugar is your friend *insulin,* a hormone produced by the pancreas. Insulin's job is to get nutrients from the blood and make them available to various tissues in the body.

Glucose is the fuel that your body uses. Insulin is in charge of getting the glucose into the cells where they can use it for energy. Think of insulin as the delivery guy — bringing glucose to the cells, opening the door, and tossing the glucose inside.

When insulin shuttles the glucose from the bloodstream into the cells, insulin *lowers* your blood-sugar level (the sugar isn't in the blood anymore; it's in the cells).

When your blood-sugar level is high, your body makes a bunch of insulin to try to bring that level down. The problem is that insulin is sometimes a little *too* good at its job.

The high cost of high insulin

When you eat a lot of high-glycemic-load foods (see "Hauling the glycemic load [GL]"), your blood sugar spikes and the pancreas has to work really hard to pump out a bunch of insulin to bring the blood-sugar level down. And it works — blood sugar drops fast. You crash. You get fatigued and sometimes a little dizzy — and hungry.

When high-glycemic-load foods cause your blood-sugar levels to spike and then drop quickly, your hormones are strapped in the front seat on this roller-coaster ride, wreaking havoc on your energy levels and even moods.

People who eat high-glycemic-load foods for years can develop a condition called insulin resistance. *Insulin resistance* occurs when the body has so much insulin all the time that it doesn't respond like it should anymore. Usually, just a little bit of insulin can bring blood sugar down, but in someone who's insulin resistant, this doesn't happen. So in an effort to lower blood-sugar levels, the body keeps producing insulin and has elevated levels of it all the time. Over time, the body requires more and more insulin to move the nutrients into the cells, and eventually the pancreas is unable to produce enough insulin to do the job. This can be very hard on the body.

Syndrome X, or *metabolic syndrome,* is a cluster of diseases caused by insulin resistance. These conditions include

- ✔ Adult-onset diabetes (Type 2)
- ✔ High blood pressure
- ✔ Hardening of the arteries and damage to arterial walls
- ✔ High ratio of bad cholesterol to good
- ✔ Elevated blood uric acid levels (which can cause gout or kidney stones)
- ✔ Weight gain and obesity
- ✔ An excess of triglycerides (fat in the bloodstream)

Excess insulin is also blamed for nutrient deficiencies, including deficiencies in calcium, magnesium, zinc, vitamin E, vitamin C, B-complex vitamins, and essential fatty acids.

Insulin also increases the amount of cortisol in the body. *Cortisol* is a stress hormone that can accelerate aging and cause other health problems.

Avoiding Nutritional Pitfalls on the Gluten-Free Diet

People often ask whether nutritional deficiencies arise as a result of being gluten-free. The answer is maybe yes and maybe no.

If you choose the healthful approach to gluten-free living that you find in this chapter, you shouldn't need to worry about nutritional deficiencies. You'll be healthier than most people who eat gluten.

However, if you eat a gluten-free diet that's mostly gluten-free "replacement" foods like breads, pizzas, pastas, cookies, brownies, and cakes — and if your "vegetables" consist of rice, corn, potatoes, and the tomatoes in the pasta sauce — then you may have some nutritional concerns.

When adopting a gluten-free lifestyle, people tend to turn to starchy stand-bys, like rice, corn, and potatoes. You gravitate toward these foods partly *because* they're starchy, sort of like the bread, pasta, and bagels you were accustomed to eating when you ate gluten. Ironically, the same foods that you crave because they fill you up and give you that satiated feeling also make you hungrier. Check out the section "Managing Your Weight When You're Gluten-Free."

Unfortunately, rice, corn, potatoes, and other starchy foods don't offer much in the way of nutrition — especially when you look at all the calories you get. Not much nutritional bang for the caloric buck, so to speak.

Other foods offer that fill-me-up satisfaction, many of which provide far more nutritional value and diversity than rice, corn, potatoes, or wheat. They include these choices:

- Amaranth
- Buckwheat
- Mesquite
- Millet
- Montina (Indian ricegrass)
- Quinoa
- Sorghum
- Teff

These alternative grains offer complete protein, fiber, and lots of vitamins and minerals. (Find out more about them in Book I, Chapter 4.)

The most common concerns focusing on nutrient deficiencies in the gluten-free diet revolve around folate or folic acid, iron, fiber, and B vitamins. The B vitamins specifically lacking in some gluten-free flours include vitamin B1 (thiamin), B2 (riboflavin), and B3 (niacin). Choosing the healthier approach earlier in this chapter is the best way to make up for any nutritional deficiencies. Supplements may work, too, but make sure they don't contain any gluten, and consult your doctor first.

Deficiencies in B-complex vitamins and iron may occur because when people were still glutenivores, they were eating lots of flour, which is usually enriched and fortified with iron, riboflavin, niacin, and thiamine. Gluten-free flours aren't enriched.

Getting the fiber you need on a gluten-free diet

Fiber is important for lots of reasons. The most well-known benefit is that it helps keep the gastrointestinal plumbing moving smoothly, and that's good for the whole gastrointestinal tract. Fiber can help reduce cholesterol and lower your chance of heart disease and cancer.

When people give up gluten and their diets consist mostly of gluten-free flours like rice and potato or tapioca flours, they're sometimes at risk of having too little fiber in their diets. If you're going to use flours, try to incorporate flax meal, Montina, chickpea, and amaranth flours into your cooking. They have much more fiber than white or even brown rice.

The most healthful diet that ensures you an adequate intake of fiber is the approach that most closely resembles the diet your ancestors ate, which is high in fruits and nonstarchy vegetables. Some good food choices include apples, kiwis, bananas, avocados, tomatoes, cabbage, broccoli, spinach, and Brussels sprouts.

Book II

Making the Switch without Losing Your Mind

The whole truth (and nothing but) about whole grains

If you're gonna do grains, the goal is whole. A grain has three parts: the germ, the endosperm, and the bran. Whole-grain foods contain all three parts:

- ✔ **Germ:** This is the part of the grain that a new plant sprouts from, and it's where you can find a lot of niacin, thiamin, riboflavin, vitamin E, magnesium, phosphorus, iron, and zinc. It also has a little protein and some fat.

- ✔ **Endosperm:** The kernel of the grain, the endosperm is the bulk of the seed. Because the seed stores its energy in the endosperm, it has most of the protein and carbohydrates as well as some vitamins and minerals.

- ✔ **Bran:** The outer layer of the seed, the bran contains most of the grain's nutrients. It's a rich source of niacin, thiamin, riboflavin, magnesium, phosphorus, iron, and zinc. This is where most of the fiber is, too.

Refined grains have been stripped of their bran and germ layers during processing, so all that's left is the endosperm. They contain some protein and fat, and there may be some fiber and nutritional value left, but most of the good stuff gets tossed out during the refining process — like the proverbial baby with the bath water.

The individual components of whole grain — vitamins, minerals, fiber, and other nutrients — work together to help protect against chronic diseases such as diabetes, heart disease, and certain cancers. Grain components are *synergistic,* meaning that each individual component is important but the value of the whole grain is greater than the sum of its parts.

Quinoa, buckwheat, and other alternative grains provide all the value that makes whole grains so nutritious.

Refined grains usually have nutrients added back in, but they're not as nutritious as a whole-grain product would be, and they lack the fiber that whole grain provides. (If the food were really nutritious, why would it need to be fortified?)

Fruits have almost twice as much fiber as whole grains, and nonstarchy vegetables have about eight times more fiber. To maximize your fill of fiber, be sure to eat the peel.

Managing Your Weight When You're Gluten-Free

Interestingly, the gluten-free diet — when done properly — can not only be your key to better health, but it may also be the key to managing your weight. In fact, it doesn't matter if you weigh too much or too little; if you're not "just right," going gluten-free may be the answer you've been looking for.

Losing or maintaining weight

For people who need to lose weight, there's no simpler and more effective way to do it than to take the Paleolithic approach covered in this chapter (see the section "Reviewing the more healthful approach" for more info). Sticking to lean meats, poultry, seafood, fish, fruits, and veggies will help un-stick those unwanted pounds.

When you go gluten-free, you eliminate refined-flour products from your diet — things like bagels, bread, pasta, and of course the sweet baked goods — and that means you're cutting out high-glycemic-index foods that offer very little in the way of nutrition but offer more than their fair share of calories. That's why people who go gluten-free the healthy way usually find their weight easier to maintain at healthy levels.

Dealing with (uh-oh) weight gain

Some people find that they gain weight when they go gluten-free — and it's no wonder! Many of them are busy discovering the wonders of the gluten-free goodie world, including gluten-free brownies, cookies, cakes, pastas, and crackers. Those are foods that may as well be applied directly to the tummy or thighs — because that's where they end up pretty quickly.

These days the gluten-free goodies are delicious — and somewhat irresistible. But for some people, eating them is strictly emotional. They tend to get carried away with these foods as a way of compensating for feelings of deprivation or restriction. They believe they're deprived because they can't eat gluten, so they "reward" themselves, or compensate, by eating extras of the goodies that they *can* eat. Before they know it, their jeans look like they belong to the neighbor's kid.

Still others experience weight gain because of the physiological changes that take place when they go gluten-free. This group of people is comprised of those who go gluten-free because they have celiac disease or gluten sensitivity. Most people with celiac disease or gluten-sensitivity don't absorb all of their nutrients, at least until they go 100 percent gluten-free. Lots of these people, while they're still eating gluten and not absorbing nutrients, become accustomed to eating far more calories than they should, because those calories aren't being absorbed, so they maintain their weight in spite of the fact that they eat far too many calories. But it's payback time after they go gluten-free. Their gut begins to heal, and they begin absorbing calories — and before they know it, they've packed on a pound (or 20).

The gluten-free diet may be the best diet on the planet. It's not actually the gluten-free-ness that gets the credit when you're talking about weight management on the gluten-free diet; it's the fact that you're adhering to a high-protein, low-glycemic, nutrient-dense diet. And following this healthy diet provides health benefits that extend far beyond being gluten-free.

Adding some pounds if you're underweight

If you've been underweight, you're likely to find that the gluten-free diet helps you gain enough to be at a healthy weight. Wait — how can it help some people *lose* weight, and help others *gain* it?

People who are underweight are often that way because they have gluten sensitivity or celiac disease and therefore are not absorbing important nutrients, including calories. That is, until they go gluten-free. Then their guts heal, and they begin to absorb those important nutrients again. After they start absorbing the calories they're consuming, they usually gain the weight they need to be at what's considered a healthy weight.

Chapter 2

Keeping a Gluten-Free-Friendly Kitchen

. . . .

In This Chapter

▶ Encouraging "glutenous" and gluten-free foods to coexist in the kitchen

▶ Keeping contaminants at bay

▶ Stocking up on handy ingredients and products

. . . .

Your idea of cooking may involve only a can opener and a microwave. Or you may have kitchen gadgets no one else knows how to use, tote mystery ingredients home from faraway lands, and subscribe to magazines most people can't pronounce. No matter how you feel about cooking, you probably spend lots of time in the kitchen.

When you're gluten-free, the kitchen needs a little extra attention. Keeping yourself safely gluten-free isn't hard, but you need to keep some special considerations in mind, especially if your kitchen contains gluten.

Sharing the Kitchen with Gluten

Some people think that the only way to be 100 percent gluten-free is to make the entire household gluten-free. Not true. Sure, doing so makes things easier — menu planning and cooking are simpler, and if the whole house is gluten-free, you don't have to worry about possible mix-ups or contamination (and no feuding between the breads). But if you choose to share your kitchen with gluten, you'll be fine.

Consider these tips for sharing a kitchen with gluten:

- **Gluten-free comes first.** If you're making two varieties of a meal —grilled cheese sandwiches, for example — make the gluten-free one first. That way, the preparation surface, knives (always plural — see "The gob drop for spreadables" section, later in this chapter), and pans stay uncontaminated. If you make the gluten-containing sandwich first, you have to either wash the pan or griddle thoroughly before making the gluten-free sandwich or use a separate pan.

- **Foil is your friend.** Using lots of aluminum foil makes your life easier. Cover cookie sheets with it, use it to separate different foods, and warm foods on foil instead of setting them directly on an oven rack. Foil is a great way to ensure your gluten-free foods aren't being contaminated.

- **Vacuum sealers save time.** You may find that you're making more homemade foods than you used to, like gluten-free breads, cookies, pizzas, and so on. Remember, homemade foods don't have preservatives in them (a good thing), so they go bad quickly (a bad thing). You can save time and money by making foods in larger quantities and then vacuum-sealing them so they stay fresh longer. Doing so is convenient, too, because you can vacuum-seal individual servings and toss them in lunches or take them on the go.

- **Freeze it.** Again, homemade foods don't have preservatives, so they don't last as long. Freeze them and then use them when you need to.

- **Use brightly colored labels.** Because you're likely to have some leftovers that are gluten-free and some that aren't, consider using brightly colored stickers or labels to stick on the storage containers so you can easily tell which leftovers are gluten-free. This is especially helpful if you have babysitters or other people in the house who may be likely to grab the wrong one.

Avoiding cross-contamination

When you're sharing a kitchen with gluten, gluten can contaminate (or *glutenate,* as some like to say) your food in several ways. Crumbs seem to throw themselves off gluten-containing breads and other foods, turning perfectly good gluten-free zones into danger zones in the blink of an eye.

Not only do crumbs fly, but preparation surfaces, pots, pans, grills, and utensils can contaminate food, too. You know those neat freaks who drive everyone nuts because they're compulsive about cleaning? Take a hard look in the mirror and embrace the reality, because that's you now. Cleanliness isn't an option anymore; it's crucial to maintaining the purity of your gluten-free lifestyle.

Crumbs: Public enemy number one

If you think ants are your biggest problem in the kitchen, think again. The ants just go marching one by one (hurrah), and although they're certainly a nuisance, they don't hurt you even if you eat them. (Don't worry, they're gluten-free.) No, enemy number one in the gluten-free-friendly kitchen is the almighty crumb. Crumbs fly off bread like sparks in a fireworks display, and they're everywhere. All the crumb-tossing blame doesn't land on the gluten-containing kind of bread — in fact, quite the opposite. Between gluten-containing and gluten-free breads, everyone knows who the real winner is in the crumb-casting competition.

So here's the deal: When you work really hard to prepare a delicious gluten-free sandwich and then set it on the counter in a pile of gluten-containing crumbs, you are, literally, eating a gluten-containing sandwich, and your efforts to find, buy, and compile gluten-free makin's are all for naught.

Even a few crumbs from gluten-containing breads or crackers can turn your gluten-free food into a toxic treat. Be diligent about cleaning crumbs, and remember the golden rule: When in doubt, leave it out. If you're not sure that your meal is uncontaminated, don't eat it.

So what about gluten-free crumbs? Do you have to be obsessive about wiping those up? Yes, if you're sharing your kitchen with gluten. Not for the sake of good hygiene, but because you can't tell whether they're gluten-free by looking at them. Thus, you can never know for sure whether you're setting your sandwich in gluten. (And then you have to consider those annoying little marching ants.)

New rules for kitchen tools

You don't need to stock up on new pots, pans, tools, and utensils, but you do need to pay attention to how you use the ones you have. For the most part, if you clean your kitchen items well, you get the gluten off them. Nonstick surfaces that clean easily and thoroughly are especially safe.

Keep in mind a couple of exceptions. It's a good idea to have separate colanders and pasta servers if you're making both gluten-containing and gluten-free pastas in your kitchen. Clearly label one as being gluten-free only. Pasta tends to leave a residue that's sometimes tricky to get off. You don't want to drain gluten-free pasta in a colander that has remnants of the gluten-containing pasta on it. Same goes for the pasta servers.

You may also want to buy separate pots, pans, or utensils if you have a favorite item and it just doesn't clean well — a special crêpe pan, for instance. If you can see (or sense) that traces of gluten could remain there and you don't want to part with the pan to get one that cleans more thoroughly, just don't use it for your gluten-free cooking. Make sure you mark your separate items well — one saying "gluten-free only" and the other saying "gluten" — so you don't get them mixed up.

Using a permanent marker may not be the latest trend in kitchen design, but it can save you from being unsure and may even spare you health-threatening mix-ups. A big, bold "GF ONLY" on your gluten-free utensils can reduce the chance of inadvertently contaminating your gluten-free foods by using the wrong kitchen items.

The gob drop for spreadables

The *gob drop* is an action (and somewhat of an art) that you need to master if you share your kitchen with gluten.

But first things first: *Spreadables* are the foodstuffs you spread onto other foodstuffs. You know — mayonnaise, butter, margarine, jelly, peanut butter, honey (unless you buy the little squeezy bear), and other things that usually fall into the condiment category. You can buy most of these condiments in squeeze bottles, but you should still learn the gob drop — you may want to buy spreadables in jars because of price or flavor (and squeezable peanut butter is just weird).

Most people dip their knives into containers, scooping out some of the spreadable, and then spread said spread onto their bread, cracker, tortilla, or other spreadee. Then they scoop a little more and continue the process. Each time the knife goes from a gluten-containing spreadee back in the spreadable, gluten crumbs get a free ride into the container, contaminating the entire tub or jar. And you know what they say about one bad apple.

That's why you need to do the gob drop. But first, toss out all the contaminated tubs and jars you have. Either keep all future tubs and jars gluten-free (by practicing the gob drop faithfully) or buy separate tubs, mark them clearly, and don't ever mix them up.

Here's how you do the gob drop to keep your spreads gluten-free:

1. **Use a knife to scoop out some of the spreadable.**

2. **Flick the spreadable onto the spreadee.**

3. **Use the knife to continue with that process until you have enough of the spreadable on the spreadee.**

4. **You may then begin spreading.**

Admittedly, the gob drop takes practice. Flick too hard, and you miss the spreadee altogether. Don't flick hard enough, and it won't come off the knife. In dire situations, you may need a second knife to scrape the spreadable off knife number one.

Of course, you can use knife number one to spread, but you can't put a knife you've spread with back into the jar or tub. If you need more of the spreadable, you have to break out another knife.

People frequently ask, "Can I put the knife back into the spreadable if I used it to spread something onto gluten-free bread?" No. Because you'll not only end up with crumbs in the spreadables, which is gross, but you'll also always wonder whether those crumbs are the gluten kind or the gluten-free kind. Resist the temptation.

Another frequently asked question is: "Do we have to do the gob drop if our entire household is gluten-free?" No (that's why this section falls under the "Sharing the Kitchen with Gluten" section), but ending up with tubs and jars full of crumbs is still really gross.

Gracious guests can lead to grief

Having too many cooks in the kitchen is bad enough, but when you're trying to keep your foods safely gluten-free and your visitors are especially "helpful," maintaining a gluten-free zone can be more than a tinge stressful. Sweet Aunt Mabel's gracious offer to help butter the bread can have you diving to protect your pristine (and well-marked) tub of margarine because you haven't yet taught her to properly execute the gob drop. And as you rescue the margarine and quickly try to decide whether teaching her the gob drop (and hovering over her so she doesn't make a mistake) would be easier than just buttering the bread yourself, Uncle Bob is getting ready to flip the burgers — and the buns — with the same spatula!

If your visitors are one-time or occasional guests, give them safe tasks to keep them busy and let them lend a hand — somewhere that won't put your gluten-free foods in peril. Have them pour the iced tea or set the table. But if they're frequent visitors, you probably need to invest the time to teach them the gob drop. Your spreadables are at risk! Your other options are to hide the tubs and jars and buy squeezables for their visit or to buy separate containers and clearly mark which ones are gluten-free.

Storing foods separately for convenience

For the most part, you don't need to have separate storage spaces for the gluten-containing and gluten-free foods unless you do so for convenience purposes. After all, simply reaching up to the gluten-free section of your pantry for a gluten-free flour mixture is easier than sorting through the shelves.

If you have kids on a gluten-free diet and others in the family still eat gluten — or if some people in the home have behavioral issues or learning disorders — then having separate storage areas can be a very good idea. For these gluten-free loved ones, it's easy to look in a pantry and be over-whelmed with all the things they can't eat, even if the things they can eat actually outnumber the things they can't.

By separating gluten-containing and gluten-free foods in the pantry, not only do you make quickly choosing from their safe shelves quite easy, but the number of things they can eat becomes more obvious to them. This can be a big psychological boost in what could otherwise be a daunting experience.

Consider marking gluten-free foods with a "GF" right when you get home from the store so the kids will have an easier time helping you put everything away in the right place.

Decoding Cryptic Labels

When someone in your family has a problem with gluten, you need to become a detective. And yes, you need the traditional magnifying glass and a notebook (or iPad!) for recording clues and crucial information. (The funny hat and curved pipe are optional.) You'll find yourself calling manufacturers to verify ingredients in their foods.

Some hidden sources of gluten include proteins made with spelt, kamut, triti-cale, farro, and durum. All these names are just varieties of wheat; tasty ones, but wheat nonetheless. Don't fall for the wheat-free claims that occasionally appear on products made from these grains.

In this section, you find out how to read food ingredient labels to ferret out hidden gluten. You discover terms that need further investigation and how to make sure that a food labeled gluten-free or one that seems gluten-free is, in fact, free of gluten. Or as free as it's possible to be!

Understanding label jargon

Every food in the supermarket that contains more than one ingredient must have a label that lists all the ingredients, along with nutrition information and some specific warnings and health claims. These labels are one line of defense against gluten, but they aren't the holy grail. You may need to do some research before you can confidently buy and eat products that are safe for you.

If only avoiding gluten was as easy as simply avoiding wheat pasta, breads, and flour! Gluten can hide in foods as diverse as salad dressing and low-fat sour cream.

 The government is helping you out a bit with label warnings. The Food Allergen Labeling and Consumer Protection Act (FALCPA) took effect in 2006. More than 160 foods are identified as allergens, but 90 percent of all food allergies are caused by just eight of them. The FALCPA requires that any product that contains one of the eight major allergenic foods clearly list that allergen on the label. Wheat is one of the eight allergens.

Woot woot! Let's hear it for labeling you can trust, now that there finally are definitive rules about what can and can't be labeled gluten-free. Until 2014, if a manufacturer wanted to slap "gluten-free" on a label, it did so — without any specific guidelines to vouch for the safety of that product. But as of August 2014, products labeled gluten-free must meet guidelines established by the Food and Drug Administration (FDA). The guidelines are lengthy, but the essence is that foods labeled gluten-free must

- Be inherently gluten-free

- Not contain gluten-containing grains

- Not be derived from a gluten-containing grain that still contains gluten

- Contain less than 20 parts per million (ppm) if there is unavoidable gluten

Say what? 20 ppm? Is it gluten-free or not? We know, it's confusing. Bottom line is that there can be trace amounts of "unavoidable" gluten even though the product is essentially gluten-free. Most researchers agree that up to 20 ppm is still safe for people with celiac disease or gluten sensitivity. Key word: *most.* Certainly this is a debate that will rage for decades, but for now it's the U.S.-accepted standard for deeming a food to be gluten-free. Although manufacturers are not required to test the product to confirm that it's below 20 ppm, they're responsible for ensuring that the product does, in fact, meet the standard. By "responsible," we mean that lawyers would happily bring it to a manufacturer's attention if a product was found to be above the 20 ppm limit.

Book II

Making the Switch without Losing Your Mind

If you eat several products containing small amounts of gluten over the course of a day, each one below 20 ppm, you can easily rise above the level of gluten that causes damage and you may experience painful and harmful symptoms. If this cumulative ingestion continues chronically, you could be causing severe harm to your body.

Here's the lesson in all of this: "Gluten-free" doesn't mean "no gluten at all." There's simply no way to guarantee zero gluten in any one product, unless you buy an apple or lemon that hasn't been coated with a wax or solution that contains gluten. Or unless you grow your own food!

There are a lot of nuances to the regulation of gluten-free labeling. First, it's a one-way voluntary law, meaning that if a product is gluten-free a manufacturer doesn't have to label it as such, but if they label it as being gluten-free, it must follow the regulatory guidelines.

It applies to all packaged food and dietary supplements, even if the product was made in another country and imported to the U.S. It does not apply to foods regulated by the U.S. Department of Agriculture (USDA), which regulates the labeling of meats, poultry, and certain egg products (it doesn't regulate labeling of shell eggs). It also does not pertain to products regulated by the Alcohol and Tobacco Tax and Trade Bureau, which regulates labeling of distilled spirits, wines containing 7 percent or more alcohol by volume, and malted beverages made with malted barley and hops.

Certification: A safety seal of approval

You've probably seen products donning a logo that "certifies" that a product is gluten-free. This is incredibly helpful for people who are new to the lifestyle and are having trouble deciphering labels, because if it's certified to be gluten-free, you can trust that it has met the most rigorous of standards.

Different organizations have different standards for certification. For instance, some require that a food contain less than 5 ppm, while others set 10 ppm as the limit (remember that researchers agree that less than 20 ppm is safe). Most of the certification programs review the ingredients, test the products, and actually go on-site to ensure that the production facilities meet stringent standards to avoid cross-contamination.

Manufacturers shell out quite a bit of cashola for certification, because they're billed for audits, inspections, and testing. You know that if a product dons a gluten-free certification logo, the manufacturer is truly committed to providing a safe product for the gluten-free community.

Cross-contamination issues

The FDA guidelines on gluten-free labeling do not define cross contamination, or cross contact. *Cross contact* refers to the contamination of gluten-free foods when they come in contact with gluten-containing ones. Cross contact can occur when crops are rotated, or during the harvest, transportation, and production processes of grain manufacture. Although there's no clear definition for cross-contact issues in the law, the final product still must fall below the 20 ppm limit in order to be labeled gluten-free.

Just because a product doesn't say "gluten-free" on the label doesn't mean it's unsafe. Not only is it voluntary for manufacturers to use the gluten-free designation, but they're forbidden from calling a food gluten-free even if it contains less than 20 ppm of gluten if that food was made with trace amounts of a gluten-containing grain. Furthermore, many products are inherently gluten-free and won't have the designation. You're not likely to see a banana labeled "gluten-free." Then again, if the marketing execs think it may sell more bananas, you just might!

On products made with flour or other grains, look for this statement on the label: "Processed in a dedicated mill." A *dedicated* mill specifically processes only one particular grain.

Rye and barley

Rye and barley, two grains that contain gluten, aren't required to be listed as an allergen like wheat is. As you know, wheat must be called out clearly on labels — but rye and barley don't have the same requirement. Products with rye and barley are not gluten-free, and may not be labeled as such. Rye is fairly easy to avoid because it's usually only listed as "rye" on labels, but barley can hide behind the generic term "natural flavors" and many others. If you see vague or generic terms on a product label, contact the manufacturer to find out exactly what ingredients are in that food.

Barley malt, especially, is in many commercially prepared products. That single ingredient is the reason many cereals aren't gluten-free. But there is hope! Many manufacturers are realizing that simple changes will let them market their products as gluten-free. What it really comes down to is this: Read every label, every single time, before you buy.

For details about the laws governing gluten-free labeling, check out the FDA's website: `www.fda.gov/Food/GuidanceRegulation/GuidanceDocumentsRegulatoryInformation/Allergens/ucm362880.htm`.

Book II

Making the Switch without Losing Your Mind

Avoiding suspect ingredients

Dozens of ingredients contain gluten. Some are obvious, like "bran" and "graham," but others are vague and nonspecific. Without some special knowledge, few people would know that "emulsifiers" can mean that gluten lurks in that product or that "vegetable protein" is a flashing red alarm for those who must avoid wheat.

You have to learn some technical terms that are used to describe gluten or that gluten can hide behind and look for them on every product you consider purchasing.

Here are just a few of the ingredients to look for on food products when you need to avoid gluten. Don't buy products with these terms:

- ✔ Bran (rice and corn bran are safe)
- ✔ Coloring
- ✔ Couscous
- ✔ Graham
- ✔ Hydrolyzed
- ✔ Kamut
- ✔ Malt (corn malt is safe)
- ✔ Natural flavors
- ✔ Soy sauce (unless specifically labeled wheat-free)
- ✔ Spelt
- ✔ Starch
- ✔ Vegetable protein

The following baking products may contain gluten. Read the label carefully before you buy them, and if any terms aren't clearly defined and identified, contact the manufacturer and find out whether the product is gluten-free. Manufacturers must list contact information on all their products.

- ✔ Cocoa and chocolate products
- ✔ Commercial dairy products
- ✔ Malted drinks and powders
- ✔ Marzipan
- ✔ Packaged bread mixes

✔ Packaged cake mixes

✔ Packaged frosting mixes

✔ Pastry fillings

✔ Pie fillings

✔ Seasoning mixes

✔ Some baking powders

Gathering Basic Foods

Here's a handy list of gluten-free items you should keep in your fridge or pantry. Check all the labels to make sure you're buying gluten-free versions.

✔ Cereals

✔ Coffee and tea (***Beware:*** Some teas have barley!)

✔ Crackers

✔ Pasta

✔ Rice

✔ Bread

✔ Breadcrumbs (either homemade or purchased)

✔ Mixes: brownie, cake, cookie

✔ Potato flakes, instant (great for coatings, thickening soups, and a quick side)

✔ Tortillas

✔ Ready-made gluten-free snacks

Look for these cans, bottles, and jars:

✔ Beans

✔ Soups, including broth or stock and bouillon

✔ Tomatoes

✔ Pasta sauce

✔ Olive oil and vegetable oil

✔ Balsamic vinegar

✔ Peanut butter

✔ Jam, jelly, or preserves

Look for the following gluten-free sauces, dressings, condiments, and other flavorings. Buy squeeze bottles when possible, and remember to mark your containers with your initials or a big "GF" so nobody sticks a crumby knife into your crumb-free products:

✔ Ketchup

✔ Mustard

✔ Mayo

✔ Barbecue sauce

✔ Salad dressings

✔ Liquid aminos

✔ Gluten-free soy sauce (tamari) and teriyaki sauce

When purchasing soy sauce and teriyaki sauce, be vigilant in looking for the gluten-free status. These products are often made with wheat, but gluten-free versions are available. The gluten-free version of soy sauce is usually called *tamari*.

Filling the fridge

Some products must be refrigerated. Pick up the following produce, meat, eggs, and dairy products:

✔ Butter

✔ Cheese

✔ Eggs

✔ Fresh fruit and vegetables

✔ Fresh meat

✔ Milk

✔ Yogurt

Unless you plan to use fresh raw meat, fish, and poultry within a day or two, put individual servings into freezer bags and freeze what you don't plan to use right away. Fresh fish, chicken, and turkey should be rinsed and patted dry with a paper towel before packaging and freezing.

Cut up carrots, pineapple, and other favorite produce and keep these foods in the fridge for a quick and naturally gluten-free snack or side.

Packing the freezer

Frozen foods have a longer shelf life than fresh and refrigerated foods, making them smart buys for kitchens of all kinds. For instance, if you like to make spur-of-the-moment smoothies, you can stock up on frozen berries; they're every bit as nutritious as fresh, and they're much easier to store and find out of season.

Here are some other gluten-free foods to keep in the freezer so they're available when you need them:

- Breads, such as sandwich bread, buns, waffles, pancakes, French toast, and muffins (gluten-free breads spoil quickly on the counter, so keep them frozen for best results)
- Ready-made pizza and pizza crust
- Frozen fruits and veggies
- Steak, chicken, and fish
- Microwaveable meals

Stocking Shortcuts

Who doesn't love shortcuts? In this section, you find products that can make your gluten-free food prep much simpler and quicker, especially when compared to assembling all the ingredients to make certain foods from scratch. But shortcuts usually cost you, and gluten-free food-prep shortcuts are no exception. Consider the savings in time these products can provide you to decide whether they're worth the higher price.

Using an all-purpose gluten-free flour blend

When you begin a gluten-free diet, you may be surprised by how many different kinds of flour are used in baking. Most people assume that eliminating gluten means less flour, but the reality is that your one all-purpose wheat flour is replaced by many specialty flours, which can include white rice flour, brown rice flour, tapioca starch, potato starch, potato flour, and sorghum flour — just to name a few. Buying an all-purpose gluten-free flour blend saves you the space of stocking the different flours; the mixing is done for you and it's all placed in one little bag, ready to go.

Brands vary greatly in taste and texture, depending on which flours the blend features. Try out a few different kinds to find the one you prefer.

Some brands of all-purpose gluten-free flour come with xanthan gum included. Xanthan gum, along with a mixture of flours, makes gluten-free baked goods come as close as possible to traditional versions. The gum simulates the gooey gluten that binds ingredients in traditional baked goods. Add about a teaspoon per cup of flour. Xanthan gum is pretty expensive for a tiny little bag, so paying a bit extra for a flour blend that includes it is usually worth it.

Purchasing polenta

Try polenta. This naturally gluten-free cornmeal porridge makes great toppings and crusts for main dishes and can be used in tasty side dishes. You can buy polenta in a bag or box in instant form, or you can buy it precooked in a roll.

Polenta is an affordable and quick-to-cook food that can be prepared in many ways and used in a wide range of meals and snacks. Polenta is a staple for gluten-free cooking for many people. Use it instead of rice, pasta, or bread.

If you've never cooked with polenta, now's a great time to give it a try. Here are some ideas for using polenta:

✔ Serve instant polenta, either plain or with herbs or cheese, as a side dish.

✔ Serve polenta instead of pasta or rice as an accompaniment to stew, stir-fry, or chili.

✔ Use polenta in a vegetarian main dish, topped with sauce or sautéed vegetables.

✔ Try instant polenta as a hot breakfast cereal, either sweet (topped with fruit, nuts, cinnamon, and milk) or savory (served with cheese and eggs).

✔ Use baked, fried, or grilled polenta rounds as a base for appetizers or hearty snacks and lunches.

✔ Use instant polenta in casseroles or as a casserole crust.

✔ Use polenta to replace the biscuit or pastry topping on potpies.

Using premade products

The single easiest — and healthiest — way to follow a gluten-free diet is to stick to naturally gluten-free foods, such as plain meats, fresh fruit and veggies, and gluten-free grains. Another way to simplify your life on a gluten-free diet is to buy some of the wonderful premade products, especially ones that aid in recipe preparation.

Here are some premade foods that are pretty easy to find, and most brands are really tasty, too:

✔ **Breads:** Bagels, muffins, baguettes, rolls, English muffins, and tortillas are all available gluten-free. Try a few brands until you find the ones you like best.

✔ **Breakfast cereals:** A few major cereal brands are becoming gluten-free, often by removing barley malt as a sweetener in a corn or rice cereal. You can usually find at least a few gluten-free cereals in any grocery store, but be sure to check the natural foods section to weigh all the options.

✔ **Crackers:** Not long ago, recipes for gluten-free crackers were pretty popular. But with so many great cracker choices available now, many people are forgoing the time and effort required for the homemade versions.

✔ **Pasta:** Unless you're feeling really ambitious, you'll likely want to buy gluten-free pasta instead of making your own. Most stores offer several choices.

✔ **Pie crust:** Find great pie crust mixes, frozen pie shells, and frozen and refrigerated ready-made foldout crusts at your local grocery store. Or if your store doesn't carry the brand you want, try using crushed gluten-free cookies or graham crackers to make a delicious crust. See Chapter 4 of Book V for directions on making crumb crusts.

- ✔ **Pizza and pizza crust:** Several brands of awesome gluten-free frozen pizzas are available. You can also find premade crusts and crust mixes in many stores.

- ✔ **Tortillas:** Corn tortillas are usually gluten-free as long as they aren't made from a mix of corn and wheat. You can also buy large tortillas made from other gluten-free grains.

Readying Your Pantry and Fridge for Baking

You want to have some basic ingredients and products specific to the gluten-free diet on hand. Admittedly, some of these items are a little pricier than their gluten-containing counterparts, and they're sometimes a little harder to find. In Chapter 3 of Book II, you find advice on where to buy them and how to save as much money as you can. But depending on how you cook (or don't), many of these items may become staples in your gluten-free-friendly kitchen.

Specialty ingredients to stock

Don't let this long list scare you. You don't need all these things; in fact, if you're not going to do any baking, you probably don't need any of them. If, however, you're planning to cook or bake gluten-free, consider having some of these ingredients on hand:

- ✔ **Arrowroot flour:** Higher in nutritional value than some other flours, arrowroot often takes the place of cornstarch.

- ✔ **Brown rice flour:** This flour still contains the bran, which makes it more nutritious than white rice flour. It has a slightly nutty taste.

- ✔ **Corn flour:** You can blend corn flour with other flours for baking, or you can mix it with cornmeal (ground corn) in cornbreads and other dishes.

- ✔ **Cornstarch:** You can use cornstarch for thickening or with other flours in baking mixtures.

- ✔ **Garbanzo/fava bean flour (or blend):** Don't let the names scare you; these are some of the best baking flours around today. They offer a great texture and extra nutritional value, and they don't taste like beans.

✓ **Gelatin powder (unflavored):** A lot of the gluten-free recipes now call for unflavored gelatin because it adds moisture and protein and it holds the ingredients together.

✓ **Guar gum:** You don't need both xanthan gum and guar gum, because you can use one in place of the other. Be aware that some people find guar gum to have a laxative effect.

✓ **Lecithin:** Lecithin is an *emulsifier,* which just means it helps ingredients blend together. Made from soy, lecithin improves aeration and the texture of baked gluten-free foods, and it makes the food a little more resistant to getting stale.

✓ **Potato starch flour:** This is not the same thing as potato flour (which tastes very much like potatoes). Potato starch is very fine, white flour. It doesn't have much flavor, so it doesn't distort the taste of your foods, but it improves the texture in baking mixes. You can use it as a thickener or with other flours in baking mixtures.

✓ **Sorghum (milo) flour:** This nutritious flour is making more of a mark in the gluten-free cooking world. Its relatively bland flavor makes it a versatile ingredient in gluten-free baking.

✓ **Soy flour:** These days, people use soy flour mostly in combination with other flours, if at all. It has a strong, distinctive flavor, which some people love but others definitely don't.

✓ **Sweet rice flour:** Some people get confused because sweet rice flour is made from *glutinous* rice, not to be confused with "glutenous" (which technically isn't a word, although this book uses it often). *Glutinous* just means "sticky." Sweet rice flour cooks differently from white rice flour, and people use it most often for thickening sauces or soups.

✓ **Tapioca flour (or starch):** This is also called *cassava flour* or *manioc.* It's great because it gives gluten-free foods a little bit of a stretch or chew that's lacking in many foods that don't contain gluten.

✓ **White rice flour:** Long considered the basic ingredient in a gluten-free diet, white rice flour is being overshadowed by more nutritious flours and flours with better consistencies, like bean, brown rice, arrowroot, and sorghum. But white rice flour is, nevertheless, a staple in the gluten-free pantry. Its bland flavor doesn't distort the taste of baked goods, and it comes in different textures (fine through regular), which affect the consistency of foods.

✓ **Xanthan gum:** A must if you're baking gluten-free breads and other baked goods, xanthan gum helps prevent crumbling.

✓ **Yeast:** Dry, active yeast is an important ingredient for gluten-free breads and other foods that need to rise. Don't use the rapid-rise yeast unless the recipe suggests it. Fresh yeast is key.

Book II

Making the Switch without Losing Your Mind

✔ **Alternative grains:** These grains are loaded with nutrients, and they're great to have on hand either as baking flours or as whole grains. Use whole grains to add flavor and texture, cook them as their own dish, or even add them to foods. Here are some alternative grains to check out:

- Amaranth
- Buckwheat
- Mesquite
- Millet
- Montina
- Quinoa
- Sorghum
- Teff

Grains — especially whole grains — have a lot of oil in them. Oil can turn rancid quickly, so when you buy whole grains and whole-grain flours, be sure to shop at stores where the turnover is high, and buy only what you plan to use within a few months. Refrigerate the flours and grains if you have the space, but pay close attention to the smell. Old flours and grains smell stale.

Mixes to have on hand

You should keep several types of gluten-free baking mixes on hand so you're always prepared. These mixes are not a compromise, nor are they "cheating." They're so good that, in many cases, the gluten-free variety would win in a side-by-side taste comparison. Best of all, with very little work on your part, your house smells like you've been baking all day!

Some people complain about the cost of mixes, but if you add up the cost of the ingredients to make baked goods from scratch (have you priced xanthan gum lately?), factor in the batches that yield only inedible hand weights, and consider that your time is at least *somewhat* valuable, the price is well worth it.

Here are some of the mixes you might want to keep handy:

✔ **All-purpose baking mix:** Several companies make various types of all-purpose baking mixes, and most are excellent. Some companies use the garbanzo/fava bean mixture, and some use mixtures of other gluten-free flours. Use these mixes for baking or as a coating for fried or baked foods.

- ✔ **Bread mixes:** Many different kinds of bread mixes are available today, most of which you can fix in a bread machine or mix by hand and cook in the oven.

- ✔ **Brownies:** The brownie mixes today are absolutely amazing. Some come with chunks of chocolate, but if they don't, you can add your own. You can also personalize them with nuts or even frosting.

- ✔ **Cakes:** Gluten-free cake mixes come in just about any flavor you want, and these days, they're all incredibly moist, light, and tasty. With slight modifications that are almost always on the package, you can make your cakes into cupcakes.

- ✔ **Chebe:** Chebe is so unique that it could've gone under several of these headings — bread, all-purpose baking mix, or pizza — so it's on its own, and it's good enough to stand alone. You can make Chebe, which comes from manioc (tapioca), into bread rolls or sticks, pizza crust, or a variety of other foods. Truly, your creativity is the only limiting factor. New varieties of Chebe have recently appeared in the marketplace.

- ✔ **Cookies:** The gluten-free cookie mixes today are fantastic. They come in just about any flavor you can dream up, and they turn out better than anything you can get from a store. Of course, you can tailor them to your tastes by adding chocolate chips or gluten-free candies.

- ✔ **Muffins:** You can make many different varieties of gluten-free muffins, including vanilla, blueberry, apple, and banana. You can also buy basic muffin mixes that you can make into any type of muffin you want.

- ✔ **Pancakes and waffles:** One mix makes both; just the proportions of ingredients change (and, of course, you need a waffle iron to make waffles).

- ✔ **Pie crusts:** In Chapter 4 of Book V, you find suggestions for making your own pie crusts from crushed cereal or cookies. But if you want something closer to the real deal, the mixes available for pie crusts are what you're looking for. These crusts are easy to make and delicious, and the mixes turn out a perfect crust every time.

- ✔ **Pizza dough:** Mixes to help you whip up a quick pizza crust are available. You just top the crust with your favorite toppings. The pizza is as good as or better than anything other people deliver.

Book II

Making the Switch without Losing Your Mind

Keep in mind that many gluten-free foods, even some of those you buy commercially, don't have preservatives in them. So unlike a store-bought pastry that has a shelf life of seven millennia, your gluten-free foods should usually be refrigerated or even frozen.

Preparing Your Kitchen for Cooking Both Ways

It goes without saying that making separate meals creates extra work for the cook (and because you're reading this book, that's probably you!). For instance, if you're having a pasta dinner and you want to make one batch of gluten-free pasta and one regular batch, you're obviously making more work for yourself, but it's probably the way to go when not everyone in the house has to be gluten-free.

These days, gluten-free pastas and other gluten-free foods are so delicious that it's just as yummy to make the gluten-free version for everyone. Sometimes, however, you'll want to make two versions of a meal, whether it's to save money or for personal preferences.

Still, cooking two versions of a meal can be easier than it sounds. Getting back to that pasta dinner, you may want to make both types of pasta but keep things simple by serving one delicious gluten-free sauce that can go on both.

Sharing is caring when you're cooking both ways, and plenty of foods are available that the whole family can share. Instead of having two varieties of everything, use gluten-free versions of shared foods like sauces, spices, condiments, and salad dressings. Doing so can certainly make your life easier and save you time in the kitchen and the grocery store.

Planning your menus for easy meal prep

It's 5 p.m., you just got home from work, and you're ready to start making dinner. You were planning to make spaghetti, but you have no gluten-free pasta in the house. Because gluten-free cooking involves special ingredients and preparation processes, you have to plan your cooking in advance and make sure you have all the ingredients on hand.

Gluten-free ingredients aren't always easy to find. For instance, if you're going to make bread and you need xanthan gum, you can't run down to the corner store and get it. And if you don't have it, you're not making bread.

Planning your work and working your plan is essential. Make menus and lists before you head for the store. (Chapter 3 of Book II has more info on where to find the items you need.) Make sure you always have appropriate ingredients on hand. You may have to order some of them online, so give yourself plenty of lead time. If a holiday is coming, plan the meal several weeks in advance in case some of the ingredients are only available on the Internet.

Using appliances to make cooking easier

Just as you don't need separate cookware, you won't need separate appliances for cooking your gluten-free foods — with one exception: You definitely want to have two toasters, or better yet, two toaster *ovens*.

Crumbs literally fly off of bread. No matter how carefully you clean, your toaster will always be home to crumbs that can contaminate your gluten-free foods. Toaster ovens beat toasters because thanks to gravity, the crumbs fall down (as opposed to getting stuck on the side of the grates in a regular toaster), and you can wipe them away or put a piece of aluminum foil on the bottom of the oven and easily get rid of them.

Toaster bags are another great invention that no shared kitchen should be without. You just put your bread into the bag, put it into the toaster, and cook as usual. You can even take the bags to restaurants with you and ask the server to toast your bread in them.

Here are four appliances that can make gluten-free cooking a whole lot easier:

✔ **Bread machine:** Unless you really love the minutiae of baking, a bread machine is a must if you want fresh-baked bread. It makes the job so much easier. You'll find delicious recipes for gluten-free breads in Chapter 6 of Book V, and some of them can be made in a bread machine. You can also buy mixes made especially for use in bread machines. The smell of fresh-baked bread in a gluten-free home is really awesome. By far, the easiest way to make homemade bread is with a machine.

Gluten-free dough is really heavy compared to regular dough. You need a bread machine with a super-strong motor, or you may catch it on fire or burn it out.

✔ **Mixer:** You don't need a special mixer, but be sure to clean the beaters and the mixer thoroughly before using this appliance to whip up gluten-free foods because residuals can hang on. Have you ever noticed that film of flour on your kitchen counter after mixing up your cookie dough? That flour floats up as well as down, getting into the underside of your mixer and just waiting to drop into the next thing you make. Clean the mixer thoroughly and shake, bang, or brush it if necessary to dislodge any hidden flour.

✔ **Food processors:** These gadgets are great, but they're really hard to clean. Be especially careful if you're mixing glutenous breadcrumbs. You may want to consider a high-end food processor that comes with multiple mixing bowls. You can use one bowl for gluten-free preparation and the other for everything else.

✔ **Rice cooker:** One tool that can be invaluable is an electric rice cooker. You'll be cooking a lot of rice, and this just makes it easy.

Book II

Making the Switch without Losing Your Mind

Changing a few techniques in your two-way kitchen

To successfully share your kitchen, you don't have to change your whole life. You just have to change a few techniques:

- ✔ Keep a few sponges within easy reach. Make sure you wash them in hot water, keep them super clean, don't use them very long, and never let them stay wet or moldy. If you keep clean sponges handy, you're more apt to wipe up the gluten crumbs that can contaminate a perfectly good gluten-free meal.

- ✔ If you use hand towels and dish towels to wipe up crumbs and clean countertops, make sure they're always clean.

- ✔ Use parchment paper or aluminum foil to cover cookie sheets, separate foods, or cover your toaster oven or broiler rack. This is a great way to make sure your gluten-free foods don't get contaminated.

- ✔ Teach everyone, even the littlest kids, how to do the gob drop (see the "The gob drop for spreadables" section earlier in this chapter for the skinny on this).

- ✔ Make gluten-free sauces and condiments that everyone can use.

- ✔ Dedicate a gluten-free area of the pantry.

- ✔ Make sure all your spices are gluten-free.

- ✔ When cooking separate meals, make sure the gluten-free version is at least as yummy as the other one.

- ✔ Cleanliness is next to godliness. Crumbs are a no-no.

- ✔ When making two varieties of a meal, make the gluten-free version first.

- ✔ Use brightly colored labels to distinguish gluten-free foods. This is especially helpful when you have babysitters or other people in the house who may grab the wrong food.

Chapter 3

Shopping within Your Gluten-Free Lifestyle

In This Chapter

▶ Developing strategies before you head to the store

▶ Figuring out what you want to buy

▶ Going places: Pick a store, any store

▶ Getting the most for your gluten-free dollar

*I*f you or someone you love had been diagnosed with celiac disease way, way back — in the early 1990s, for instance — you'd have faced a much tougher proposition than you do today. There was no Internet, and no books or other ready source of information. And certainly there was no distinctive labeling on food nor ready lists of what to avoid.

Finding gluten-free products really *is* easier than you may think, and thanks to improved labeling laws and manufacturer awareness, it's getting easier all the time.

In this chapter, you get the help you need to figure out what to buy. Then you get guidance on where to shop, how to shop, and — this is important — how to save money on gluten-free foods. You can find important shopping tips to save you time, money, and frustration.

Knowing What You Want

One of the best things you can do to make shopping easier when you're enjoying a gluten-free lifestyle is plan ahead. If you try to wing it, especially at first, you end up spending hours in the grocery store walking in circles, trying to figure out what to eat and what to buy, and *then* worrying about whether the food's gluten-free.

Not only do planning meals ahead of time and making shopping lists save you time and headaches in the store, but these steps also give you the peace of mind that the meals you're planning are, in fact, gluten-free.

Planning your meals

You've probably heard the dictum *plan your work, and work your plan*. Same thing goes for meals, although *plan your meals and eat 'em* isn't quite as catchy or clever.

Most people think planning meals sounds like a great idea, and they're able to pull it off once or twice. But for the most part, they're spontaneous and impulsive. They see something in the store that looks particularly appealing (and because they're usually starving while they're shopping, *everything* looks good), and they toss it in the cart. But planning meals helps you strategize before you head to the store.

When you're planning your meals, try not to think in terms of cutting out gluten, but instead think of how you can make substitutions. Think about the things you love to eat — with or without gluten — and build around those foods, making the substitutions you need to make to convert gluten-containing meals into gluten-free ones.

Sitting down and making a meal plan is tough, but it pays off in spades when you're at the store and you find your busy weekdays speeding by. You may find some of these tips helpful:

- ✔ **Have the whole family eat gluten-free.** Even if some members of your family are still gluten-eaters, make your life simpler by planning most, if not all, of the family meals to be gluten-free. This planning isn't hard if you follow the *if man made it, don't eat it* approach of eating meats, fruits, vegetables, and other natural foods. And even if your meal includes things like pasta, the gluten-free varieties these days are so delicious that the entire family will love them — and may not even know the difference.

- ✔ **Plan a few days' menus at once.** Look through cookbooks (no, they don't have to be gluten-free ones — for inspiration on making *anything* gluten-free, see Chapter 4 of this Book) and at individual recipes for inspiration. Remember, the gluten-free diet is *not* all about rice, corn, and potatoes. In fact, the more variety, the better. Variety isn't just the spice of life; it's important from a nutritional standpoint. Rice, corn, and potatoes don't offer much nutritionally.

- ✔ **Plan a marathon cooking day.** Maybe you designate Sundays to be your day in the kitchen. With the week's worth of meals already in mind, you can prepare several meals at once, saving yourself time shopping, cooking, *and* cleaning up during the week. Because you'll have menu ideas fresh in your hand and food won't go to waste, you'll probably save money, too.

- ✔ **Use foods that can do double-duty.** If you're planning to cook a large roasting chicken for dinner one night, you can count on leftovers for chicken stir-fry the next night.

- ✔ **Plan meals you can cook in a slow cooker.** Slow cookers are great for complete one-course meals. And walking into a house that smells like you've been cooking all day is a great way to say "welcome home!"

Book II

Making the Switch without Losing Your Mind

Have the whole family help with menu planning. Nothing is more frustrating than spending a weekend planning, shopping, and cooking only to hear moans and groans about how what used to be someone's favorite food is now "gross." Let them offer suggestions — for that matter, enlist help with the cooking and cleanup, too.

Making lists

Your spontaneity is exactly what food manufacturers are banking on. They want you to be impulsive, and that's why they tempt you with the delicious-but-oh-so-bad-for-you, high-profit-margin foods at the end of aisles and checkout stands. (Find out more about store layout in the section titled "Navigating the Aisles," because you need to know the marketing secrets so you don't get sucked in.) How many times have you roamed the grocery store thinking of yummy, healthy meals to make for the week, only to get home with dozens of bags of groceries, unable to remember a single meal? Yeah, me too.

At the risk of sounding a little elementary here, shopping lists are really helpful. Not only do they remind you of foods and ingredients you need, but they also help prevent impulse shopping.

Keep a running list of what you're running low on or what you need to buy next time you're at the store. Make sure the list is handy for everyone in the family so no one whines that you "forgot" a favorite food (when you didn't even know that *was* a favorite food).

As you do your menu planning, add the ingredients you need for your week's worth of meals to the list. If you need to call manufacturers to find out whether some of the ingredients are gluten-free, now's the best time to do it (if the product's not sitting in front of you, you can usually find the manufacturer's phone number online). Don't wait till you're in the store, because you may find that the company's customer service representatives have all gone home for the day.

If you're a coupon-clipper, clip your coupons and refer to your grocery list and the store ads. Can you replace items on your list with ones that are on sale or that you have coupons for? You may even find that the coupons provide inspiration for meal planning. What you don't want to do is buy things just *because* you have coupons. Use them only for things you really need.

Don't forget the snacks! Whether your idea of a snack is ice cream or raisins, snacks are an important part of your day. When you're making your shopping list, encourage your family members to add their favorite snacks — preferably the healthy kind — so you don't have to hear that "There's nothing to eat in this house!"

Deciding What to Buy

Obviously, the most important considerations for figuring out what to buy are what you like, what you're going to make, and whether it's gluten-free.

Keep in mind the two kinds of gluten-free foods: foods that companies make as specialty items and foods that are naturally gluten-free.

Checking out gluten-free specialty products

Gluten-free specialty items come from companies that specifically market some or all of their products to the wheat-free/gluten-free community. Most of the time, these products are foods that would normally have gluten in them — such as pasta, bread, crackers, cookies, and brownies — but have been formulated to be gluten-free.

The specialty products are almost always labeled *gluten-free,* so you don't have to question their safety as far as your dietary restrictions are concerned. The companies that make these products generally make several product lines and sell their foods by mail, online, or at specialty retailers. These days, "regular" grocery stores are starting to carry more of these specialty items.

Wheat has to be called out on the label, so it's pretty easy to avoid. But remember that *wheat-free* doesn't mean *gluten-free.* If you see a package labeled *wheat-free,* the contents may still contain barley, rye, oats, or derivatives of those ingredients. Read the label carefully to see whether it lists other forms of gluten besides wheat.

Remembering naturally gluten-free foods

Many people think the gluten-free lifestyle limits them to buying foods that say *gluten-free* on the label. This is *so* not true! Limiting yourself to those foods is ultrarestrictive, and it also means you're overlooking lots of foods that are inherently — or naturally — gluten-free, some of which are the most nutritious of all. These are foods that contain no gluten, although the distributor doesn't necessarily market them as such. They include the obvious players — meat, poultry, fish, seafood, fruits, vegetables, and nuts — but they also include some products that seem like they may have gluten in them but don't.

Book II

Making the Switch without Losing Your Mind

Many foods, including most candies, chips, popcorn, deli foods, condiments, and spices, are inherently gluten-free. Even some commercial cereals are gluten-free but aren't labeled as such. (What? A cereal without malt flavoring?)

Asian foods — like rice wraps, many Thai foods, and most fish or oyster sauces — are good examples of foods that are often inherently gluten-free (remember, though, that soy sauce usually has wheat in it). Mexican and other ethnic cuisines also offer a lot of naturally gluten-free foods. So although they don't say *gluten-free* on the label, they are, in fact, often safe on the gluten-free diet.

The best foods are those without a label: meat, seafood, produce, and so on. But many other foods are gluten-free and don't say so on the label. Read the list of ingredients, and if you don't see anything blatantly off-limits, call the manufacturer to confirm that the food is gluten-free. You'll be surprised at how often you find products that you can safely enjoy.

If you wear reading glasses, bring them to the store. You have to do lots of label reading, and you want to have your glasses handy so you can read all the ingredients.

Asking for opinions

The last thing you want to do is spend gobs of money on specialty items and expensive foods only to find that they taste more like cardboard than cake. Because gluten-free foods can be pricey, and because some are great and some are awful, asking around about gluten-free foods and getting opinions from others who've tried them is more important than ever. Of course, opinions vary, and what one person loves, another may hate, but opinions can be valuable, especially if you hear several of them.

If you want to hear opinions on products, you have a lot of options. Try some of these places:

- ✔ **Support groups:** If you attend support group meetings, ask the members whether they've ever tried a particular product or whether they have suggestions for, say, brownies. You can get lots of helpful ideas this way.

- ✔ **Listserv:** You can subscribe to free e-mail lists (we go into detail about these in Book I, Chapter 5). Posting questions and comments about gluten-free products is a valuable part of belonging to these lists.

- ✔ **Online rating systems:** Some of the online shopping websites offer customer ratings. See how many stars a product has, and read the comments to help you decide whether you want to buy it.

- ✔ **Shoppers:** If you see people at a store buying a product you haven't tried, ask whether they've tried it and what they like or don't like about it. At the same time, if you've tried a product and see someone looking at it, speak up. He or she will appreciate the input.

- ✔ **Store staff:** Sometimes the store staff members are very knowledgeable about products. Ask them whether they've tried a particular product and what they like or don't like about it. Be careful, though — sometimes a staffer sounds knowledgeable but isn't. Make sure you know your facts well enough to tell the difference.

When you find products that you and your family love and have confirmed to be gluten-free, save the label or part of the packaging. Keep the labels in a binder and create divided sections such as "Soup," "Candy," or whatever category you like. Then, bring the binder with you to the store so you can quickly spot the items again and rest easy, knowing that you like the product and that it is, in fact, gluten-free.

Deciding Where to Shop

So you know what meals you want to make, you have at least some idea of what foods you want to buy, and you may even have a list in hand. Where do you get all this stuff (some of which you've never heard of)? Well, for most of your shopping needs, you can pick a store — any store — because you're not as limited as you may think.

"Regular" grocery stores

You can do most of your shopping at "regular" grocery stores — yep, the kind you find on every corner in most cities. If you're surprised by this, don't be. Remember, your best bet is to eat mostly foods that are naturally healthy and inherently gluten-free, and you can find those at your friendly neighborhood grocery store.

Obviously, these stores are more convenient and less expensive than specialty stores. But from a psychological standpoint, you have a couple of other, less tangible reasons for shopping at a regular grocery store.

First, a gluten-free diet can seem restrictive and even daunting to some people, and some even find it to be somewhat isolating (hopefully not when they're finished with *this* book). Being forced to shop only at specialty stores or online confirms those feelings of isolation and despair. Being able to shop at "regular" stores and buy "regular" brands that everyone else is buying is really liberating for people who feel this way.

If you have kids on the gluten-free diet, considering the psychological impact of shopping at regular grocery stores is even more important. Kids want to be like all the other kids and eat brands (and junk foods) that all the other kids eat. And that's okay — feeling that way is perfectly normal. For most kids, fitting in ranks right up there with breathing. Shopping at "regular" grocery stores gives them the sense of normalcy that they crave.

Regular brands aside, many major grocery stores are starting to carry more gluten-free specialty items; some even have entire gluten-free sections. If you have some favorite specialty products that you want your local store to carry, don't hesitate to ask the manager whether the store can carry them. How often you get a positive response may surprise you, and the manager may be surprised at how much interest customers have in the gluten-free products.

You may also be pleased to know that many of the regular grocery chains have lists of the gluten-free products they carry, both name brand and generic. Some of the stores post the lists on their websites, and others offer the lists if you call their customer service numbers.

Natural foods stores

Most natural foods stores are well aware of the growing interest in gluten-free products, and they're stocking up to meet the increasing demand. You can find all the meats and vegetables (usually organic) that are such a big part of the gluten-free diet, but you can also find lots of gluten-free specialty items. Some natural foods stores even have dedicated gluten-free sections.

Because natural foods stores have become so popular, they've expanded their offerings and generally provide a huge array of exotic and gourmet health foods, supplements, and even cosmetics and household goods. Shopping at some of these places is more like being in a fun zone than a food zone.

Farmers' markets

Coming soon to a corner near you! Farmers' markets are popping up everywhere (not just next to farms), offering fresh produce, eggs, meat, fish, honey, nuts, and other (inherently gluten-free) items, usually at prices far below those of most retailers. The foods are ripe, organic is the rule rather than the exception, and the generous samples that sellers pass out are enough to count as lunch.

You can also feel good knowing you're supporting local farmers and the environment: The food is usually grown without pesticides, and not having to ship the foods long distances uses less energy and gasoline.

Ethnic markets

You want a gluten-free kind of a thrill? Go to an Asian market — the more authentic, the better — and check out all the stuff that's gluten-free. Don't forget the Thai and Indian aisles. Truly, the selection is amazing. Sauces, rice wraps, tapioca noodles, rice candies, things you've never heard of, and things that you may wonder about for years — all gluten-free. Of course, they're not labeled as such, but that's okay. If the label is in English, you can see for yourself that gluten isn't in many of the foods. Asians use very little wheat in their products.

Other ethnic cuisines may surprise and delight as well. Mexican is just one of the many other cultures that use lots of inherently gluten-free ingredients in their cooking. Explore new cultures without ever leaving your country and experience a thrill of the gluten-free variety.

Gluten-free retail stores

Once only a dream for those who've been gluten-free for a long time, gluten-free stores are finally a reality. Entire stores filled with gluten-free foods, books about being gluten-free, cookbooks, and other important resources are beginning to pop up, and they're thriving. You'll be seeing more and more of these, so keep your eyes open for a store opening near you.

Websites and catalogs

You can do all your gluten-free shopping from the comfort of your favorite easy chair, any time, day or night — you can even be in your comfiest jammies, if you want. Some great websites specialize in selling gluten-free products, and within just a few minutes, you can place your order. A couple of days later, your shipment arrives at your doorstep — and you may be so excited to rip open that big box of gluten-free goodies, you feel like a kid at the holidays!

All the gluten-free specialty food manufacturers have websites, so if you know a specific brand you want to buy, you can go to the site and see what they have to offer (you can find the sites with a quick Google search). But here are a few sites you can buy several different brands from:

✔ www.glutenfreemall.com

✔ www.glutenfree.com

✔ www.amazon.com (search under "Grocery" for gluten-free)

Yep, even Amazon.com has gluten-free products you can buy.

Some sites allow you to sort out other allergens, too, so you can narrow down the products that are, for instance, gluten-free, casein-free, corn-free, and soy-free. Some sites also provide customer rating systems. They give you an average customer rating and specific comments about a product. This type of a customer rating system is invaluable in helping you decide which products to buy.

If you don't have a computer, most companies offer a toll-free number, and some will send you a free catalog so you can order by phone or fax.

Navigating the Aisles

You thought grocery shopping was just a matter of steering the cart up and down the aisles, didn't you? And you probably even thought *you* were in control of your purchases, right? Actually, for decades now, grocery store psychologists have been studying ways to get people to spend more, and they've come up with subtle and subliminal ways to turn us all into Stepford Shoppers, falling victim to strategically placed temptations scattered about the store like land mines.

Copy a safe and forbidden ingredients list off the Internet (try the "Safe Gluten-Free Food List/Unsafe Foods & Ingredients" link at www.celiac.com) and bring it with you to the store. You may need it when you're reading ingredients on product labels.

Perusing the perimeter

One of the best ways to avoid some of those glaring gluten temptations at the store is to shop the perimeter. Store layouts are predictable; produce, dairy, meat, and other staples are as far from the front door of the store as possible so that you have to walk past all the more expensive (and usually less nutritious) foods before you get to what you really want.

For the most part, the gluten-free items on your list are along the perimeter of the store. If your store has a good health food aisle, you may be able to find gluten-free pastas, mixes, cereals, bars, and other items. Your best bet in general, though, is to stick to the fruits, vegetables, meats, and dairy items — most of which are around the outsides. Just think of how much time you can save by not having to go through the cracker, cookie, and bread aisles!

Sorting through the health food aisle

At first, the health food aisles may seem to be the best bet for finding gluten-free foods. Not necessarily.

Health food aisles are full of product labels screaming *whole grain* or *multi-grain*. Lots of "healthy" foods are loaded with whole grains to provide fiber and nutrients, and although the gluten-free diet sometimes allows whole grains like brown rice, millet, or quinoa, for instance, most of the whole grains in those products contain gluten.

Health food sections do offer some benefits. The longer a food's ingredients list is, the less likely it is to be gluten-free, and health food aisles are good places to find items that have short ingredients lists. Read them carefully!

The major grocery stores are starting to carry a larger variety of gluten-free specialty products in their health food aisles. If your favorite grocery store carries gluten-free products, tell the manager how much you appreciate it and even make suggestions for products the store could carry that it doesn't. Chances are, store managers are "testing" the gluten-free products, and your feedback may be valuable in making sure the stores continue to carry them.

Planning impulsive purchases

High-powered grocery store psychologists have spent billions of retail-funded dollars on studies that finally concluded with a shocking revelation: Shoppers are impulsive. So the stores capitalize on your impulsivity by planning your impulsive purchases. "Planned impulsivity" may at first seem to be an oxymoron, but it's exactly what stores are creating when they strategize everything from where to place items to what music they play in the background.

Book II

Making the Switch without Losing Your Mind

Don't tell me you haven't fallen for the marketing. You're at the store for just a few items ("I'll just use a hand basket"), and you walk out with a cartload of things you didn't even know you wanted. You're captivated by flashing coupon dispensers, in-aisle displays, free samples, and heavily loaded end caps at the end of each aisle — all of which are there because the psychologists have done their homework. And don't forget the fact that your kids are the primary targets, as they tend to be quite influential when you make your impulsive purchases.

Rarely are these so-called *impulse* purchases directing you toward healthy foods, much less gluten-free ones. If you're having a hard time sticking to the diet, or if you find being tempted by the gluttonous gluten products out there to be daunting, be aware of the efforts to snare you at the stores, and have your guard up against impulsive, gluten-containing purchases.

Living Gluten-Free — Affordably

One of the most common complaints about the gluten-free diet is that it's more expensive — but it doesn't need to be. Yes, a loaf of regular bread is less than half the cost of a loaf of gluten-free bread. And gluten-free crackers and cookies are often smaller *and* twice the price of regular ones. It's easy to pay more than your fair share in shipping expenses. But you have ways to save significant amounts of money when you're enjoying a gluten-free lifestyle. So before you take a second mortgage on your house to finance this diet, take note of these tips that can save you a bunch.

Scaling back on specialties

Most of the "extra expense" of the gluten-free diet is in the high cost of specialty items. We're not suggesting you celebrate little Preston's birthday with store-bought rice crackers to save the expense of making a gluten-free cake. You need to have *some* specialty items on hand, and cakes or special-occasion treats are definitely among them.

But if you find you're spending way too much money to accommodate this diet, take a look at how many and what types of specialty items you buy. Breads, crackers, cookies, cakes, pizzas, pretzels, donuts — they're pricey, for sure. But you don't need them. You can substitute store-bought chips for a fraction of the cost of gluten-free pretzels. Even as high-priced as they are, candies and candy bars that you can get at any grocery store are far cheaper than specialty treats.

And really, most of the specialty items aren't good for you, anyway — they're high-calorie, high-glycemic-index foods (they raise your blood sugar quickly — see Book II, Chapter 1 for more on that) that provide very little nutritional value. If you follow the more nutritious approach to gluten-free eating in Chapter 1 of Book II, you find very little room for these expensive indulgences.

Some of the specialty items people buy are unnecessary. Gluten-free vanilla is a good example: All vanilla is gluten-free! You don't need to buy it as a specialty item.

Some specialty items may be important to have on hand — pasta, some special-occasion treats, and maybe some bread or bagels, for instance. But in general, most people buy more specialty items than they need, and it definitely puts a burden on the budget.

Saving on shipping

If you do buy specialty items, you can find ways to save on shipping. For one, you can ask your local grocery or natural foods store to carry the product you want — that way, the store pays for the shipping, not you.

If you're ordering online, order from a company that sells many different brands of products. That way, you pay one shipping charge for several different brands. Buying one or two products at a time from individual manufacturers costs you a fortune in shipping.

Going generic

Don't assume that generics are off-limits on this diet. Most of the time, generic products are as clearly labeled as major brands, and sometimes a toll-free number is listed on the package so you can call to confirm whether the item is gluten-free. Usually, generics are labeled as being *distributed by* a large grocery chain or distribution company. Dig a little — call toll-free information or go on the Internet to get a phone number for the large grocery chain or distribution company. Most of the time, you can locate a customer service representative who can help you find out more about the ingredients.

If the generics are a store brand, chances are good that you'll be able to get lots of information about the products. Some of the large grocery chains have lists of their gluten-free generics, and sometimes those lists are even available online. If you want more information about a store's generic products, call its toll-free number and ask to talk with the head of quality control or the nutrition department.

Book II

Making the Switch without Losing Your Mind

Eating nutritiously

Some people think that eating nutritious foods is more expensive. Not true. Fresh produce and meats do seem expensive — they are! But chips and other processed, blood-sugar-raising foods — which not only are worthless nutritionally but also cause weight gain and make you hungrier — are a complete waste of money. Chapter 1 of Book II is loaded with information on being gluten-free nutritiously.

Buy nutritious foods, but buy only what you need. Most nutritious foods are also perishable, and if you don't use them within a few days, fresh produce isn't so fresh anymore.

Eating in

Eating out at restaurants or fast-food places eats through a budget in no time. Eating at home not only ensures that your meal is, in fact, gluten-free, but it also saves you money.

Sure, planning and preparing home-cooked meals takes time, but the money you save and the peace of mind knowing your meals are nutritious and gluten-free are well worth it.

Using gluten-free mixes

The gluten-free mixes for baked goods like brownies, cakes, cookies, and breads may seem expensive, and they are. But compare them to the cost of buying several different types of specialty flours, xanthan gum (a must-have in gluten-free baking recipes), and other ingredients you need to make those homemade baked goods, and then add on the cost of the failed attempts (you *will* have some failures), and suddenly, the surefire-taste-delicious-and-always-turn-out-right mixes seem like a bargain.

Developing good shopping habits

You can do a lot to save time and money when you shop. Here's a list to get you started:

- **Don't shop when you're hungry.** If you shop on an empty stomach, you're more vulnerable to impulse purchases.

- **Bring a list.** Planning before you head to the grocery store keeps you focused on the healthy and gluten-free foods you need and makes you less likely to impulsively buy things you don't need.

- **Stock up when you can.** Buying food in larger quantities is almost always cheaper if you can afford to do so and if you have somewhere to store the food. Remember that gluten-free foods often have a short shelf life, so if you're going to stock up on premade products, make sure you have room in your freezer.

- **Consider co-ops.** Co-ops aren't in all parts of the country, but if you have one nearby, they're a great way to save money. The idea is that a group of people form a cooperative, buy food in bulk, and then offer the food to others to buy. Usually, anyone can become a member for a small charge (nonmembers can buy, too, but usually for a surcharge). The focus is nearly always on healthy foods.

- **Join membership clubs.** Membership clubs are usually the big warehouse-type stores. One of the world's largest has recently begun carrying a large selection of gluten-free products. These stores are especially good if you want to buy in bulk, because most of their products are supersized.

- **Use coupons, flyers, rebates, and frequent-shopper programs.** Using coupons isn't just a fun way to annoy the people behind you. You can save hundreds of dollars a year by taking advantage of product incentives. Even if you're a less-than-enthusiastic coupon clipper, try to find a few to use each week, and don't forget to check the circulars that are at the front of the stores. They always list weekly specials, and they're usually for the meats and produce, which are gluten-free. If the store is out of an advertised special, ask for a rain check. You can get the sale price when the store has more of the product in stock.

✔ **Dare to compare.** Always look at the unit price of a product, not just the package price. Stores list unit prices on the price tags on the grocery shelves. The package price tells you only the cost of the entire item, whereas the unit price shows the cost per pound, ounce, and so on. This way, when you compare the price of one item to another, you're comparing apples to apples.

   If you don't have one already on your pocket protector, you may want to consider bringing a small (or large, if you're more the analytical type) calculator with you. Most stores offer cost-per-unit prices, but sometimes they mix up the units, so one item — juice, for instance — will be in cost per ounce, while its competitor is in cost per box. If you have your handy-dandy calculator with you, you can make an accurate comparison and choose the best value.

✔ **Keep your eye on the scanner.** So you may have to forego the magazine that tells which celeb is giving birth to alien twins or how to lose all the weight you want in 23 seconds, but watching to make sure that the scanner rings up the correct price is important. Stores do make mistakes. And a lot of times, believe it or not, those mistakes are not in your favor.

✔ **If possible, don't shop with your kids.** Yeah, they're adorable, but they're enemy number one when you're trying to resist the impulsive shopping that grocery stores are counting on. Kids are their primary targets. Notice where the sugary cereals are located — right at eye level for an irresistible 5-year-old. Grocery stores are counting on your kids to lure you into impulsive purchases of high-profit-margin treats like cereals and snack foods.

✔ **Buy generics.** Lots of generic products are gluten-free. Some stores have lists of their gluten-free generics available at the customer service desk or on the Internet.

Book II

Making the Switch without Losing Your Mind

Chapter 4

Cooking and Baking Tips and Techniques

· ·

· ·

Some unique cooking tips and techniques can help in your gluten-free cooking adventures, and you find them in this chapter. Every recipe you find in this book walks you step by step from ingredients to *yum!,* but if you prefer to cook without the safety net of recipes, you're still okay. The tips and techniques in this chapter apply to you and your creative culinary efforts.

The same goes for baking: After you discover how to bake tender and delectable gluten-free products using the recipes in this book, you'll naturally be curious about transforming your own favorite recipes into safe and healthy foods you can enjoy. Everyone has a favorite bread, cookie, cake, or pie that Grandma or Mom used to make.

In this chapter, you find out how to convert your favorite traditional, wheat-based recipes for baked goods into gluten-free delights. First, try some of the recipes in this book just so you understand how gluten-free baking works. There's nothing like hands-on experience to make you a better baker.

When you feel comfortable with the process, tackle a simple recipe. And as your confidence grows, you'll be able to convert more of your old-fashioned wheat recipes into yummy gluten-free treats.

Creatively Gluten-Free: Improvising in the Kitchen

Finding out how to improvise and cook *anything* gluten-free has a lot of value. Sometimes that means modifying a recipe for something that normally has gluten in it so that it's gluten-free. Other times, that means throwing caution to the wind and doing without a recipe altogether.

No single ingredient is more important in gluten-free cooking than creativity. You may not always have ingredients on hand to make the gluten-free dish you want to make. You may not have a recipe handy for a meal you have in mind. You may think you have no way to convert your old favorite standby into a gluten-free goodie. Don't let any of those things stop you. Cooking gluten-free is actually easy if you improvise, explore alternatives, and stretch the boundaries of your creativity in the kitchen.

Adapting any dish to be gluten-free

Pop quiz: You're standing in line at the grocery store, mindlessly perusing the magazines offering valuable, up-to-date, star-struck gossip and surefire ways to lose all your belly fat in less than ten minutes, when the cover of your favorite cooking magazine catches your eye. It's a beautiful photo of (insert favorite food here), glistening with — agh! — gluten! You:

(A) Leave the store in tears, feeling sorry for yourself as you pathetically choke down a rice cake.

(B) Buy the magazine as a reminder of a past life of gluten-gluttony.

(C) Delight in knowing that because you or someone you love bought you this copy of *Gluten-Free All-in-One For Dummies,* you can easily and confi-dently modify that recipe to be deliciously gluten-free.

The right answer is, of course, C. You can modify nearly any dish to be gluten-free. Some dishes are easier than others — baked goods are the tough-est, so we deal with those last. You can go one of two ways when you're adapting a dish to be gluten-free: with a recipe or without.

Starting with a recipe

If you're following a recipe for something that's not gluten-free and you want to convert it, start by reviewing the list of ingredients the recipe calls for. Make a note of those that usually have gluten in them. Then, using the sub-stitutions in this chapter or some of your own, substitute gluten-free ingredi-ents as you need to.

For the most part, when you make substitutions, measurements convert equally — with the exception of flours, which you find in the section "Discovering Key Alternative Flours."

Don't have the right substitutions? Improvise. For instance, if a recipe calls for dredging something in flour before sautéing and you don't have any gluten-free flours, maybe you have a gluten-free mix that would work. Pancake mix or even muffin mix can work quite well as a substitute for a flour coating.

Cooking without a recipe

If you're not using a recipe, creativity once again prevails. Say you want to make chicken nuggets. You certainly don't need a recipe for that; just slice some chicken and figure out what you want to coat it in before frying or baking. Put some of your favorite gluten-free barbecue potato chips in a plastic bag, and crunch them up. Now you have a coating!

At the risk of belaboring a point, you have to be creative. The substitution ideas in this chapter are just that — ideas. Coming up with substitutions that work for your convenience, preference, and budget is up to you.

Avoiding cross-contamination when cooking

After you've worked hard to create a delicious gluten-free meal, you wouldn't go dust a bunch of wheat flour all over it, would you? Of course not. Yet sometimes the *way* you cook food can contaminate it as though you had done just that, and you may not be aware that your food is being contaminated.

Cooking gluten-containing foods at the same time as gluten-free ones is okay, but be aware that cross-contamination during the cooking process is a very real consideration. Be careful not to glutenate (contaminate with gluten) your food inadvertently. Watch out for a few pitfalls:

✔ **Cooking utensils:** You can't flip a gluten-containing hamburger bun with a spatula and then flip a burger. Well, you can, but that burger is no longer gluten-free. Same thing goes for tossing the pasta and stirring the sauce. Use separate utensils while you're cooking, and keep track of which one is which.

✔ **Double-duty cooking surfaces:** If you're cooking gluten-containing and gluten-free foods on the same griddle, grills, or cookie sheets or in the same pans, cook the gluten-free version first. If that just doesn't work, you can use the same cooking surface for both versions, but be sure to find a clean spot for your gluten-free foods.

✔ **Frying oil:** When you fry breaded products in oil, bits of the breading or batter stay in the oil when you're finished frying. So if you fry gluten-containing foods in oil, don't use that same oil to fry your gluten-free foods. Either fry the gluten-free foods first or use completely separate pans and fresh oil for the gluten-free foods.

If you're cooking both glutenous and gluten-free foods in your fryer, you'll need to be extra diligent when you're cleaning it to make sure you get all the gluten out. If your fryer isn't easy to clean thoroughly, you may want to consider having separate fryers.

Using standby substitutions

To convert a recipe that usually contains gluten into one that's gluten-free, you need to make some simple substitutions. For the most part, with the exception of flours you use when making baked goods, the substitutions are simple — just swap one for the other. You find out about flours for baked goods separately, in the upcoming section "Discovering Key Alternative Flours."

✔ **Beer:** Some foods, especially deep-fried foods, may call for beer in the recipe. You can use either the gluten-free beers available online or try cider instead.

✔ **Binders:** A binder is just something that holds foodstuff together. Because gluten provides elasticity and stretch to baked goods, adding binders to foods that don't have gluten-containing flours in them is a good idea. Binders include xanthan gum, guar gum, gelatin powder (this is cool, too, because it adds protein and moisture), and eggs.

✔ **Breadcrumbs:** No-brainer here. Anyone who's ever eaten a piece of gluten-free bread (especially without toasting it) knows that bread-crumbs aren't hard to come by. You can buy gluten-free breadcrumbs from specialty stores or online, but if you can't or don't want to get those, consider using any gluten-free bread: Put the bread in a plastic bag and smoosh it into the size of crumbs you want. You can even toast the crumbs if you want added crunch or need dry breadcrumbs instead of fresh ones. Crushed cereals work well in place of breadcrumbs, too. Also consider using mashed potato flakes or quinoa flakes.

✔ **Bun:** Consider using a lettuce wrap, corn tortilla, or, of course, gluten-free bread. Some good gluten-free buns are available online and at specialty shops.

✔ **Coatings:** If a recipe calls for some type of coating, you have several options. You can despair and not make the dish (Ha! Kidding!) or consider using any of the gluten-free flours listed in the section "Discovering Key Alternative Flours," as well as any versatile gluten-free mix you have lying around, such as a mix for bread, muffins, or pancakes. Cornmeal or corn flour *(masa)* with seasonings mixed in adds an interesting texture, and crushed barbecue potato chips (gluten-free, of course) are a favorite. You may also want to look into commercial brands of Cajun-style coatings, usually marketed as seafood seasonings. Many of those are just cornmeal with some spices added.

✔ **"Cream of" soups:** Use chicken broth and sour cream or half-and-half. If you're going for ultra-nutritious, blend some cooked cauliflower in the blender and use that for the "cream of" part. Remember to add the food the soup is a cream of — mushroom, celery, potato, and so on — to complete it.

✔ **Croutons:** Homemade croutons are actually very easy to make. Most recipes for croutons suggest you use stale bread, but it's not a good idea to do that for gluten-free bread, because you'd probably end up with crumbled crouton crumbs instead. Cut fresh gluten-free bread into the size cubes you want and deep-fry them. After you drain and cool them, roll them in Parmesan cheese, spices, or any other flavoring you like.

✔ **Fillers:** *Filler* is a highly technical culinary term for something that fills stuff in. Yum. Generally not something you hope to see on a label, fillers aren't always a bad thing; they may be in meatloaf, for example, where the recipe often calls for breadcrumbs, crackers, and other filler-type materials to add, well, *filling.* Gluten-free bread or breadcrumbs provides an obvious substitution here, but also consider leftover corn bread, mashed potato flakes, or even an unsweetened cereal that you've crushed up.

✔ **Flour:** Many recipes call for flour, usually to serve as a thickener (see the suggested thickeners in this list). Also consider using gluten-free flours such as rice flour, sweet rice flour (they're different), potato starch, sorghum flour, garbanzo/fava bean flour, and Montina (Indian ricegrass flour).

✔ **Flour tortillas:** The obvious substitution here is corn tortillas. Some new gluten-free flour tortillas are on the market now, and you can find recipes for homemade tortillas online or in cookbooks. Other wrap substitutions include rice wraps (found in Asian markets and featured in a few recipes in this book) or lettuce.

✔ **Pie crust:** One of the easiest ways to make a pie crust is to smash your favorite cereal into tiny crumbs, add some butter (and sugar, if the cereal isn't sweet enough), and then press the mixture into the bottom of a pie pan. Some good gluten-free crackers and cookies work well the same way. Some pie crusts are supposed to be cooked before adding the pie filling, and others aren't. The fact that the crust is gluten-free doesn't change, regardless of whether you need to cook the crust before filling the pie. Also check out some of the gluten-free pie crust mixes available on the Internet and at specialty stores.

✔ **Sandwich squeezers:** These items are what are otherwise known as the bread "ends" of a sandwich, and you have lots of alternatives to bread. Try a lettuce wrap, corn tortilla, waffle, or pancake (the toaster-oven variety is great for this). Of course gluten-free bread works, too, if you can find a variety you like.

✔ **"Special" sauce:** The secret's out: You can make their "special" sauce with just mayo and ketchup, both of which are gluten-free!

✔ **Soy sauce:** Most soy sauce has wheat in it (and the label clearly indicates wheat), but you can find brands that are wheat-free. (By the way, *tamari* — a thicker, Japanese soy sauce — is not always wheat-free, so check the label.) Either use a wheat-free soy sauce or try Bragg Liquid Aminos. You may also want to get adventurous and try an Asian sauce like fish sauce (careful — it's really fishy!) or oyster sauce.

✔ **Teriyaki:** Because most soy sauce has wheat in it, most teriyaki (which is made from soy sauce) does, too. A few brands of wheat-free teriyaki sauces are available, but don't be afraid to make your own.

✔ **Thickeners:** Many recipes call for flour as a thickener, but lots of alternatives are available. For sweet things, try using a dry pudding mix or gelatin. ClearJel works well with acidic ingredients (unlike cornstarch), tolerates high temperatures, and doesn't cause pie fillings to "weep" during storage. Arrowroot flour, agar, tapioca starch, and cornstarch are also excellent thickeners. So is sweet rice flour, which comes from sticky or glutinous rice (despite the name, it really is gluten-free). And remember that muffin or cake mix you have lying around. Not only do mixes thicken the recipe, but the sweet flavor is a pleasant surprise. You can find more information on using gluten-free thickeners in the section "Thickening with gluten-free starches and flours."

Discovering Key Alternative Flours

Certain flours are most often used in gluten-free baking because they work well, especially in combination. Just like baking with wheat flour, you choose gluten-free flours based on the product you're making.

This section covers the different gluten-free flours and their characteristics, the type of crumb they produce, and their protein, fiber, and carbohydrate content. Study these lists to find out about the flours that are going to become a part of your kitchen. The more you know about them, the better gluten-free baker you'll be!

Flours for delicate baked goods

When you're making delicate, gluten-free baked goods, you're starting out ahead. In these types of recipes — for cookies, cakes, muffins, and quick breads — you don't want a lot of gluten formation. The flours you choose should be fairly low in protein with a mild flavor. And you want to add some starch to balance the product structure. Remember to follow the basic 70 percent protein flour to 30 percent starch ratio for the best baked goods.

What follows are some of the best flours to use for delicate baked goods, in order of increasing protein content.

Book II

Making the Switch without Losing Your Mind

White rice flour

This flour, made from white rice, is white and basically flavorless. Like brown rice flour, it provides crunch unless it's very finely ground. It has 2.4 grams of protein, 1 gram of fiber, and 31.7 grams of carbohydrates per ¼ cup. You almost always want to combine it with other gluten-free flours in baking recipes. Try it in shortbread for a wonderfully crumbly texture. Look for superfine white rice flour in specialty stores, Asian markets, and online.

Coconut flour

This flour is white and slightly sweet tasting, yet mild. It's made from dried and ground coconut. It's high in healthy monounsaturated fats and works best in recipes with eggs. This flour is also very absorbent and needs a lot of liquid. In fact, many recipes with coconut flour call for using a 1:1 ratio of flour to liquid. It has 3 grams of protein, 12 grams of fiber, and 6 grams of carbs per ¼ cup.

Almond flour

This flour, sometimes called almond meal, has a wonderfully nutty yet mild and slightly sweet taste. The flour is white or ivory and produces a tender, moist crumb, very similar to wheat flour. It's high in fat, but like coconut flour, the fat is of the healthier monounsaturated variety. Also, like coconut flour, almond flour works best in recipes with eggs (to provide more structure). It has 6 grams of protein, 3 grams of fiber, and 6 grams of carbs per ¼ cup. Because it's high in fat, store it in the fridge or freezer. Bring the flour to room temperature before using in a recipe.

Cashew flour

This flour has a naturally nutty and sweet taste and produces soft and tender baked goods because it's made from dried, ground cashews. It's a good choice for mimicking the flavor of wheat flour. Try this flour in chocolate chip cookies or brownies. Cashew flour has 10 grams of protein, 2 grams of fiber, and 16 grams of carbs per ¼ cup.

Flours for yeast breads and rolls

Yeast breads and rolls need more structure than delicate baked goods, so you should use higher-protein flours to make them. You also want more flavor in these breads because the flavor of wheat breads is, well, mostly of wheat. The combination of these flours produces some very yummy bread. After you've tried these flours, you'll feel sorry for people who only eat wheat breads!

This section presents the best flours to use for yeast breads and rolls, in order of increasing protein content.

Corn flour

Corn flour is yellow because it's made from dried and ground corn. It adds strength to doughs and batters and a nice depth of flavor. It tastes sweet, slightly nutty, and, well, a little bit like corn! Corn flour contains 2 grams of protein, 6 grams of fiber, and 22 grams of carbs per ¼ cup.

Brown rice flour

Brown rice flour, made from unhulled rice grains, has a medium protein content and a nutty taste, but it's pretty bland and mild. Unless it's finely ground, the flour provides some crunch to baked goods. Look for superfine brown rice flour at stores. It has 2.9 grams of protein, 2 grams of fiber, and 30 grams of carbs per ¼ cup.

Buckwheat flour

Buckwheat flour is confusing at first. Because its name includes "wheat," many people think it has gluten. But the buckwheat plant isn't a grain; it's a fruit seed that's related to rhubarb. This seed is very good for you; it can help reduce the risk of diabetes and control blood pressure.

Store-bought buckwheat flour is roasted before grinding, creating a lovely dark brown color and an earthy flavor. It produces a tender and sweet crumb that's firm because of high protein content. Buckwheat flour has 3.8 grams of protein, 6 grams of fiber, and 21.2 grams of carbs per ¼ cup.

Raw buckwheat flour can be difficult to find, but you can make your own flour from raw (green) buckwheat groats. Just grind the groats in a coffee grinder or mill. It has a naturally sweet flavor.

Sorghum flour

Sorghum is a cereal grain, but it contains no gluten. It was used for years as animal feed, but it's very nutritious. This flour has the most wheatlike taste and a very high protein and insoluble fiber content. It's a pale brown flour with a dark brown fleck. Often used in flour blends, sorghum flour produces a firm but tender structure. It contains 4 grams of protein, 3 grams of fiber, and 25 grams of carbs per ¼ cup.

Quinoa flour

The quinoa plant is an ancient cereal grain. Quinoa is unusual because it's one of the only plants that provides 100 percent of all the amino acids the human body needs. The brown seed is coated with a bitter substance called *saponin* that must be rinsed off before using. The flour has the saponin removed.

This flour is pale brown with a strong flavor, so add only small amounts unless you really enjoy the taste. It can be bitter and tastes quite nutty. It adds great strength to batters and doughs. It contains 4 grams of protein, 4 grams of fiber, and 21 grams of carbs per ¼ cup.

Amaranth

Amaranth is actually an herb. Its seeds are dried and ground to make flour. Amaranth flour is brown with a nutty but mild flavor. It adds an earthy and grassy taste to baked goods and strength to doughs and batters. Amaranth flour has 4 grams of protein, 3 grams of fiber, and 20 grams of carbs per ¼ cup.

Always cook amaranth grains before you eat them because, in a raw state, amaranth has compounds that block the absorption of nutrients.

Teff flour

Teff is another ancient, nutritious grain. Teff is native to Ethiopia, and the flour comes in two colors: dark brown and ivory. It's very high in fiber and contains a good amount of iron, calcium, and B vitamins. Teff flour produces a tender crumb and adds moisture to gluten-free baked goods. The dark brown teff flour has a nutty taste reminiscent of cocoa powder. Ivory teff flour has a much lighter flavor. Teff flour contains 5 grams of protein, 6 grams of fiber, and 32 grams of carbs per ¼ cup.

White bean flour

This flour is made from white beans. You can also find black bean flour, but it's usually used to make bean dips and fillings. White bean flour is white or ivory, produces a tender crumb, and has a mild flavor. It's very high in protein, with 7 grams per ¼ cup. It has 8 grams of fiber and only 20 grams of carbs per ¼ cup.

Book II

Making the Switch without Losing Your Mind

Fava (or garfava) flour

This flour is a blend of garbanzo bean flour and fava bean flour. Garbanzo beans, also known as chickpeas, are a legume with a sweet flavor. Fava beans, used mostly in Italian cooking, are an ancient pea. This flour blend has a strong taste often described as "beany" and a high protein content. It's usually used in small quantities because of its strong taste. It has 9 grams of protein, 3 grams of fiber, and 23 grams of carbs per ¼ cup.

Soy flour

This flour is made from roasted soybeans and is high in protein. Because it's also high in healthy fats, you should store it in the fridge or freezer. It has a mild and nutty flavor but can also taste beany. It adds tenderness and moistness to baked goods. It helps baked goods brown; in fact, you should watch foods made with soy flour to prevent over-browning. This flour has 12 grams of protein, 5 grams of fiber, and 10 grams of carbs per ¼ cup.

Flours for quick breads

Quick breads need more structure than cakes and cookies but less structure than yeast breads and rolls. Though you still want to maintain the 70 percent flours with protein to 30 percent flours with starch ratio, you can choose flours with a lower protein content for quick breads and muffins.

The following are the best flours to use to make the best gluten-free quick breads and muffins, in order of increasing protein content.

Millet flour

You may think of millet as bird food, but it has been nourishing populations for generations. The tiny seed has a nutritional profile similar to wheat. Millet flour is soft with a low protein content. It has a light ivory color, so it's a good choice for light-colored baked goods, and it produces a soft crumb, so it's a good choice for tender quick breads. Millet flour has a slightly sweet flavor. It has 3 grams of protein, 4 grams of fiber, and 22 grams of carbs per ¼ cup.

Sweet rice flour

Sweet rice is also known as *glutinous rice.* The flour doesn't contain any gluten; this name just refers to the rice's stickiness. This flour is bland and mild. It works very well when combined with brown rice flour because it's more finely ground, and the sweet rice flour creates a sticky structure that helps tender quick breads hold together. It contains 3 grams of protein, 1 gram of fiber, and 24 grams of carbs per ¼ cup.

Flour weight chart

One of the key methods for successful gluten-free baking is substituting flours by weight, not by volume. If you've baked a lot in the past, you're used to measuring flours by volume; that is, by cups and tablespoons. One cup of all-purpose wheat flour weighs 125 grams. Gluten-free flours, however, weigh anywhere from 112 to 160 grams per cup.

That difference in weight doesn't sound like a lot, but baking experts have found that a few grams more or less of any one flour makes a huge difference in the end product. When bakers discovered that measuring flours by weight and not by volume was the key to delicious breads, cakes, and cookies, the world of gluten-free baking changed forever.

If you're a stickler for math, you'll find that in the conversion of grams to cups or vice versa, there will be differences of up to 2 grams. This occurs because we developed the recipes with grams and then converted to cups. Rounding, because scales can't measure less than 1 gram, create these tiny differences. That amount of flour (equivalent to the weight of two small paper clips, or about ¼ of an ounce) won't make a difference in the recipes.

To successfully work with gluten-free flours and starches, you must weigh them. And you need to know how much each of these flours (and starches) weighs. When substituting one flour or starch for another, always substitute by weight. That means that if a recipe calls for 140 grams of millet flour, which is 1 cup, you don't use 1 cup of brown rice flour. You use 140 grams of brown rice flour. Table 4-1 shows you substitution weights.

Book II

Making the Switch without Losing Your Mind

Table 4-1			Flour Weights			
Flour	*1 Cup*	*¾ Cup*	*½ Cup*	*⅓ Cup*	*¼ Cup*	*1 Tbsp.*
All-purpose wheat flour	125 grams	94 grams	62 grams	42 grams	31 grams	8 grams
Blanched almond flour	112 grams	84 grams	56 grams	38 grams	28 grams	7 grams
Amaranth flour	120 grams	90 grams	60 grams	42 grams	30 grams	8 grams
Brown rice flour	135 grams	101 grams	68 grams	45 grams	36 grams	9 grams
Roasted buckwheat flour	120 grams	90 grams	60 grams	42 grams	30 grams	8 grams
Cake wheat flour	114 grams	85 grams	57 grams	38 grams	28 grams	7 grams

(continued)

Table 4-1 *(continued)*

Flour	1 Cup	¾ Cup	½ Cup	⅓ Cup	¼ Cup	1 Tbsp.
Coconut flour	112 grams	84 grams	56 grams	38 grams	28 grams	7 grams
Corn flour	116 grams	87 grams	58 grams	38 grams	28 grams	7 grams
Garfava flour	120 grams	90 grams	60 grams	42 grams	30 grams	8 grams
High-Protein Bread Flour Mix*	131 grams	99 grams	66 grams	43 grams	33 grams	8 grams
Millet flour	125 grams	94 grams	62 grams	42 grams	31 grams	8 grams
Oat flour	120 grams	90 grams	60 grams	42 grams	30 grams	8 grams
Quinoa flour	120 grams	90 grams	60 grams	42 grams	30 grams	8 grams
Sorghum flour	123 grams	92 grams	62 grams	42 grams	30 grams	8 grams
Soy flour	112 grams	84 grams	56 grams	38 grams	28 grams	7 grams
Superfine brown rice flour	160 grams	120 grams	80 grams	53 grams	40 grams	10 grams
Sweet rice flour	155 grams	116 grams	78 grams	53 grams	39 grams	10 grams
Teff flour	120 grams	90 grams	60 grams	42 grams	30 grams	8 grams
White bean flour	128 grams	96 grams	64 grams	43 grams	32 grams	8 grams
White Flour Mix*	148 grams	111 grams	74 grams	49 grams	37 grams	9 grams
White rice flour	160 grams	120 grams	80 grams	53 grams	40 grams	10 grams
Whole-Grain Flour Mix*	135 grams	101 grams	68 grams	45 grams	34 grams	9 grams

*These mixes appear in Chapter 2 of Book V.

Cooking with Wheat Alternatives

Most gluten-free cooking is pretty straightforward. You just substitute gluten-free ingredients for the gluten-containing ones and, for the most part, you're set. The process is a little different for baked goods, as you find later in this chapter. But most gluten-free cooking isn't much different from "regular" cooking, especially if you follow the theme of this chapter and let your creative side take over.

Incorporating alternative gluten-free grains

Not only are the gluten-free grains and grain alternatives in Book I, Chapter 4 ultra-nutritious, but they add unique flavors and textures to foods, too. For the most part, cooking them is just like cooking other grains. But you need to know a few things to perfect the art of using alternative gluten-free grains.

When cooking gluten-free grains as whole grains (as opposed to using them as a flour in baked goods), you find these alternative grains cook like most whole grains — just toss them in boiling water, reduce the heat so the water simmers, and you're set. The grain-to-water proportion and cooking times are really the only things that vary. Table 4-2 has some approximations of amounts of liquids and cooking time; you can modify them to suit your preferences.

Table 4-2	Cooking Alternative Grains	
Gluten-Free Grain (1 Cup)	*Water or Chicken Broth*	*Cooking Time*
Amaranth	2½ cups	20 to 25 minutes
Brown rice (long or short grain)	3 cups	40 minutes
Buckwheat	2 cups	15 to 20 minutes
Corn (grits)	3 cups	5 to 10 minutes
Millet	3 cups	35 to 45 minutes
Quinoa	2 cups	15 to 20 minutes
Teff	2 cups	15 to 20 minutes
White rice	2 cups	15 minutes
Wild rice	4 cups	45 minutes

Quinoa, millet, teff, amaranth, buckwheat, and the other alternative grains are great additions to soups, stuffing, and other foods. You can use alternative grains in other places, too, whether you precook them or simply toss them in with the other ingredients:

✔ **Snacks:** Using a little oil in a pan, you can pop amaranth grains on the stove like popcorn and eat them seasoned or plain.

✔ **Soups:** Use buckwheat, quinoa, or millet in soups instead of rice or noodles. No need to cook the grains first; just add them to the soup as you're cooking it. Remember, they absorb the liquid and double in volume. Whole amaranth and teff are too small, and they may seem gritty in soups, although both work well to thicken soups if you use the flour form of them.

✔ **Stuffing:** Use the larger alternative grains, such as cooked quinoa, millet, or buckwheat, instead of breadcrumbs or croutons in stuffing. Season the stuffing to your taste and then stuff vegetables, poultry, or pork tenderloins.

Thickening with gluten-free starches and flours

People usually use starch-based thickeners such as cornstarch, arrowroot, and tapioca to thicken their sauces and gravies. Starch thickeners give food a transparent, glistening sheen, which looks great for pie fillings and in glazes. The thickeners don't always look quite right in gravy or sauce, though, so knowing which ones to use is important.

To thicken with gluten-free starches, mix the starch with an equal amount of cold liquid until it forms a paste. Then whisk the paste into the liquid you're trying to thicken. After you add the thickener to the liquid, cook it for at least 30 seconds or so to get rid of the starchy flavor. But be careful you don't overcook it — liquids that you thicken with these starches may get thin again if you cook them too long or at too high of a temperature.

Some of these flours have the advantage of working well with foods that are acidic. Acidic foods include canned or glazed fruits, citrus, tomatoes, and vinegar. Bananas, figs, avocados, and potatoes are examples of foods that aren't acidic (they're alkaline).

Take a look at your options for thickeners:

✔ **Arrowroot:** If you're looking for that shiny gloss for dessert sauces or glazes, arrowroot is a good bet. Use arrowroot if you're thickening an acidic liquid but not if you're using dairy products (it makes them slimy). Arrowroot has the most neutral taste of all the starch thickeners, so if you're worried that a thickener may change or mask the flavor of your dish, use arrowroot. You can freeze the sauces you make with arrowroot.

✔ **ClearJel:** This modified cornstarch works especially well for fruit pie fillings because it blends well with acidic ingredients, tolerates high temperatures, and doesn't cause pie fillings to "weep" during storage. It also doesn't begin thickening until the liquid begins to cool, which allows the heat to be more evenly distributed within the jar if you're canning.

✔ **Cornstarch:** Cornstarch is the best choice for thickening dairy-based sauces, but don't use it for acidic foods. Cornstarch isn't as shiny as tapioca or arrowroot. Don't use cornstarch if you're freezing the sauce, or the sauce will get spongy.

- ✔ **Potato starch:** Usually used to thicken soups and gravies, potato starch doesn't work well in liquids that you boil. Unlike cornstarch and some other grain-based foods, potato starch is a permitted ingredient for Passover.

  Potato flour and potato starch flour are different. Potato flour is heavy and tastes much like potatoes. Potato starch flour is fine, with a bland taste. It's great to mix with other flours for baking or to use as a thickener for soups or gravies.

- ✔ **Tapioca:** You can use pearl tapioca or tapioca granules to thicken puddings and pies, but they don't completely dissolve when you cook them, so you end up with tiny gelatinous balls. If you like the balls, you can also use instant tapioca to thicken soups, gravies, and stews. If you don't like them, you can get tapioca starch, which is already finely ground. Tapioca gives a glossy sheen and can tolerate prolonged cooking and freezing.

Book II

Making the Switch without Losing Your Mind

You can use any of the alternative grains to thicken sauces, gravies, stews, puddings — anything! Depending on what you're making, you can use whole grains or flours as a thickener. You probably want to use a flour instead of whole grain to thicken something like gravy, but whole grains add lots of nutrition and work well to thicken soups and stews.

When you're using these flours or starches as thickeners, substitution amounts are a little different. Instead of 1 tablespoon of all-purpose flour, use these amounts:

- ✔ **Agar:** ½ tablespoon
- ✔ **Arrowroot:** 2 teaspoons
- ✔ **Cornstarch:** ½ tablespoon
- ✔ **Gelatin powder:** ½ tablespoon
- ✔ **Rice flour (brown or white):** 1 tablespoon
- ✔ **Sweet potato flour:** 1 tablespoon

Cutting out casein, too

Lots of people are eliminating both gluten and casein (pronounced "*kay-seen*"). While it may seem doubly difficult to have to eliminate both of these items from your diet, it's well worth it for many people.

Casein is the protein found in milk — not just cow's milk but sheep and goat's milk as well.

Casein is not to be confused with lactose. Lactose is a sugar found in dairy products. An enzyme our bodies produce, called lactase, breaks down casein in most cases. Many people don't have enough lactase to break down the lactose, though, so they become "lactose intolerant." It's pretty easy these days to find products that are lactose-free, but "lactose-free" doesn't mean "casein-free."

Here's a partial list of things to watch out for if you're avoiding casein:

- Milk
- Cream
- Cheese
- Cream cheese
- Sour cream
- Butter
- Yogurt
- Ice cream and ice milk
- Sherbet (some)

- Chocolate
- Cream of (insert variety) soups and veggies
- Cereal
- Bread
- "Vegetarian" cheese (some)
- "Vegetarian" meats (some)
- Whey

You may assume "cheese-free" to mean "casein-free," since casein is found in milk products like cheese. But that assumption is wrong. Sometimes casein (in some form) is added back to the product to enhance the consistency or its cooking properties (for instance, casein helps cheese melt better).

Also watch out for other forms of casein, including ingredients that have the word *caseinate* in them (such as ammonium caseinate, iron caseinate, magnesium caseinate, and so on).

If a food is certified as "kosher nondairy" or "kosher pareve," it's casein-free.

Adjusting the Dough or Batter

When you're converting a traditional wheat recipe into a gluten-free recipe, be sure to read the traditional recipe carefully. Make note of the types of flour used and any other possible gluten products or ingredients called for, and list alternatives you can use.

Then jump right in, following these tips and tricks. With time, you'll be turning out delicious recipes from your past, altered to fit your new gluten-free lifestyle.

Converting traditional dough and batter recipes to gluten-free

You can make lots of easy changes to a traditional recipe to convert it to a desired gluten-free treat. You just need some knowledge about the chemistry of the recipe, a little practice, and a lot of patience.

Here are some important points to keep in mind when converting a traditional wheat batter or dough to a gluten-free batter or dough:

✔ Always weigh your flours. Remember that a cup of all-purpose flour weighs 125 grams. If a recipe calls for a cup of all-purpose wheat flour, substitute 125 grams of an alternative flour. That means that sometimes you'll use less than a cup, sometimes more. Weighing is crucial.

✔ Always combine alternative flours. Don't substitute all-brown rice flour for all-purpose wheat flour, for instance. A combination of different flours provides the best results.

✔ When substituting flours, use higher-protein flours for bread recipes, pie crusts, and pizza crusts. Use lower-protein flours and more starches for cookies, cakes, dumplings, and soufflés.

✔ Remember the 70 percent protein flour to 30 percent starch flour ratio. This is a general guide for any gluten-free baked good. The protein provides the structure, and the starch provides tenderness and a fine crumb.

✔ Many recipes taste better with brown sugar instead of granulated sugar. Honey is a good addition to use; replace some of the liquid in the recipe with honey or maple syrup.

✔ Add more liquid to the wheat recipe you're converting. Start out with a couple of tablespoons of extra liquid. After you make the recipes in this book, you'll know what a good gluten-free batter should look like. Measure the ingredients carefully and write down what you added, along with the quantities.

✔ Add a tiny bit of an acidic ingredient such as vitamin C powder, sour cream, or buttermilk. Gluten-free flours aren't as acidic as wheat flours, so baking soda doesn't work quite as well. Vitamin C powder is a good choice for those who can't use cow's milk in recipes.

✔ Baking powder can make some gluten-free baked goods taste a little tinny. Look for baking powders made with calcium, not aluminum. And try to find double-acting baking powder, which creates carbon dioxide when mixed with water and also when heated, which means your baked goods get a lift when the batter is mixed and in the oven! Always make sure that your baking powder and baking soda are labeled gluten-free. Consider making your own baking powder by combining equal amounts of baking soda and cream of tartar.

Book II

Making the
Switch
without
Losing
Your Mind

✔ You may want to increase the leavening. Add a bit more baking powder, baking soda, or yeast to the traditional wheat recipe. Start by adding 25 percent more.

✔ Use yogurt or buttermilk to replace some of the liquid in the traditional recipe. Doing so helps make gluten-free baked goods, especially cakes and quick breads, fluffier.

✔ Think about using carbonated water in recipes. Doing so helps give the texture an extra boost without adding any more leavening, which can make baked goods bitter or sour.

✔ Puréed fruits and vegetables help add flavor and also add *pectin,* a natural substance found in produce that thickens liquid. Like gelatin, pectin increases moisture, too. Substitute these products for some of the liquid in a traditional wheat recipe.

✔ Add an extra egg, egg white, or egg replacer. The protein in the egg helps build the structure along with the gluten-free flours. In fact, you can replace some of the liquid in the traditional recipe with egg whites. One egg white is about 2 tablespoons.

✔ Increase flavorings. Double the vanilla and add more of any extract called for, and increase the amount of spices slightly. Just don't go overboard! Increase by 10 percent at first. If you like the results, you can add more the next time.

✔ Flavorful liquids can improve gluten-free breads, cakes, and cookies. Use cold coffee, molasses, fruit juice, honey, coconut milk, vanilla soy milk, nut milks, and vegetable juices to replace some or all of the liquid in a wheat recipe.

✔ Think about including an additive in your gluten-free doughs and batters. Xanthan or guar gum, gelatin, sweet whey, eggs, raw buckwheat flour, chia slurries, and flaxseed slurries are excellent additions that can give your baked goods more structure and a better, finer crumb.

You may have to try several times before you successfully convert your favorite recipe into a gluten-free treat. Just remember that experimenting in the kitchen is a learning experience and can be fun when you approach it with a light attitude. Think of it as exploring a new world, and you're in charge. The more you learn, the easier converting recipes is!

Mixing gluten-free batters

You make most gluten-free recipes the same way as traditional wheat recipes, although you can skip some steps. For instance, adding liquid and flour alternatively to a creamed butter and flour mixture isn't necessary. You can just combine all the ingredients and beat for a few minutes. That saves you lots of time and work in the kitchen.

Keep these points in mind when mixing gluten-free doughs and batters:

- ✔ Always stir the flours, starches, gums, salt, and yeast or baking powder together until they're one color so that everything is evenly distributed before proceeding with the recipe. Use a wire whisk to make sure the dry ingredients are well combined. No one wants to bite into a cookie and get a chunk of sorghum flour or xanthan gum!

- ✔ Beat the batter longer than the traditional recipe suggests. Because the recipe has no gluten to overdevelop, you don't have to worry about creating a tough product. But these flours need a little extra time to absorb water and hydrate properly so they form a nice crumb. And beating adds air to your recipes, which creates the airy texture you're looking for.

- ✔ You mix most gluten-free quick breads like wheat quick breads — just until the ingredients are combined.

- ✔ You usually beat cookie doughs and batters for a minute or two to hydrate the dough and form the crumb structure.

- ✔ Beat cakes for a minute or two. Folding in beaten egg whites can help make the cakes fluffier and lighter.

- ✔ Beat bread doughs and yeast breads with a mixer, using the paddle attachment, for several minutes to add air and develop the protein structure. You don't knead gluten-free bread doughs, because they're soft and sticky.

- ✔ For pie crust, you may need to add more flour until a soft dough forms. Chill the dough before rolling it out.

- ✔ A food processor can help mix doughs thoroughly and in little time. Process the ingredients until they're well mixed. Add a few more seconds of processing time if the recipe tells you to beat by hand or with a mixer for a few minutes.

Book II

Making the Switch without Losing Your Mind

Using baking mixes

Baking mixes are a great choice for gluten-free baking. Having a mix on hand means you'll be more likely to make cookies or a cake because you can just reach for a mix instead of hauling out three or four bags of gluten-free flours.

This book has recipes for lots of gluten-free baking mixes. Two of them, White Flour Mix and Whole-Grain Flour Mix (both in Chapter 2 of Book V), are used in many of the recipes. Make up a batch of each of these mixes to make gluten-free baking much easier. You can make your own mixes after you get more experience in the kitchen. Just follow the 70 percent protein flour to

30 percent starch flour rule, measure by weight, and mix the ingredients really well before storing.

You can find lots of commercial gluten-free baking mixes on the market, too. Most work very well. Before you buy a commercial gluten-free mix, be sure to read product reviews from Amazon.com or other online stores. Avoid mixes with poor reviews to save time and money.

You can use many of the baking mixes in Book V, Chapter 2 to substitute for flours in any recipe. For instance, use the Light Cakey Corn Bread Mix in your grandmother's recipe for corn bread baked in a cast-iron skillet. Use the High-Protein Bread Flour Mix in your mom's recipe for Parker House rolls. And use the Cookie Mix without Gums in your aunt's recipe for sugar cookies.

If you don't keep a 100 percent gluten-free kitchen, using baking mixes helps you avoid cross-contamination. Think about making wheat-based baking mixes, too, on a different day from your gluten-free baking. Flour dust can hang in the air for 24 to 48 hours after use, so spread out the different types of baking. Never bake a gluten-free recipe and a wheat recipe on the same day, unless, of course, you bake the gluten-free recipe first and remove it from the kitchen while you bake the wheat product. But remember, your cleanup must be impeccable!

Handling and Baking the Dough

After you adjust your gluten-free dough or batter ingredient list, you need to mix the dough, shape it, bake it, and cool it. You handle gluten-free baked goods a bit differently from wheat-based baked goods.

In this section, you find out about handling the doughs, shaping them, choosing products to help form the doughs, setting baking times and temperatures, and knowing the best ways to cool and store your delicious gluten-free baked goods.

Working with gluten-free doughs

Gluten-free doughs are much softer and stickier than wheat doughs, and they need a little help to form. Fortunately, regular supermarkets have all the supplies you need to handle your doughs and batters with ease.

Here are some tips for handling gluten-free doughs:

✔ Chill cookie doughs before you bake them. The rest time helps the dough firm up so it's easier to shape and holds its shape in the oven. And it gives the flour more time to hydrate so the cookie is more tender.

✔ Grease pans or cookie sheets well and flour them with a tiny bit of gluten-free flour or starch. Or you can use parchment paper or Silpat liners to line cookie sheets and baking pans. Gluten-free doughs are stickier than wheat doughs so they can use the extra help.

✔ Piping bags can be your best friend in the kitchen. Because gluten-free doughs are much softer and stickier than wheat-based doughs, using a piping bag can help you form breadsticks, cookies, and rolls with ease.

✔ Ice cream scoops are another wonderful appliance to help you handle gluten-free doughs.

✔ Plastic wrap and parchment paper are also your friends in the gluten-free kitchen. You use these products to shape doughs and wrap them for chilling in the fridge.

✔ Because they're about the consistency of thick cake batter, you need to place gluten-free doughs and batters into pans and forms before you bake them. The pans give the dough structure and help hold it in the correct form while the structure sets. Have fun with your gluten-free recipes by choosing pans with unusual or fun shapes.

✔ Use a smaller pan than the one called for in the traditional recipe. Make two breads in 5-x-3-inch pans rather than one large loaf in a 9-x-5-inch pan. Make sure that you fill the pan with the same proportion of batter or dough as called for in the original recipe.

✔ Don't use dark-colored or Teflon pans. These types of pans hold more heat than shiny light metal or glass baking pans, and the bottoms and sides of your beautiful creations may burn before the inside is done.

Baking and cooling doughs

When you're ready to bake, be sure that your oven is properly calibrated before you begin. This is an essential step whether you're baking with wheat or gluten-free flours. An oven temperature that's off by 25 degrees or more can ruin your breads, cakes, cookies, and pies. Follow the manufacturer's instructions to calibrate your oven.

For the best gluten-free baked goods, try these tips for baking methods, times, and temperatures:

- ✔ Use the middle oven rack unless the recipe tells you to bake on a higher or lower rack. On the middle rack, the oven heat circulates evenly around the pans.

- ✔ As a general rule, don't bake more than one pan at a time. If you stack cookie sheets on two racks in a conventional oven, the top sheet will have underbaked bottoms, and the bottom sheet will have underbaked tops. You can rotate pans after half of the baking time has elapsed if you're in full Christmas cookie production! However, you can stack sheets or pans in a convection oven because the fans in that type of oven circulate the air more efficiently.

- ✔ Preheat pizza stones and cast-iron pans before you add your gluten-free doughs and batters. In fact, bread recipes turn out with a wonderful crust and light interior when you use a heavy pot with a lid.

- ✔ Brush your gluten-free creations with milk or eggs (if dairy or eggs aren't a problem) to help them brown just before you put them into the oven. Olive oil helps baked goods brown, too.

- ✔ You bake most gluten-free baked goods at the same temperature as wheat products. If you find that your breads or cakes aren't quite done inside, lower the temperature by 25 degrees and increase the time by five minutes or so.

- ✔ Don't overbake gluten-free products. They don't brown quite the same as wheat products. Use touch and temperature tests to judge doneness.

- ✔ Set the timer for a few minutes less than the baking time calls for in the traditional wheat recipe.

- ✔ Remove the baked goods from the pans quickly so the breads, cakes, and cookies don't steam. Cool them on a wire rack.

- ✔ For a nice, crisp crust on yeast breads, after you remove the bread from the pan, put it back in the oven, directly on the rack, for a minute or two. This helps drive off excess moisture in the crust and also browns the bread evenly.

- ✔ Angel food cakes and sponge cakes are cooled in a specific way: hung upside down like a bat! These cakes have very delicate structures. Cooling them upside down helps stretch the protein and starch web as it cools so it doesn't shrink and collapse. Place a funnel or glass pop bottle on the counter and carefully balance the tube pan upside down.

- ✔ Cool baked goods completely before you wrap and store them. If you wrap a bread or cake before it's cool, water collects on the product's surface, making it soggy.

Managing Expectations

When you find out that you must avoid gluten for the rest of your life, you may think that biting into a slice of tender bread with a crisp crust and a fluffy texture is a sensation you'll never experience again.

With the tips and tricks in this book, you *can* have that experience again. But no matter how good a gluten-free recipe is, it will never be the same as a wheat recipe. It can be even better! Nothing beats homemade treats. Making them healthy is a bonus.

In this section, you get a grip on flavor differences, texture differences, and visual differences between wheat-based and gluten-free baked goods. At first the change may take some adjustment, but you'll soon learn to love the taste, texture, and look of gluten-free cakes, cookies, pies, and desserts.

Book II

Making the Switch without Losing Your Mind

Flavor differences

Wheat flour is known for its consistency; it's consistent in the way it behaves in recipes, consistent in its look, and consistent in taste. That's where gluten-free flours have an advantage: They all have a different taste!

When you transition to a gluten-free diet, the number of alternative flours and starches can seem dizzying. As you bake, you'll discover the flours and starches you like best.

Some flours are naturally sweet, others are nutty, and others have a strong flavor. When you're just getting started baking gluten-free, try as many as you can. And keep notes about which flours you like and which you don't.

The point is to be flexible. No gluten-free recipe ever tastes exactly the same as a wheat flour recipe. But remember that homemade gluten-free baked goods taste better than anything made in a factory, mass-produced, or made in a supermarket bakery.

Texture differences

Texture is the elephant in the room for gluten-free baked goods. Huge improvements were made when flour combinations and additives were added to the mix. Measuring according to weight instead of volume represented the next step forward. Even with these changes, gluten-free baked goods don't have quite the same texture as wheat-based products. To get the best texture from your gluten-free baked products, try these tips:

- Eat breads and rolls warm. Of course, nothing's better than eating these products warm from the oven, but you can reheat breads and rolls before serving for better texture. Microwave rolls for 8 to 10 seconds apiece on high power. Wrap breads in foil and reheat them in a 350 degree oven for 9 to 12 minutes. But don't try this more than once! Reheating makes starch go stale faster, so multiple reheating creates a tough and dry bread or roll.

- Some gluten-free flours have a slightly gritty texture, especially brown rice flour. Sweet rice flour from Asian markets is incredibly fine textured. But corn flour, teff flour, and quinoa flours are all a bit gritty. Use less of these flours or grind them in a food processor for a finer texture.

- Some gluten-free baked goods can be denser than their wheat cousins, although many of the newer gluten-free recipes are wonderfully light. To adjust to this fact, bake recipes that are naturally denser. A whole-grain bread will always be denser than a white bread. It's also better for you, with more fiber and vitamins.

- If your breads aren't as soft or tender as you'd like, toast them. Nothing's better than toasted homemade bread spread with a little softened butter or whipped honey.

- If you're not completely happy with the texture of your gluten-free baked goods, freeze them. Freezing firms structure and can help keep products moist for a longer period. In fact, some products, such as brownies and soft cookies, taste delectable when frozen and partially thawed.

Visual differences

Many gluten-free baked goods look a little different from wheat baked goods. The breads may not rise quite as high, and cookies and pastries may be flatter. Browning is a little different, too. But you may be surprised at how appetizing these gluten-free treats look. The crumb of gluten-free breads and cakes is very similar to wheat products. Pie crusts are just as flaky, and cookies can be crackled and golden-brown. Here are some ways to improve the look of your gluten-free baked goods:

- You can get a more evenly browned look by brushing doughs and batters with a beaten egg or any kind of milk before you put them into the oven.

- Use muffin tins or baking rings when making rolls and biscuits to help the softer batters and doughs hold their shape.

- Use piping bags and ice cream scoops to shape cookies and rolls. A thicker batter or dough produces a puffier product.

Book III
Gluten-Free Starts for Meals . . . or Days

Peanut Butter

Don't touch knife to bread. Flick it.

(1) (2)

Discover how to stock a dorm room with easy, gluten-free staples at www.dummies.com/extras/glutenfreeaio.

Contents at a Glance

Chapter 1

Breakfast and Brunch, Reimagined

In This Chapter

▶ Adding sizzle to your morning

▶ Cereal, pancakes, and beyond

▶ Morning fare that's out of the box but in your diet

*I*f you eat dinner at 6 p.m. and wake up at 7 a.m., you'll have fasted for more than 13 hours before you sit down to breakfast. At that point, your body's blood sugar levels are screaming for nourishment. Eating breakfast jump-starts your metabolism so it works harder and more efficiently all day. Simply put, never skip breakfast.

Forget the excuse, "I don't have time for breakfast." There are foods that you can take in the car and eat as you commute to work. At the very least, you can grab a piece of fruit, a container of yogurt, and a health bar. Some foods can be prepared the night before so that, in the morning, you can put them in the oven while you shower, and they're ready by the time you're dressed. Now, did that cover all the "I don't have time for breakfast" excuses? Besides, after making the recipes in this chapter, you'll wake up each morning anticipating your first meal of the day.

Many of the recipes in this chapter call for a flour mixture. See Book V, Chapter 2 for a no-fail gluten-free recipe.

Starting the Day the Gluten-Free Way

Most people climb out of bed, shuffle into the kitchen, and pop some bread into the toaster or pour a bowl of cereal — you can, too. You just have to make sure your bread and cereal are gluten-free.

If you have gluten eaters in the house, you need to be certain that your toast is not contaminated by their toast crumbs. The easiest way to do this is to have two toasters or to use Toast-It! Bags. With these bags, you insert the bread into the bag, and then insert the bag into the toaster. The bag allows heat to penetrate so the bread will toast, but no crumbs or essence of crumbs can cling to the toaster. These bags are great to take with you when you're traveling so you can have toast on the road without fear of cross-contamination.

But you are about to realize that breakfast is so much more than mere bread and cereal.

Gluten-Free Granola

Prep time: 30 min • **Cook time:** 2 hr • **Yield:** 12 servings

Ingredients	Directions
2 cups puffed rice cereal	**1** Preheat the oven to 250 degrees.
2 cups puffed corn cereal	**2** In a large bowl, combine the puffed rice cereal, puffed corn cereal, Perky's Nutty Rice cereal, Kashi Cranberry Sunshine cereal, and peanuts.
1 cup Perky's Crunchy Rice cereal	
1 cup Kashi Cranberry Sunshine cereal	
1 cup roasted peanuts	**3** In a small saucepan, heat the vanilla extract, light corn syrup, honey, and oil over medium heat (it just needs to get warm so it flows more easily; don't overheat it). Stir the mixture occasionally as it heats.
2 teaspoons vanilla extract	
½ cup light corn syrup	
½ cup honey	**4** Pour the warm honey mixture over the dry ingredients, making sure it all gets mixed up.
¼ cup vegetable oil	
½ cup raisins	**5** Place the mixture on large baking sheets that you've coated with nonstick spray. Bake the granola for 2 hours, stirring every 15 minutes to keep the mixture from sticking.
½ cup dried cranberries	
Nonstick cooking spray	
	6 Carefully add the raisins and cranberries to the hot granola, folding them into the mixture so they're well mixed. Let the granola cool to room temperature, and serve.

Per serving: Calories 288 (From Fat 98); Fat 11g (Saturated 1g); Cholesterol 0mg; Sodium 91mg; Carbohydrate 46g (Dietary Fiber 3g); Protein 5g.

Tip: Homemade granola tends to go stale quickly. Extend the life of your homemade granola by using a vacuum-packing system to seal and store several individual-sized servings. Too late? If your granola has already gone stale, use it to make Honey Oat Bars (see recipe in Book V, Chapter 3).

Pumpkin Pecan Parfait

Prep time: 5 min • **Yield:** 1 serving

Ingredients	Directions
1 cup plain yogurt	*1* In a small bowl, stir together the yogurt, pumpkin, and cinnamon.
2 tablespoons pumpkin puree	
¼ teaspoon cinnamon	*2* In a large drinking glass, layer half the yogurt mixture, half the pecans, and half the honey. Repeat.
¼ cup chopped pecans	
1 tablespoon honey	

Per serving: Calories 436 (From Fat 228); Fat 25g (Saturated 4g); Cholesterol 15mg; Sodium 174mg; Carbohydrate 42g (Dietary Fiber 5g); Protein 16g.

Note: Make sure you purchase plain pumpkin puree and not pumpkin pie filling for this recipe.

Vary It! To make this dairy-free, try almond yogurt.

Vary It! Use vanilla-flavored yogurt and cut the honey to ½ tablespoon or just a drizzle.

Banana Split Breakfast

Prep time: 5 min • **Yield:** 1 serving

Ingredients	*Directions*
1 banana	**1** Slice the banana lengthwise and place it in a bowl.
½ cup plain Greek yogurt	**2** Spoon the yogurt onto the banana.
2 tablespoons 100% fruit preserves	**3** Warm the preserves in the microwave for about 10 seconds. Spoon them over the yogurt and banana.
¼ cup fresh berries	
2 tablespoons slivered almonds	**4** Top the banana and yogurt with fresh berries and almonds.

Per serving: Calories 357 (From Fat 88); Fat 10g (Saturated 2g); Cholesterol 8mg; Sodium 34mg; Carbohydrate 58g (Dietary Fiber 7g); Protein 14g.

Vary It! Instead of preserves, warm up a touch of nut butter or your favorite chocolate hazelnut spread and top your banana split breakfast with these decadent alternatives.

Vary It! If you have trouble with dairy, make this with Greek yogurt made with almond milk.

Cinnamon Breakfast Cereal

Prep time: 4 min • **Cook time:** 5 min • **Yield:** 2 servings

Ingredients	Directions
2 cups cooked brown rice 1 cup milk 2 tablespoons brown sugar ⅛ teaspoon cinnamon ¾ teaspoon vanilla 2 tablespoons maple syrup 1 tablespoon butter 2 tablespoons raisins ⅓ cup toasted pecan pieces	*1* Place all the ingredients in the top of a double boiler over boiling water, stirring frequently, for about 5 minutes. *2* When the cereal is thoroughly warmed, spoon it into 2 serving bowls.

Per serving: Calories 605; Fat 25g (Saturated 7g); Cholesterol 27mg; Sodium 108mg; Carbohydrates 88g (Dietary Fiber 6g); Protein 11g.

Tip: To speed things up in the morning, cook the rice the night before or use leftover dinner rice.

Note: If you prefer a more liquid cereal, add more warmed milk.

Perfect Pancakes

Prep time: 5 min • **Cook time:** 15 min • **Yield:** 5 servings (2 pancakes each)

Ingredients	Directions
1¼ cups all-purpose flour	**1** In a medium bowl, mix together the flour, sugar, baking powder, baking soda, and salt.
½ tablespoon sugar	
1 teaspoon baking powder	**2** Add the eggs, butter or oil, milk, and vanilla to the flour mixture. Stir to thoroughly combine the batter.
½ teaspoon baking soda	
¼ teaspoon salt	**3** Spray a flat pan or griddle with nonstick cooking spray and heat the pan over medium to medium-high heat.
2 eggs, beaten	
2 tablespoons melted butter or vegetable oil	**4** For each pancake, ladle ¼ cup batter onto the hot pan. When the pancakes begin to puff, form small bubbles, and become lightly browned on the edges (after about a minute), flip the pancakes over with a spatula and cook the other side.
1 cup milk	
½ teaspoon vanilla extract	
Butter for serving	
Maple syrup for serving	**5** Serve the pancakes with butter and a touch of maple syrup.

Per serving: Calories 206 (From Fat 83); Fat 9g (Saturated 5g); Cholesterol 93mg; Sodium 368mg; Carbohydrate 26g (Dietary Fiber 3g); Protein 7g.

Tip: Make your own pancake mix by measuring and mixing the dry ingredients (Step 1) and storing them in a plastic bag. Be sure to write the rest of the ingredients and directions on the bag.

Vary It! Throw a handful of fresh blueberries or mini chocolate chips into the batter while mixing to sweeten your cakes. Or add the mix-ins to individual pancakes in the pan, and you can make multiple variations from a single batch.

Note: Leftover pancakes save well in the refrigerator or freezer. After they cool, layer the pancakes with plastic wrap and seal them in a plastic bag. Reheat them in the microwave or toaster oven when you're ready to enjoy the leftovers.

Cornmeal Pancakes

Prep time: 15 min • **Cook time:** 5 min • **Yield:** 4–5 servings

Ingredients	Directions
3 eggs	*1* Preheat the griddle over medium heat.
1 cup buttermilk	*2* In a large bowl, beat the eggs until they're light and fluffy and then add the buttermilk, corn bread mix, and oil. Beat until the batter is uniform and all one color. Because this batter has no gluten, the pancakes won't get tough no matter how long you beat!
1½ cups Light Cakey Corn Bread Mix without shortening (see Book V, Chapter 2)	
¼ cup vegetable or neutral oil like safflower or sunflower	
	3 Sprinkle the griddle with a few drops of water. When the water sizzles and disappears quickly, the griddle is ready.
	4 Grease the griddle with unsalted butter. Pour the batter onto the griddle, using a ¼-cup measuring cup.
	5 Cook until the batter rises, the pancake edges set and look cooked, and bubbles form on the surface, about 2 to 5 minutes.
	6 Carefully turn the pancakes with a spatula and cook for 2 minutes longer. Serve immediately.

Per serving: Calories 512 (From Fat 301); Fat 33g (Saturated 11g); Cholesterol 200mg; Sodium 495mg; Carbohydrate 46g (Dietary Fiber 3g); Protein 10g.

Note: You can substitute other types of milk for the buttermilk in this recipe, including almond milk, rice milk, and soy milk. Because buttermilk is more acidic than these other milk types, add a teaspoon of lemon juice to the milk and let it sit for a few minutes before using.

Whole-Grain Buttermilk Waffles

Prep time: 15 min • **Cook time:** 8 min • **Yield:** 4 waffles

Ingredients	Directions
3 eggs	*1* In a medium bowl, beat together the eggs, butter, sugar, vanilla, and buttermilk until combined.
4 tablespoons butter, melted and cooled, or neutral oil like sunflower or safflower	*2* In a large bowl, combine the Whole-Grain Flour Mix, White Flour Mix, baking powder, baking soda, and salt; mix well.
2 tablespoons sugar	
1 teaspoon vanilla	*3* Pour the wet ingredients into the dry ingredients and mix just until combined.
1 cup buttermilk	
1¼ cups minus 1 teaspoon (166 grams) Whole-Grain Flour Mix (see Book V, Chapter 2)	*4* Preheat a waffle iron according to the appliance's instructions. The iron has to be hot for the best waffle texture.
½ cup minus 1 teaspoon (71 grams) White Flour Mix (see Book V, Chapter 2)	*5* Spray the waffle iron with nonstick cooking spray.
1 tablespoon baking powder	*6* Add enough batter to evenly cover the bottom waffle surface. The amount you use depends on your waffle iron; follow the instructions. Close the iron and bake until the steaming stops, about 7 to 8 minutes.
½ teaspoon baking soda	
¼ teaspoon salt	

Per serving: Calories 398 (From Fat 151); Fat 17g (Saturated 9g); Cholesterol 193mg; Sodium 702mg; Carbohydrate 53g (Dietary Fiber 2g); Protein 11g.

Note: Be sure to read the instructions that come with your waffle iron. All waffle irons cook different amounts of batter and for different times. A general rule is to cook until the steam stops coming out of the sides of the iron.

Note: The first waffle often sticks. If it does stick, use a rubber spatula on the unplugged waffle iron to pry it off. The next waffle should come off clean because the butter in the batter helps to grease the iron as it cooks.

Vegan Flax Raisin Muffins

Prep time: 26 min • **Cook time:** 30 min • **Yield:** 18 muffins

Ingredients	Directions
1 cup (150 grams) dark raisins	*1* Preheat the oven to 350 degrees. Grease 18 muffin cups or line them with paper liners.
¼ cup golden flaxseeds	
1½ cups plus 1 teaspoon (206 grams) Whole-Grain Flour Mix (see Book V, Chapter 2)	*2* Place the raisins in a small bowl; pour hot water over them to cover and soak for 15 minutes; drain.
1 cup minus 2 teaspoons (142 grams) White Flour Mix (see Book V, Chapter 2)	*3* Start the food processor and add the flaxseeds through the feed tube while it's running to break them up. You can either grind them to a fine powder or just break the seed coats to add texture to the muffins.
⅓ cup packed light brown sugar	
2 teaspoons baking powder	*4* Add the drained raisins to the food processor and puree.
1 teaspoon baking soda	
½ teaspoon sea salt	*5* In a medium bowl, combine the Whole-Grain Flour Mix, White Flour Mix, brown sugar, baking powder, baking soda, and salt and mix until the mixture is one color.
⅓ cup neutral oil	
1 teaspoon vanilla	
1⅓ cups applesauce	*6* Add the mixed flours, olive oil, vanilla, and applesauce to the food processor with the raisins and flaxseeds. Process until completely combined.
	7 Spoon the batter into the prepared muffin cups, filling each ⅔ full.
	8 Bake for 28 to 30 minutes, or until the muffins spring back when lightly touched and are golden-brown.
	9 Cool the muffins in the pan for 3 minutes and then move them to a wire rack to cool completely.

Per serving: Calories 171 (From Fat 45); Fat 5g (Saturated 1g); Cholesterol 0mg; Sodium 182mg; Carbohydrate 31g (Dietary Fiber 2g); Protein 2g.

Vary It! You can use other dried fruits in place of the raisins; just substitute the same weight. Dried apricots, pears, or mangoes are yummy. Weigh, hydrate, and puree.

Breakfast Bread Pudding

Prep time: 10 min plus refrigeration time • **Cook time:** 20 min • **Yield:** 9 servings

Ingredients	*Directions*
4 eggs	*1* In a large bowl, whisk together the eggs, whole milk, cinnamon, vanilla, ½ cup of the brown sugar, and baking powder.
⅔ cup whole milk	
½ teaspoon cinnamon	
4 teaspoons vanilla	*2* Cut the bread slices into small cubes, and then stir them into the egg mixture. Cover the mixture and refrigerate it for at least 2 hours.
½ cup plus 1 tablespoon brown sugar	
¼ teaspoon baking powder	*3* In a small bowl, stir the raisins into the rum. Cover the mixture and let it cure at room temperature for at least 2 hours.
6 slices bread	
¾ cup raisins	
2 tablespoons dark rum	*4* Preheat the oven to 400 degrees. Spray a 9-x-9-inch baking pan with cooking spray.
Nonstick cooking spray	
1 banana, sliced thinly	*5* Stir the raisins into the bread mixture.
2 teaspoons cinnamon sugar	
3 tablespoons maple syrup	*6* Spoon half of the soaked bread into the prepared pan. Slice the banana on top of the bread and sprinkle with remaining 1 tablespoon brown sugar. Spoon the remaining bread over the banana slices, pouring any remaining egg mixture on top. Press down gently on the bread cubes to even out the top.
	7 Sprinkle the top of the pudding with cinnamon sugar.
	8 Bake the pudding at 400 degrees for 20 minutes, or until the top is lightly browned. Remove the pudding from the oven and drizzle it with maple syrup. Cool the pudding for 10 minutes before cutting.

Per serving: Calories 239; Fat 5g (Saturated 1g); Cholesterol 96mg; Sodium 72mg; Carbohydrate 43g (Dietary Fiber 2g); Protein 4g.

Note: Because of the soaking time required, assemble this the night before.

Vary It! Use orange juice in place of the rum.

Baked Chocolate Lava Oatmeal

Prep time: 5 min • **Cook time:** 25 min • **Yield:** 12 servings

Ingredients	Directions
2 cups rolled oats (not instant)	**1** Preheat the oven to 375 degrees.
¼ cup butter	
½ cup brown sugar	**2** Combine the oats, butter, brown sugar, eggs, milk, vanilla, and baking powder in a microwave-safe dish. Stir until well mixed.
2 eggs	
2 cups milk	**3** Microwave the oatmeal mixture on high for 4 minutes.
1 teaspoon vanilla	
1 teaspoon baking powder	**4** Place 12 paper muffin cups in a regular muffin pan. Fill each paper cup halfway with the oatmeal mixture.
¼ cup (12 teaspoons) chocolate hazelnut spread	
1 banana, sliced into 12 pieces	**5** On top of each muffin cup of oatmeal, place 1 teaspoon of the chocolate hazelnut spread and 1 slice of banana.
	6 Top each muffin cup with the remaining oatmeal mixture.
	7 Bake for 15 minutes.

Per serving: Calories 191 (From Fat 74); Fat 8g (Saturated 4g); Cholesterol 47mg; Sodium 69mg; Carbohydrate 25g (Dietary Fiber 2g); Protein 5g.

Vary It! Use jam, almond butter, or peanut butter instead of chocolate hazelnut spread for a different version of this decadent breakfast.

Tip! Freeze your leftovers. When you're ready to enjoy an oatmeal cup, reheat it in the microwave for about 1 minute.

Cinnamon Apple Fritters

Prep time: 20 min • **Cook time:** 4 min • **Yield:** 8–10 fritters

Ingredients	*Directions*
3 eggs	*1* Beat the eggs in a large bowl with a spout. Add the flours, salt, maple syrup, baking powder, and cinnamon and beat for 1 minute.
1 cup minus 2 tablespoons (107 grams) sorghum flour	
⅓ cup (55 grams) sweet rice flour	*2* Beat in the buttermilk and ½ teaspoon vanilla. Stir in the apple and let the batter rest while the oil preheats.
⅓ cup minus 1 teaspoon (41 grams) brown rice flour	
1 cup minus 2 tablespoons minus 1 teaspoon (105 grams) tapioca flour	*3* Heat the safflower oil in a large frying pan. Line a cookie sheet with a few pieces of newspaper and then top with paper towels.
½ teaspoon salt	*4* In a shallow bowl, combine the powdered sugar, 1 teaspoon vanilla, and milk and mix until smooth; set this glaze aside.
1 tablespoon plus 1 teaspoon maple syrup	
1 teaspoon baking powder	*5* Check the oil temperature; it should be at 365 degrees.
1½ teaspoons cinnamon	
⅔ cup minus 1 tablespoon buttermilk	*6* Carefully drizzle ¼ cup of the dough into the oil. Drizzle the batter in one direction and then perpendicular to the first layer, leaving holes for the oil to penetrate so the fritter cooks evenly.
½ teaspoon plus 1 teaspoon vanilla	
1 small Granny Smith apple, peeled and minced	*7* Fry the fritter for 2 to 3 minutes, until the top edges start to turn brown. Flip the fritter and cook for another minute until browned.
2 cups safflower oil for frying	
1 cup powdered sugar	*8* Remove the fritter with tongs to the prepared cookie sheet; let it rest for 30 seconds and then flip to drain.
1 tablespoon milk	
	9 Repeat with the remaining batter. As the fritters start to cool, you can dip them into the powdered sugar glaze. Let them stand on a wire rack until the glaze hardens. Store at room temperature for three days.

Per serving: Calories 260 (From Fat 117); Fat 13g (Saturated 1g); Cholesterol 65mg; Sodium 190mg; Carbohydrate 34g (Dietary Fiber 1g); Protein 4g.

Brunch Pizza

Prep time: 10 min • **Cook time:** 20 min • **Yield:** 8 servings

Ingredients	Directions
8 eggs	*1* Preheat the oven to 400 degrees. Spray a 14-inch pizza pan with nonstick cooking spray (or use any similar size of low-rimmed, oven-safe pan).
20-ounce package refrigerated hash browns	
A dash of salt	*2* In a medium bowl, beat 1 egg and then stir in the hash browns. Spread the hash browns in the prepared pizza pan all the way to the edges. Pat down the hash-brown crust with the back of a spoon. Sprinkle the crust with a dash of salt and pepper and bake it for 15 minutes.
A dash of black pepper	
½ cup milk	
1½ cups shredded cheddar cheese	
¼ cup chopped green bell peppers	*3* While the crust is baking, whisk together the remaining 7 eggs and the milk in a microwave-safe bowl. Cook the eggs in the microwave on high for 3 minutes. Stir. Cook an additional 3 minutes. Stir the eggs again.
¼ cup sliced mushrooms	
¼ cup bacon (a couple of slices), cooked and crumbled	*4* When the crust is baked, remove it from the oven and spread the egg mixture evenly over the crust.
¼ cup chopped ham, fully cooked	
¼ cup cooked spinach	*5* Top the eggs with cheese, bell peppers, mushrooms, bacon, ham, and spinach. Return the pan to the oven and bake for another 5 minutes, or until the cheese is melted. Cut the pizza into 8 wedges.

Per serving: Calories 188 (From Fat 92); Fat 10g (Saturated 4g); Cholesterol 200mg; Sodium 310mg; Carbohydrate 12g (Dietary Fiber 1g); Protein 12g.

Tip: You can use refrigerated Simply Potatoes shredded hash browns for this recipe. If using frozen hash browns, check them for gluten-free status and defrost them before using them.

Tip: If you want to soften the bell peppers and mushrooms, cook them quickly with a touch of oil in a pan heated to medium-high — a quick sauté. Stir and cook them until they reach your desired softness and then toss them on the pizza in Step 5.

Vary It! Use any toppings that sound good. Try green onions, tomatoes, sausage, and broccoli.

Note: A pizza pan and a pizza cutter are helpful for this recipe, but you can make a rectangular version on a cookie sheet and cut the pizza with a knife.

Note: This pizza provides plenty to share with friends or roommates. If you're saving the extras for yourself, seal up the leftovers in plastic wrap or a zipper bag and store them in the fridge. Reheat a slice in the microwave on high for about 45 seconds.

Vary It!: Use egg substitute or egg whites if you want to reduce fat and calories: 2 egg whites = 1 whole egg, or 2 egg yolks = 1 whole egg, or ¼ cup egg substitute = 1 whole egg.

Make-Ahead Brunch Casserole

Prep time: 20 min • **Cook time:** 35 min • **Yield:** 6 servings

Ingredients	Directions
Nonstick cooking spray	**1** Preheat the oven to 375 degrees. Lightly spray a 9-x-9-inch baking dish with cooking spray.
3 large Idaho potatoes, boiled, peeled, and diced	
5 hard-boiled eggs, peeled and diced	**2** Place the diced potatoes, eggs, ham, green pepper, and onion in the baking dish.
¾ pound low-salt ham, cut into ½-inch cubes	**3** Sprinkle the parsley, pepper, and 1 cup of cheese on top; using a spoon, toss the ingredients lightly to distribute the cheese evenly.
¼ green pepper, minced	
½ medium onion, minced	
2 tablespoons chopped fresh parsley	**4** In a small bowl, stir together the melted butter, cornstarch, and sour cream (the mixture will be thick). Spoon tablespoonfuls of the mixture on top of the casserole. With the back of the spoon, smooth the topping to cover the casserole evenly.
¼ teaspoon pepper	
1 cup plus 2 tablespoons grated sharp cheddar cheese	
2 tablespoons butter, melted	**5** Sprinkle the top with the remaining 2 tablespoons of cheese and paprika.
2½ tablespoons cornstarch	
8-ounce container sour cream	**6** Bake the casserole for 35 minutes. Let the dish set for 5 minutes before serving.
Paprika	

Per serving: Calories 524; Fat 28g (Saturated 10g); Cholesterol 281mg; Sodium 722mg; Carbohydrate 42g (Dietary Fiber 4g); Protein 26g.

Tip: Assemble this dish the day before, and just pop it in the oven before your friends arrive.

Note: This recipe is for a 9-x-9-inch dish, but you can easily double the ingredients to fit a 9-x-13-inch pan for a larger crowd.

Note: Some nonstick cooking sprays contain flour. Check the label carefully!

Potato Tomato Pie

Prep time: 15 min • **Cook time:** 65 min • **Yield:** 8 servings

Ingredients	Directions
Nonstick cooking spray	*1* Preheat the oven to 400 degrees. Spray a 9-inch pie plate with cooking spray.
2 cups firmly packed grated raw potatoes	
¼ teaspoon salt	*2* Place the raw potatoes in a colander or sieve. Sprinkle them with salt and let them set for 5 minutes.
2 eggs	
¼ cup grated onion	*3* In a medium bowl, whisk the eggs. Squeeze out the excess water from the potatoes and add them to the eggs. Stir in the onion.
3 or 4 medium tomatoes, sliced ⅛-inch thick	
½ teaspoon oregano	*4* Put the mixture into the prepared pie plate. Using the back of a spoon, pat the mixture onto the bottom and sides of the pan.
¼ teaspoon pepper	
1 teaspoon Italian seasoning	
8 slices bacon, cooked crisp and crumbled	*5* Bake the crust for 35 minutes. Remove the pan from the oven and reduce the oven temperature to 350 degrees.
¾ cup grated Parmesan cheese	
¾ cup mayonnaise	*6* Layer half of the tomato slices onto the bottom of the baked crust. Sprinkle with half of the pepper and Italian seasoning and half of the bacon. Repeat the layer with the remaining tomatoes, pepper, Italian seasoning, and bacon.
⅓ cup seasoned breadcrumbs	
	7 In a small bowl, stir together the cheese and mayonnaise. Drop this mixture in dollops on top of the tomatoes and then spread it carefully to cover the top of the pie.
	8 Sprinkle the breadcrumbs on top of the pie. Bake the pie uncovered for 30 minutes, or until the breadcrumbs begin to brown.

Per serving: Calories 222; Fat 15g (Saturated 4g); Cholesterol 76mg; Sodium 645mg; Carbohydrate 14g (Dietary Fiber 1g); Protein 9g.

Note: You can serve this delicious pie at a brunch, as a side dish for dinner, and even as a main entree with a tossed salad.

Eggs in a Bread Basket

Prep time: 5 min • **Cook time:** 5 min • **Yield:** 4 servings

Ingredients	Directions
4 slices bread **4 tablespoons margarine** **4 eggs**	**1** Heat a griddle or large nonstick frying pan over medium-high heat. While the pan is heating, butter both sides of each piece of bread.
	2 In the center of each bread slice, cut out a circle about the size of an egg. You can use a knife to cut the circle, or use a cookie cutter to make cute shapes.
	3 Make sure the pan or griddle is hot enough that if you put a drop of water on it, the water sizzles. When the pan or griddle is hot, put all the bread — slices and cutouts — on the pan or griddle to fry.
	4 When the bottom side of the bread is golden brown, after about 2 minutes, flip each slice and cutout.
	5 Crack an egg into the hole in the center of each slice of bread. You may find that you have too much egg and that it covers the bread. That's okay.
	6 When the second side of the bread is golden brown, after about 2 minutes, flip it over again to cook the egg on the other side. Cook the egg until it's at the firmness you enjoy, and serve the "eggs in a basket" with the cooked cutouts as decorative additions.

Per serving: Calories 318 (From Fat 205); Fat 23g (Saturated 5g); Cholesterol 213mg; Sodium 196mg; Carbohydrate 21g (Dietary Fiber 1g); Protein 7g.

Vary It! If you'd like to cut out a lot of the cholesterol, toss the egg yolks and simply make this recipe with the whites.

Pepperoni Frittata

Prep time: 10 min • **Cook time:** 5 min • **Yield:** 6 servings

Ingredients	*Directions*
1 tablespoon olive oil	*1* Preheat the broiler. Wrap the handle of a 10-inch nonstick skillet with foil.
1½ cups thinly sliced broccoli florets	
¼ cup sliced green onion	*2* Heat the oil in the skillet. Add the broccoli, green onion, salt, pepper, Italian seasoning, thyme, dill, and parsley. Cook the vegetables and seasonings over medium-high heat, stirring, until the broccoli florets are tender-crisp. Sprinkle pepperoni over broccoli.
¼ teaspoon salt	
¼ teaspoon pepper	
½ teaspoon dried Italian seasoning	
¼ teaspoon dried thyme	*3* In a small bowl, whisk together the eggs, cornstarch, and milk until they're very light. Pour the mixture over the vegetables.
¼ teaspoon dried dill	
1 tablespoon snipped fresh parsley	*4* As the eggs begin to set, run a rubber spatula around the edge of the skillet, lifting the egg mixture to allow the uncooked portions to flow underneath. Continue cooking and lifting the edges until the eggs are nearly set. (The top surface will still be moist.)
10 slices pizza pepperoni, chopped	
6 eggs	
3 tablespoons cornstarch	*5* Sprinkle the top of the frittata with cheese.
1½ tablespoons milk	
¾ cup shredded Swiss cheese	*6* Place the skillet under the broiler and broil the frittata for 1 to 2 minutes until the top is set and the cheese has melted. Cut the frittata into wedges to serve.

Per serving: *Calories 197; Fat 13g (Saturated 5g); Cholesterol 229mg; Sodium 261mg; Carbohydrate 10g (Dietary Fiber 1g); Protein 12g.*

Vary It! Use cooked, crumbled sausage in place of the pepperoni. Instead of the broccoli, try asparagus tips. Substitute cheddar or mozzarella cheese for the Swiss cheese.

Curried Chard with "Poached" Egg

Prep time: 10 min • **Cook time:** 10 min • **Yield:** 4 servings

Ingredients	Directions
2 large bunches fresh Swiss chard, rinsed	*1* Remove stems from chard and chop into ½-inch pieces. Layer the chard leaves in a stack and chop into strips.
1 tablespoon olive oil	
1 large garlic clove, minced	*2* In a 10-inch nonstick skillet, heat olive oil over medium heat. Add garlic, cumin, ginger, mustard seeds, pepper, and cardamon, and sauté for 1 minute. Add chard stems and sauté until tender, stirring occasionally. Add chard leaves and continue to sauté until tender.
½ teaspoon cumin	
½ teaspoon ground ginger	
½ teaspoon yellow mustard seeds	
⅛ teaspoon fresh black pepper	*3* Use a large spoon to make four indentations in the cooked chard. Crack open one egg into each indention. Sprinkle with fresh ground black pepper. Place a lid over the mixture to allow the steam to cook eggs to soft stage, approximately 5 minutes, until egg white solidifies from transparency to opaque.
⅛ teaspoon cardamom	
4 eggs	
	4 Divide the contents of the skillet into four servings and serve immediately.

Per serving: Calories 141; Fat 9g (Saturated 2g); Cholesterol 186mg; Sodium 341mg; Carbohydrate 8g (Dietary Fiber 4g); Protein 9g.

Tip: Wash chard leaves and stems before using to remove dirt and sand clinging to them.

Note: Swiss chard comes in a few varieties and is a source of many different antioxidants and phytonutrients. It's low in calories, high in fiber — some say it's a vegetable with a PhD!

Breakfast Quiche

Prep time: 15 min • **Cook time:** 45 min • **Yield:** 4 servings

Ingredients	Directions
3 cups frozen hash browns, thawed	**1** Preheat the oven to 325 degrees.
⅓ cup melted butter	**2** To prepare the crust, mix the hash browns and butter carefully, making sure the potatoes don't turn to mush.
Nonstick cooking spray	
5 eggs	**3** Spray a 9-inch pie plate or quiche pan with nonstick spray. Press the potato-butter mixture evenly on the bottom and sides of the pan.
¾ cup milk	
1 cup cooked diced ham	
⅓ cup diced onion	**4** In a large mixing bowl, beat the eggs with an electric mixer for 2 minutes on low speed. Add the milk, ham, onion, cheeses, basil, and salt and pepper. Stir until they're well mixed.
1 cup grated Swiss cheese	
¼ cup grated cheddar cheese	
¼ cup grated Monterey Jack cheese	**5** Pour the egg mixture into the crust, and bake it for 45 minutes. To test whether the quiche is done, insert a knife in the center. If it comes out clean, the quiche is ready.
2 teaspoons chopped fresh basil	
Salt and pepper to taste	

Per serving: Calories 585 (From Fat 392); Fat 44g (Saturated 23g); Cholesterol 368mg; Sodium 808mg; Carbohydrate 22g (Dietary Fiber 1g); Protein 29g.

Tip: To add nutritional value and flavor, add any cut-up veggies and meats you like to this recipe.

Crab Quiche

Prep time: 10 min • **Cook time:** 20 min • **Yield:** 6 servings

Ingredients	Directions
Nonstick cooking spray	**1** Preheat the oven to 375 degrees. Spray a 9-inch pie plate with cooking spray.
3 eggs	
2 green onions, chopped	**2** In a large bowl, whisk together the eggs, green onions, yogurt, cornstarch, basil, dill, parsley, salt, and pepper until they're thoroughly blended.
¼ cup plain low-fat yogurt	
2 teaspoons cornstarch	
¼ teaspoon dried basil	
½ teaspoon dried dill	**3** Stir in the broccoli, crabmeat, and Romano and Swiss cheeses.
2 tablespoons fresh parsley, minced	
⅛ teaspoon salt	**4** Spread the mixture evenly in the prepared pie plate.
⅛ teaspoon pepper	
¾ cup (½ of a 10-ounce box) chopped broccoli, thawed	**5** Lay the tomato slices neatly across the top of the quiche and then sprinkle them with breadcrumbs.
4.25-ounce can flaked crabmeat, drained (beware gluten-containing imitation crab)	**6** Bake the quiche, uncovered, for 20 minutes, or until a knife inserted in the center comes out clean. Let the quiche stand for 5 minutes before cutting.
2 tablespoons grated Romano cheese	
¼ cup (1 ounce) shredded Swiss cheese	
2 plum tomatoes, sliced thin	
¼ cup breadcrumbs	

Per serving: Calories 123; Fat 6g (Saturated 3g); Cholesterol 133mg; Sodium 299mg; Carbohydrate 7g (Dietary Fiber 1g); Protein 12g.

Note: You can make a pie crust for this quiche, but it isn't needed.

Vary It! Use a 6-ounce can of salmon in place of the crabmeat with equally excellent results.

Mini Pancetta Quiches

Prep time: 20 min • **Cook time:** 25 min • **Yield:** 36 servings

Ingredients	Directions
2 tablespoons (16 grams) cornstarch	**1** Preheat the oven to 425 degrees. Spray 36 mini muffin cups with nonstick cooking spray and set aside.
2 tablespoons (14 grams) tapioca flour	**2** In a blender or food processor, combine the cornstarch, tapioca flour, milk, cream, eggs, salt, thyme, and pepper. Blend until smooth and set aside.
¾ cup milk	
⅓ cup heavy cream	**3** In a medium skillet, heat the olive oil over medium heat. Add the pancetta; cook and stir until the cubes are crispy, about 5 to 7 minutes. Add the shallot, cook for 2 minutes, and then drain well on paper towels.
3 eggs	
½ teaspoon salt	
1 teaspoon dried thyme leaves	
⅛ teaspoon pepper	**4** Divide the pancetta mixture and fontina cheese among the mini muffin cups.
1 tablespoon olive oil	
6 ounces diced pancetta	**5** Spoon about 1 tablespoon of the egg mixture into each mini muffin cup, over the pancetta mixture and fontina cheese. Sprinkle each mini quiche with a bit of Parmesan cheese.
1 shallot, minced	
1 cup shredded fontina cheese	
¼ cup grated Parmesan cheese	**6** Bake for 15 to 20 minutes, or until the quiches are light golden-brown and set.
	7 Let the quiches cool in the muffin tins for 5 minutes and then run a sharp knife around the edge of each mini quiche and remove from the tin. Serve warm.

Per serving: Calories 37 (From Fat 26); Fat 3g (Saturated 1g); Cholesterol 21mg; Sodium 95mg; Carbohydrate 1g (Dietary Fiber 0g); Protein 2g.

Vary It! You can use just about any filling and any cheese in these tiny crustless quiches. Some chopped cooked chicken or tiny shrimp would be delicious. Use vegan cheese, Cheddar cheese, Swiss cheese, or Gouda cheese — just be sure that you're buying gluten-free versions.

Maple Soufflé

Prep time: 10 min • **Cook time:** 40 min • **Yield:** 4 servings

Ingredients	Directions
6 large eggs, separated	**1** Preheat the oven to 350 degrees.
6 tablespoons maple syrup	**2** In a small mixing bowl, use the mixer to whip the egg whites on high speed until soft peaks form. Set the bowl aside.
¼ teaspoon cinnamon	
⅛ teaspoon salt	
¼ cup small-curd cottage cheese	**3** In a large mixing bowl, use the mixer to whip the egg yolks about 3 minutes until they're thick. Whip in the maple syrup, cinnamon, salt, and cottage cheese until blended.
2 tablespoons butter, melted	
⅓ cup sliced almonds	**4** Fold the egg whites into the egg yolk mixture.
	5 Brush the melted butter on the bottom and sides of a 9-x-1½-inch round straight-sided soufflé dish. Pour the egg mixture into the prepared pan. Sprinkle the top with almonds.
	6 Bake for 40 minutes, or until the top is puffed and lightly browned.
	7 Cut into wedges to serve.

Per serving: Calories 240; Fat 13g (Saturated 5g); Cholesterol 60mg; Sodium 123mg; Carbohydrate 16g (Dietary Fiber 1g); Protein 7g.

Tip: Drizzle a little maple syrup over the top of each piece for a perfect presentation.

Simple, Stylin' Smoothie

Prep time: 4 min • **Yield:** 3 cups

Ingredients	Directions
½ cup milk	*1* Put all the ingredients in a blender.
1 cup strawberry yogurt	
2 ripe bananas	*2* Mix until smooth.
1 teaspoon honey	
¼ cup ice cubes	

Per serving: Calories 141 (From Fat 18); Fat 2g (Saturated 1g); Cholesterol 9mg; Sodium 41mg; Carbohydrate 29g (Dietary Fiber 2g); Protein 4g. (Based on three 1-cup servings.)

Vary It! Remember, you can make a smoothie countless ways — be creative, and use ingredients you have on hand, especially those that are a little too ripe to eat plain. Play with the portion sizes and types of ingredients you use to get the taste and nutritional value that suits you. The only fruit that doesn't work well is citrus.

Piña Colada Smoothie

Prep time: 5 min • **Yield:** 1 serving

Ingredients	Directions
1 cup refrigerated coconut milk	**1** Combine the coconut milk, pineapple chunks, honey, and ice cubes in a blender.
½ cup pineapple chunks	
2 tablespoons honey	**2** Blend the ingredients on high for 30 seconds or until they're smooth.
1 cup ice cubes	

Per serving: Calories 284 (From Fat 46); Fat 5g (Saturated 5g); Cholesterol 0mg; Sodium 33mg; Carbohydrate 62g (Dietary Fiber 1g); Protein 2g.

Broiled Grapefruit

Prep time: 1 min • **Cook time:** 5 min • **Yield:** 1 serving

Ingredients	Directions
1 grapefruit, cut in half **2 tablespoons brown sugar**	**1** Section out the grapefruit, carefully cutting between the membranes with a sharp knife.
	2 Place the two halves of the grapefruit on a baking sheet lined with aluminum foil.
	3 Sprinkle brown sugar on top of each grapefruit half and broil in the oven or toaster oven until bubbly, about 5 minutes. If you use a toaster oven, this dish cooks a little faster because the food is closer to the heat. Watch to make sure your grapefruit isn't browning too quickly.

Per serving: *Calories 194 (From Fat 2); Fat 0g (Saturated 0g); Cholesterol 0mg; Sodium 13mg; Carbohydrate 51g (Dietary Fiber 3g); Protein 1g.*

Cranberry Pear Bundt Coffeecake

Prep time: 25 min • **Cook time:** 1 hr • **Yield:** 16 servings

Ingredients	Directions
2 tablespoons plus 6 tablespoons unsalted butter, melted	**1** Preheat the oven to 350 degrees. Brush a 12-inch Bundt pan with 2 tablespoons melted butter and sprinkle with ¼ cup sugar, coating every crack and crevice.
¼ cup plus ¼ cup sugar	
1¼ cups plus 1 teaspoon (189 grams) White Flour Mix (see Book V, Chapter 2)	**2** In a medium bowl, combine the White Flour Mix, Whole-Grain Flour Mix, ¼ cup sugar, baking powder, baking soda, nutmeg, and salt and mix well with a wire whisk.
⅓ cup plus 1 tablespoon (54 grams) Whole-Grain Flour Mix (see Book V, Chapter 2)	
2 teaspoons baking powder	**3** Use 3 tablespoons of this mixture to toss with the pears and cranberries; set aside.
1 teaspoon baking soda	**4** In a large bowl, beat the eggs with sour cream, 6 tablespoons melted butter, and vanilla until combined. Add the flour mixture and stir until well blended.
¼ teaspoon ground nutmeg	
¼ teaspoon salt	
2 pears, peeled and diced	
1 cup fresh or frozen cranberries	**5** Fold in the coated fruits.
4 eggs	**6** Pour the batter into the prepared pan. Place in the oven on the bottom rack.
1 cup sour cream	
1 teaspoon vanilla	**7** Bake for 55 to 60 minutes, or until the cake springs back when lightly touched and starts to pull away from the sides of the pan.
	8 Let the cake cool in the pan for 3 minutes and then gently shake the pan to make sure the cake is released. Turn onto a wire rack and let the cake cool completely before storing it in an airtight container.

Per serving: Calories 173 (From Fat 91); Fat 10g (Saturated 6g); Cholesterol 75mg; Sodium 188mg; Carbohydrate 19g (Dietary Fiber 1g); Protein 3g.

Note: This is an excellent breakfast treat for fall mornings. The combination of tart cranberries and sweet pears is special. The cake's flavor develops overnight, so bake it the day before for the best flavor.

Breakfast Biscuit Bread

Prep time: 15 min plus rising time • **Cook time:** 35 min • **Yield:** 1 loaf (12 slices)

Ingredients	Directions
Nonstick cooking spray	**1** Preheat the oven to 200 degrees. When the oven reaches that temperature, turn it off. Spray a 4-x-8-inch baking pan with cooking spray.
¼ cup cornstarch	
¼ cup sorghum flour	
½ cup plus 2 tablespoons flour mixture (See Book V, Chapter 2)	**2** Place the cornstarch, sorghum flour, flour mixture, flaxseed meal, salt, cinnamon, sugar, and yeast in a medium mixing bowl. With a whisk, stir the ingredients to blend thoroughly.
1 tablespoon light flaxseed meal	
½ teaspoon salt	**3** With a rubber spatula, stir in the vinegar, honey, melted butter, egg, egg whites, and buttermilk.
¾ teaspoon cinnamon	
2½ tablespoons granulated sugar	**4** Stir in the warm water last.
¾ teaspoon active dry yeast	**5** Turn on the mixer and slowly increase the speed to high. Beat the batter for 3 minutes. (It will be more of a batter than a dough consistency.)
½ teaspoon cider vinegar	
1 tablespoon honey	**6** Spoon the batter into the prepared baking pan.
4 teaspoons melted butter, cooled	**7** Cover the pan with wax paper that has been sprayed with cooking spray. Place the pan in the oven to rise for 40 minutes.
1 egg, at room temperature	
2 egg whites, at room temperature	**8** Remove the pan from the oven and preheat the oven to 350 degrees. When the oven reaches that temperature, remove the wax paper from the bread.
2 tablespoons buttermilk, at room temperature	
¼ cup warm water (110 degrees)	**9** Bake the bread for 35 to 40 minutes, or until baked through.
	10 Let the bread set for 5 minutes. Then remove the bread from the pan and allow it to cool on a wire rack.

Per slice: Calories 93; Fat 2g (Saturated 1g); Cholesterol 21mg; Sodium 125mg; Carbohydrate 17g (Dietary Fiber 1g); Protein 2g.

Lemon Cranberry Cornmeal Scones

Prep time: 25 min • **Cook time:** 23 min • **Yield:** 12 scones

Ingredients	Directions
¾ cup whole milk plain yogurt	*1* Preheat the oven to 425 degrees. Line two cookie sheets with Silpat liners or parchment paper.
1 cup dried cranberries	
6 tablespoons unsalted butter, softened	*2* In a small bowl, combine the yogurt with the dried cranberries and set aside to plump for a few minutes.
½ cup sugar	
1 cup plus 3 tablespoons (177 grams) White Flour Mix (see Book V, Chapter 2)	*3* In a large mixing bowl, beat the butter until it's light and fluffy. Gradually add the sugar, beating on high, until the mixture is light and creamy, about 3 to 6 minutes.
½ cup plus 2 tablespoons minus 1 teaspoon (83 grams) Whole-Grain Flour Mix (see Book V, Chapter 2)	*4* Beat in the flour mixes, cornmeal, baking powder, salt, and lemon rind. The mixture will be dry and sandy.
1 cup (142 grams) yellow or white cornmeal	*5* Beat in the eggs and the lemon juice.
1 tablespoon baking powder	
½ teaspoon salt	*6* Add the yogurt and cranberries and beat for 1 minute, until a dough forms.
1 teaspoon grated lemon rind	
2 eggs	*7* Scoop out the batter with a ⅓-cup ice-cream scoop (Number 10) and place six on each prepared cookie sheet, leaving plenty of room to spread. Sprinkle with a bit of coarse sugar (if desired).
2 teaspoons lemon juice	
Coarse sugar for topping (optional)	*8* Place pans in the oven and lower the temperature to 350 degrees. Bake for 22 to 25 minutes, or until just barely browned. Move scones to a wire rack to cool. Serve warm.

Per serving: Calories 274 (From Fat 98); Fat 11g (Saturated 6g); Cholesterol 79mg; Sodium 316mg; Carbohydrate 43g (Dietary Fiber 1g); Protein 4g.

Vary It! If you prefer a different dried fruit, go ahead and use it. Dried blueberries or cherries are good choices; just be sure to rehydrate them in the yogurt before using.

Note: If you don't like the crunch of cornmeal, you can substitute the same weight of corn flour. But don't substitute cup for cup because corn flour weighs much more than cornmeal.

Chapter 2

Putting Together Appetizers and Snacks That Please

In This Chapter

▶ Pleasing crowds while you keep your diet on track

▶ Making easy-to-grab nibbles

▶ Trying out snazzy snacks and awesome apps

Appetizers, hors d'oeuvres, starters, antipasto, gustus, mezethes, tapas, maza, mezze, zakuski, dim sum, smorgasbord . . . an appetizer by any other name is still an appetizer.

It seems a little ironic that we *eat* to build an appetite, but that's the idea. Appetizers are small servings of foods served before a meal to whet the appetite, or they can be served alone to enable people to dawdle over small servings of different dishes. Serving appetizers stretches out a social gathering while guests circulate, talk, bond, and mingle. This chapter gives you several gluten-free appetizers you can serve before your next meal or gathering.

Choosing the Right Appetizers for the Occasion

Conjure up in your mind all those appetizers you've been offered at parties over the years. Celery sticks with plain cream cheese. Crackers with spray cheese. Chips and dip made from sour cream and onion soup mix. Herring in dill sauce. Aren't you tired of these things? Wouldn't you rather serve something with more character and spice? Something a bit more memorable?

Bland appetizers merely fill the belly, whereas appetizers with pizzazz actually assault the senses and get guests craving more.

Be creative in your food choice. Balance hot and cold dishes, rich and mild foods, and try to include at least one vegetarian offering. Assortment is the key. Pick foods that are party-friendly — people will most likely be walking around, so you don't want to serve foods that are too sticky, messy, or greasy. Better choices are items that people can pick up easily and eat with two fingers.

Here are a few ideas to get your creative juices flowing:

- ✔ Consider serving something where people can participate, like assembling their own mini-tacos on corn tortillas or in corn taco shells and adding their own toppings, fillings, or condiments.

- ✔ Rice papers (available at Asian markets), when soaked in water for 2 minutes, become very pliable and make the perfect wrapper for appetizers. You can use these wrappers to make mini-Reuben wraps with pastrami and Swiss cheese and a dab of gluten-free brown mustard (to be served hot or cold). Or spread the rice papers with cream cheese, and then top with gluten-free chunky salsa, shredded lettuce, crisp-cooked bacon, and some guacamole. Roll them up for one delicious appetizer.

- ✔ A great assemble-ahead appetizer is eggplant pizza. Brown slices of eggplant in your broiler, top with a small amount of gluten-free spaghetti sauce, sprinkle with Italian seasoning, and then top off with a slice of provolone cheese. Pop it in the microwave to melt the cheese, and it's ready to serve.

- ✔ In the summertime, make use of your grill. Early in the day, assemble mini-kebabs (shrimp, chicken, beef, veggies), or wrap mushrooms in bacon and brush them with gluten-free barbecue sauce. Let your friends grill their own appetizers.

To add some sanity to the day of the party, choose appetizers that you can make ahead and store in the refrigerator or freezer until it's time to serve them. If guests are coming for dinner, choose lighter appetizers so people don't fill up on them, but prepare enough so that your guests stay busy munching and meandering in the living room or family room (so they'll stay out of your kitchen and let you work at plating the dinner). Plan on about four appetizers per person. If you're offering two appetizers, that would average two of each selection per person. If you're only serving appetizers, then you'd better make a bit larger quantity of each. Figure on eight to nine pieces per guest.

If you're hosting a party, chances are that most of your guests aren't on a gluten-free diet. But hey, it's your party! Make gluten-free appetizers that everyone can enjoy!

Shrimp Deviled Eggs

Prep time: 10 min • **Cook time:** 11 min • **Yield:** 6 servings

Ingredients	Directions
3 eggs	**1** Place the eggs in a single layer in a medium saucepan with enough cold water to cover them. Add a teaspoon of salt to the pan to help prevent the eggshells from cracking. Bring the water to a boil over high heat. As soon as the water starts to boil, let the eggs cook for exactly 11 minutes, and then remove the pan from the heat. Set the pan in the sink and run cold water over the eggs to stop them from further cooking.
1 teaspoon plus dash of salt	
8 large cocktail shrimp, cooked and deveined	
2 tablespoons plus 1 teaspoon mayonnaise	
¼ teaspoon mustard	
¼ teaspoon dried dill	**2** Dice the shrimp and set them aside.
¼ teaspoon lemon juice	
⅛ teaspoon pepper	**3** Peel the eggs and cut them in half lengthwise. Carefully remove the yolks and place them in a medium bowl. Set the egg whites aside.
Paprika	
	4 Mash the yolks with the back of a fork. Add the mayonnaise, mustard, dill, lemon juice, pepper, and a dash of salt and stir until the mixture is smooth.
	5 Stir in the shrimp until it's evenly distributed.
	6 With a small spoon, refill the egg white halves, mounding the yolk mixture on top.
	7 Sprinkle the tops lightly with paprika, cover, and refrigerate until serving time.

Per serving: Calories 68; Fat 5g (Saturated 1g); Cholesterol 122mg; Sodium 116mg; Carbohydrate 2g (Dietary Fiber 0g); Protein 5g.

Feta Supreme Spread

Prep time: 5 min plus refrigeration time • **Yield:** 2 cups

Ingredients	Directions
8 ounces feta cheese	**1** With a fork, crumble the feta cheese in a medium bowl.
1½ tablespoons fresh lemon juice (1 lemon)	**2** Add the lemon juice, red wine vinegar, olive oil, oregano, garlic powder, cumin, and pepper and continue to blend with a fork until everything is mixed.
1 tablespoon red wine vinegar	
3 tablespoons olive oil	**3** Cover the bowl with plastic wrap and refrigerate the spread for several hours.
½ teaspoon dried oregano	
¼ teaspoon garlic powder	
⅛ teaspoon cumin	
¼ teaspoon pepper	

Per serving: Calories 121; Fat 11g (Saturated 5g); Cholesterol 25mg; Sodium 316mg; Carbohydrate 2g (Dietary Fiber 0g); Protein 4g.

Tip: Make this spread ahead so it has plenty of time for the flavors to blend.

Note: Slather this spread on gluten-free pita wedges or gluten-free crackers to make an easy appetizer. You can also use it as a sandwich spread or sprinkled over a Greek salad.

Spicy Corn Fritters

Prep time: 15 min • **Cook time:** 25 min • **Yield:** 4 servings

Ingredients	Directions
1 cup canned corn	*1* Put the corn, chilies, garlic, lime leaves, cilantro, eggs, polenta, and green beans into a large bowl; mix them thoroughly. Use your hands to form balls about the size of golf balls. Set them on a plate.
2 fresh red chilies, seeded and finely chopped	
1 teaspoon minced garlic (about 2 cloves)	*2* Heat the peanut oil in a wok, skillet, or deep fryer to a high heat. You'll know the oil is hot enough when you add a small drop of water into the oil and it pops. (Be careful, though. More than a drop, and it may pop and burn you.)
10 kaffir lime leaves, finely chopped (found in Thai section of Asian markets)	
3 tablespoons chopped fresh cilantro	*3* Turning the fritters occasionally, cook them in the oil until they're brown and crispy on the outside (about 7 minutes). Remove the fritters from the wok, skillet, or deep fryer with a slotted spoon, and let them drain on paper towels.
2 eggs, beaten	
½ cup premade polenta (about 4 ounces)	
¼ cup finely sliced green beans	
½ cup peanut oil (for frying)	

Per serving: Calories 294 (From Fat 149); Fat 17g (Saturated 3g); Cholesterol 106mg; Sodium 226mg; Carbohydrate 28g (Dietary Fiber 4g); Protein 7g.

Crabmeat Dip

Prep time: 10 min plus refrigeration time • **Yield:** 2 cups

Ingredients	Directions
4.5-ounce can crabmeat, drained and flaked (beware gluten-containing imitation crab)	*1* In a medium bowl, stir together all the ingredients, mixing well to blend thoroughly.
1 hard-boiled egg, shelled and minced	*2* Cover and chill the dip for at least 2 hours for flavors to blend.
¼ cup mayonnaise	
¼ cup sour cream	
1 teaspoon lemon juice	
½ teaspoon dry mustard	
¼ teaspoon dried dill	
1 green onion, minced	
¼ teaspoon Worcestershire sauce	
½ teaspoon dried parsley	
¼ teaspoon salt	
⅛ teaspoon pepper	

Per serving: *Calories 88; Fat 7g (Saturated 2g); Cholesterol 59mg; Sodium 284mg; Carbohydrate 3g (Dietary Fiber 0g); Protein 4g.*

Artichoke and Spinach Dip

Prep time: 10 min • **Cook time:** 25 min • **Yield:** 12 servings

Ingredients	Directions
8-ounce package cream cheese	**1** Preheat the oven to 350 degrees. Let the cream cheese warm to room temperature.
¼ cup mayonnaise	
½ teaspoon minced garlic (about 1 clove)	**2** In a large bowl, cream together the cream cheese, mayonnaise, garlic, basil, salt, and pepper. Setting aside a few teaspoons of each cheese to use as a topping, add the Parmesan, Romano, and mozzarella cheeses. Mix until everything is well blended.
1 teaspoon fresh basil	
Salt and pepper to taste	
½ cup shredded Parmesan cheese	**3** Add the artichoke hearts and spinach, and mix again.
½ cup grated Romano cheese	**4** Spray a 1-quart ovenproof serving dish with nonstick spray, pour in the dip, and top it with the cheese you set aside in Step 2.
¼ cup grated mozzarella cheese	
14-ounce jar artichoke hearts, drained and chopped	**5** Bake the dip for about 25 minutes or until the top begins to brown and the cheese melts.
½ cup spinach, drained and chopped	
Nonstick cooking spray	

Per serving: Calories 139 (From Fat 111); Fat 12g (Saturated 6g); Cholesterol 30mg; Sodium 292mg; Carbohydrate 3g (Dietary Fiber 0g); Protein 5g.

Note: Processed cheeses may contain gluten. Make sure that you're choosing gluten-free versions.

Guacamole

Prep time: 15 min • **Yield:** 6 servings

Ingredients	*Directions*
2 ripe avocados	*1* Peel the avocados, remove the flesh from the pits, and cube the avocado flesh. Save the pits.
1 small-to-medium ripe tomato, diced	
½ small red onion, chopped	*2* In a medium bowl, combine the avocado flesh, tomato, onion, jalapeño, lime juice, cilantro, Worcestershire sauce, and salt and pepper.
½ teaspoon finely cut jalapeño pepper	
4 tablespoons lime juice	*3* Mix all the ingredients well, keeping the guacamole lumpy. Place the avocado pit in the dip and remove the pit just before serving.
2 teaspoons chopped cilantro	
2 teaspoons Worcestershire sauce	
Salt and pepper to taste	

Per serving: Calories 104 (From Fat 76); Fat 8g (Saturated 2g); Cholesterol 0mg; Sodium 117mg; Carbohydrate 8g (Dietary Fiber 5g); Protein 2g.

Mango Salsa

Prep time: 20 min • **Yield:** 6 servings

Ingredients	Directions
1 ripe mango, peeled, pitted, and diced (about 1 cup)	*1* Combine the mango, onion, jalapeño, tomato, cilantro, lime juice, and salt and pepper in a bowl; mix them until well blended. Don't mix so hard that you mash the mango — the salsa should contain chunks.
½ medium red onion, finely chopped	
1 jalapeño pepper, minced	*2* Chill the salsa for an hour or more to blend all the flavors.
1 large tomato, diced	
¼ cup fresh cilantro, chopped	
4 tablespoons fresh lime juice	
Salt and pepper to taste	

Per serving: Calories 35 (From Fat 2); Fat 0g (Saturated 0g); Cholesterol 0mg; Sodium 101mg; Carbohydrate 9g (Dietary Fiber 1g); Protein 1g.

Tortilla Sticks

Prep time: 5 min • **Cook time:** 8 min • **Yield:** 20 pieces

Ingredients	Directions
2 (8-inch) rice flour tortillas	**1** Preheat the oven to 400 degrees. Spray a nonstick cookie sheet with nonstick spray.
2 tablespoons butter, melted	**2** Brush one side of each tortilla with the melted butter, then sprinkle with the cheese, garlic powder, and Italian seasoning. Press toppings into the tortillas so they will adhere.
3 tablespoons grated Parmesan cheese	
⅛ teaspoon garlic powder	**3** With a clean pair of scissors, cut each tortilla into 10 (¾-inch wide) strips. Place strips on the baking sheet.
¼ teaspoon Italian seasoning	**4** Bake for 8 minutes or until strips are light golden and crisp.

Per serving: Calories 26; Fat 2g (Saturated 0.8g); Cholesterol 4mg; Sodium 35mg; Carbohydrate 2g (Dietary Fiber 0g); Protein 1g.

Note: These sticks are perfect for snacking hot from the oven, but they're also the perfect accompaniment for soups or a pasta dinner.

Vary It! Tortilla sticks are also tasty when sprinkled with sesame seeds before baking.

Artichoke Squares

Prep time: 10 min • **Cook time:** 35 min • **Yield:** 16 pieces

Ingredients	Directions
3 tablespoons olive oil	*1* Preheat the oven to 325 degrees. Oil an 8-inch-square baking dish.
8 green onions, sliced thin	*2* Add the olive oil to a small skillet and sauté the onion and garlic over medium heat until they're soft. Let the mixture cool slightly.
½ teaspoon minced garlic	
4 eggs	*3* With a whisk, whip the eggs in a large bowl until they're frothy. Stir the mint, dill, and Worcestershire sauce into the eggs.
½ teaspoon dried mint	
1 teaspoon dried dill	
1 teaspoon Worcestershire sauce	*4* Stir in the artichokes, cheese, onions, and garlic.
15-ounce can artichoke quarters, drained and chopped	*5* Smooth the mixture into the prepared baking dish. Sprinkle the breadcrumbs over the top.
1 cup shredded Swiss cheese	*6* Bake for 35 minutes, or until the breadcrumbs are lightly browned.
3 tablespoons seasoned breadcrumbs	*7* Let the dish cool slightly before cutting.

Per serving: Calories 76; Fat 6g (Saturated 2g); Cholesterol 59mg; Sodium 64mg; Carbohydrate 3g (Dietary Fiber 1g); Protein 4g.

Tip: Don't buy marinated artichokes or this dish will be too bitter.

Note: You can assemble these squares ahead of time; they bake by themselves while you prepare for company, and you usually don't need forks to enjoy them.

Cajun Stuffed Mushrooms

Prep time: 15 min • **Cook time:** 35 min • **Yield:** 24 mushroom caps

Ingredients	Directions
Nonstick cooking spray	**1** Preheat the oven to 350 degrees. Line an 8-x-11-inch baking dish with foil; spray the foil with nonstick cooking spray.
24 large mushrooms	
½ pound spicy sausage	
1 cup chopped onion	**2** Clean the mushrooms, removing the stems. Set the caps aside. Chop the stems.
¼ cup minced green bell pepper	
½ teaspoon garlic powder	**3** In a large skillet, brown the sausage, onion, green bell pepper, and mushroom stems over medium heat, breaking the meat up with a fork. Stir in the garlic powder, Cajun seasoning, parsley, and cumin.
¾ teaspoon Cajun seasoning	
2 teaspoons dried parsley	
½ teaspoon cumin	**4** Pile the stuffing into the mushroom caps. Set the caps, stuffing side up, in the prepared baking dish.
1 cup mayonnaise	
¾ cup grated Parmesan cheese	**5** In a small bowl, stir together the mayonnaise and Parmesan cheese. Spoon the mixture on top of each mushroom cap.
	6 Bake the mushrooms for 35 minutes, or until the cheese is golden.

Per mushroom: *Calories 8; Fat 7g (Saturated 2g); Cholesterol 7mg; Sodium 143mg; Carbohydrate 1g (Dietary Fiber 0g); Protein 2g.*

Tip: If you thrive on five-alarm foods that virtually disintegrate your taste buds, then use gluten-free hot sausage and add more Cajun seasoning.

Spicy Buffalo Wings

Prep time: 5 min • **Cook time:** 10 min • **Yield:** 2 dozen wings

Ingredients	Directions
1½ cups gluten-free flour mixture (see Book V, Chapter 2) 2 teaspoons seasoned salt, divided 24 chicken wings Oil for frying ½ cup red wine vinegar ½ cup honey 2 tablespoons molasses 3 tablespoons ketchup 3 tablespoons Cholula or your favorite hot sauce	*1* Put the flour mixture and 1 teaspoon of the seasoned salt in a gallon-size plastic bag, and shake the bag to mix them. Add the wings (about five at a time) and shake the bag to coat them well. *2* Heat the oil over medium-high heat in a heavy skillet. Fry the wings in about 2 inches of hot oil for approximately 5 minutes, until they're crispy on the outside. Break open a wing and make sure the meat inside isn't pink. Cook the wings longer if the meat is still pink. Drain the wings on paper towels. *3* Prepare the sauce by mixing the remaining teaspoon of seasoned salt, red wine vinegar, honey, molasses, ketchup, and hot sauce in a medium bowl. *4* Dip the cooked wings in the mixture to coat them with the sauce.

Per serving: *Calories 176 (From Fat 102); Fat 11g (Saturated 2g); Cholesterol 29mg; Sodium 178mg; Carbohydrate 9g (Dietary Fiber 0g); Protein 9g.*

Tip: For an easier recipe, use commercial wing or hot sauces. Simply coat and cook the wings as indicated in Steps 1 and 2, and then coat the wings with sauce as indicated in Step 4.

Almond Hummus

Prep time: 10 min plus refrigeration time • **Yield:** 1½ cups

Ingredients	Directions
Nonstick cooking spray	*1* Over medium heat, sauté the almonds in a small skillet that has been sprayed with cooking spray. Stir frequently until the almonds are browned.
¼ cup blanched slivered almonds	
15-ounce can garbanzo beans, rinsed and drained	*2* Place the almonds into a blender and puree until smooth. Then add the remaining ingredients, pureeing until smooth. You may need to scrape down the sides of the blender during this process. Depending on your personal taste, you may want to add more lemon juice.
2 tablespoons olive oil	
½ teaspoon dried dill	
1 teaspoon cumin	*3* Spoon the mixture into a serving bowl. Cover and refrigerate the hummus for several hours to allow the flavors to blend.
2 tablespoons fresh chopped parsley	
¼ teaspoon salt	
¼ teaspoon pepper	
3 tablespoons fresh lemon juice	
¼ teaspoon chicken bouillon granules	
¼ cup water	

Per serving: *Calories 149; Fat 9g (Saturated 1g); Cholesterol 0mg; Sodium 186mg; Carbohydrate 14g (Dietary Fiber 3g); Protein 6g.*

Note: Spread this hummus on gluten-free crackers, on flatbread, or even on a sandwich topped with roasted red peppers, chopped kalamata olives, and crumbled feta cheese.

Trail Mix Bars

Prep time: 10 min • **Cook time:** 10 min • **Yield:** 24 servings

Ingredients	Directions
½ cup sesame seeds	**1** In a small, dry skillet, heat the sesame seeds over medium heat, stirring often, until they're lightly browned. Place the browned seeds in a medium bowl. Repeat with the sunflower seeds, then the coconut, and then the almonds.
½ cup sunflower seeds	
½ cup coconut	
½ cup slivered almonds	
½ cup raisins	**2** Stir the raisins and cinnamon into the seed mixture.
½ teaspoon cinnamon	
2½ tablespoons butter	**3** In a small saucepan, warm the butter, honey, and brown sugar over medium heat to soft-ball stage, or 238 degrees on a candy thermometer. At this temperature, a small amount of this syrup dropped into cold water will form a soft, flexible ball. If you remove the ball from the water, it will flatten like a pancake after a few moments in your hand.
2 tablespoons honey	
2 tablespoons brown sugar	
Nonstick cooking spray	
	4 Pour the syrup over the seed mixture. Using a rubber spatula, blend the ingredients well to coat evenly.
	5 Press the mix into a 9-inch-square pan that has been sprayed with cooking spray and let it cool slightly.
	6 Cut the trail mixture into 24 pieces before the bars have completely cooled. Store the bars in an airtight container.

Per serving: Calories 91; Fat 6g (Saturated 2g); Cholesterol 3mg; Sodium 16mg; Carbohydrate 8g (Dietary Fiber 1g); Protein 2g.

Vary It! In place of the raisins (or in addition to the raisins), you can use dried cranberries, cut-up dates, or dried apricots.

Nutty Granola Pie

Prep time: 5 min • **Cook time:** Less than 1 min • **Yield:** 8 servings

Ingredients	*Directions*
1 cup oats	*1* Spray a 9-inch pie plate with cooking spray.
1 cup crisp rice cereal	
½ cup pecans	*2* Mix the oats, rice cereal, pecans, and raisins in the prepared pie plate. Pour honey over the mixture and stir until it's well coated. Press the mixture firmly into the pie plate.
¼ cup raisins	
½ cup honey	
¼ cup nut butter	
	3 Heat the nut butter in the microwave on high until it's runny, about 30 seconds. Drizzle the heated nut butter over the mixture.
	4 Refrigerate the pie until it's cool. Then cut it into 8 wedges.
	5 Store leftovers (as if!) covered in the refrigerator.

Per serving: Calories 241 (From Fat 87); Fat 10g (Saturated 1g); Cholesterol 0mg; Sodium 72mg; Carbohydrate 38g (Dietary Fiber 3g); Protein 5g.

Tip: To press a sticky mixture easily into a pan, place your hand in a small plastic bag (glove-like) and spray the bag with cooking spray. You can now press mess-free. Or if you don't have a bag, just coat your fingers with cooking spray so the mixture doesn't stick to you while pressing.

Note: Check the rice cereal for gluten-free status.

Sweet and Salty Trail Mix

Prep time: 5 min • **Yield:** 8 servings (½ cup each)

Ingredients	Directions
2 cups roasted, salted whole almonds **1 cup dried apples** **½ cup yogurt-covered raisins** **½ cup golden raisins** **½ cup dried cranberries**	*1* Combine the almonds, apples, yogurt-covered raisins, golden raisins, and cranberries in an airtight container. Shake to mix.

Per serving: Calories 336 (From Fat 177); Fat 20g (Saturated 3g); Cholesterol 0mg; Sodium 134mg; Carbohydrate 36g (Dietary Fiber 6g); Protein 9g.

Note: Store this mix in an airtight container until it's gone.

Cinnamon-Glazed Pecans

Prep time: 5 min • **Cook time:** 1 hr • **Yield:** 8 servings (¼ cup each)

Ingredients	*Directions*
1 egg white, at room temperature	*1* Preheat the oven to 200 degrees. Line a baking pan with parchment paper or aluminum foil.
8 ounces pecan halves	*2* In a deep bowl, beat the egg white with an electric hand mixer on high until the egg white is stiff. The egg should turn foamy and white and hold its shape when you lift out the beater.
2 tablespoons cinnamon	
½ cup white sugar	
	3 Carefully stir the pecans into the egg white. Stir together the cinnamon and sugar and add the mixture to the pecans, stirring until the nuts are evenly coated.
	4 Pour the mixture in the prepared baking pan. Bake the mixture for about 1 hour, stirring every 15 minutes, until the coating is hardened on pecans.
	5 Let the pecans cool. Store them in an airtight container with a lid.

Per serving: Calories 251 (From Fat 184); Fat 21g (Saturated 2g); Cholesterol 0mg; Sodium 7mg; Carbohydrate 18g (Dietary Fiber 4g); Protein 3g.

Tip: To separate egg white from yolk, crack the egg gently and use the two halves of the shell to hold in the yolk while the white runs into a bowl. Discard the yolk or use it in another recipe. Take care to fully separate the white from the yolk — the white won't whip up like it needs to if there's yolk in the mixture.

Tip: Whipping egg whites is most effective with room-temperature egg whites. Leave your egg out of the fridge for at least 15 minutes for best results.

Tip: If you cover the pan in parchment before pouring on the glazed pecans, the food won't stick during baking and you won't even have to wash the pan afterward!

Spicy Almonds

Prep time: 15 min • **Cook time:** 15 min • **Yield:** 3 cups

Ingredients	Directions
¼ cup butter	**1** Preheat the oven to 350 degrees.
2 tablespoons Worcestershire sauce	**2** Melt the butter in a medium saucepan.
2 tablespoons soy sauce	**3** Remove the pan from the heat and stir in the Worcestershire sauce, soy sauce, cumin, salt, garlic powder, pepper, and sugar.
1 teaspoon cumin	
1 teaspoon coarse salt	
1 teaspoon garlic powder	**4** Add the almonds and stir until they are evenly coated.
½ teaspoon cayenne pepper	
½ teaspoon sugar	**5** Transfer the mixture to a shallow baking sheet.
3 cups whole almonds	**6** Bake the almonds at 350 degrees for 15 minutes, stirring once halfway through baking.
	7 Let the almonds cool thoroughly before storing in an airtight container.

Per serving: Calories 247; Fat 22g (Saturated 4g); Cholesterol 10mg; Sodium 417mg; Carbohydrate 8g (Dietary Fiber 4g); Protein 8g.

Tip: For added decadence, sprinkle the hot almonds with ½ teaspoon of coarse salt as soon as they come out of the oven. They should keep for up to 3 weeks in an airtight container.

Honey Cinnamon Grahams

Prep time: 10 min • **Cook time:** 9–11 min • **Yield:** 24 crackers

Ingredients	Directions
¾ cup gluten-free flour mixture (see Book V, Chapter 2)	**1** Preheat the oven to 325 degrees.
¼ cup coconut flour	**2** In a medium bowl, whisk together the flour mixture, coconut flour, salt, cinnamon, and baking powder.
½ teaspoon salt	
½ teaspoon cinnamon	**3** In a large mixing bowl, use the mixer to whip together the butter, honey, sugar, vanilla, and milk.
1 teaspoon baking powder	
¼ cup butter, softened	**4** Slowly add the dry ingredients to the butter mixture. Mix on medium speed until blended. (You may have to add a few more drops of milk if the dough won't hold together. The dough should be pliable.)
2 tablespoons honey	
⅓ cup brown sugar	
1 teaspoon vanilla	**5** Lightly spray 2 baking sheets with the cooking spray.
1 tablespoon milk	
Nonstick cooking spray	**6** On a sheet of plastic wrap, roll out the dough with a rolling pin to ¼-inch thick. Cut the dough into 2-inch squares and place the crackers on the prepared baking sheets.
1 teaspoon cinnamon sugar	
	7 Prick the top of each cracker several times with the tines of a fork.
	8 Sprinkle the tops with cinnamon sugar.
	9 Bake the crackers for 9 to 11 minutes until the edges are barely beginning to brown. Remove the crackers to a wire rack to cool. Store in an airtight container.

Per serving: Calories 69; Fat 2g (Saturated 1g); Cholesterol 5mg; Sodium 85mg; Carbohydrate 14g (Dietary Fiber 1g); Protein 0g.

Tip: Watch the crackers closely in the oven. You want to bake them until the edges are just beginning to show signs of browning. Overbaking causes these crackers to get too hard.

Note: If you keep your coconut flour in the freezer, it may pack together. Take it out of the freezer the night before you plan to use it.

Perky Popcorn

Prep time: 20 min • **Cook time:** 35 min • **Yield:** 10 cups

Ingredients	*Directions*
2½ quarts (10 cups) popped popcorn	*1* Preheat the oven to 250 degrees.
¾ cup pecan pieces	*2* Combine the popcorn and pecans in a large roasting pan that has been sprayed with cooking spray.
Nonstick cooking spray	
1 cup brown sugar	*3* In a medium saucepan, stir together the brown sugar, water, butter, salt, and corn syrup.
½ cup water	
¼ cup butter	*4* Cook the syrup over medium heat, stirring occasionally with a wooden spoon, until the mixture comes to a full boil.
¼ teaspoon salt	
¼ cup light corn syrup (or other liquid sweetener, such as agave, honey, or brown rice syrup)	*5* Insert a candy thermometer into the pan, making sure the bulb at the bottom doesn't touch the bottom of the saucepan.
¼ teaspoon baking soda	*6* Continue cooking the syrup until it reaches 238 degrees, soft-ball stage. (This will take 3 to 5 minutes.)
	7 Remove the pan from the heat. Stir in the baking soda. The mixture will thicken immediately.
	8 Pour the mixture over the popcorn and pecans, stirring until all the popcorn is coated.
	9 Bake the popcorn for 35 minutes, stirring every 10 minutes.

10 Remove the popcorn from the roasting pan and spread it out on wax paper to cool completely.

11 When the popcorn is cool, break it into pieces and store it in a tightly covered container.

Per serving: Calories 235; Fat 11g (Saturated 4g); Cholesterol 12mg; Sodium 137mg; Carbohydrate 35g (Dietary Fiber 2g); Protein 2g.

Cheesy Crisps

Prep time: 7 min • **Cook time:** 30 min • **Yield:** 36 crackers

Ingredients	Directions
Nonstick cooking spray	*1* Preheat the oven to 325 degrees. Spray a baking sheet with cooking spray.
1½ cups spiced flax crackers	
1½ cups shredded sharp cheddar cheese	*2* Place the crackers in a food processor and grind them to a fine meal.
¼ cup water	*3* Add the cheese and water. Continue to process until the ingredients are well blended and a dough is formed.
	4 Remove the dough and form it into a ball.
	5 Place the dough between two sheets of plastic wrap and roll it out to ¼-inch thickness.
	6 Transfer the dough to the prepared baking sheet.
	7 Using a knife or pastry wheel, cut the dough into small squares or diamonds; don't separate or spread the pieces apart.
	8 Bake the dough for 30 minutes, or until the crackers are crisp and the edges are just beginning to brown.
	9 Remove the crackers from the oven and let them set for 3 minutes. Then break or cut the crackers along the lines and remove them to a cooling rack.

Per cracker: Calories 24; Fat 2g (Saturated 1g); Cholesterol 5mg; Sodium 37mg; Carbohydrate 0g (Dietary Fiber 0g); Protein 1g.

Tip: To measure the 1½ cups of crackers, break the whole crackers into bits and squish them into a measuring cup.

Note: The crackers used in this recipe were Foods Alive Mexican Harvest Flax Crackers.

Note: Shredded cheese may contain gluten. Make sure you're choosing a gluten-free option.

Chapter 3

Sensational Salads

Most people know that plain green salads are gluten-free — and, of course, you can have steamed or boiled vegetables — but even hard-core veggie fans get tired of those things pretty quickly. In this section, you find ways to dress up delicious and nutritious veggie salads and make fast salad meals a snap.

But another kind of salad falls somewhere between a salad and a side. This is the kind without any lettucelike substances at all; instead, it features potatoes, pasta, rice, and other alternative salad makin's. Potato salad, for instance: Is it a side or a salad? You think about that while checking out some ways to snazz up your salads — sides — whatever.

Serving Salads with Green, Leafy Stuff

Veggie salads are a great way to combine interesting grains, fruits, vegetables, and meats in one dish. As a side or a complete meal, salads are nutritious and delicious, and they're especially great on a hot, summer day, when they make for a cool, quick dinner (without making you resort to cereal and milk).

Most of these salads start with a basic bed of greens or a variety of lettuce types. Prewashed bagged greens make these salads even simpler, but of course you can use any type of lettuce you want. Remember that the darker the lettuce, the more nutritious it probably is.

From there, the options are endless. Here are a few favorites:

- **Caesar Salad:** Start with romaine lettuce and add Caesar dressing. You can buy it or use the easy recipe in this chapter. Remember to add freshly grated Parmesan cheese.

- **Cool as a Cucumber Salad:** In a medium-sized bowl, mix finely chopped cucumber (peeled and seeded) with plain yogurt, onion powder, lemon juice, and black pepper. Put it over a bed of greens and top it with diced tomatoes.

- **Grilled Garlic Chicken Salad:** In a small bowl, mix ¾ cup Italian salad dressing with 2 teaspoons minced garlic and a dash of crushed red pepper flakes. Add sliced red bell pepper and sliced mushrooms to the dressing, and toss them so they're well coated. Fish the peppers and mushrooms out of the dressing, setting aside the remaining dressing, and grill the peppers and mushrooms as you grill your chicken. Place salad greens on plates and add the grilled vegetables and chicken. Drizzle the remaining dressing on top.

- **Thai Beef Salad:** Start with a bed of greens and add ¼ cup mint leaves (torn into large pieces), half a cucumber (peeled and sliced), several thinly sliced pieces of grilled flank steak, 2 tablespoons chopped peanuts, and lime wedges (for garnish). Top the salad with an Asian salad dressing, like the one in this chapter.

- **Tomato and Basil Salad:** Over a bed of greens, add sliced beefsteak tomatoes topped with torn pieces of a large, fresh basil leaf. If you'd like, add a slice of mozzarella. Then drizzle the salad with a balsamic vinaigrette dressing.

- **Warm Beet Salad:** In a large saucepan, cook some green beans in boiling water until they're tender, about 8 minutes. Add a 16-ounce can of sliced beets (drained), and cook them over medium heat until they're heated through. Drain the beans and the beets. Meanwhile, in a screw-top glass jar, combine about 3 tablespoons orange juice, 3 tablespoons extra-virgin olive oil, 1 tablespoon balsamic vinegar, 2 teaspoons minced garlic, and a dash of white pepper. Shake the dressing well. Lay out some mixed greens, place the beans and beets on top of them, and coat the veggies with the dressing.

Dressing it up with dressings

Lots of commercially available salad dressings are gluten-free. People used to think that most salad dressings were off-limits for those on a gluten-free diet, but that was because they thought vinegar wasn't allowed. Now that they know vinegar (with the exception of malt vinegar) is okay, store shelves are loaded with options. (Although you do still need to be vigilant — not all dressings are gluten-free.) But if you'd prefer to make your own dressings — because you like to, because doing so saves money, or because the dressing has more wholesome ingredients that way — the recipes in this section should get you started in the right direction.

No time for recipes? You can toss together these quick and easy dressings for your salads:

- ✔ **Roasted Red Pepper Vinaigrette:** Mix chopped roasted red pepper with white wine vinegar, minced garlic, chopped flat-leaf parsley, extra-virgin olive oil, and salt and pepper.

- ✔ **Garbanzo Vinaigrette:** Mix coarsely mashed garbanzo beans (chickpeas) with sherry vinegar, minced shallots, chopped chives and parsley, extra-virgin olive oil, and salt and pepper.

- ✔ **Lemon Parmesan Dressing:** Mix fresh lemon juice and freshly grated Parmesan cheese with mayonnaise, minced garlic, extra-virgin olive oil, and salt and pepper.

- ✔ **Pesto Vinaigrette:** Mix pesto sauce with white wine vinegar, extra-virgin olive oil, and salt and pepper.

Book III

Gluten-Free Starts for Meals . . . or Days

Finishing off your salad with some fixin's

Toss it in to mix it up. You can add lots of goodies to your salad to perk it up and provide more nutrition at the same time:

- ✔ **Beans and legumes:** Try green beans, kidney beans, black beans, or garbanzo beans (chickpeas). Not only do they add flavor, but they add lots of fiber, too.

- ✔ **Bok choy:** Oh, boy — bok choy (Chinese white cabbage) is loaded with nutrients, and new shredded varieties are great on salads.

- ✔ **Cherry tomatoes:** Several varieties of cherry tomatoes are available, and they come in all different colors and shapes.

- ✔ **Crumbled bacon:** Of course, bacon adds some fat, but it also adds flavor.

✔ **Crumbled cheese:** Be creative, using cheeses like *queso seco* (Mexican dry cheese), *queso fresco* (fresh Mexican cheese), or freshly grated Romano or Parmesan.

✔ **Diced ham or turkey:** A little less fatty than bacon, these meats add protein and flavor to a salad — but be careful, because some of them contain gluten.

✔ **Fruit:** Grapes, pineapple, melons, kiwi — a variety of fruits can liven up a salad.

✔ **Greens:** Iceberg lettuce is boring and relatively worthless, nutritionally speaking. Consider radicchio, romaine, kale, spinach, arugula, and other greens to increase the vitamin, mineral, and fiber content — not to mention flavor.

✔ **Jicama:** Somewhere between an apple and a potato, jicama (pronounced *hee*-cuh-muh) adds crunch, flavor, and lots of fiber.

✔ **Mushrooms:** Buy them sliced to make preparing salads easier on yourself. They add lots of minerals and an interesting flavor.

✔ **Nuts:** Any kind of nut will do. They add nutrients, crunch, and flavor.

✔ **Olives:** If you use chopped olives, you can spread them around the salad and get just as much flavor without as many calories.

✔ **Onions:** Red onions and scallions are two of the most popular varieties to put on salads. Onions and other white vegetables add nutrients, too.

✔ **Radishes:** Not only do these add a zip to your salad, but they have potassium and vitamin C.

✔ **Raisins:** Also try similar toppings, like dried cranberries.

✔ **Raw broccoli:** New packaged broccoli slaws make adding flavor and crunch easy. Broccoli is loaded with cancer-fighting nutrients and calcium.

✔ **Shredded cabbage:** In the same family as broccoli, cabbage contains nutrients that are important for cancer prevention.

✔ **Sprouts:** Loaded with fiber and nutrients, sprouts are a great addition to any salad. And they're easy to grow yourself.

Asian Salad Dressing

Prep time: 5 min • **Yield:** 8 servings

Ingredients	Directions
½ cup rice vinegar	*1* Combine the vinegar, soy sauce, water, sesame oil, and sesame seeds in a jar with a tight-fitting lid, and shake the mixture well.
¼ cup soy sauce	
2 tablespoons water	
1 teaspoon sesame oil	*2* Add the canola oil and shake again.
1 teaspoon toasted sesame seeds	
⅓ cup canola oil	

Per serving: Calories 94 (From Fat 90); Fat 10g (Saturated 1g); Cholesterol 0mg; Sodium 460mg; Carbohydrate 0g (Dietary Fiber 0g); Protein 1g.

Caesar Salad Dressing

Prep time: 5 min • **Yield:** 8 servings

Ingredients	Directions
1 egg	*1* Place the egg in a microwaveable dish and cover it with a paper towel. Heat the egg in the microwave on high for 10 seconds.
½ cup lemon juice	
½ cup extra-virgin olive oil	
2 teaspoons minced garlic (about 4 cloves)	*2* Combine the egg, lemon juice, olive oil, garlic, Worcestershire sauce, Parmesan, anchovies, and pepper in a blender or small food processor, and process the dressing until smooth. If it's too runny, add a little Parmesan cheese. If it's too thick, add a little more lemon juice or olive oil.
2 tablespoons Worcestershire sauce	
¾ cup fresh Parmesan cheese	
2-ounce can anchovies	
1 teaspoon freshly grated pepper	

Per serving: Calories 186 (From Fat 154); Fat 17g (Saturated 4g); Cholesterol 39mg; Sodium 450mg; Carbohydrate 3g (Dietary Fiber 0g); Protein 6g.

Creamy Green Anchovy Salad Dressing

Prep time: 5 min • **Yield:** 8 servings

Ingredients	Directions
2 cups mayonnaise	*1* Mix the mayonnaise, anchovies, green onion, parsley, chives, rice vinegar, tarragon, and lemon juice in a blender or food processor.
5 anchovy fillets, minced	
1 chopped green onion	
2 teaspoons fresh parsley	*2* Process the mixture until the dressing is smooth. Refrigerate it until you're ready to serve.
2 teaspoons chopped fresh chives	
1 tablespoon rice vinegar	
2 teaspoons chopped fresh tarragon	
2 teaspoons lemon juice	

Per serving: *Calories 402 (From Fat 397); Fat 44g (Saturated 7g); Cholesterol 35mg; Sodium 406mg; Carbohydrate 2g (Dietary Fiber 0g); Protein 1g.*

Quinoa Crunch

Prep time: 15 min • **Yield:** 6 servings

Ingredients	Directions
¼ cup lime juice	**1** Make a vinaigrette by whisking together the lime juice, white pepper, black pepper, jalapeño, coarse salt, and olive oil. Set aside the mixture.
¼ teaspoon white pepper	
¼ teaspoon freshly ground black pepper	
¼ cup sliced marinated jalapeño pepper	**2** Place the quinoa in a fine sieve and wash it under running water, rubbing it with your hands for a few minutes. Drain the water.
¼ teaspoon coarse salt	
¼ cup olive oil	**3** In a large pot, combine the water and quinoa. Bring the mixture to a boil, lower the heat, and simmer it uncovered for about 10 to 15 minutes, or until the quinoa is barely tender. Don't overcook it. Strain the quinoa, drain it thoroughly, and let it cool. Don't rinse it.
3 cups water	
1½ cups quinoa	
¾ cup peeled, seeded, and diced cucumber	
¾ cup seeded and diced tomato	**4** Mix the quinoa in with the cucumber, tomato, red bell pepper, yellow bell pepper, green onions, parsley, mint, and vinaigrette. Add a little salt and pepper to taste (you don't need much, because this dish has plenty of flavor). Serve it at room temperature or cold.
¾ cup sliced red bell pepper	
¼ cup sliced yellow bell pepper	
¼ cup sliced green onions, white part only	
¼ cup chopped fresh Italian parsley	
¼ cup chopped fresh mint	
Salt and pepper to taste	

Per serving: Calories 260 (From Fat 105); Fat 12g (Saturated 2g); Cholesterol 0mg; Sodium 240mg; Carbohydrate 34g (Dietary Fiber 4g); Protein 7g.

Breezy Caprese Salad

Prep time: 5 min • **Yield:** 2 servings

Ingredients	Directions
1 large tomato	*1* Slice the tomato and the mozzarella into ¼-inch thick slices.
4 ounces fresh mozzarella cheese	
5 to 7 baby spinach leaves	*2* Alternate the tomato, cheese, and spinach leaves on a plate, stacking them and overlapping them slightly.
1 tablespoon olive oil	
4 teaspoons balsamic vinegar	*3* Drizzle the arranged cheese and veggies with oil, balsamic vinegar, salt, and pepper.
Salt to taste	
Black pepper to taste	

Per serving: Calories 249 (From Fat 191); Fat 21g (Saturated 9g); Cholesterol 41mg; Sodium 191mg; Carbohydrate 6g (Dietary Fiber 1g); Protein 11g.

Tip: Get the freshest ingredients possible for the best flavor in this dish. It's a great salad to enjoy after a trip to a farmers' market.

Vary It! Use fresh basil leaves instead of spinach if you prefer a more powerful flavor.

Rice Salad with Red Peppers, Garbanzo Beans, and Feta

Prep time: 15 min • **Resting time:** 1 hr • **Yield:** 6 servings

Ingredients	Directions
½ cup lemon juice	*1* Make the dressing by whisking together the lemon juice, garlic, olive oil, and salt and pepper.
2 teaspoons minced garlic (about 4 cloves)	
¼ cup extra-virgin olive oil	*2* In a large serving bowl, combine the rice, garbanzo beans, feta cheese, parsley, dill, green onions, and red bell peppers.
Salt and pepper to taste	
3 cups cooked rice, cooled to room temperature	
15-ounce can garbanzo beans (chickpeas), drained	*3* Pour the dressing over the rice mixture and mix well. Let it sit at least an hour before serving. Serve at room temperature or cold.
1 cup finely diced feta cheese	
½ cup chopped fresh parsley	
¼ cup chopped fresh dill	
4 green onions, washed, ends removed, thinly sliced	
½ cup roasted red bell peppers	

Per serving: Calories 308 (From Fat 137); Fat 15g (Saturated 5g); Cholesterol 22mg; Sodium 561mg; Carbohydrate 35g (Dietary Fiber 3g); Protein 8g.

Sweet-Potato Potato Salad

Prep time: 15 min • **Cook time:** 20 min • **Chill time:** 2 hr • **Yield:** 6 servings

Ingredients	*Directions*
2 pounds sweet potatoes, peeled and cooked	**1** Peel and dice the sweet potatoes. Steam them for 20 minutes, or until they're tender but not mushy.
3 tablespoons canned chopped green chilies	**2** In a large serving bowl, mix the sweet potatoes, green chilies, red bell pepper, cilantro, paprika, and mayonnaise. Chill the potato salad for at least 2 hours; serve it cold.
½ cup chopped red bell pepper	
2 tablespoons chopped cilantro	
Dash paprika	
⅓ cup mayonnaise	

Per serving: Calories 216 (From Fat 90); Fat 10g (Saturated 2g); Cholesterol 7mg; Sodium 112mg; Carbohydrate 30g (Dietary Fiber 3g); Protein 2g.

Greek Veggie Salad

Prep time: 5 min • **Chill time:** 30 min • **Yield:** 2 servings

Ingredients	Directions
1 large tomato, diced	**1** Mix the tomato, cucumber, onion, olives, cheese, oil, lemon juice, oregano, salt, and pepper in a serving bowl.
1 large cucumber, diced	
¼ of a red onion, diced	
8 Kalamata olives, sliced in half and pitted	**2** Refrigerate for at least 30 minutes and serve the salad chilled.
¼ cup crumbled feta cheese	
2 tablespoons olive oil	
1 teaspoon lemon juice	
½ teaspoon oregano	
Salt to taste	
Black pepper to taste	

Per serving: Calories 254 (From Fat 198); Fat 22g (Saturated 5g); Cholesterol 17mg; Sodium 611mg; Carbohydrate 12g (Dietary Fiber 3g); Protein 5g.

Tip: Enjoy this Greek treat as a side salad or top it with some chopped grilled chicken to make it a complete meal!

Marinated Artichoke Salad

Prep time: 5 min plus refrigeration time • **Yield:** 6 servings

Ingredients	*Directions*
7.5-ounce jar marinated artichokes, reserve juice	*1* Combine the artichokes, mushrooms, tomato, and broccoli in a large bowl.
8-ounce jar marinated button mushrooms, reserve juice	*2* In a small bowl, whisk together the juices from the artichokes and mushrooms, the salt, pepper, dill, oregano, mint, and oil. Pour the dressing over the vegetables and toss to coat evenly.
1 large tomato, cut into chunks	
3 cups broccoli florets	
¼ teaspoon salt	*3* Cover and refrigerate the salad for several hours to allow the flavors to blend.
¼ teaspoon pepper	
¼ teaspoon dried dill	
¼ teaspoon dried oregano	
⅛ teaspoon dried mint	
3 tablespoons olive oil	

Per serving: Calories 95; Fat 7g (Saturated 1g); Cholesterol 0mg; Sodium 265mg; Carbohydrate 7g (Dietary Fiber 3g); Protein 3g.

Note: Marinated salads need "bonding" time in the refrigerator to meld all the flavors together.

Minestrone Salad

Prep time: 15 min • **Cook time:** 8 min plus refrigeration time • **Yield:** 8 servings

Ingredients	*Directions*
½ cup rice pasta shells	*1* In a medium saucepan, boil the pasta according to the package directions; drain.
3 tablespoons olive oil	
2 tablespoons cider vinegar	*2* In a large bowl, whisk together the oil, vinegars, parsley, oregano, basil, mint, salt, pepper, and sugar. Add the pasta and the kidney beans, carrot, zucchini, green bell pepper, onion, and pepperoni. Toss well to coat the pasta and veggies evenly with the dressing.
1 tablespoon balsamic vinegar	
1 tablespoon dried parsley	
¾ teaspoon dried oregano	
½ teaspoon dried basil	*3* Cover the salad and refrigerate it for several hours to allow the flavors to blend.
½ teaspoon dried mint	
¼ teaspoon salt	
¼ teaspoon pepper	
½ teaspoon sugar	
15.5-ounce can light red kidney beans, rinsed and drained	
1 carrot, sliced thin	
1 medium zucchini, sliced thin	
½ green bell pepper, chopped	
1 medium yellow onion, sliced thin	
⅛ pound pepperoni, slices halved	

Per serving: Calories 149; Fat 8g (Saturated 2g); Cholesterol 8mg; Sodium 318mg; Carbohydrate 15g (Dietary Fiber 4g); Protein 4g.

Tip: Don't rinse the pasta if you want the dressing to stick to it.

Note: This tasty salad should be made ahead and then refrigerated to allow the flavors to blend.

Luscious Lentil Salad

Prep time: 10 min • **Cook time:** 15 min plus refrigeration time • **Yield:** 4 servings

Ingredients	Directions
⅓ **pound lentils**	*1* Place the lentils in a small saucepan and cover with water. Bring the water to a rolling boil, and boil about 15 minutes, or until the lentils are tender but not mushy. Rinse the lentils under cold water, and then drain.
3 tablespoons olive oil	
2 tablespoons balsamic vinegar	
¼ **teaspoon salt**	
⅛ **teaspoon pepper**	*2* Place the lentils in a medium bowl. Add the oil, vinegar, salt, pepper, dill, mint, oregano, onion, green bell pepper, celery, carrot, and parsley to the bowl. Stir the lentils well to coat them evenly.
¼ **teaspoon dried dill**	
⅛ **teaspoon dried mint**	
¼ **teaspoon dried oregano**	
1 small onion, chopped	*3* Cover the salad and refrigerate it for 2 hours to allow the flavors to blend.
¼ **green bell pepper, chopped**	
1 rib celery, sliced thin	
½ **carrot, sliced thin**	
1 tablespoon chopped fresh parsley	

Per serving: Calories 168; Fat 10g (Saturated 1g); Cholesterol 0mg; Sodium 163mg; Carbohydrate 15g (Dietary Fiber 5g); Protein 5g.

Potato Salad Niçoise

Prep time: 35 min • **Cook time:** 15 min plus refrigeration time • **Yield:** 4 servings

Ingredients	*Directions*
16 small white gourmet potatoes or small red-skinned potatoes	*1* Place potatoes in a medium saucepan. Cover with water and bring to a boil. Boil for 20 minutes or until potatoes are just fork tender. Rinse in cold water to cool them down. When cool, slide off the skins and discard skins.
4 eggs	
2 cups frozen, cut green beans	
2 green onions, sliced thin	*2* Place eggs in a small saucepan. Cover with water and bring to a boil. Boil for 11 minutes and then remove eggs to a colander and rinse well with cold water. When cool enough to handle, peel eggs, discarding shells. Quarter eggs and set aside.
4 Roma tomatoes, sliced	
12 pitted black olives	
1 teaspoon brown mustard	
¼ teaspoon garlic powder	*3* Place the green beans in a medium saucepan and cover with water. Bring to a boil and cook until they're fork tender; rinse the green beans in cold water and then drain them and place in a large bowl.
¼ teaspoon salt	
¼ teaspoon pepper	
2 teaspoons dried parsley	*4* Quarter the potatoes and add them to the green beans. Add the green onions, tomatoes, and olives to the bowl.
½ teaspoon Italian seasoning	
2 tablespoons cider vinegar	
¼ cup olive oil	*5* In a small bowl, whisk together the mustard, garlic powder, salt, pepper, parsley, Italian seasoning, vinegar, and oil; pour the dressing over the potato mixture and gently blend to distribute the dressing evenly. Cover the potato salad and refrigerate it for 2 hours.
Gluten-Free Croutons (see the following recipe)	
	6 Just before serving, toss in the Gluten-Free Croutons (see the following recipe) and garnish with the egg wedges.

Gluten-Free Croutons

Ingredients	Directions
⅛ teaspoon salt	*1* Preheat the oven to 300 degrees. In a medium bowl, whisk together the salt, pepper, Italian seasoning, garlic powder, cheese, and oil.
⅛ teaspoon pepper	
¼ teaspoon Italian seasoning	
¼ teaspoon garlic powder	*2* Cut the bread into ½-inch cubes. Add the bread cubes to the bowl and toss them until the oil mixture is evenly distributed.
1 teaspoon grated Romano cheese	
2 tablespoons olive oil	*3* Spoon the bread cubes onto a baking sheet and bake them for 35 minutes, or until the bread is toasted, stirring occasionally. Watch closely so that the cubes don't burn.
3 slices bread	

Per serving: Calories 570; Fat 28g (Saturated 5g); Cholesterol 212mg; Sodium 657mg; Carbohydrate 68g (Dietary Fiber 10g); Protein 15g.

Note: The beauty of this salad is that you can make it ahead, cover it, and refrigerate it until serving time.

Grilled Romaine Salad with Crab Red Pepper Salsa

Prep time: 10 min • **Cook time:** 10 min • **Yield:** 4 servings

Ingredients	Directions
1 large red bell pepper	*1* Preheat grill to high heat. Place whole red bell pepper on grill grates and turn until entire pepper is charred and blistered. Place pepper in a brown paper bag and let stand for 5 minutes. Peel the skin from the pepper, discard the seeds and core. Rinse under cold water to remove residue. Chop the red pepper and place in a small glass bowl.
2 green onions, trimmed and sliced	
½ cup chopped fresh cilantro	
1 tablespoon lime juice	
½ tablespoon olive oil	*2* Gently toss the chopped red bell peppers with the green onions, cilantro, lime juice, olive oil, and crabmeat. Set aside.
1 cup fresh lump crabmeat	
2 heads romaine lettuce, washed and dried thoroughly	*3* Cut each head of romaine lettuce lengthwise into two pieces with the core intact. Lightly spray the romaine with olive oil spray and place on grill for 2 to 3 minutes on each side until very lightly charred. Romaine will be slightly wilted and lightly brown.
Nonstick olive oil cooking spray	
Freshly ground pepper to taste	
	4 Place the grilled romaine lettuce on individual plates and top with the crab red pepper salsa.

Per serving: Calories 77; Fat 4g (Saturated 0g); Cholesterol 18mg; Sodium 186mg; Carbohydrate 9g (Dietary Fiber 3g); Protein 7g.

Tip: To save time, use store-bought roasted red bell peppers. Roasting peppers and letting them rest in a paper bag allows them to sweat, which makes it easier to remove the charred skin. Roasting gives them a smoky, rich, sweet flavor.

Note: This salad needs no dressing but you could drizzle one of your favorite oil and vinegar based dressings over top.

Vary It! Omit crab red pepper salsa and instead sprinkle romaine with chopped tomatoes and goat cheese. Top with balsamic vinaigrette.

Marinated Steak Salad

Prep time: 10 min plus refrigeration time • **Cook time:** 15 min • **Yield:** 8 servings

Ingredients	Directions
3 tablespoons soy sauce	**1** In a small bowl, whisk together the soy sauce, balsamic vinegar, ginger, water, and oil.
3 tablespoons balsamic vinegar	
¼ teaspoon ginger	**2** Pour half of the mixture into a self-seal plastic bag. Cover the remaining mixture in a bowl and refrigerate.
¼ cup water	
2 tablespoons olive oil	**3** Place the steak in the self-seal plastic bag with the marinade, turning to coat. Seal the bag and marinate the meat in the refrigerator for 2 hours.
1½ pound well-trimmed beef sirloin steak, 1 inch thick	
6 cups baby spinach leaves	**4** Preheat the broiler.
½ cup thin, diagonally cut carrot slices	**5** Remove the steak from the marinade and place the meat on a broiler pan. Broil the steak for 15 minutes (medium rare) or to desired doneness, turning once. Let the meat stand 5 minutes, and then carve it into thin slices.
½ cup thinly sliced cucumber	
½ cup thinly sliced radishes	
1 cup small broccoli florets	
24 pea pods, blanched	**6** Distribute the spinach leaves evenly onto 8 salad dishes. Top with the carrot, cucumber, and radish slices. Sprinkle the salads with the broccoli and place the pea pods on the salads.
4 teaspoons sesame seeds	
	7 Sprinkle the salads with the reserved dressing. Top with the steak slices and then sprinkle with the sesame seeds.

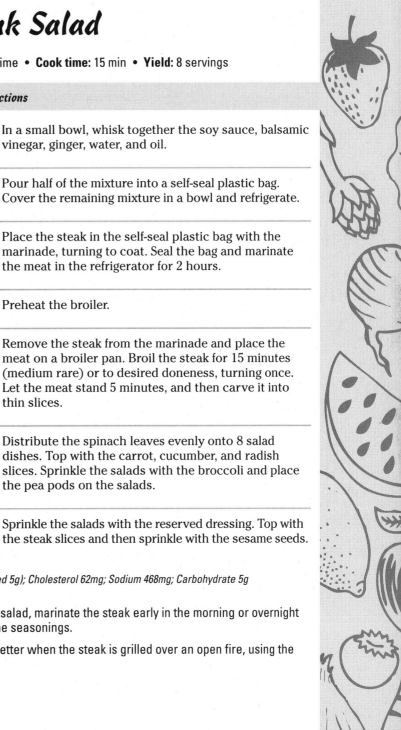

Per serving: Calories 245; Fat 13g (Saturated 5g); Cholesterol 62mg; Sodium 468mg; Carbohydrate 5g (Dietary Fiber 2g); Protein 27g.

Tip: To get the most flavor from this salad, marinate the steak early in the morning or overnight so it will absorb all the essence of the seasonings.

Note: Although this recipe is even better when the steak is grilled over an open fire, using the broiler is a good alternative.

Taco Salad

Prep time: 5 min • **Cook time:** About 10 min • **Yield:** 2 servings

Ingredients	Directions
1 cup (about 3 ounces) ground beef	**1** Heat a small skillet over medium heat. Brown the ground beef with garlic salt and chili powder, breaking apart the meat with a large spoon or spatula as it cooks.
1 teaspoon garlic salt	
1 teaspoon chili powder	
3 cups shredded lettuce	**2** Drain any fat from the pan. Pat the beef with a paper towel to absorb any remaining grease.
1 tomato, diced	
1 avocado, diced	**3** In a medium bowl, combine the cooked beef, shredded lettuce, tomato, avocado, olives, corn, cilantro, cheese, and salsa.
2 tablespoons sliced black olives	
¼ cup canned corn, drained	
2 tablespoons fresh cilantro	**4** Top the salad with crushed tortilla chips and add a drizzle of ranch dressing.
¼ cup shredded cheddar cheese	
½ cup salsa	
1 cup crushed corn tortilla chips	
Drizzle of ranch dressing	

Per serving: Calories 442 (From Fat 237); Fat 26g (Saturated 8g); Cholesterol 30mg; Sodium 1,222mg; Carbohydrate 38g (Dietary Fiber 13g); Protein 20g.

Tip: Turn this into a no-cook recipe by using leftover meat in this salad.

Tip: Heat things up by using a hot salsa, hot sauce, or a dash of cayenne pepper.

Vary It! Use cooked chicken instead of beef for a spicy chicken taco twist, or leave out the meat altogether.

Chapter 4

Simmering Soups and Stews

Whoever invented soups was a genius. What other food concoction allows you to dump almost anything into some water, cover it, and let it cook all by itself, and then call it a meal?

Soup is the ideal solution for gardeners. In late summer, when you have more vegetables than you know what to do with, when you can't even *give* away all that stuff hanging off vines and popping up through the ground, consider chopping up that yield and making a huge pot of soup. Soup is a cornucopia of nutrition and tastes.

No Glutens and Swimming with Flavor

As the old-time theme song from one of the large soup companies used to say about soup, MMMMM . . . MMMMM . . . GOOD! If you steam vegetables to serve as a side dish, the water used to steam them (which is overflowing with nutrients from these veggies) is poured down the drain. With soup, all the nutrients that these natural foods exude during cooking remain in the broth, and you just know that has to be healthy and good for you.

If soups have one drawback, it's that for the broths to be palatable, it seems like you have to dump in half the salt shaker. Still, you have options. The best option is to reduce the amount of salt used and use more herbs and spices for flavoring. Here are some tips for using herbs and spices:

- ✔ Fresh herbs are much more potent and impart more flavor than dried ones, so less is needed. But fresh herbs vary greatly in strength and the amount of flavor they exude.

- ✔ Dominant, strong flavors include cardamom, curry, ginger, hot peppers, black pepper, mustard, rosemary, cloves, and sage.

- ✔ Medium flavors are found in basil, celery seed, cumin, dill, fennel, tarragon, garlic, marjoram, mint, oregano, thyme, and turmeric.

- ✔ Then there are herbs that you can use by the bushelful. They add a very mild flavor, like parsley, chives, and chervil.

- ✔ Usually ¼ teaspoon of dried or powdered herbs equals ¾ to 1 teaspoon of fresh herbs that are cut or crumbled.

The recipes that follow can help you think beyond chicken noodle (albeit gluten-free noodle) soup. We don't mean to demean or berate chicken soup. At the first sign of a sniffle or sneeze, chances are you reach for chicken soup and hot tea. The medicinal effects of this soup are more than just an old wives' tale. Chicken soup has been prescribed for the common cold as far back as the ancient Egyptians.

If your soup is too thin for your liking, stir in a small amount of gluten-free instant potato flakes to thicken it up almost instantly. If it's too greasy, lay a few lettuce leaves on top of the broth to absorb the fat. And if you plan to freeze the soup, hold off adding any pasta to it until you thaw and reheat it, or the gluten-free pasta may get too soft and fall apart.

Grandma's Chicken Tortilla Soup

Prep time: 5 min • **Cook time:** 25 min • **Yield:** 8 servings

Ingredients	Directions
1 tablespoon vegetable oil	*1* Heat the oil in a large pot over medium heat. Sauté the chicken, onion, carrots, bell pepper, and rice for about 5 minutes. The chicken will continue cooking in the soup.
1 pound chicken breasts, cut into ½-inch strips	
½ of a medium onion, diced	
½ cup thinly sliced carrots	*2* Add the chicken broth and let the soup come to a simmer, with small bubbles just beginning to break the surface.
¼ of a green bell pepper, diced	
⅓ cup white rice (not instant)	*3* Add the tomatoes to the pot. Reduce the heat to medium-low and cover the pot. Simmer the soup until the rice is tender, about 20 minutes.
32 ounces nonfat gluten-free chicken broth	
15-ounce can diced tomatoes	
15-ounce can pinto beans, drained and rinsed	*4* Add the beans, corn, and cilantro to the soup. Taste the soup and add salt as needed. When the soup returns to a simmer, it's ready to serve.
15-ounce can corn, drained	
3 to 4 fresh cilantro sprigs, chopped	*5* Top each bowlful of soup with crushed tortilla chips.
Salt to taste	
1 cup crushed corn tortilla chips	

Per serving: Calories 238 (From Fat 61); Fat 7g (Saturated 1g); Cholesterol 34mg; Sodium 844mg; Carbohydrate 28g (Dietary Fiber 5g); Protein 17g.

Note: You can use 2 cups fresh or frozen corn instead of canned without adjusting cooking time. Corn cooks quickly, and the crispness of fresh corn is nice. For softer kernels, add fresh corn to the soup a few minutes earlier than indicated in the recipe.

Tip: Top this soup with your favorite toppings. Try grated cheddar cheese, sliced avocado, sour cream, black olives, chopped tomatoes, and even shredded lettuce.

Note: Cover and refrigerate this soup for up to a few days. Reheat it in the microwave or in a pot on the stove over medium heat until it's steaming.

Loaded Baked Potato Soup

Prep time: 5 min • **Cook time:** 20 min • **Yield:** 4 servings

Ingredients	Directions
2 large russet potatoes	**1** Wash the potatoes and pat them dry. Microwave the potatoes on high for 6 to 8 minutes on a microwave-safe plate, until the potatoes are soft when you pierce them with a fork.
1½ cups gluten-free chicken broth	
2½ cups low-fat milk	
⅓ cup plus 2 tablespoons shredded cheddar cheese	**2** Cut the potatoes in half and let them cool for a few minutes. Scoop out the middle of the potatoes and coarsely mash the insides with a potato masher or a fork. Discard the skin.
1 tablespoon dried onion flakes	
Salt to taste	**3** In a large pot, combine the potatoes, chicken broth, milk, ⅓ cup of the cheese, onion flakes, and salt and pepper. Cook on medium-low, until the soup is warm and the cheese is melted, stirring often. Don't boil the soup.
Black pepper to taste	
2 tablespoons low-fat sour cream	
3 slices bacon, cooked and crumbled	**4** Divide the soup into four bowls and top each serving with the remaining cheese and the sour cream, bacon, and chives.
2 tablespoons chopped fresh chives	

Per serving: Calories 264 (From Fat 98); Fat 11g (Saturated 5g); Cholesterol 28mg; Sodium 695mg; Carbohydrate 29g (Dietary Fiber 2g); Protein 13g.

Vary It! Use low-fat turkey bacon to cut the fat content in this soup. Just be sure to check the labels. Some versions contain gluten.

Note: Cover and refrigerate this soup for up to 3 days. Reheat it in a bowl for about a minute in the microwave, or heat it in a pot on the stove over medium heat until the soup is steamy.

Creamy Tomato Basil Soup

Prep time: 5 min • **Cook time:** 15 min • **Yield:** 4 servings

Ingredients	Directions
28-ounce can crushed tomatoes	**1** In a large uncovered pot, cook the tomatoes, basil, broth, milk, garlic salt, and pepper over medium heat for 10 to 15 minutes.
10 to 15 fresh basil leaves, finely chopped, or 1 tablespoon dried	
2 cups gluten-free chicken or vegetable broth	**2** Top the soup with gluten-free croutons.
1½ cups fat-free milk	
½ teaspoon garlic salt	
Black pepper to taste	
Gluten-free croutons	

Per serving: Calories 142 (From Fat 33); Fat 4g (Saturated 1g); Cholesterol 4mg; Sodium 929mg; Carbohydrate 23g (Dietary Fiber 4g); Protein 7g.

Note: To use fresh tomatoes, peel and seed about 4 tomatoes and pulse them in the blender with the fresh basil leaves; then follow the directions as stated in the recipe.

Vary It! Add ¼ cup shredded cheddar or Parmesan cheese while cooking, or sprinkle cheese on top before serving.

Note: Cover and store this soup in the fridge for up to a week.

Lamb and Rice Soup

Prep time: 10 min • **Cook time:** 1¾ hr • **Yield:** 6 servings

Ingredients	Directions
1 tablespoon olive oil	**1** In a large saucepan over medium heat, sauté the celery and onion in oil slowly, stirring often, until the vegetables are softened.
¾ cup chopped celery	
1 onion, chopped	
1½ pounds lamb bone-in shoulder steak	**2** Add the lamb, water, parsley, and bouillon cubes.
8 cups water	**3** Bring the liquid to a boil, and then lower the heat to medium-low, cover the pan, and simmer for 1½ hours until the lamb is very tender.
2 tablespoons minced fresh parsley	
2 chicken bouillon cubes	**4** Remove the lamb and cut the meat into tiny pieces. Discard the bones and any fat. Add the lamb to the saucepan.
¾ teaspoon salt	
¼ teaspoon pepper	
⅓ cup uncooked rice	**5** Stir in the salt, pepper, and rice. Cover the pan and simmer the soup for 15 minutes until the rice is tender.
3 eggs, at room temperature	**6** In a large mixing bowl, use the electric mixer to whip the eggs for 3 minutes. Add the lemon juice.
3 tablespoons fresh lemon juice	
	7 Very gradually, drizzle the hot broth from the soup into the eggs, whipping the mixture on high to blend. (The easiest way to add the broth to the eggs is to tip the pan slightly so the broth comes to the top and then dip it out with a soup ladle.) When the bowl feels warm to the touch, lower the mixer speed to medium and continue slowly adding most of the broth from the saucepan.
	8 Slowly pour the egg mixture back into the saucepan with the lamb, stirring constantly. Simmer the soup on low for 1 minute, stirring constantly. Serve immediately.

Per serving: Calories 231; Fat 12g (Saturated 4g); Cholesterol 154mg; Sodium 655mg; Carbohydrate 11g (Dietary Fiber 1g); Protein 19g.

Tip: Add the hot broth slowly to the eggs to prevent curdling.

Three Bean Soup

Prep time: 10 min • **Cook time:** 1 hr • **Yield:** 6 servings

Ingredients	Directions
3 tablespoons olive oil	*1* In a large saucepan, sauté the onion, garlic, celery, carrots, green bell pepper, and parsley in the oil over medium heat, stirring often, until the vegetables are soft.
1 cup chopped onion	
1 clove garlic, minced	
1 cup chopped celery	
1 cup chopped carrot	*2* Place ⅓ of the navy beans in a small bowl and mash them with the back of a fork.
½ cup chopped green bell pepper	
¼ cup fresh chopped parsley	*3* Stir the mashed beans plus the remaining navy beans, black beans, kidney beans, bay leaf, salt, pepper, tomato sauce, and water into the saucepan. Stir to blend. Bring the ingredients to a boil, and then lower the heat and simmer, covered, for 1 hour. Remove the bay leaf before serving.
15.5-ounce can navy beans, rinsed and drained	
15.5-ounce can black beans, rinsed and drained	
15.5-ounce can light kidney beans, rinsed and drained	
1 bay leaf	
1¼ teaspoon salt	
¼ teaspoon pepper	
8-ounce can tomato sauce	
6 cups water	

Per serving: Calories 277; Fat 8g (Saturated 1g); Cholesterol 0mg; Sodium 1,452mg; Carbohydrate 41g (Dietary Fiber 14g); Protein 13g.

Tip: Using canned beans in this recipe cuts down on the prep time of this soup without cutting down on taste. By mashing a few of the beans, the soup becomes thicker.

Spinach Lentil Soup

Prep time: 20 min • **Cook time:** 50 min • **Yield:** 6 servings

Ingredients	Directions
1 pound brown lentils	**1** Place the lentils in a large saucepan and cover them with water. Cook the lentils on high until the water comes to a boil. Remove the pan from the heat and drain the lentils in a colander. Rinse them well under cold running water and drain again.
8 cups water	
2 tablespoons olive oil	
½ cup chopped celery	
⅓ cup chopped carrots	**2** In the same saucepan, over medium heat, sauté the celery, carrots, onion, and garlic in the oil. Stir the mixture frequently until the vegetables are tender but not browned.
1 large onion, chopped	
1 clove garlic, minced	
3 sprigs fresh parsley, chopped	**3** Add the lentils, parsley, bay leaves, spinach, and 8 cups of water. Bring the contents to a boil, skimming off any foam as needed.
2 bay leaves	
10-ounce box chopped spinach, thawed	**4** Lower the heat, cover the pan, and simmer for 40 minutes, or until the lentils are very soft, adding more water if needed.
8 cups water	
8-ounce can tomato sauce	
1¼ teaspoon salt	**5** Stir in the tomato sauce, salt, pepper, and vinegar. Continue to simmer the soup for 10 minutes. Discard the bay leaves before serving.
¼ teaspoon pepper	
2 teaspoons cider vinegar	

Per serving: Calories 155; Fat 5g (Saturated 1g); Cholesterol 0mg; Sodium 698mg; Carbohydrate 22g (Dietary Fiber 8g); Protein 8g.

Tip: Adding a teeny amount of cider vinegar makes all the difference in the world in the taste of this creation. If the tomato sauce and salt are added too early, the lentils may not cook thoroughly.

Cabbage Soup

Prep time: 15 min • **Cook time:** 1 hr • **Yield:** 12 servings

Ingredients	Directions
6 medium onions, chopped	*1* Place all the ingredients in a large saucepan.
2 cloves garlic, minced	
1 large green bell pepper, seeded and chopped	*2* Bring the ingredients to a rapid boil, and then reduce the heat, cover the pan, and let the soup simmer for 1 hour.
14.5-ounce can diced tomatoes with juice	
1 medium head of cabbage, cored and chopped	*3* Discard the bay leaves before serving.
½ bunch parsley, chopped	
3 large carrots, sliced thin	
8 stalks celery, sliced thin	
½ teaspoon salt	
¼ teaspoon pepper	
4 cups chicken bouillon	
1 cup water	
2 bay leaves	

Per serving: Calories 78; Fat 2g (Saturated 0g); Cholesterol 0mg; Sodium 540mg; Carbohydrate 16g (Dietary Fiber 5g); Protein 3g.

Lean Beef Chili

Prep time: 10 min • **Cook time:** 20 min • **Yield:** 6 servings

Ingredients	Directions
1 tablespoon olive oil	**1** In a large saucepan over medium-high heat, sauté the ground beef, green pepper, onion, celery, and garlic in the oil, breaking the meat up with a fork as it cooks.
1 pound 90 percent lean ground beef	
½ medium green bell pepper, chopped	**2** Stir in the remaining ingredients except the cheese. Bring the ingredients to a boil, and then reduce the heat. Cover the pan and simmer, stirring occasionally, for 15 to 20 minutes, until the broth thickens.
1 medium onion, chopped	
1 rib celery, chopped	
2 cloves garlic, minced	**3** Stir in the cheese until it's melted.
8-ounce can tomato sauce	
15-ounce can diced tomatoes	
1½ cups water	
15-ounce can kidney beans with liquid	
15-ounce can black beans, rinsed and drained	
1½ teaspoons chili powder	
1 teaspoon cumin	
¼ teaspoon cayenne pepper	
½ teaspoon salt	
¼ teaspoon pepper	
¼ cup grated Parmesan cheese	

Per serving: Calories 329; Fat 10g (Saturated 4g); Cholesterol 49mg; Sodium 1,039mg; Carbohydrate 34g (Dietary Fiber 10g); Protein 26g.

Tip: This chili is beyond mouth warming and tongue tingling. After an initial tasting, you can add more chili powder or a few drops of gluten-free hot pepper sauce if you like your tongue to blister and swell and your throat to be on fire.

Note: You can adorn your bowl with a dollop of sour cream, chopped green onions, cheddar cheese, or whatever you like.

Hobo Stew

Prep time: 10 min • **Cook time:** 7 hr • **Yield:** 6 servings

Ingredients	Directions
1 to 1½ pounds stew meat	*1* Preheat the oven to 250 degrees.
1 large russet potato, peeled and cut into large cubes	
1 large sweet potato, peeled and cut into large cubes	*2* Combine all ingredients in a 3-quart Dutch oven and place in the oven for 6 to 7 hours. Don't lift lid until baking is complete.
1 small package baby carrots	
1 large onion, sliced	
2½-pound can diced tomatoes	
1 cup tomato juice	
2 slices gluten-free bread	
Dash salt	
¾ tablespoon sugar	
1 tablespoon arrowroot flour or other thickening agent, such as cornstarch	

Per serving: Calories 308; Fat 8g (Saturated 2g); Cholesterol 47mg; Sodium 543mg; Carbohydrate 42g (Dietary Fiber 6g); Protein 19g.

Tip: Stew can also be made in a slow cooker and cooked on the low temperature setting for 7 to 8 hours or on the high setting for 3 to 4 hours.

Note: Sweet potatoes are a wonderful addition to a more traditional stew. They're nutritious, they contain a large amount of beta carotene, and they have a low-glycemic index — plus, they're easy on the budget.

Black Bean Chili

Prep time: 32 min • **Cook time:** 45 min • **Yield:** 8 servings

Ingredients	Directions
3 tablespoons cooking oil	**1** Heat 1 tablespoon of the cooking oil in a large Dutch oven for about 1 minute on medium heat.
1 pound lean steak, cut into 1-inch cubes	
½ cup dry cooking sherry	**2** In a large pot, sear the steak cubes over medium-high heat in the cooking oil to brown the outside, leaving the inside rare. You may need to do this in two batches, depending on how large your pot is.
1 small onion, chopped	
2 stalks celery, chopped	**3** Add the cooking sherry and cook another minute.
2 carrots, chopped	
Two 15-ounce cans black beans (drain most, but not all, of the juice)	**4** Remove the steak-sherry mixture from the pot, place it in another bowl, and set aside.
One 15-ounce can chili beans (drain most, but not all, of the juice)	**5** Heat the remaining 2 tablespoons of oil in the same Dutch oven you used to cook the steak. Heat for about 1 minute on medium heat.
One 14.5-ounce can diced tomatoes (some have flavorings; choose one you like if you want extra flavor)	**6** Add the chopped onion, celery, and carrots to the oil, and sauté for about 2 minutes.
One 4-ounce can diced green chilies	**7** Add the steak–sherry mixture to the chopped veggies in the Dutch oven.
2 tablespoons brown sugar (light or dark)	
2 tablespoons honey	**8** Add the beans, tomatoes, chilies, brown sugar, honey, cumin, chili powder, and red chili flakes (if you like the heat).
1 tablespoon cumin	
4 tablespoons chili powder	

Red chili flakes to taste (optional)

Salt and pepper to taste

9 Stir and let it simmer on medium heat for 2 hours, stirring every 20 minutes or so.

10 Season with salt and pepper to taste.

Per serving: Calories 280 (From Fat 79); Fat 9g (Saturated 1g); Cholesterol 29mg; Sodium 505mg; Carbohydrate 32g (Dietary Fiber 9g); Protein 19g.

Tip: Most grocery stores carry a trio of chopped veggies, including onions, celery, and carrots. You may spend a tad more, but you'll save yourself some prep time by letting someone else do the chopping.

New England Clam Chowder

Prep time: 30 min • **Cook time:** 45 min • **Yield:** 8 servings

Ingredients	Directions
3 cups fish stock	**1** In a large pot, simmer the stock and the wine over medium heat. Add the thyme, bay leaf, and parsley. Add the clams, cover the soup, and cook until the clams open (about 8 minutes for smaller clams and up to 15 minutes for large clams).
1 cup dry white wine	
½ teaspoon dried thyme	
1 bay leaf	
½ teaspoon dried parsley	**2** Remove the clams from the pot, take the clams out of the shells, and set the clams aside.
8 pounds fresh, cleaned clams (still in the shell)	
¼ pound sliced bacon, cut in 1-inch pieces	**3** In another large pot, cook the bacon until the pieces begin to get crispy. Remove the pieces with a slotted spoon and set them aside. Discard all the fat except a teaspoon or so.
2 medium onions, chopped	
1½ pounds red potatoes, peeled and diced	**4** Add the onion to the bacon fat, turn the heat to low, and cook the onions till they're soft but not brown (about 15 minutes).
2 cups heavy cream	
Pepper to taste	**5** In that same large pot, add the strained cooking liquid and the potatoes. Simmer the soup gently until the potatoes are cooked through — about another 20 minutes or so.
	6 Add the clams, bacon, and cream to the soup, and add pepper to taste.

Per serving: Calories 412 (From Fat 238); Fat 27g (Saturated 15g); Cholesterol 132mg; Sodium 316mg; Carbohydrate 18g (Dietary Fiber 2g); Protein 24g.

Tip: To clean the clams, let them sit in fresh water for a few hours. Or you can rinse them in a few changes of fresh water, letting them sit in the water a few minutes between changes.

Vary It! You've probably seen restaurants serve clam chowder in bread bowls and figured those days are gone now that you're gluten-free. Well, try this: Heat your oven to 425 degrees and mix up a batch of gluten-free bread. (Recipes abound in Book V.) Using ovenproof bowls as molds, press a layer of bread dough about ½-inch thick into each bowl. Bake the bowls until the bread is golden brown, about 20 minutes. Peel the bread out of the bowl-mold and pour clam chowder into your bread bowl. See? You can have your bowl and eat it, too.

Book IV

Main Courses with Meat and Without

Contents at a Glance

Chapter 1

Bringing Beef, Lamb, and Pork to the Table

In This Chapter

▶ Using tips for buying and preparing meat

▶ Working with various cuts of meat

▶ Making delectable dishes with beef, lamb, and pork

Recipes in This Chapter

▶ Shredded Pork

▶ Steak and Peanut Pepper Pasta

▶ Best Spare Ribs You'll Ever Eat!

▶ Lamburgers with Tzatziki Sauce

▶ Meatballs in Wine Sauce

▶ Ham with Glazed Bananas

▶ Best-Ever Sloppy Joes

▶ Reuben Quesadillas

▶ Pepperoni Squares

▶ Macaroni and Sausage Casserole

▶ Cheeseburger Casserole

▶ Tex-Mex Pizza

▶ Meat and Vegetable Pasties

*Y*es, meat is gluten-free . . . initially. If you buy roasts, chops, or any other whole piece of meat, you don't need to be concerned from a gluten standpoint. If, however, you pick up a package of marinated beef kebabs or preseasoned pork tenderloin, you'll need to check what ingredients have been used in the marinade and seasonings.

When you buy meat from the deli department, be careful. Most of the premium meats sold there are solid meat, but some of the less expensive brands may use extenders. *Extenders* are inexpensive fillers and binders that can include wheat; they can enhance the flavor of processed meats, but they're primarily added to expand and extend the product. These fillers must be listed on the label, and manufacturers must list wheat on the label — so if you're reading carefully, you'll find it.

And then there's the enigma surrounding ground meats. If you pick up a package that says "ground beef," wouldn't you assume it was just beef that was ground up? Well, that may not necessarily be so. Some (granted, not many) meat processors add fillers that contain wheat products to their ground meats. Again, the ingredients in the fillers must be listed on the package ingredient label, but you still have to read the label to make sure it's safe for you to eat.

Eying the Main Attractions: Beef, Pork, and Lamb

Three grades of beef are sold in grocery stores: prime, choice, and select.

- ✔ **Prime** is juicier and more tender than the other two grades because it has the most *marbling* (a fancy word for "fat specks").

- ✔ **Choice** beef is moderately marbled and generally slightly more "mature" than prime beef. It's the most popular grade purchased because it isn't as expensive as prime and it's more tender than select.

- ✔ **Select** is the leanest, so ultimately it's the healthiest, but because it has the least amount of marbling, it's usually tougher, less juicy, and less flavorful.

On one hand, you have tender, juicy, flavorful; on the other hand, you have healthier. And then you have the beef that's in the middle of the road. It's really a matter of preference.

Pork today is 35 percent to 50 percent leaner than it was just 30 years ago. Unfortunately, pork dries out when it's overcooked, primarily because of the lower fat content. You can avoid overcooking pork by paying close attention to the internal temperature with an accurate instant-read thermometer. Pork is cooked through when the thermometer registers 160 degrees. Always let the meat *rest* (that's a fancy word for letting it sit for a few minutes after it's cooked) before serving or carving so the juices can be reabsorbed into the center.

If you aren't partial to the taste of lamb, chances are you tasted mutton. Meat from older sheep is called *mutton,* and most people think it tastes disgusting, whereas the taste of spring lamb is succulent, delicious, and moist. When buying leg of lamb, you may find it challenging to figure out how much you need because of the bone. You're safe if you buy 1 pound for every two people to be served.

Shredded Pork

Prep time: 15 min • **Cook time:** 4–5 hr • **Yield:** 4 servings

Ingredients	Directions
2 pounds boneless pork shoulder-blade roast	*1* Trim the fat from the pork. Place all the meat in the slow cooker, cutting the pork roast into pieces if it doesn't fit. Add the chicken broth, onions, jalapeño peppers, garlic, coriander, cumin, oregano, and salt and pepper.
1 cup chicken broth	
2 large onions, cut into quarters	
4 jalapeño peppers, sliced	*2* Cover and cook the pork on the high-heat setting for 4 to 5 hours. Use a slotted spoon to get the meat out of the liquid; discard the liquid. When the meat cools, use two forks to shred it.
3 teaspoons minced garlic (about 6 cloves)	
2 teaspoons ground coriander	
2 teaspoons ground cumin	
2 teaspoons dried, crushed oregano	
Salt and pepper to taste	

Per serving: Calories 393 (From Fat 194); Fat 22g (Saturated 7g); Cholesterol 133mg; Sodium 510mg; Carbohydrate 9g (Dietary Fiber 3g); Protein 39g.

Tip: You can use shredded pork to make a variety of meals. Dress it up with condiments and extras such as sour cream, shredded lettuce, refried beans, olives, salsa, diced tomatoes, jalapeño peppers, spicy carrots, and guacamole, and use it for the following:

- Burritos
- Enchiladas
- Fajitas
- Nachos
- Quesadillas
- Salads
- Sandwiches
- Tacos
- Tostadas

Steak and Peanut Pepper Pasta

Prep time: 2 hr and 25 min • **Cook time:** 15 min • **Yield:** 4 servings

Ingredients	Directions
½ cup rice wine vinegar	**1** Preheat the grill or set the oven to broil. If you're using a gas grill, heat on high for 10 minutes, and then reduce the heat to medium-low. If you plan to broil the steak, move the oven rack so it's about 5 inches from the top of the oven.
½ cup olive oil	
4 tablespoons soy sauce	
4 tablespoons peanut butter	
2 tablespoons chopped fresh cilantro	**2** Combine the vinegar, oil, soy sauce, peanut butter, cilantro, garlic, and red pepper in a blender. Cover and blend the dressing until it's well mixed.
1 teaspoon minced garlic (about 2 cloves)	
½ teaspoon crushed red pepper	**3** Trim the fat from the meat. Put the steak in a shallow dish and pour about one-third of the dressing from Step 2 over the meat. Cover and marinate the meat in the refrigerator for 2 hours, turning occasionally. Chill the remaining dressing.
1 pound lean top sirloin steak	
4 ounces fine noodles	**4** Drain the meat, discarding the dressing it was marinating in. Grill or broil the steak until it's cooked the way you like it, turning once halfway through. This should take about 8 to 12 minutes, depending on the thickness of the meat and how you like your steak cooked.
1½ cups shredded cabbage	
1½ cups bok choy, thinly sliced	
1 cup spinach	
1 cup carrots, shredded or thinly sliced	**5** Cook the noodles according to the package directions, making sure they're *al dente* (slightly firm and not over-cooked). Drain them and set them aside.
½ cucumber, thinly sliced (for garnish)	
½ yellow summer squash, halved and thinly sliced (for garnish)	**6** While the meat is cooking, combine the noodles, cabbage, bok choy, spinach, and carrots in a medium-sized mixing bowl. Add about half of the remaining dressing to the pasta-veggie mixture and stir until it's well mixed.
¼ cup chopped peanuts	

7 When the meat is done, slice it into thin slices across the grain. To assemble this dish, serve the pasta-veggie mixture on each person's plate. Put a few slices of meat on top of the noodle mixture. Garnish the dish with a few slices of cucumber and squash. Drizzle the remaining dressing mixture over each plate, and top with peanuts.

Per serving: Calories 573 (From Fat 333); Fat 37g (Saturated 7g); Cholesterol 64mg; Sodium 1,229mg; Carbohydrate 30g (Dietary Fiber 4g); Protein 33g.

Tip: Instead of shredding the veggies, buy a shredded broccoli-carrot-cabbage mixture. You can use any veggies you want, as long as they're thinly shredded.

Best Spare Ribs You'll Ever Eat!

Prep time: 1 hr • **Cook time:** 40 min • **Yield:** 4 servings

Ingredients	Directions
1 tablespoon brown sugar	**1** Early in the day (or the day before), put the sugar and vinegar in a large Dutch oven. Reduce over medium heat about 8 minutes until the vinegar and sugar form a syrup. (Watch carefully because the syrup will suddenly darken in color.)
¼ cup cider vinegar	
5 cups water	
1 tablespoon beef bouillon granules	
2 tablespoons molasses	**2** Immediately add the water and bouillon granules. Stir in the molasses, ketchup, dry mustard, Worcestershire sauce, cloves, chili powder, and cayenne pepper. Bring it to a boil.
¼ cup ketchup	
2 teaspoons dry mustard	
1 teaspoon Worcestershire sauce	**3** Cut each slab of ribs into smaller sections. Add them to the pan and simmer for 20 minutes.
⅛ teaspoon cloves	
½ teaspoon chili powder	**4** Remove the pan from the heat. Remove the ribs and place them in a dish. Cover and refrigerate.
¼ teaspoon cayenne pepper	
3 pounds baby back ribs (2 slabs)	**5** Cook the liquid over medium heat until it becomes thick and syrupy (about 25 minutes), stirring constantly during the last 5 minutes.
	6 Remove the pan from the heat and pour the sauce into a bowl. (Yield will be about 1 cup of basting sauce.) Cool the sauce, and then cover and refrigerate it.
	7 Before dinner, preheat the oven to 350 degrees.
	8 Place the ribs on a nonstick baking dish, with the underside facing up.
	9 Baste well with the sauce and bake for 20 minutes. Turn the ribs over and baste generously. Continue to bake for 20 to 25 minutes.

Per serving: Calories 607; Fat 28g (Saturated 10g); Cholesterol 218mg; Sodium 673mg; Carbohydrate 16g (Dietary Fiber 0g); Protein 67g.

Lamburgers with Tzatziki Sauce

Prep time: 10 min • **Cook time:** 12 min • **Yield:** 4 servings

Ingredients	Directions
4 tablespoons plain Greek yogurt	*1* Preheat gas grill on high.
2 tablespoons cucumber, finely minced	*2* In a small bowl, make the tzatziki sauce by blending together the yogurt, cucumber, garlic, 1 teaspoon lemon zest, and dill. Refrigerate.
1 teaspoon minced garlic	
1 teaspoon plus 1 teaspoon lemon zest	*3* In mixing bowl, combine ground lamb, herbs, 1 teaspoon lemon zest, breadcrumbs, salt, and pepper until well blended. Divide mixture and gently shape into four 1-inch burger patties.
½ teaspoon dried dill	
1 pound ground lamb	
1 teaspoon dried basil	*4* Transfer burgers to hot grill and cook for 4 to 5 minutes each side until browned and cooked through. Let sit for 5 minutes.
½ teaspoon dried chives	
½ teaspoon dried rosemary	
½ teaspoon dried thyme	*5* Place burgers on burger buns and top with tzatziki sauce, spinach, tomato, and red onion.
½ cup breadcrumbs	
Salt and pepper to taste	
4 burger buns	
1 cup baby spinach	
1 tomato, sliced	
1 small red onion, sliced	

Per serving: Calories 635; Fat 32g (Saturated 8g); Cholesterol 76mg; Sodium 340mg; Carbohydrate 62g (Dietary Fiber 3g); Protein 25g.

Tip: A loosely packed patty makes a juicier burger. When cooking, flip only once to prevent losing more juices than necessary.

Vary It! If you have difficulty finding ground lamb, choose a shoulder cut or lamb stew meat and have your butcher trim and grind it.

Meatballs in Wine Sauce

Prep time: 15 min • **Cook time:** 40 min • **Yield:** 4 servings

Ingredients	Directions
2 slices porous bread, toasted 1 pound lean ground beef	**1** Crumble the toast into a medium bowl. Add the ground beef, egg, salt, pepper, and garlic. Mix thoroughly.
1 egg ¼ teaspoon salt ¼ teaspoon pepper	**2** Form the meat mixture into small balls, and then roll into football-shaped ovals. You should have about 24 meatballs.
2 cloves garlic, minced 2 tablespoons butter	**3** In a large skillet over medium heat, brown the meatballs in butter, turning frequently.
3 ounces (½ of a 6-ounce can) tomato paste ½ teaspoon sugar ½ cup red wine 1½ cups water	**4** Add the tomato paste, sugar, red wine, and water, cover, and simmer for 30 minutes, adding more water only if needed.

Per serving: Calories 310; Fat 14g (Saturated 7g); Cholesterol 137mg; Sodium 478mg; Carbohydrate 12g (Dietary Fiber 2g); Protein 26g.

Tip: Use the most porous bread you can find for toasting.

Note: This is one recipe where you can't take a shortcut by substituting garlic powder for the cloves of garlic.

Ham with Glazed Bananas

Prep time: 5 min • **Cook time:** 5 min • **Yield:** 4 servings

Ingredients	Directions
3 tablespoons plus 1 tablespoon butter	*1* Melt 3 tablespoons of butter in a nonstick medium skillet. Stir in the brown sugar until it melts.
3 tablespoons brown sugar	
¼ cup dark corn syrup	*2* Stir in the corn syrup and cinnamon and bring it to a gentle simmer. Slice the bananas into the syrup and simmer for 2 minutes.
½ teaspoon cinnamon	
2 large bananas, peeled	*3* In a medium skillet, melt 1 tablespoon of butter. Add the ham pieces and brown quickly on each side, turning once.
8-ounce ham steak, cut into 4 pieces	
	4 Place the ham slices on a serving dish and top with the banana glaze.

Per serving: Calories 335; Fat 14g (Saturated 8g); Cholesterol 53mg; Sodium 786mg; Carbohydrate 43g (Dietary Fiber 2g); Protein 13g.

Tip: Select fairly firm bananas so they don't get too soft when cooked.

Note: If the ham you select has skin or rind encircling it, cut it off before preparing this dish.

Best-Ever Sloppy Joes

Prep time: 15 min • **Cook time:** 10 min • **Yield:** 4 servings

Ingredients	*Directions*
1 tablespoon olive oil	**1** In a medium skillet over medium-high heat, brown the ground beef, onion, and green bell pepper in oil, breaking up the meat with a fork.
1 pound lean ground beef	
1 medium onion, diced	
¼ green bell pepper, diced	**2** Stir in the chili powder, cayenne pepper, paprika, cumin, mustard, garlic powder, salt, pepper, brown sugar, vinegar, Worcestershire sauce, and tomato sauce and simmer for 10 minutes, stirring often.
1 teaspoon chili powder	
¼ teaspoon cayenne pepper	
1 teaspoon paprika	
½ teaspoon cumin	
1 teaspoon yellow mustard	
½ teaspoon garlic powder	
¼ teaspoon salt	
¼ teaspoon pepper	
1 tablespoon brown sugar	
2 teaspoons cider vinegar	
2 tablespoons Worcestershire sauce	
8-ounce can tomato sauce	

Per serving: Calories 257; Fat 10g (Saturated 3g); Cholesterol 68mg; Sodium 829mg; Carbohydrate 16g (Dietary Fiber 3g); Protein 3g.

Note: Double, triple, or quadruple this recipe when you host a big crowd. Spoon several heaping spoonfuls of hamburger mix on top of a toasted bun.

Reuben Quesadillas

Prep time: 5 min • **Cook time:** 5 min • **Yield:** 6 servings

Ingredients	Directions
Three 10-inch tortillas, cut in half	*1* Spread 3 of the tortilla halves with ½ teaspoon of mustard.
1½ teaspoons hot mustard	*2* Divide the corned beef in thirds; lay 1 portion on each of 3 halves of the tortilla.
8 ounces deli corned beef, sliced thin	*3* Divide the sauerkraut in thirds; lay 1 portion on top of the corned beef on each tortilla.
8-ounce can sauerkraut, drained and rinsed	*4* Lay 2 slices of Swiss cheese on top of the sauerkraut on each quesadilla.
6 slices low-fat Swiss cheese	*5* Cover each quesadilla with the remaining 3 tortilla halves.
	6 Cut each tortilla semicircle in half to make a total of 6 halves.
	7 Place the quesadillas in a large skillet that has been prewarmed over medium-high heat, and toast the quesadillas on each side until the tortillas are lightly browned and the cheese is melted.

Per serving: Calories 232; Fat 10g (Saturated 3g); Cholesterol 47mg; Sodium 7,143mg; Carbohydrate 16g (Dietary Fiber 1g); Protein 24g.

Note: These quesadillas are great eaten fresh off the griddle, but you can also make them ahead and pack them in a bag for lunchtime.

Vary It! You can substitute different ingredients for the contents of the quesadilla, using pastrami in place of the corned beef and/or provolone cheese in place of Swiss. If you aren't a fan of sauerkraut, substitute cole slaw.

Pepperoni Squares

Prep time: 15 min • **Cook time:** 40 min • **Yield:** 6 servings

Ingredients	Directions
Nonstick cooking spray	**1** Preheat the oven to 400 degrees. Spray a 9-x-9-inch baking dish with cooking spray.
1 tablespoon olive oil	
½ cup chopped onion	**2** In a small skillet, sauté the onions and green bell pepper in oil over medium heat, stirring often, until the vegetables are soft.
⅓ cup chopped green bell pepper	
2 eggs	**3** In a medium mixing bowl, use the mixer to whip together the eggs and milk. Add the flour and beat the mixture until it's smooth and thickened. Stir in the reserved onion and green bell pepper, parsley, red pepper flakes, mozzarella cheese, salt, pepper, Italian seasoning, and pepperoni.
¾ cup whole milk	
¾ cup gluten-free flour mixture (see Book V, Chapter 2)	
1½ tablespoons dried parsley	
⅛ teaspoon red pepper flakes	**4** Transfer the mixture to the prepared baking pan and bake for 40 minutes. Cut into 6 pieces.
½ cup shredded mozzarella cheese	
⅛ teaspoon salt	**5** In a microwave-safe bowl, warm the spaghetti sauce to serve as a dipping sauce for the Pepperoni Squares.
Dash pepper	
½ teaspoon Italian seasoning	
2 ounces pizza pepperoni, slices quartered	
1 cup spaghetti sauce	

Per serving: Calories 229; Fat 11g (Saturated 3g); Cholesterol 84mg; Sodium 510mg; Carbohydrate 25g (Dietary Fiber 4g); Protein 8g.

Tip: If you cut the pieces smaller (24 pieces per pan), you can serve the squares as an appetizer.

Note: These squares can be prepared the night before, covered, and refrigerated. Just before serving, pop them in the oven.

Macaroni and Sausage Casserole

Prep time: 20 min • **Cook time:** 30 min • **Yield:** 8 servings

Ingredients	*Directions*
Nonstick cooking spray	*1* Preheat the oven to 325 degrees. Spray a 9-x-13-inch baking dish with cooking spray.
1 pound sausage (regular or spicy)	
1 medium onion, diced	*2* In a large skillet, brown the sausage and onion over medium-high heat, breaking up the meat with a fork. Remove the skillet from the heat and drain off the fat.
3 cups pasta shells	
8-ounce jar processed cheese	*3* Boil the pasta in water in a large saucepan until it's barely tender and then drain. Return the pasta to the saucepan and immediately stir in the cheese so it melts.
18-ounce can cream of mushroom soup	
¼ teaspoon pepper	*4* Stir in the sausage, soup, and pepper.
¾ cup breadcrumbs	*5* Spoon the mixture into the prepared baking dish.
2 tablespoons melted butter	*6* In a small bowl, stir together the breadcrumbs and melted butter. Sprinkle this over the macaroni and sausage.
	7 Bake the casserole for 30 minutes until hot and bubbly and the breadcrumbs start to brown a little.

Per serving: Calories 333; Fat 17g (Saturated 9g); Cholesterol 51mg; Sodium 1,233mg; Carbohydrate 31g (Dietary Fiber 1g); Protein 15g.

Cheeseburger Casserole

Prep time: 25 min • **Cook time:** 50 min • **Yield:** 6 servings

Ingredients	Directions
1 tablespoon olive oil	*1* Preheat the oven to 375 degrees. Spray a 2-quart casserole with nonstick cooking spray and set aside.
1 onion, chopped	
3 cloves garlic, minced	*2* In a large skillet, heat the olive oil over medium heat. Add the onion and garlic and cook for 5 minutes, stirring frequently. Add the ground beef and cook, stirring to break up the meat, until the beef is browned, about 6 to 8 minutes. Drain off the fat.
1¼ pounds lean ground beef	
One 8-ounce can tomato sauce	
2 tablespoons tomato paste	*3* Add the tomato sauce, tomato paste, ketchup, mustard, thyme, salt, and pepper and simmer for 10 minutes.
⅓ cup ketchup	
¼ cup mustard	
1 teaspoon dried thyme leaves	*4* Meanwhile, in a medium bowl, combine the Whole-Grain Flour Mix, White Flour Mix, baking powder, and ½ teaspoon salt.
Salt and pepper to taste	
1¼ cups minus 1 teaspoon (165 grams) Whole-Grain Flour Mix (see Book V, Chapter 2)	*5* In a small bowl, combine the eggs, butter, and milk and beat until combined.
⅓ cup minus 1 teaspoon (45 grams) White Flour Mix (see Book V, Chapter 2)	*6* Stir the egg mixture into the flour mixture just until combined.
1 teaspoon baking powder	*7* Stir the cheese cubes into the hot beef mixture and pour into the prepared casserole. Spoon the batter onto the beef mixture in six sections. Sprinkle with Parmesan cheese.
½ teaspoon salt	
2 eggs	
⅓ cup butter, melted	
⅓ cup milk	*8* Bake for 25 to 30 minutes, or until the topping is light golden-brown and set.
4 ounces cheddar cheese, cubed	
3 tablespoons grated Parmesan cheese	

Per serving: *Calories 583 (From Fat 309); Fat 34g (Saturated 16g); Cholesterol 180mg; Sodium 972mg; Carbohydrate 40g (Dietary Fiber 3g); Protein 30g.*

Note: The mustard flavor is strong in this recipe. If you love mustard, you'll love it! If not, reduce the mustard amount to 1 to 2 tablespoons.

Tex-Mex Pizza

Prep time: 30 min • **Cook time:** 35 min • **Yield:** 8 servings

Ingredients	*Directions*
1 recipe Cornmeal Pizza Crust (see Book V, Chapter 6)	*1* Preheat the oven to 425 degrees. Prepare the Cornmeal Pizza Crust and bake it for 10 minutes, and then set aside.
½ pound ground pork sausage	
1 small onion, chopped	*2* In a large saucepan, cook the ground pork sausage with the onion, garlic, and jalapeño pepper until the sausage is thoroughly cooked, about 5 to 7 minutes, stirring to break up the sausage. Drain well.
2 cloves garlic, minced	
1 jalapeño pepper, minced	
1 cup refried beans (from 16-ounce can)	*3* Stir in the refried beans, taco sauce, chili powder, salt, cumin, and red pepper flakes. Remove from heat.
½ cup taco sauce	
2 teaspoons chili powder	*4* Spread the bean mixture over the crust and top with the cheeses. Bake for 15 to 20 minutes, or until the crust is golden-brown and the cheeses are melted and starting to brown.
½ teaspoon salt	
½ teaspoon cumin	
¼ teaspoon crushed red pepper flakes	
1 cup shredded cheddar cheese	*5* While the pizza is baking, combine the avocado, tomato, and green onion.
½ cup shredded pepper jack cheese	*6* Let the pizza cool for 3 to 5 minutes before cutting it into wedges to serve. Top with the avocado mixture.
1 avocado, peeled and diced	
1 ripe tomato, chopped	
¼ cup chopped green onion	

Per serving: Calories 412 (From Fat 164); Fat 18g (Saturated 7g); Cholesterol 35mg; Sodium 859mg; Carbohydrate 49g (Dietary Fiber 9g); Protein 15g.

Note: To make your own chili powder, combine 1 teaspoon ground cumin, 1 teaspoon dried ground chiles, 1 teaspoon smoked paprika, 1 teaspoon ground oregano, 1 teaspoon garlic powder, 1 teaspoon salt, 1 teaspoon onion powder, ½ teaspoon black pepper, and ½ teaspoon cayenne pepper. Blend well and store in an airtight container. And make sure all these ingredients are gluten-free, too!

Meat and Vegetable Pasties

Prep time: 40 min, plus rest time • **Cook time:** 50 min • **Yield:** 8 servings

Ingredients	Directions
1 cup (123 grams) sorghum flour	*1* In a large bowl, combine the sorghum flour, tapioca flour, sweet rice flour, 1 teaspoon salt, sugar, baking powder, and gelatin or xanthan gum. Cut in the shortening until large crumbs form.
¾ cup (94 grams) tapioca flour	
½ cup (78 grams) sweet rice flour	
1 teaspoon plus ½ teaspoon salt	*2* Add the water until the dough forms a ball. Let rest, covered, for 1 hour.
1 tablespoon sugar	
½ teaspoon baking powder	*3* Roll the dough out to ¼-inch thickness. Using a 6-inch saucer, cut out circles of dough.
½ teaspoon unflavored gelatin or 1 teaspoon xanthan gum	
1 cup solid shortening	*4* For the filling, melt the butter in a large skillet over medium heat. Add the beef and cook until browned, about 3 to 4 minutes.
¼ cup ice water	
1 tablespoon butter	
1 pound boneless sirloin, cubed	*5* Add the turnips, potatoes, carrots, and onion. Cook for 10 to 12 minutes, until the vegetables are crisp-tender. Add ½ teaspoon salt, parsley, and pepper; cool for 15 minutes.
½ cup cubed turnips	
½ cup cubed potatoes	
½ cup cubed carrots	*6* Preheat the oven to 400 degrees. Put ½ cup filling on one side of each circle of dough. Fold the dough over to cover the filling and crimp the edges. Place on a cookie sheet.
1 onion, diced	
2 tablespoons minced parsley	*7* Bake for 35 to 40 minutes, or until golden-brown.
¼ teaspoon pepper	

Per serving: Calories 475 (From Fat 268); Fat 30g (Saturated 8g); Cholesterol 37mg; Sodium 499mg; Carbohydrate 41g (Dietary Fiber 2g); Protein 15g.

Vary It!: For a vegetarian pasty, omit the beef and butter. Add 2 cloves minced garlic and ¼ pound mushrooms, chopped, to the vegetable mixture. Cook the vegetable mixture in 1 tablespoon olive oil until it's crisp-tender and then proceed with the recipe.

Chapter 2

Building Great Dishes from Turkey and Chicken

In This Chapter

▷ Using turkey for more than holiday dinners

▷ Starting with chicken for tasty main courses

▷ Using smart tips for cooking with poultry

A barbecued chicken leg is hot off the grill, dripping with sauce, and sitting on your plate. You're starving, and the aroma is activating all your sensory glands. Are you really going to use your fork and knife? Or are you going to dive down with both hands and pick it up? According to Emily Post, "Birds are not eaten with the fingers in company!" Fortunately, Miss Manners counters with the advice that hands can definitely be used in the enjoyment and consumption of said bird. (Like any of us really cares what either of them has to say!)

Few foods are as versatile as chicken. First, you need to decide what kind of chicken to buy — free-range or farm-raised, light meat or dark meat, whole chickens or separate parts, diced or shredded or strips, fresh or frozen, pre-marinated or plain, bone-in or boned. After you've made these decisions, then you have to figure out how you're going to prepare the bird. It can be grilled, stewed, baked, roasted, stuffed, broiled, boiled, oven-fried, deep-fried, pan-fried, microwaved, or cooked in a slow cooker. With all these choices, picking just one can be difficult.

The recipes in this chapter come to your rescue. They take America's favorite food and dress it up in new ways. Now the only decision you have to make is which of these recipes you're going to make first!

Making Poultry with Pizzazz

You may not realize just how versatile poultry really is. Not only do these birds soak up flavors from marinades and rubs, providing an array of flavors and taste experiences, but your fine (formerly feathered) friends in and of themselves are oozing with options. White meat or dark? Breast or thigh? Skin or no skin? Don't underestimate the significance of these choices — to people with a preference, white meat versus dark is an entirely different bird.

Chicken is a great source of protein, as well as niacin, vitamins B-6 and B-12, vitamin D, iron, and zinc. Ounce for ounce, skinless chicken is one of the lowest-fat meats around. Although breast meat definitely has the lowest fat content, even skinless dark meat is comparatively low in fat, and most of the fat it does have is unsaturated — the good kind.

Dark meat is dark because birds use their leg and wing muscles more, so those muscles require more oxygen. *Myoglobin* is an iron-containing protein that transfers oxygen from the blood to the muscles, changing the color of the meat — and providing you with more iron.

Sizzling Chicken and Walnuts

Prep time: 15 min • **Cook time:** 10 min • **Yield:** 4 servings

Ingredients	Directions
2 tablespoons peanut oil	*1* In a large wok skillet, heat oil over medium-high heat and sauté chicken for about 3 minutes or until browned. Remove from pan.
3 boneless and skinless chicken breasts, cut into bite-size strips	
3 green onions, cut in diagonal slices	*2* Add onions and celery and sauté quickly. Add chicken back to pan. Add butter, walnuts, and lemon zest. Cook uncovered for several minutes while continuing to stir.
2 medium celery sticks, cut in diagonal slices	
½ to 1 tablespoon butter	*3* Add soy sauce and lemon juice. Stir until chicken is coated.
¾ cup walnut halves	
1 teaspoon lemon zest	*4* Serve with cooked brown rice.
2 tablespoons soy sauce	
1 tablespoon fresh lemon juice	
2 cups cooked brown rice	

Per serving: Calories 424; Fat 24g (Saturated 4g); Cholesterol 59mg; Sodium 540mg; Carbohydrate 27g (Dietary Fiber 4g); Protein 27g.

Tip: When stir-frying, it's best to have all your ingredients prepped ahead and ready to use because the cooking takes so little time that you won't have time for prep after you start cooking. Don't overcrowd your dish with too many ingredients to get the perfect searing.

Note: Walnuts are high in alpha-linolenic acid, a heart healthy omega-3 fatty acid that may help prevent heart attacks.

Corn Chip Chicken

Prep time: 10 min • **Cook time:** 45 min • **Yield:** 5 servings

Ingredients	Directions
9.75-ounce bag corn chips	*1* Preheat the oven to 375 degrees.
¼ teaspoon pepper	
½ teaspoon Cajun seasoning	*2* Pour half of the corn chips into a blender and puree; pour the fine crumbs into a self-seal plastic bag. Repeat with the second half of corn chips.
¼ teaspoon garlic powder	
1 teaspoon paprika	*3* Add the pepper, Cajun seasoning, garlic powder, and paprika to the corn chips and mix well to distribute the spices evenly.
4 tablespoons melted butter	
5 whole chicken legs (leg and thigh)	*4* Dip one chicken piece into the melted butter, and then place it in the bag. Seal the bag and shake it to coat the chicken with crumbs. Repeat with the remaining chicken pieces.
	5 Place the chicken in an 8-x-11-inch baking dish.
	6 Bake the chicken for 40 to 45 minutes, or until the chicken is just cooked through. (You don't need to turn the chicken pieces during cooking.)

Per serving (breaded without skin): Calories 630; Fat 35g (Saturated 12g); Cholesterol 170mg; Sodium 540mg; Carbohydrate 32g (Dietary Fiber 4g); Protein 41g.

Tip: You can bread the chicken ahead, cover it, and refrigerate it until baking time.

Vary It! This recipe uses chicken legs, but you can use the pieces your family likes best.

Lemon Caper Chicken

Prep time: 20 min • **Cook time:** 25 min • **Yield:** 4 servings

Ingredients	Directions
4 boneless, skinless chicken breasts **4 tablespoons olive oil, divided** **¼ cup rice flour** **Salt and pepper to taste** **3 green onions, chopped** **1 teaspoon minced garlic (about 2 cloves)** **¼ cup chicken broth** **½ cup dry sherry** **¼ cup freshly squeezed lemon juice** **4 tablespoons capers, drained and rinsed** **2 tablespoons unsalted butter**	*1* Pound the chicken breasts to an even thickness — about ½ inch is good. If you don't have a meat tenderizer, you can use any other heavy, manageable object, like an iron skillet. *2* Put enough olive oil into a large skillet to coat the bottom of the pan. This will probably require about 2 tablespoons. Heat the oil over medium-high heat. *3* Dredge the chicken breasts in rice flour and season the chicken with salt and pepper. *4* Brown the chicken, about 3 minutes on each side. If your pan isn't big enough, you may need to do this in a couple of batches. Make sure you have enough oil in the pan at all times (you'll probably have to add another tablespoon of oil during cooking). Transfer the chicken to a warm serving platter and cover it with foil. *5* Clean the pan to get the residual flour out, or use a new skillet. Reduce the heat to low and add the rest of the olive oil to the skillet (you should have about 1 tablespoon left). Add the green onions, garlic, chicken broth, sherry, lemon juice, and capers. Turn up the heat to medium-high and simmer until the liquid has reduced to half (about 5 minutes). *6* Tilt the pan so the liquid pools on one side, and whisk in the butter until the sauce is smooth. Pour the sauce over the chicken breasts and serve immediately.

Per serving: Calories 362 (From Fat 205); Fat 23g (Saturated 6g); Cholesterol 89mg; Sodium 529mg; Carbohydrate 11g (Dietary Fiber 1g); Protein 28g.

Date-Night Chicken Carbonara

Prep time: 5 min • **Cook time:** 20 min • **Yield:** 2 servings

Ingredients	Directions
4 ounces pasta	*1* Cook and drain the pasta according to the package directions.
3 slices bacon	
6-ounce boneless, skinless chicken breast, cut into small chunks	*2* While the pasta is cooking, add the bacon and chicken to a large skillet over medium heat. Stir the chicken and turn the bacon to cook all sides, heating until the chicken is no longer pink and the bacon is crispy.
1 tablespoon butter	
¾ cup chicken broth	
¾ cup sour cream	*3* Remove the chicken and bacon from the pan and set them aside on paper towels. Crumble the bacon. Wipe out any extra grease from the pan with a paper towel.
½ cup Parmesan cheese	
1 cup peas	*4* Add the butter, chicken broth, sour cream, and Parmesan cheese to the pan. Cook over medium-low heat until the butter is melted and the sauce is hot.
½ teaspoon garlic salt	
½ teaspoon black pepper	
	5 Add the peas and the cooked chicken and bacon to the sauce and cook about another minute. Stir in the garlic salt and pepper.
	6 Pour the sauce over the pasta and serve it immediately.

Per serving: Calories 764 (From Fat 344); Fat 38g (Saturated 21g); Cholesterol 126mg; Sodium 1,296mg; Carbohydrate 60g (Dietary Fiber 5g); Protein 40g.

Tip: Cut the chicken with a sharp knife on a cutting board, holding the chicken in place with a fork. Using the fork ensures that you don't have to touch the raw chicken with your hands.

Vary It! Use asparagus spears instead of peas. Cook them separately and then add them to the sauce in Step 5.

Tip: Use 2 cups precooked roasted or grilled chicken instead of cooking the raw chicken to speed up the meal prep.

30-Minute Paella

Prep time: 5 min • **Cook time:** 25 min • **Yield:** 4 servings

Ingredients	Directions
6-ounce boneless, skinless chicken breast, roughly diced	**1** Heat a large skillet (one that has a lid) over medium-high heat. Cook the chicken and sausage uncovered, stirring now and then, until the meat is browned, about 5 minutes. Remove the chicken and sausage from the skillet and set aside.
8 ounces chorizo sausage links, thickly sliced	
½ of a green bell pepper, diced	
½ of a red bell pepper, diced	**2** Wipe almost all the grease out of the skillet, leaving about a teaspoon's worth in the pan. Return the skillet to the burner.
1 medium onion, diced	
2 cups uncooked rice	**3** Add the green bell pepper, red bell pepper, and onion to the skillet. Cook them for about 2 to 3 minutes, until they're brown.
2 cups water	
15-ounce can crushed tomatoes	
1 chicken bouillon cube	**4** Stir in the rice, water, tomatoes, chicken bouillon, garlic salt, and oregano, and add the chicken and sausage back to the skillet. Cover the skillet with the lid and reduce the heat to low. Simmer for 10 minutes.
1 teaspoon garlic salt	
½ teaspoon dried oregano	
12 small (about 4 ounces) frozen precooked shrimp	**5** Add the shrimp and peas to the skillet. Simmer, uncovered, for 10 minutes or until the liquid is evaporated.
1 cup frozen peas	

Per serving: Calories 775 (From Fat 216); Fat 24g (Saturated 9g); Cholesterol 97mg; Sodium 1,613mg; Carbohydrate 98g (Dietary Fiber 6g); Protein 37g.

Note: Bags of shrimp usually list the shrimp size based on the number of shrimp per pound, so lower numbers mean larger shrimp. Small shrimp are usually labeled 51/60, meaning there are 51 to 60 shrimp per pound; in this case, each shrimp weighs about 0.3 ounces or a little less.

Creole Chicken

Prep time: 10 min • **Cook time:** 50 min • **Yield:** 4 servings

Ingredients

1 tablespoon olive oil

2 cloves garlic, minced

1 medium onion, thinly sliced

2 ribs celery, thinly sliced

½ green bell pepper, finely diced

1 tablespoon dried parsley

8-ounce can tomato sauce

1 cup water

2 bay leaves

½ teaspoon salt

⅛ rounded teaspoon cayenne pepper

Four 5-ounce bone-in skinless chicken breasts

Directions

1 Preheat the oven to 350 degrees.

2 In a medium skillet over medium heat, sauté the garlic, onion, celery, and green bell pepper in oil, stirring frequently, until tender (about 4 minutes).

3 Stir in the parsley, tomato sauce, water, bay leaves, salt, and cayenne pepper. Simmer 2 more minutes.

4 Place the chicken in a 9-x-9-inch baking dish. Pour the sauce over the chicken.

5 Bake the chicken for 35 minutes and then cover with foil and bake another 15 minutes until the chicken is very tender.

Per serving: Calories 194; Fat 5g (Saturated 0g); Cholesterol 68mg; Sodium 707mg; Carbohydrate 8g (Dietary Fiber 2g); Protein 29g.

Tip: If you like really spicy hot food, add more cayenne pepper.

Slow Cooker Chicken with Spinach and Mushrooms

Prep time: 5 min • **Cook time:** 8 hr • **Yield:** 4 servings

Ingredients	Directions
Two 10-ounce boxes frozen, chopped spinach, thawed	**1** Stir together all the ingredients, except the chicken, in the slow cooker.
8-ounce can sliced mushrooms, with liquid	
18-ounce can cream of mushroom soup	**2** Add the chicken thighs and stir them in so they're covered with the sauce.
¼ cup sherry	
1 packet dry onion soup mix	**3** Cover and cook on low for 8 hours.
½ teaspoon pepper	
¼ teaspoon dried thyme	
Four 5-ounce skinless chicken thighs	

Per serving: Calories 401; Fat 9g (Saturated 2g); Cholesterol 63mg; Sodium 1,520mg; Carbohydrate 19g (Dietary Fiber 6g); Protein 21g.

Parmesan Chicken with Fresh Tomato Salsa

Prep time: 15 min • **Cook time:** 15 min • **Yield:** 4 servings

Ingredients	Directions
Four 4-ounce boneless skinless chicken breasts	**1** On a cutting board and using the meat mallet, pound the thicker portion of each chicken breast to make the thickness of the pieces uniform.
8 teaspoons sherry	
¼ teaspoon plus ¼ teaspoon pepper	**2** Pour the sherry into a shallow bowl.
2 cups coarsely shredded Parmesan cheese (do not use canned grated cheese)	**3** Mix ¼ teaspoon of pepper, the cheese, and breadcrumbs together on a sheet of wax paper.
⅛ cup breadcrumbs	**4** Dip each chicken breast in the sherry, moistening both sides, and then press the breasts firmly into the cheese mixture, covering both sides of each breast. Use a meat mallet to help the cheese adhere to the meat.
1 tablespoon plus 3 tablespoons olive oil	
½ medium onion, chopped	
½ small green bell pepper, chopped	**5** In a medium skillet over medium heat, sauté the onion, green bell pepper, and garlic in 1 tablespoon of olive oil, stirring frequently, until the vegetables are tender. Stir in the Italian seasoning, salt, ¼ teaspoon of pepper, tomatoes, and parsley. Continue cooking until the mixture is heated through.
½ teaspoon minced garlic	
2 teaspoons Italian seasoning	
¼ teaspoon salt	
4 plum Roma tomatoes, chopped	**6** Preheat a large nonstick skillet over medium-high heat. Add 3 tablespoons of oil. Set the breasts in the skillet and cook 5 to 6 minutes per side, until the cheese is light golden and the chicken is cooked through.
2 tablespoons minced fresh parsley	

7 Remove the breasts from the skillet and set on paper towels to drain the excess oil.

8 To serve, place the chicken breasts on a serving platter and spoon the tomato salsa over the chicken breasts.

Per serving: Calories 449; Fat 26g (Saturated 10g); Cholesterol 83mg; Sodium 1,034mg; Carbohydrate 61g (Dietary Fiber 1g); Protein 38g.

Tip: To get the cheese coating to stick to the chicken, pound the cheese in with the flat side of a meat mallet.

Cashew Roasted Chicken Salad

Prep time: 10 min • **Yield:** 1 serving

Ingredients	Directions
2 tablespoons plain Greek yogurt	*1* In a medium bowl, stir together the yogurt, lemon juice, salt, and pepper. Add the cooked chicken, celery, parsley, and capers. Mix well.
1 teaspoon lemon juice	
Salt to taste	
Black pepper to taste	*2* Place the mixture on a bed of two or three leaves of lettuce.
1 cup shredded cooked chicken	
1 stalk celery, finely chopped	*3* Sprinkle chopped cashews on top.
1 tablespoon chopped flat-leaf parsley	
1 teaspoon capers	
2 or 3 leaves of lettuce, torn	
½ cup chopped cashews	

Per serving: Calories 696 (From Fat 385); Fat 43g (Saturated 10g); Cholesterol 127mg; Sodium 570mg; Carbohydrate 28g (Dietary Fiber 4g); Protein 55g.

Tip: You can easily make this salad into two chicken salad sandwiches with some sliced bread.

Note: Capers are small, green, berry-like flower buds that add a nice, tangy flavor that pairs well with lemon. You can find them in small jars near the olives in the grocery store. You can skip this ingredient if you don't have any, but adding them to dishes with lemon brings an extra zing.

Note: Store leftovers covered in the fridge for no more than a day or two.

Turkey Roll-Ups

Prep time: 10 min, plus refrigeration time • **Yield:** 4 servings

Ingredients	Directions
10-inch tortilla	**1** Spread the mayonnaise on one side of the tortilla. Along one edge, layer the turkey and cheese on top of the mayonnaise. Along that same edge, lay out the peppers and cucumber. Sprinkle the spinach leaves over all.
1 tablespoon mayonnaise	
2 ounces deli turkey breast, sliced thin	
2 ounces provolone cheese, sliced thin	**2** Tightly roll up the tortilla. Wrap it in a damp paper towel, then in wax paper, and refrigerate for several hours.
2 red bell peppers, roasted and sliced (or use canned, prepared red roasted bell peppers)	
1 small cucumber, sliced very thin	**3** When you're ready to serve the roll-up, remove the paper towel and wax paper, and slice the tortilla into 8 slices.
½ cup baby spinach leaves	

Per serving: Calories 135; Fat 6g (Saturated 3g); Cholesterol 26mg; Sodium 291mg; Carbohydrate 10g (Dietary Fiber 1g); Protein 11g.

Chicken Pot Pie

Prep time: 40 min • **Cook time:** 60 min • **Yield:** 8–10 servings

Ingredients	Directions
½ recipe Butter Pie Crust (see Book V, Chapter 4)	**1** Preheat the oven to 425 degrees. Grease a deep-dish metal pie plate or shallow casserole dish and place it on a cookie sheet.
3 tablespoons butter	
⅛ cup (53 grams) sweet rice flour	**2** Prepare the Butter Pie Crust and roll it out in a circle large enough to cover the pie plate or dish; refrigerate.
½ cup dry white wine	
1 cup milk	**3** For the sauce, melt the butter in a medium saucepan over medium heat. Add the sweet rice flour and cook for 1 minute. Add the wine and cook until the wine evaporates, about 3 to 5 minutes. Add the milk and chicken stock, whisking constantly until smooth, about 3 to 5 minutes.
1 cup chicken stock	
4 tablespoons olive oil	
3 boneless, skinless chicken breasts, diced	
1 large onion, diced	**4** Simmer the sauce until it thickens, about 3 to 4 minutes. Remove it from the heat and set aside.
3 carrots, diced	
3 celery stalks, sliced	**5** For the filling, in a large saucepan, heat the olive oil over medium heat. Add the chicken and onions and cook, stirring, until the chicken is done and the onions are crisp-tender, about 6 to 8 minutes.
¾ cup green peas	
1 teaspoon chopped fresh thyme	
2 tablespoons minced fresh parsley	**6** Add the carrots and celery and cook another 2 to 3 minutes.
	7 Place the chicken mixture into the prepared pie plate. Top with the peas and herbs.

8 Pour the sauce over the chicken and vegetables and top with the pie crust.

9 Immediately place the cookie sheet/pie plate into the oven. Bake for 10 minutes, reduce the heat to 350 degrees, and bake 25 to 30 minutes more, until the crust is golden-brown and the filling is bubbly.

Per serving: *Calories 357 (From Fat 178); Fat 20g (Saturated 8g); Cholesterol 59mg; Sodium 294mg; Carbohydrate 31g (Dietary Fiber 3g); Protein 15g.*

Southwest Black Bean and Turkey Burger

Prep time: 10 min • **Cook time:** 11 min • **Yield:** 1 serving

Ingredients	Directions
3 ounces lean ground turkey	**1** In a medium bowl, combine the turkey, beans, garlic salt, chili powder, and cumin. Form the mixture into a patty about ½-inch thick.
¼ cup canned black beans, drained and lightly mashed	
¼ teaspoon garlic salt	**2** Heat the oil in a small skillet over medium heat. When the skillet is hot, place the patty in the skillet.
¼ teaspoon chili powder	
¼ teaspoon ground cumin	**3** Cook the patty about 4 to 5 minutes on each side, or until it's no longer pink in the center. Make sure the patty is well done. Top the burger with cheese for the final minute or 2 of cooking, until the cheese is melted.
1 teaspoon vegetable oil	
1 slice pepper jack cheese	
1 hamburger bun	
3 avocado slices	**4** Heat the bun in the microwave on high for 20 seconds (if frozen) or 10 seconds (if thawed).
1 teaspoon fat-free sour cream	
1 teaspoon salsa	**5** Slide the burger onto the bun and top it with avocado slices, sour cream, and a touch of salsa.

Per serving: Calories 679 (From Fat 345); Fat 38g (Saturated 9g); Cholesterol 80mg; Sodium 721mg; Carbohydrate 55g (Dietary Fiber 7g); Protein 31g.

Note: Lean turkey burgers can be dry. The beans add some moisture and make for a moist and delicious burger!

Tip: Add a little bit of oil when cooking lean turkey to ensure it doesn't stick to the pan.

Chapter 3

Swimming in Ideas for Fish and Seafood

In This Chapter

▶ Getting the basics on cooking with fish and seafood

▶ Discovering great main dishes and casseroles

▶ Running through great recipes for fish and seafood

Some people think fish is fish. But, oh, how wrong they are. Think of the options. Do you want to cook it with dry heat (baking, barbecuing, blackening, bronzing, broiling, microwaving), or use moist heat (steaming, poaching), or fry the fish (deep-frying, pan-frying)? When you've made up your mind about how to cook it, then you're confronted with further queries: Should it be marinated? Stuffed? Breaded? Basted? Glazed? Served with a sauce?

Before you become totally overwhelmed with choices, take a look at some of the recipes in this chapter and realize that fish can make a fabulous dish!

Reeling in Compliments with Fish and Seafood Dishes

Unlike meat, fish is naturally tender and requires short cook times at a high temperature. All fish and seafood are naturally gluten-free. Below are some general guidelines for cooking fish:

✔ Measure fish at its thickest part.

✔ Allow 10 minutes of cook time per inch of thickness for fresh fish.

- ✔ Allow 20 minutes of cook time per inch of thickness for frozen fish.

- ✔ Fish is ready when it's opaque but still juicy. Sometimes if you cook a fillet until it flakes easily with a fork, it will be overdone and dried out.

- ✔ Raw fish is *translucent,* kind of like frosted glass. You certainly can't look through it, but it's not solid either. Cooked fish is *opaque* and solid, meaning you can't see through it at all.

- ✔ Baking fish in an aluminum pan can create a chemical reaction that leaves the fish tasting acidic. It's best to bake fish in a glass or stainless steel pan.

- ✔ *Do not overcook* or the fish will become tough.

Fish is loaded with great nutrients, such as healthy omega-3s and protein, but nearly all fish and shellfish contain traces of mercury as well. For most people, the risk from mercury isn't of concern, but pregnant women, nursing mothers, and young children would be prudent to avoid those fish that contain higher levels of mercury. Those fish include shark, swordfish, king mackerel, and tilefish. Fish and shellfish low in mercury include shrimp, canned light tuna, salmon, Pollock, and catfish. Albacore ("white" tuna) has more mercury than canned light tuna.

Broiling, Baking, and Poaching Fish

Preparing fish by baking, broiling, and poaching it are healthy ways to serve it to your family and friends. This section focuses on several easy recipes.

The good news: Fish is a highly nutritious food commodity. It provides protein, far fewer calories than meat, and is rich in omega-3 fatty acids. (Isn't it odd that you're always being told to stay away from fatty foods, yet certain fatty acids are good for you?)

Omega-3 has many health benefits, including lowering triglycerides and helping to prevent heart disease and blood clots; improving brain function; helping with high blood pressure, diabetes, strokes, depression, arthritis, allergies, circulation problems, ADHD, Alzheimer's disease, skin disorders, and gout; and lowering the risk of osteoporosis in post-menopausal women. The primary source for this fatty acid is fatty fish, such as salmon, mackerel, sardines, and herring. Opt to buy fish that comes from the deep sea (as opposed to farm-raised) so it will be as pollutant-free as possible.

Sesame Pretzel Fish

Prep time: 10 min • **Cook time:** 20 min • **Yield:** 4 servings

Ingredients	Directions
Nonstick cooking spray	**1** Preheat the oven to 400 degrees. Spray a 9-x-13-inch baking dish with cooking spray.
Two 2.65-ounce bags sesame pretzel rings	**2** Puree 1 bag of pretzels at a time in a blender; empty the crumbs into a gallon-size self-seal plastic bag.
½ teaspoon salt	
¼ teaspoon pepper	**3** Add the salt, pepper, dill, and garlic powder to the plastic bag; seal the bag and shake well to mix the ingredients.
¾ teaspoon dried dill	
¼ teaspoon garlic powder	
½ cup fresh lemon juice (about 3 whole lemons)	**4** In a shallow bowl, whisk together the lemon juice and brown mustard.
1½ tablespoons brown mustard	**5** Rinse the fillets and pat them dry. Place the fillets in the lemon-mustard mixture and let them marinate for 3 minutes.
Four 5-ounce fillets of bass	
	6 Remove the bass and place the fillets in the bag with the crumbs. Seal the bag and shake it to coat the fillets evenly.
	7 Place each piece of fish in a single layer in the prepared baking dish and bake the fillets for 20 minutes.

Per serving: Calories 403; Fat 16g (Saturated 5g); Cholesterol 129mg; Sodium 963mg; Carbohydrate 24g (Dietary Fiber 2g); Protein 39g.

Tip: Ground pretzels, especially ones with sesame seeds, make an excellent coating for oven-baked chicken, too!

Note: The fish may be prepared ahead, covered with plastic wrap, and refrigerated until you're ready to bake it.

Vary It! If bass is not available, you can substitute orange roughy. Orange roughy is not as thick as bass, so you may have to reduce the baking time.

Tequila-Lime Shrimp and Scallops

Prep time: 2 min • **Cook time:** 10 min • **Yield:** 4 servings

Ingredients	Directions
1 pound medium shrimp, cooked, peeled, and deveined	*1* If your shrimp or scallops are frozen, thaw and rinse them. If the scallops are as large as an egg or larger, cut them in half and set them aside.
½ pound sea scallops	
¼ cup lime juice	*2* In a large glass, ceramic, or stainless steel mixing bowl, stir together the lime juice, lemon juice, cilantro, 1 tablespoon oil, tequila, garlic, hot sauce, cumin, and oregano. Add the shrimp and scallops.
¼ cup lemon juice	
¼ cup chopped fresh cilantro	
2 tablespoons olive oil, divided	
¼ cup tequila	*3* In a large skillet over medium-high heat, cook the onion, green bell pepper, and red bell pepper in the remaining tablespoon of oil until they begin to get soft, about 4 minutes.
2 teaspoons minced garlic (about 4 cloves)	
2 teaspoons hot sauce	*4* Add the shrimp-scallop mixture to the skillet, and bring everything to a boil. Cook and stir the mixture for about 3 minutes, until some of the liquid has burned off and the scallops are cooked.
½ teaspoon ground cumin	
½ teaspoon dried oregano	
1 large onion, cut into thin wedges	
1 green bell pepper, cut into bite-size strips	*5* Serve the seafood over rice, over pasta, or in the wrap of your choice, and garnish it with lime wedges.
1 red bell pepper, cut into bite-size strips	
4 lime wedges (for garnish)	

Per serving: Calories 397 (From Fat 205); Fat 23g (Saturated 10g); Cholesterol 181mg; Sodium 499mg; Carbohydrate 12g (Dietary Fiber 2g); Protein 36g.

Seafood Sole

Prep time: 15 min • **Cook time:** 30 min • **Yield:** 4 servings

Ingredients	Directions
Nonstick cooking spray 1 tablespoon butter ½ cup onion, chopped 7-ounce can sliced mushrooms, drained ½ pound fresh, cooked medium shrimp, cut in half 6-ounce can lump crabmeat, drained (avoid imitation, which can contain gluten) Four 6-ounce sole or flounder fillets ¼ teaspoon salt ¼ teaspoon pepper ¼ teaspoon paprika 18-ounce can ready-to-serve cream of mushroom soup ¼ teaspoon chicken bouillon granules 2 teaspoons cornstarch ¼ cup shredded sharp white cheddar cheese 1 tablespoon dried parsley	*1* Preheat the oven to 400 degrees. Lightly grease a 9-x-9-inch baking dish with cooking spray. *2* Melt the butter in a large saucepan; add the onions and mushrooms and sauté them over medium heat until they're soft. Stir in the shrimp and crabmeat and heat the mixture. *3* Rinse the fillets and pat them dry. Sprinkle the fillets with salt, pepper, and paprika, and lay them in the prepared baking dish. Spoon the shrimp mixture over the fillets. *4* In a medium bowl, stir together the soup, bouillon granules, and cornstarch until the ingredients are blended. Stir in the cheese and parsley. Pour the mixture over the casserole. *5* Bake the casserole for 30 minutes.

Per serving: Calories 418; Fat 16g (Saturated 7g); Cholesterol 178mg; Sodium 1,414mg; Carbohydrate 13g (Dietary Fiber 1g); Protein 54g.

Tip: If you prepare this dish for company, you may opt to stuff each piece of fish with the seafood mixture, and then roll it up, secure it with a toothpick, and pour the sauce over the top before baking.

Note: Be sure to use lump crabmeat because imitation crabmeat usually isn't gluten-free.

Salmon Crepes

Prep time: 15 min • **Cook time:** 10–15 min • **Yield:** 4 servings

Ingredients	Directions
Nonstick cooking spray	*1* Preheat the oven to 400 degrees. Using the cooking spray, grease a 9-x-9-inch baking dish.
1½ tablespoons butter	
1 green onion, sliced thin	*2* In a medium saucepan, sauté the onion in butter over medium heat until the onion is soft but not browned. Remove the pan from the heat.
1 tablespoon cornstarch	
½ teaspoon salt	
⅛ teaspoon pepper	*3* In a small bowl, stir together the cornstarch, salt, pepper, thyme, dill, and half-and-half until well blended, and then add it to the butter and onions in the pan. Stir until blended.
⅛ teaspoon dried thyme	
⅛ teaspoon dried dill	
¾ cup half-and-half	
1 egg	*4* Return the pan to the heat and cook the contents over medium heat, stirring constantly, until the mixture has thickened. Remove the pan from the heat.
2 teaspoons sherry	
6-ounce can salmon, drained	
4-ounce can mushroom stems and pieces, drained	*5* In a medium bowl, whip the egg with a whisk. Very slowly, drizzle the half-and-half mixture into the egg, whisking constantly, until ¾ of the *roux* (the half-and-half mixture) has been incorporated. Stir the egg mixture into the remaining roux in the pan. Cook 1 minute over medium heat, stirring constantly, and then remove the pan from the heat.
8 crepes (see the recipe in Book V, Chapter 5)	
1 tablespoon grated Romano cheese	
	6 Pour ¾ of the sauce into a medium bowl. Stir the sherry into the remaining sauce in the pan and set it aside.

7 Stir the salmon and mushrooms into the bowl with the reserved sauce.

8 Place a heaping tablespoon of the salmon mixture down the center of each crepe. Roll up the crepes, jelly-roll style, and place them in a single layer in the prepared baking dish. Pour the remaining sauce over the tops of the crepes, and then sprinkle with cheese.

9 Bake the crepes for 10 to 15 minutes, or until they're heated through.

Per serving of 2 crepes: Calories 217; Fat 15g (Saturated 9g); Cholesterol 122mg; Sodium 473mg; Carbohydrate 9g (Dietary Fiber 1g); Protein 13g.

Seafood au Gratin

Prep time: 15 min • **Cook time:** 30 min • **Yield:** 6 servings

Ingredients	Directions
Nonstick cooking spray	*1* Preheat the oven to 325 degrees. Grease a 9-x-13-inch glass baking dish with cooking spray.
3 tablespoons butter	
2 tablespoons cornstarch	*2* In a medium saucepan, melt the butter.
¼ cup plus 1¾ cups half-and-half	*3* In a small bowl, stir the cornstarch together with ¼ cup of the half-and-half until the mixture is smooth. Stir this into the butter in the pan.
¼ teaspoon salt	
1 teaspoon dried parsley	
⅛ teaspoon dried red pepper flakes	*4* Add the remaining half-and-half, salt, parsley, red pepper flakes, and dried onion to the cornstarch mixture. Over medium heat, cook the mixture, stirring constantly with a whisk, until the mixture has thickened.
1 teaspoon minced dried onion	
¾ cup shredded cheddar cheese	*5* Stir in the cheddar cheese until it melts. Remove from heat.
¼ cup sherry	
14-ounce can quartered artichoke hearts	*6* Drain the artichoke hearts, reserving the liquid. Stir the sherry and the artichoke juice into the sauce in the saucepan.
Juice from artichokes	
¾ pound crabmeat pieces (beware gluten-containing imitation crab)	*7* Place the artichoke hearts, crabmeat, shrimp, and scallops in the prepared baking dish.
½ pound raw shrimp, peeled and deveined	
½ pound sea scallops, sliced into medallions	*8* Pour the cream sauce over the seafood. Sprinkle the top with almonds, Parmesan cheese, and very lightly with paprika.
⅓ cup slivered almonds	
¼ cup grated Parmesan cheese	*9* Bake for 30 minutes.
Paprika to taste	

Per serving: *Calories 461; Fat 27g (Saturated 15g); Cholesterol 183mg; Sodium 667mg; Carbohydrate 16g (Dietary Fiber 4g); Protein 37g.*

Tip: Don't substitute milk for the half-and-half, or the sauce won't be as thick and rich.

Note: Use real crabmeat; the imitation crabmeat may not be gluten-free.

New Orleans Shrimp Casserole

Prep time: 50 min • **Cook time:** 40 min • **Yield:** 4 servings

Ingredients	*Directions*
½ recipe Butter Pie Crust (see Book V, Chapter 4)	*1* Prepare the Butter Pie Crust, roll out into a 10-inch circle, and refrigerate.
¼ cup butter	
½ cup chopped celery	*2* Preheat the oven to 425 degrees.
1 onion, chopped	
3 cloves garlic, minced	*3* In a large skillet, melt the butter over medium heat. Add the celery, onion, garlic, and red bell pepper; cook and stir until crisp-tender, about 5 to 6 minutes.
1 red bell pepper, chopped	
2 tablespoons (18 grams) sweet rice flour	*4* Add the sweet rice flour, White Flour Mix, celery salt, pepper, and paprika; cook and stir for 2 minutes.
2 tablespoons (20 grams) White Flour Mix (see Book V, Chapter 2)	*5* Add the wine or chicken broth and tomatoes. Cook, stirring occasionally, over medium heat until thickened, about 3 to 5 minutes.
½ teaspoon celery salt	
¼ teaspoon black pepper	
½ teaspoon paprika	*6* Add the shrimp to the mixture; cook and stir for 4 to 5 minutes, until the shrimp curl and turn pink. Stir in the peas and cheddar and Gouda cheeses; remove from the heat and pour into a 2-quart casserole dish.
¼ cup dry white wine or chicken broth	
One 14-ounce can diced tomatoes, undrained	*7* Immediately top with the Butter Pie Crust; crimp the edges if desired. Sprinkle the crust with Parmesan cheese.
3 cups 30-count uncooked peeled shrimp	

1 cup baby frozen peas, thawed

1 cup shredded cheddar cheese

½ cup shredded Gouda cheese

2 tablespoons grated Parmesan cheese (do not use canned Parmesan, which often contains gluten)

8 Bake for 18 to 23 minutes, or until the casserole is bubbly and the crust is golden-brown.

Per serving: Calories 727 (From Fat 351); Fat 39g (Saturated 24g); Cholesterol 317mg; Sodium 1,161mg; Carbohydrate 55g (Dietary Fiber 6g); Protein 41g.

Coconut-Crusted Mahi-Mahi

Prep time: 5 min • **Cook time:** 15 min • **Yield:** 4 servings

Ingredients	Directions
½ cup panko breadcrumbs	**1** Preheat the oven to 400 degrees. Line a baking sheet with parchment paper or foil sprayed with nonstick cooking spray.
¼ cup sweetened, flaked coconut	
1 tablespoon gluten-free all-purpose flour	**2** In a shallow dish, mix the breadcrumbs, coconut, flour, cayenne pepper, salt, and pepper.
¼ teaspoon cayenne pepper	
Salt to taste	**3** One at a time, dip the mahi-mahi fillets in water and roll them in the breadcrumb mix. Pat down the bread-crumb mixture on top of the fish to ensure liberal coverage.
Black pepper to taste	
Four 6-ounce mahi-mahi fillets	
2 tablespoons melted butter or olive oil	**4** Place the mahi-mahi fillets on the baking sheet and drizzle them with melted butter or olive oil.
	5 Bake the mahi-mahi for about 15 minutes, until the crust is golden and the fish flakes with a fork.

Per serving: Calories 247 (From Fat 82); Fat 9g (Saturated 5g); Cholesterol 149mg; Sodium 318mg; Carbohydrate 6g (Dietary Fiber 1g); Protein 34g.

Tip: If your mahi-mahi is frozen, be sure to thaw it before cooking. It's tough to get coating to stick to frozen fish, and frozen fish takes longer to cook and gets watery in the oven.

Tip: If you can't find gluten-free panko, you can use cracker crumbs or other gluten-free breadcrumbs.

Tip: Serve your mahi-mahi with vegetables and hot rice.

Potato Nests with Shrimp

Prep time: 20 min • **Cook time:** 20 min • **Yield:** 8 servings

Ingredients	Directions
Nonstick cooking spray	*1* Preheat the oven to 450 degrees. Coat 8 cupcake tins with cooking spray.
4 medium russet potatoes, shredded	
¼ teaspoon plus ¼ teaspoon salt	*2* In a medium bowl, toss together the shredded potatoes, ¼ teaspoon of salt, and the melted butter until the potatoes are evenly coated.
3 tablespoons melted butter	
1 tablespoon olive oil	*3* Press the mixture onto the bottom and sides of the prepared cupcake tins. Bake for 15 to 20 minutes until golden.
¼ cup chopped onions	
¾ cup sliced fresh mushrooms	*4* Heat the oil in a medium saucepan over medium-high heat; sauté the onions and mushrooms until they're lightly browned.
¼ cup whole milk	
8 ounces cream cheese, cubed	
2 tablespoons dried parsley	*5* Stir in the milk, cream cheese, parsley, ¼ teaspoon of salt, pepper, and pimento. Stir the mixture until the cheese melts.
⅛ teaspoon pepper	
2 tablespoons chopped pimento	
1 pound small cooked shrimp	*6* Stir in the shrimp and wine, simmering just until the ingredients are warmed. Serve in the potato nests.
¼ cup dry white wine	

Per serving: Calories 314; Fat 17g (Saturated 10g); Cholesterol 269mg; Sodium 213mg; Carbohydrate 22g (Dietary Fiber 1g); Protein 16g.

Tuna Fish Sandwich Like No Other

Prep time: 8 min • **Cook time:** 3 min • **Yield:** 4 servings

Ingredients	Directions
4 slices bread (see Book V, Chapter 6 for gluten-free recipes)	**1** Preheat the broiler. Place the bread slices in a 9-x-13-inch baking dish.
¼ green bell pepper, cut into thin julienne strips	**2** On each slice of bread, layer the green bell pepper, onion, spinach leaves, and tomato slices, dividing evenly.
⅛ red onion, sliced thin	
½ cup baby spinach leaves	**3** In a small bowl, blend the pepper, Italian seasoning, tuna, and Italian dressing. Spoon the mixture on top of the tomato slices.
2 small plum tomatoes, sliced thin	
⅛ teaspoon pepper	
¼ teaspoon Italian seasoning	**4** Cut the artichoke hearts in half. Lay 4 halves on each sandwich.
6.5-ounce can water-pack chunk tuna, drained	**5** Lay 1 slice of pepper cheese on top of each sandwich.
2 teaspoons Italian dressing	
8 artichoke hearts	**6** Broil the sandwiches about 3 minutes or just until the cheese is melted.
4 slices pepper cheese	

Per serving: Calories 429; Fat 15g (Saturated 9g); Cholesterol 40mg; Sodium 632mg; Carbohydrate 50g (Dietary Fiber 3g); Protein 24g.

Note: Try this filling on bread, in a pita or tortilla, or even spoon it atop shredded lettuce. You won't want to go back to the old tuna-and-mayo rendition.

Antipasto Lettuce Wraps

Prep time: 6 min • **Yield:** 4 servings

Ingredients	Directions
2 tablespoons olive oil	*1* In a medium bowl, whisk together the olive oil, vinegar, garlic powder, pepper, and oregano. Add the onion, green bell pepper, red bell peppers, tuna fish, pepperoni, and artichokes and stir to blend.
2 tablespoons cider vinegar	
¼ teaspoon garlic powder	
⅛ teaspoon pepper	
¾ teaspoon dried oregano	*2* Spoon the mixture into 8 endive leaves to form boat sandwiches.
1 small onion, minced	
¼ green bell pepper, chopped	
3 red bell peppers, roasted and sliced thin (or use canned, prepared roasted red bell peppers)	
6.5-ounce can tuna fish, drained	
2 ounces pizza pepperoni, slices halved	
6-ounce jar marinated artichokes, drained and cut in half	
8 Belgian endive leaves	

Per serving: Calories 232; Fat 17g (Saturated 3g); Cholesterol 28mg; Sodium 720mg; Carbohydrate 6g (Dietary Fiber 1g); Protein 15g.

Tuna Broccoli Casserole

Prep time: 15 min • **Cook time:** 25 min • **Yield:** 6 servings

Ingredients	Directions
Nonstick cooking spray	**1** Preheat the oven to 400 degrees. Using the cooking spray, grease a 9-x-9-inch baking dish.
2 cups rice seashell pasta	
2 tablespoons cornstarch	**2** In a medium saucepan, cook the pasta according to package directions, and then rinse and drain it.
1 teaspoon chicken bouillon granules	
1 teaspoon dried minced onion	**3** In a large bowl, stir together the cornstarch, bouillon granules, dried onion, thyme, parsley, pepper, and salt.
¼ teaspoon dried thyme	
1 tablespoon dried parsley	**4** Add the pasta, tuna, pimento, soup, milk, broccoli, and ½ cup of the cheese to the bowl. Stir to mix well.
¼ teaspoon pepper	
⅛ teaspoon salt	**5** Spoon the mixture into the prepared baking dish.
12-ounce can tuna packed in water, drained	
4-ounce jar chopped pimento, drained	**6** In a small bowl, stir together the remaining ¾ cup of cheese, breadcrumbs, and paprika. Sprinkle this mixture on top of the casserole.
18-ounce can cream of mushroom soup	
3 tablespoons whole milk	**7** Bake the casserole for 25 minutes.
10-ounce box frozen chopped broccoli, thawed	
½ cup plus ¾ cup shredded Monterey Jack cheese	
¼ cup seasoned breadcrumbs	
¼ teaspoon paprika	

Per serving: Calories 385; Fat 13g (Saturated 7g); Cholesterol 40mg; Sodium 406mg; Carbohydrate 41g (Dietary Fiber 3g); Protein 26g.

Tip: Because companies change their recipes and ingredients regularly, check the soup label ingredients to make sure it's gluten-free.

Chapter 4

Making Marvelous, Meatless Mains

In This Chapter

▶ Giving vegetables center stage

▶ Cooking with gluten-free pastas and grains

▶ Finding unexpected combinations for mouthwatering meals

Meatless dishes are perceived to be a challenge on a gluten-free diet because so many vegetarian or vegan dishes use pasta. The good news is that lots of really great gluten-free pastas are available; the other good news is that veggies are gluten-free! All of them!

Veggin' Out with Main Dishes

Veggies add flavor, nutrition, and color to a dinner plate. For a festive presentation, sprinkle the dish with minced parsley before putting the vegetables on the plate. If you want to get really wild and crazy, add some edible flowers, like nasturtiums.

Cooking vegetables is somewhat of an art. Here are a few suggestions to keep in mind:

✔ All vegetables that grow above ground can start cooking in boiling water.

✔ For those that grow beneath the ground (beets, turnips, and so on), start in cold water.

- ✔ Many vegetables can be grilled (leeks, onions, asparagus, eggplant, and so on). Just slather them with a little olive oil and some seasonings before grilling.

- ✔ Salted eggplant absorbs less fat than unsalted eggplant when it's fried or sautéed. Sprinkle the slices with salt and place them in a colander in the sink. Let them set for 30 minutes, and then rinse the slices in cool water and pat them dry with paper towels.

- ✔ Peeled sweet potatoes can be substituted for white potatoes in many recipes.

- ✔ Whether you steam, grill, roast, stir-fry, or pan-fry your veggies, try to include them in as many meals as possible.

Packing Some Punch with Pastas and Starches

While veggies may be good for us, face it — nothing beats a great bowl of pasta or a side of potatoes. The gluten-free pastas taste every bit as good as traditional wheat pasta if you take a little care with the preparation. When boiling gluten-free pasta, add a little oil to the pot of water. Oil helps prevent the pasta from sticking together. Also add some salt. Salt raises the temperature of the boiling water, enabling the pasta to cook more quickly without falling apart.

The alternative flour pastas and macaronis become gooey and mushy if you overcook them. As soon as they're *al dente* (a fancy word for "just about tender"), remove the pan from the stove, drain off the water, and then rinse the pasta under cold running water (unless a recipe directs otherwise).

To serve the pasta with a sauce, add some sauce to the pot you used to cook the pasta and bring it to a boil. Add the rinsed and drained pasta, and then heat, stirring occasionally, just until the strands are hot, and serve immediately. If you're going to use the pasta in a casserole that will be baked, you don't need to reheat the pasta after you drain it.

The variety of alternative pastas available is increasing almost daily. Corn and rice are still the mainstays. Corn pasta is a bit coarser and grainier, takes a little longer to cook, and has a more distinctive taste. It also holds together better. Rice pasta has no distinctive taste, so it absorbs the sauce's flavor. It cooks more quickly than the corn-based products, so you need to pay close attention when it nears al dente. If it's overcooked, it can fall apart — but cooked al dente, it's fabulous.

Although rice and corn are the most common alternative pastas on the grocery shelves, you can also buy gluten-free pasta that's made from the following flours:

- ✔ White sweet potato
- ✔ Milo
- ✔ Water chestnut
- ✔ Arrowroot
- ✔ Yam
- ✔ Lotus
- ✔ Cassava
- ✔ Quinoa
- ✔ Amaranth
- ✔ Buckwheat
- ✔ Lentil
- ✔ Black bean

After corn and rice pasta, lentil definitely weighs in as the next most popular. It's darker in color, but the taste is very good and it resists the mushy factor. Quinoa pasta is pretty widely available these days, too, and is *loaded* with nutrition!

Buckwheat pasta often has wheat flour added to it. Don't assume the buckwheat pasta is pure buckwheat. Be sure to read the label!

Anyone who is vegan or vegetarian has already discovered some of the fascinating and delectable things that can be done with vegetables. A meat-and-potatoes person may need a little more convincing that it's possible to fill an empty stomach *and* enjoy the meal with no meat present. This section includes a few entrees that will convince anyone that meat isn't needed to satisfy the tummy at mealtime.

If you're innovative, select a vegetable large enough to stuff. Hollow it out, chop up the center, and sauté with onions and green bell pepper. Add "something" (rice, pasta, and/or veggies) to the onions and peppers, restuff the vegetable, and top it off with gluten-free breadcrumbs, shredded cheese, or a sauce, and then bake. Each time you opt to do this, select a different veggie for the shell, a different filling, and a different topping.

Gluten-free lasagna noodles are another source for creativity. *Parboil* (partially cook by boiling) the noodles *slightly,* and then drain. (If the noodles are fully cooked, they'll fall apart when you assemble the casserole.) Don't rinse the noodles because they need to keep the starch intact for a cohesive finished product. If you use enough sauce in the casserole, you don't even need to parboil. Simply lay the noodles in a pan, top with a filling of your choice, repeat the layers, spread with a sauce, and bake.

Vegan Lasagne

Prep time: 15 min • **Cook time:** 90 min • **Yield:** 10 servings

Ingredients	Directions
½ cup rice (or vegan) cream cheese	**1** Preheat the oven to 350 degrees.
½ cup rice (or vegan) mozzarella	**2** In a large mixing bowl, combine the rice cream cheese, mozzarella, and Parmesan. In a medium bowl, mix together the pasta sauce, basil, onion powder, pepper, and salt. Set aside both mixtures.
½ cup rice (or vegan) Parmesan	
Two 24-ounce jars pasta sauce	
¼ cup fresh chopped basil	**3** Heat a large skillet over medium-high heat. Cook the spinach, zucchini, olives, mushrooms, and onions in Bragg Liquid Aminos for 4 minutes or until the onions begin to soften. Don't overcook (remember, the veggies will still cook when the lasagne bakes). Set aside this mixture.
1 teaspoon onion powder	
¼ teaspoon white pepper	
Sea salt to taste	
½ cup chopped spinach	**4** Spray a shallow 9-by-13-inch baking dish with nonstick spray. In the baking dish, layer the lasagne as follows: Place one-third of the sauce on the bottom of the dish, followed by a layer of uncooked noodles (just enough to cover the sauce), half the cheese mixture, and half the vegetable mixture. Repeat this layering process with another third of the sauce, another layer of noodles, most of the remaining cheese, and the rest of the vegetables. Finish with the last third of sauce on the top.
½ cup diced zucchini	
¼ cup sliced black olives	
¼ cup sliced mushrooms	
¼ cup chopped onions	
1 tablespoon Bragg Liquid Aminos	
Nonstick cooking spray	**5** Top the lasagne with a thin layer of mozzarella and Parmesan.
10-ounce package lasagna noodles, uncooked	**6** Cover the lasagne with aluminum foil and bake it for 1 hour. Remove the foil and bake the lasagne 30 minutes longer or until its top is golden brown. Cool the lasagne for at least 15 minutes before cutting into it.

Per serving: Calories 313 (From Fat 53); Fat 6g (Saturated 1g); Cholesterol 0mg; Sodium 1,002mg; Carbohydrate 51g (Dietary Fiber 3g); Protein 11g.

Tip: Be creative and use whatever veggies and other "stuffing" ingredients you like.

Tip: If your sauce isn't flavorful enough, try adding a teaspoon of minced garlic.

Spinach Lasagne

Prep time: 35 min • **Cook time:** 45 min • **Yield:** 6 servings

Ingredients	Directions
½ cup hot water	**1** Preheat the oven to 350 degrees.
1 chicken bouillon cube	**2** In a small bowl, stir together the hot water and bouillon cube until the cube dissolves.
1 medium onion, chopped	**3** In a medium saucepan over medium heat, sauté the onion and garlic in oil until tender, stirring frequently.
2 teaspoons fresh minced garlic	
1 tablespoon olive oil	**4** Stir in the broth (bouillon cube and water), spaghetti sauce, Italian seasoning, and pepper; simmer slowly for 15 minutes.
2½ cups spaghetti sauce	
¾ teaspoon Italian seasoning	**5** In a medium bowl, stir together the cottage cheese, yogurt, Romano cheese, and spinach.
¼ teaspoon pepper	
1½ cups small curd cottage cheese	**6** In a medium saucepan, boil the noodles according to the package directions, boiling only for 10 minutes. Drain the water and rinse the noodles very quickly with cold water so they're cool enough to handle (you want them to retain their starch).
½ cup plain yogurt	
¼ cup grated Romano cheese	
10-ounce box frozen chopped spinach, thawed and squeezed dry	**7** Spread ¼ of the sauce in an 8-x-11-inch baking dish. Lay 1 layer of noodles on top of the sauce. Spread ½ of the spinach mixture over the noodles, and then ⅓ of the mozzarella. Repeat the layers, ending with the sauce and mozzarella.
8-ounce box lasagna noodles	
1½ cups shredded mozzarella cheese	**8** Bake the lasagne uncovered for 45 minutes. Let the lasagne set for 10 minutes before cutting.

Per serving: Calories 388; Fat 14g (Saturated 6g); Cholesterol 29mg; Sodium 911mg; Carbohydrate 45g (Dietary Fiber 5g); Protein 22g.

Tip: Take care not to overcook the noodles when parboiling them.

Fresh Harvest Penne

Prep time: 30 min • **Cook time:** 50 min • **Yield:** 8 servings

Ingredients	Directions
16-ounce package penne (or any cut) pasta	*1* Cook the pasta as directed, being careful not to overcook it.
2 tablespoons olive oil	*2* In a large frying pan, heat the olive oil over medium heat. Add the onion, zucchini, and squash, and sauté, stirring often, for about 5 minutes.
½ medium red onion, diced	
¾ cup thickly sliced zucchini	*3* Add the garlic and eggplant to the pan, and continue stirring frequently.
¾ cup thickly sliced yellow squash	
1 tablespoon minced garlic (about 6 cloves)	*4* When the eggplant begins to get soft, after about 5 minutes, reduce the heat to low and add the tomatoes. Continue stirring the mixture for 3 to 4 minutes.
1 cup ½-inch eggplant cubes	
2 medium tomatoes, diced	*5* Drain the pasta. In a large serving bowl, combine the pasta, vegetables, basil, and Parmesan cheese.
⅓ cup fresh basil, chopped	
⅓ cup freshly grated Parmesan cheese	

Per serving: Calories 252 (From Fat 51); Fat 6g (Saturated 1g); Cholesterol 3mg; Sodium 64mg; Carbohydrate 46g (Dietary Fiber 8g); Protein 6g.

Cheese Enchiladas

Prep time: 25 min • **Cook time:** 1 hr • **Yield:** 6 servings

Ingredients	*Directions*
2 cups grated cheddar cheese	*1* Preheat the oven to 350 degrees.
2 cups grated Monterey Jack cheese	*2* Combine the cheddar, Monterey Jack, garlic powder, and 2 teaspoons of the cumin; set the mixture aside.
1 teaspoon garlic powder	*3* To make the enchilada sauce, heat 1 tablespoon of the cooking oil in a large skillet over medium-high heat. Add the minced onion and garlic, and sauté them until they're soft, about 4 minutes. Add the tomato sauce, chili powder, oregano, hot sauce, and remaining teaspoon of cumin. Cover the sauce and simmer it for about 30 minutes.
3 teaspoons cumin, divided	
3 tablespoons cooking oil, divided	
1 small white onion, finely minced	
2 teaspoons minced garlic (about 4 cloves)	*4* When the sauce is finished, spray a 9-by-13-inch baking dish with nonstick spray, and then pour about ⅔ cup of the sauce into it. Set aside the remaining enchilada sauce for Step 6.
4 cups tomato sauce	
3 tablespoons chili powder	*5* In a small skillet, heat the remaining 2 tablespoons of cooking oil (or enough oil to generously cover the bottom of the pan) over medium-high heat.
1 teaspoon oregano	
2 teaspoons hot sauce	*6* Briefly dip one corn tortilla into the hot oil to soften it (about 5 seconds), making sure both sides get coated, and then dip it in the enchilada sauce, coating both sides. Lay the tortilla flat on a plate or cutting board, and put about ⅓ cup of the cheese mixture down the center of the tortilla (lengthwise). Roll up the tortilla, and put it seam-side down into the baking dish.
Nonstick cooking spray	
12 corn tortillas	
¼ cup sliced black olives	

7 Repeat Steps 5 and 6 for each enchilada, laying the enchiladas side by side in the baking dish. Pour the rest of the enchilada sauce over the rolled-up enchiladas, and sprinkle any remaining cheese mixture over them. Add the sliced black olives on top of the cheese.

8 Bake the enchiladas for 20 to 30 minutes, until the cheese is melted and bubbly.

Per serving: Calories 548 (From Fat 306); Fat 34g (Saturated 16g); Cholesterol 73mg; Sodium 1,640mg; Carbohydrate 41g (Dietary Fiber 7g); Protein 25g.

Enchilada Casserole

Prep time: 15 min • **Cook time:** 20 min • **Yield:** 6 servings

Ingredients	Directions
Nonstick cooking spray	**1** Preheat the oven to 350 degrees. Spray a 7-x-11-inch baking pan with cooking spray.
8-ounce can tomato sauce	**2** In a large skillet over medium-high heat, stir together the tomato sauce, water, and hot pepper sauce. Bring it to a boil, and then lower the heat and let it simmer for 3 minutes. Remove the skillet from the heat and let the sauce cool slightly.
⅓ cup water	
5 drops hot pepper sauce	
½ medium onion, diced	**3** In a small skillet, sauté the onions, garlic, and green bell pepper in the oil over medium heat until the vegetables are softened but not browned. Stir frequently. Remove the skillet from the heat and let the veggies cool.
1 clove garlic, minced	
½ cup diced green bell pepper	
2 teaspoons olive oil	**4** In a medium bowl, stir together the onion mixture, parsley, salt, pepper, chili powder, oregano, cumin, Monterey Jack cheese, and ½ cup of cheddar cheese.
3 tablespoons fresh chopped parsley	
⅛ teaspoon salt	**5** Dip each tortilla quickly into the tomato sauce to coat both sides. Lay the tortilla on a flat surface and spread with 1 tablespoon of the refried beans.
⅛ teaspoon pepper	
2½ teaspoons chili powder	
½ teaspoon dried oregano	**6** Spoon the cheese mixture on top of the beans, dividing evenly among the 6 tortillas.
½ teaspoon cumin	
1 cup shredded Monterey Jack cheese	**7** Roll the tortillas and arrange them in the prepared baking dish. Pour the remaining tomato sauce over the tortillas, and then sprinkle them with the remaining 2 tablespoons of cheddar cheese.
½ cup plus 2 tablespoons shredded sharp cheddar cheese	
Six 9-inch corn tortillas	**8** Cover the pan with foil and bake for 20 minutes.
6 tablespoons refried beans	

Per serving: Calories 239; Fat 13g (Saturated 7g); Cholesterol 29mg; Sodium 619mg; Carbohydrate 21g (Dietary Fiber 5g); Protein 12g.

Tip: When dipping the tortillas in the tomato sauce, do it quickly or the tortillas will get so soft they may fall apart.

Note: Keep these enchiladas covered in the refrigerator to pop in the oven, toaster oven, or microwave.

Eggplant Morocco

Prep time: 45 min • **Cook time:** 40 min • **Yield:** 4 servings

Ingredients	Directions
1 teaspoon whole cumin seeds (or ground cumin)	**1** Toast and grind the cumin seeds. This step is optional (you can use ground cumin if you prefer), but if you want traditional Moroccan food, you'll toast and grind. Just put the cumin seeds in a skillet over medium heat and stir until they're dark brown and begin to smell good (about 5 minutes). Remove them from the pan right away so they don't burn. Cool the seeds, and use a coffee or spice grinder to grind them.
2 medium eggplants	
1 small red onion, chopped	
2 teaspoons red wine vinegar	
1 teaspoon lemon juice	
1 teaspoon sugar	**2** Put the eggplant in an oven-safe baking dish and bake at 350 degrees for about 30 minutes. The skin will darken and the insides will be tender.
2 tablespoons olive oil (extra-virgin is best)	
2 tablespoons parsley	**3** When the eggplant is cool enough to handle, scrape the insides out of the skin and place on a cutting board. Chop the eggplant into ½-inch cubes. Be sure to cut off and throw away the stem.
Salt to taste	
Black pepper to taste	
	4 Mix together ½ teaspoon of cumin, the eggplant, onion, vinegar, lemon juice, sugar, oil, and ½ tablespoon parsley.
	5 Put the mixture into a serving dish and top with the rest of the cumin, parsley, and salt and pepper.

Per serving: Calories 99 (From Fat 64); Fat 7g (Saturated 1g); Cholesterol 0mg; Sodium 151mg; Carbohydrate 9g (Dietary Fiber 3g); Protein 1g.

Spinach Pie

Prep time: 15 min • **Cook time:** 45 min • **Yield:** 12 servings

Ingredients	Directions
Nonstick cooking spray	*1* Preheat the oven to 350 degrees. Spray a 9-inch pie plate with cooking spray.
3 tablespoons butter	
1 medium onion, chopped	*2* Melt the butter in a large skillet over medium heat. Add the onion and sauté until tender, about 8 minutes.
3 large eggs	
16-ounce container small-curd cottage cheese	*3* In a large bowl, whisk the eggs lightly.
1 cup shredded mozzarella cheese	*4* Stir in the cottage cheese, mozzarella cheese, Parmesan cheese, salt, pepper, and dill.
1 cup grated Parmesan cheese	
¼ teaspoon salt	*5* Stir in the onions and spinach until everything is well blended.
½ teaspoon pepper	
1 teaspoon dried dill	*6* Spoon the mixture into the prepared pie plate.
10-ounce box frozen chopped spinach, thawed and squeezed dry	*7* Bake the pie for 45 minutes, or until a knife inserted near the center comes out clean. If the pie begins to brown too much on top before being cooked through, cover it with a piece of foil.
	8 Let the pie rest for 10 minutes before cutting it into 12 wedges.

Per serving: Calories 177; Fat 11g (Saturated 7g); Cholesterol 81mg; Sodium 484mg; Carbohydrate 4g (Dietary Fiber 1g); Protein 16g.

Tip: You can prepare this dish ahead, cover and refrigerate it, and then bake it just before dinner.

Stuffed Acorn Squash

Prep time: 15 min • **Cook time:** 1 hr • **Yield:** 2 servings

Ingredients	Directions
1 large acorn squash, halved and seeded	**1** Preheat the oven to 375 degrees.
1 cup water	**2** Place the squash, cut-side down, on a small baking dish.
2 tablespoons butter, melted	
½ teaspoon bottled lemon juice	**3** Pour the water onto the bottom of the dish and bake for 35 minutes. Remove the squash from the oven and discard the water in the pan.
¼ teaspoon cinnamon	
2 tablespoons brown sugar	**4** In a bowl, stir together the butter, lemon juice, cinnamon, brown sugar, apple, and pecans.
1 medium red or golden delicious apple, peeled, cored, and chopped fine	**5** Mound the apple mixture on top of the squash halves, dividing evenly.
2 tablespoons chopped pecans	**6** Place the squash back in the baking dish, cut-side up, and continue baking it for another 30 to 35 minutes or until the flesh is tender when poked with a fork. If the top browns too much, cover it with foil during the last 15 minutes of baking.

Per serving: Calories 294; Fat 14g (Saturated 8g); Cholesterol 30mg; Sodium 94mg; Carbohydrate 45g (Dietary Fiber 5g); Protein 3g.

Tip: The easiest way to half the squash is to take a strong, pointed knife and first make jabs that cut through the skin around the center of the vegetable. Then take a butcher knife and press down along the "jabbed" line.

Cranberries and Yams

Prep time: 15 min • **Cook time:** 20 min • **Yield:** 4 servings

Ingredients	Directions
Nonstick cooking spray	**1** Preheat the oven to 450 degrees. Spray a baking sheet with cooking spray.
2 large yams, peeled	
¼ teaspoon cinnamon	**2** Cut each yam in half crosswise and then into wedges.
¼ teaspoon plus ⅛ teaspoon salt	**3** In a plastic, self-seal bag, combine the cinnamon, ¼ teaspoon of salt, cumin, pepper, and garlic powder.
¼ teaspoon cumin	
⅛ teaspoon pepper	**4** Add the yams. Seal the bag and shake it until the yams are evenly coated.
¼ teaspoon garlic powder	
2 tablespoons dried cranberries	**5** Lay the yam wedges in a single layer on the prepared baking sheet.
2 teaspoons butter	**6** Bake the yams for 30 to 35 minutes, or until the wedges are very tender, turning the yams once during baking.
1 large pear, peeled, cored, and cut into ½-inch cubes	
¼ cup coarsely chopped pecans	**7** While the yams bake, place the cranberries in a bowl of hot water to soak and soften for 5 minutes. Drain.
¼ teaspoon ginger	**8** Melt the butter in a large nonstick skillet.
1 teaspoon brown sugar	**9** Add the pears and pecans and sauté them over medium heat until the pears are tender and golden, about 4 minutes, stirring frequently.
½ teaspoon balsamic vinegar	
	10 Stir in the cranberries, ginger, brown sugar, vinegar and remaining ⅛ teaspoon of salt, and heat until the sauce is warmed.
	11 To serve, spoon the cranberry sauce over the yams.

Per serving: Calories 186; Fat 7g (Saturated 2g); Cholesterol 5mg; Sodium 279mg; Carbohydrate 31g (Dietary Fiber 5g); Protein 2g.

Carrot and Zucchini Latkes

Prep time: 15 min • **Cook time:** 10 min • **Yield:** 6 latkes

Ingredients	Directions
½ pound carrots	**1** Grate the carrots, zucchini, and onion using the large holes of a box grater.
1 medium zucchini	
1 small onion	**2** Place the vegetables in the center of several paper towels. Bring up the ends of the towels and twist them together to form a pouch. Holding the pouch over the sink, squeeze out the excess moisture from the vegetables.
1 egg	
1 tablespoon plus 1 teaspoon cornstarch	
¼ teaspoon salt	
¼ teaspoon pepper	**3** Place the vegetables in a medium bowl. Add the egg, cornstarch, salt, pepper, dill, Romano cheese, and breadcrumbs, and mix well.
¼ teaspoon dried dill	
1 tablespoon grated Romano cheese	**4** Heat the oil in a large skillet over medium heat.
¼ cup Italian seasoned breadcrumbs	**5** For each latke, spoon 1 large spoonful of the mixture carefully into the pan. Immediately use the side and back of the spoon to form the mixture into a flat round. Cook about 4 minutes per side, or until browned.
2 tablespoons olive oil	
	6 Remove the latke from the skillet; drain on a paper towel. Repeat with the remaining mixture.

Per serving: Calories 204; Fat 11g (Saturated 2g); Cholesterol 72mg; Sodium 345mg; Carbohydrate 23g (Dietary Fiber 3g); Protein 5g.

Tip: The breadcrumbs in the recipe are readily available at most health food stores. The breadcrumbs will stay fresher longer if you keep the unused portion in the freezer.

Note: The only thing that these latkes are missing is a dollop of sour cream on top. (As long as it's gluten-free, and not all of them are.) Enjoy these latkes as a side dish, or serve several as a main entree.

Roasted Asparagus with Mustard Dressing

Prep time: 6 min • **Cook time:** 15 min • **Yield:** 4 servings

Ingredients	Directions
1 bunch thin asparagus (approximately 28 stalks)	*1* Preheat the oven to 400 degrees.
1 tablespoon plus 3 tablespoons olive oil	*2* Wash the asparagus, and break off and discard the tough ends. Place the stalks in a baking dish.
2 tablespoons brown mustard	
¼ teaspoon salt	*3* Drizzle the stalks with 1 tablespoon of oil and toss to coat evenly. Spread the asparagus in a single layer.
⅛ teaspoon pepper	
1 tablespoon balsamic vinegar	*4* Bake the asparagus for 10 minutes, or until they're almost tender-crisp.
1 teaspoon sugar	*5* In a small bowl, whisk together the remaining 3 tablespoons of oil, mustard, salt, pepper, vinegar, and sugar.
	6 Pour the mustard glaze over the asparagus and return it to the oven for 5 minutes.

Per serving: Calories 160; Fat 14g (Saturated 2g); Cholesterol 0mg; Sodium 237mg; Carbohydrate 7g (Dietary Fiber 1g); Protein 3g.

Tip: Cover and refrigerate any leftovers because they're also amazing when served cold.

Buckwheat Stuffed Bell Peppers

Prep time: 20 min • **Cook time:** 1 hr • **Yield:** 6 servings

Ingredients	Directions
1 cup roasted buckwheat (kasha) groats, rinsed well 1½ cups vegetable stock 2 tablespoons olive oil, divided ½ red bell pepper, diced 1 cup baby spinach 2 cups frozen edamame, thawed 1 cup frozen corn, thawed ¼ cup chia seeds Fresh ground pepper and salt to taste 6 whole bell peppers, combination of red, green, and yellow, cored with tops removed 6 tablespoons rice vinegar 3 tablespoons soy sauce 2 tablespoons sesame oil 2 tablespoons chopped fresh cilantro 1 tablespoon fresh ginger, peeled and minced ½ teaspoon sugar	**1** Preheat the oven to 350 degrees. In a medium saucepan, add the vegetable stock. Bring to boil over medium-high heat. Add kasha to the boiling water and stir well with a wooden spoon. Reduce the heat to simmer, cover pan, and cook until all the liquid is absorbed, about 10 to 15 minutes. **2** In a medium skillet, add 1 tablespoon olive oil and diced red bell pepper and sauté on high heat for 2 minutes. Remove from heat and combine peppers with spinach, edamame, corn, chia seeds, pepper, and salt. Add mixture to the cooked buckwheat. **3** Rub remaining oil over cored bell peppers. Prebake the peppers in a glass baking pan for 15 minutes to soften. Remove from oven and fill the peppers with the kasha mixture, pressing firmly to fill the cavity. Place in baking pan, cover with foil, and bake for an additional 40 minutes. **4** In a small glass bowl, whisk together the rice vinegar, soy sauce, sesame oil, cilantro, ginger, and sugar. Drizzle sauce over peppers when ready to serve.

Per serving: Calories 341; Fat 14g (Saturated 2g); Cholesterol 0mg; Sodium 839mg; Carbohydrate 45g (Dietary Fiber 10g); Protein 13g.

Tip: Many grocery stores now carry buckwheat. Even though it doesn't naturally contain gluten, grains can be contaminated in the farming and production processes. Also sometimes vegetable stock can have gluten-containing ingredients, such as malt, malt flavoring, or hydrolyzed wheat protein, so read labels.

Note: With a delicious nutty flavor, buckwheat is easy to cook and super nutritious. It's loaded with fiber and low in saturated fat, cholesterol, and sodium. Don't overcook buckwheat, or it will become mushy.

Twice-Baked Sweet Potatoes

Prep time: 15 min • **Cook time:** 90 min • **Yield:** 4 servings

Ingredients	*Directions*
2 large sweet potatoes or yams, cut in half lengthwise	*1* Preheat the oven to 375 degrees.
Nonstick cooking spray	*2* Put the halves of the potatoes together to form a whole potato, and wrap each potato in foil.
3 tablespoons milk	
3 tablespoons maple syrup	*3* Bake the potatoes for about 1 hour until they're tender but not mushy.
½ teaspoon vanilla	
¼ teaspoon salt	*4* Cool the potatoes slightly, and then scoop out the centers, leaving enough potato to hold the shape of the skin. Place the scooped-out centers in a large mixing bowl.
1 egg	
3 tablespoons gluten-free flour mixture (see Book V Chapter 2 for white or whole-wheat versions)	*5* Lower the oven temperature to 325 degrees. Spray an 8-x-11-inch baking dish with cooking spray.
3 tablespoons brown sugar	*6* Using a mixer, whip the potato pulp until it's smooth. Add the milk, maple syrup, vanilla, salt, and egg, and continue to whip until the pulp is light and fluffy.
3 tablespoons butter, melted	
3 tablespoons finely chopped pecans	*7* Spoon the filling into the potato shells, dividing evenly.
	8 Place the shells in the prepared baking dish.
	9 In a small bowl, use a fork to blend together the flour mixture and brown sugar. Add the butter and continue to blend with the fork until the dry ingredients are evenly moistened.

10   Stir in the pecans.

11   Crumble sugar mixture over the potatoes. Bake the potatoes for 30 minutes.

Per serving: *Calories 384; Fat 21g (Saturated 7g); Cholesterol 77mg; Sodium 238mg; Carbohydrate 46g (Dietary Fiber 3g); Protein 5g.*

Tip: Sweet potatoes have a relatively low-glycemic index (see Book II, Chapter 1 for more info), making them far healthier for you than white potatoes.

The Ultimate Macaroni and Cheese

Prep time: 30 min • **Cook time:** 30 min • **Yield:** 9 servings

Ingredients	Directions
Nonstick cooking spray	**1** Preheat the oven to 350 degrees. Spray a 9-x-9-inch baking dish with cooking spray.
8-ounce box rice penne pasta	
2 cups milk	**2** In a medium saucepan, cook the pasta as the package directs, boiling only for 6 minutes. Rinse and drain the pasta.
½ cup whipping cream	
4 tablespoons butter	
1 teaspoon salt	**3** In the same saucepan, stir together the milk and whipping cream. Remove ½ cup of the milk mixture and set it aside.
¾ cup shredded Romano cheese, divided	
	4 Bring the remaining milk mixture to a simmer and add the drained pasta.
	5 Cook the milk and pasta over medium heat, stirring frequently, about 10 minutes, or until the mixture thickens and most of the milk is absorbed.
	6 Add the butter and salt and stir until the butter melts.
	7 In the prepared baking dish, layer half of the macaroni, and then half of the cheese. Repeat the layers.
	8 Pour the reserved milk over the top of the pasta.
	9 Bake for 30 minutes, or until the top begins to brown around the edges. Let the dish cool for 10 minutes before serving.

Per serving: Calories 227; Fat 12g (Saturated 7g); Cholesterol 36mg; Sodium 326mg; Carbohydrate 23g (Dietary Fiber 0g); Protein 7g.

Tip: You can assemble this dish ahead and freeze it (thaw it before baking), or you can cover and refrigerate it until shortly before dinner.

Cheese-Stuffed Zucchini

Prep time: 20 min • **Cook time:** 45 min • **Yield:** 4 servings

Ingredients	Directions
Nonstick cooking spray	*1* Preheat the oven to 350 degrees. Spray a 9-x-9-inch baking dish with cooking spray.
2 medium zucchini, each cut in half lengthwise	
2 teaspoons olive oil	*2* Carefully remove the pulp from each zucchini half, leaving a ¼-inch thick shell. Chop the pulp.
1 cup finely chopped onion	
1 cup finely chopped green bell pepper	*3* Heat the oil in a large nonstick skillet. Add the onion, green bell pepper, and garlic. Sauté over medium heat, stirring frequently, until the vegetables are soft (about 5 minutes).
2 cloves garlic, minced	
1 cup finely chopped plum tomatoes	*4* Stir the tomatoes, zucchini pulp, oregano, parsley, salt, pepper, dill, and mint into the onion mixture. Reduce the heat and cook over medium-low heat for 5 minutes, stirring occasionally. Remove from the heat; cool for 5 minutes.
¾ teaspoon dried oregano	
¼ cup chopped fresh parsley	
¼ teaspoon salt	*5* Stir in the cheese.
¼ teaspoon pepper	
¼ teaspoon dried dill	*6* Stuff each zucchini shell with about ½ cup of the onion mixture. Sprinkle the tops with breadcrumbs.
¼ teaspoon dried mint	
¾ cup crumbled feta cheese	*7* Set the zucchini "boats" in the prepared baking dish.
4 teaspoons Italian seasoned breadcrumbs	
	8 Bake the zucchini for 30 minutes, or until the breadcrumbs are lightly browned and the shells are tender.

Per serving: Calories 165; Fat 9g (Saturated 5g); Cholesterol 25mg; Sodium 610mg; Carbohydrate 17g (Dietary Fiber 4g); Protein 7g.

Tip: You can also serve this as a side dish.

Note: If you grow your own zucchini, try stuffing the flowers from the plant before the vegetable begins to develop. Pick the flowers when they are large, wash them well, and then stuff and bake them.

Quinoa-Stuffed Tomatoes

Prep time: 30 min • **Cook time:** 20 min • **Yield:** 4 servings

Ingredients	Directions
4 large tomatoes	**1** Preheat the oven to 350 degrees.
1 cup water	
2 teaspoons butter	**2** Cut ½ inch off the stem side of each tomato and discard the lid. Hollow out the insides.
2 teaspoons olive oil	
½ teaspoon minced garlic	**3** Place the tomato shells in a 9-x-9-inch baking dish, cut-side down.
2 green onions, minced	
½ teaspoon salt	**4** Pour the water around the tomatoes, cover the dish with foil, and bake the tomatoes for 15 to 20 minutes until the skins are slightly softened but firm enough to hold their shape. Remove the tomatoes from the oven and drain off the hot water.
¼ teaspoon pepper	
½ teaspoon dried dill	
¼ teaspoon dried thyme	
¼ teaspoon dried mint	
2 teaspoons dried parsley	**5** In a large nonstick saucepan, sauté the garlic and onions in the butter and oil over medium-high heat until the onion is tender, stirring frequently.
14-ounce can chicken broth	
½ cup uncooked quinoa	**6** Stir in the salt, pepper, dill, thyme, mint, and parsley.
2 tablespoons fresh lemon juice	**7** Add the chicken broth and bring it to a boil.
10-ounce box frozen chopped spinach, thawed and drained well	**8** Lower the heat to medium-low, stir in the quinoa, cover the pan, and simmer the broth slowly for 20 minutes, or until the broth has been absorbed and the quinoa is tender.
3 tablespoons crumbled feta cheese	**9** With a fork, stir in the lemon juice and spinach until everything is well combined. Stir in the feta cheese.

10 Stuff the tomatoes with the quinoa mixture. Cover the pan with foil.

11 Bake the stuffed tomatoes for 20 minutes.

Per serving: Calories 222; Fat 10g (Saturated 4g); Cholesterol 17mg; Sodium 815mg; Carbohydrate 28g (Dietary Fiber 6g); Protein 11g.

Tip: Select large, ripe (but not too soft) tomatoes for this recipe because, after they're baked, they need to be firm enough to hold their shape yet soft enough to cut easily with a fork. You don't use the tomato pulp in this recipe, so place the pulp in a self-seal bag to use in a stew or pasta sauce another day.

Vegetable Cheese Calzone

Prep time: 40 min • **Cook time:** 45 min • **Yield:** 4 servings

Ingredients	Directions
1 recipe Basic Pizza Dough (see Book V, Chapter 6)	**1** Make the Basic Pizza Dough and divide it into four parts. Roll out each piece onto a piece of parchment paper into a 10-inch circle.
2 tablespoons olive oil	
1 red bell pepper, diced	**2** In a large skillet, heat the olive oil over medium heat. Add the bell pepper, zucchini, and spinach and cook until soft, about 8 to 9 minutes. Let cool completely.
1 zucchini, diced	
1 cup frozen chopped spinach, thawed and well drained	
½ cup grated mozzarella cheese	**3** Divide the vegetable mixture among the dough circles, leaving the outer inch of dough filling-free.
¼ cup grated Parmesan cheese	**4** Top each circle with 2 tablespoons mozzarella cheese, 1 tablespoon Parmesan cheese, 1 tablespoon kalamata olives, and 2 tablespoons artichoke hearts.
¼ cup sliced kalamata olives	
½ cup chopped artichoke hearts	**5** Fold one side of the calzone over the other and crimp well around the edges.
	6 Let rise for 30 minutes. Preheat the oven to 425 degrees.
	7 Bake the calzones for 35 to 40 minutes, until well browned.

Per serving: Calories 507 (From Fat 167); Fat 19g (Saturated 5g); Cholesterol 15mg; Sodium 922mg; Carbohydrate 76g (Dietary Fiber 5g); Protein 14g.

Vary It! Use your favorite vegetables in this easy recipe.

Spinach and Goat Cheese Stuffed Rolls

Prep time: 30 min, plus chilling time • **Cook time:** 25 min • **Yield:** 6 servings

Ingredients	Directions
4 ounces goat cheese with herbs, crumbled	*1* In a medium bowl, combine the goat cheese, spinach, and pepper until combined. Place the mixture onto plastic wrap and form it into a 10-inch-long log. Chill the log while you make the dough.
8 ounces frozen chopped spinach, thawed and well drained	
¼ teaspoon pepper	*2* For the dough, in a large bowl, combine the yeast, sugar, Whole-Grain Flour Mix, White Flour Mix, buckwheat flour (or xanthan gum), and salt and mix until the dough is one color.
1½ teaspoons active dry yeast	
1½ teaspoons sugar	
½ cup plus 1 tablespoon plus 2 teaspoons (83 grams) Whole-Grain Flour Mix (see Book V, Chapter 2)	*3* Add the egg, butter or shortening, and water and beat well for 1 minute.
½ cup minus 1 teaspoon (71 grams) White Flour Mix (see Book V, Chapter 2)	*4* Roll the dough onto parchment paper to ½-inch thickness, a 12-x-6-inch rectangle. Chill the dough for a half hour to let it rise slightly and firm.
2 tablespoons (20 grams) raw buckwheat flour or ¾ teaspoon xanthan gum	*5* Preheat the oven to 425 degrees.
¼ teaspoon salt	*6* Remove the dough and goat cheese filling from the fridge. Remove the plastic from the goat cheese log and place the log in the center of the dough. Flatten the cheese mixture slightly.
1 egg	
¼ cup butter or butter-flavored shortening	*7* Fold in the ends of the dough and then the sides to encase the filling. Leave a gap at the center so the filling shows.
2 tablespoons water	
	8 Bake for 15 minutes, rotate the pan, and bake 10 to 12 minutes longer, or until the crust is golden-brown. Let the roll cool completely before slicing to serve.

Per serving: Calories 263 (From Fat 132); Fat 15g (Saturated 9g); Cholesterol 71mg; Sodium 240mg; Carbohydrate 27g (Dietary Fiber 2g); Protein 9g.

Note: Make sure that the spinach is really well drained. Squeeze the spinach until no more liquid comes out. Press it in a kitchen towel or between paper towels to make sure it's really dry.

Vegetarian Herb-Topped Biscuit Casserole

Prep time: 45 min • **Cook time:** 50 min • **Yield:** 8 servings

Ingredients	Directions
1 recipe Herbed Cream Biscuits (see Book V, Chapter 5) **2 tablespoons plus ¼ cup olive oil** **1 onion, diced** **2 sweet potatoes, peeled and diced** **2 russet potatoes, peeled and diced** **1 zucchini, diced** **1 red bell pepper, diced** **1 cup sliced button or crimini mushrooms** **1 cup rinsed and drained garbanzo beans** **3 cloves garlic, minced** **3 tablespoons minus 1 teaspoon (27 grams) sweet rice flour** **2 tablespoons minced fresh rosemary** **2 cups milk or light cream**	*1* Preheat the oven to 400 degrees. Grease a 9-x-13-inch pan with nonstick cooking spray. Prepare the biscuits and set aside. *2* Cook the 2 tablespoons olive oil and onion in a large frying pan over medium heat for 1 to 2 minutes, until the onion starts to soften. Add the sweet potatoes, russet potatoes, and zucchini. Cook and stir until the potatoes begin to brown, about 8 to 10 minutes. *3* Add the red bell pepper, mushrooms, and garbanzo beans and cook for 1 minute longer. Pour into the prepared pan. *4* In another medium saucepan, heat ¼ cup olive oil over medium heat. Add the garlic and cook for 30 seconds, until the garlic is fragrant. *5* Stir in the sweet rice flour and cook for 30 seconds. Add the rosemary and milk and cook over medium heat, stirring constantly with a wire whisk, until the gravy is thickened and smooth, about 5 to 6 minutes. *6* Pour the gravy over the vegetables in a casserole dish and immediately top with the biscuits. *7* Bake for 25 to 30 minutes, until the casserole is bubbly and the biscuits are golden-brown. Serve immediately.

Per serving: Calories 513 (From Fat 248); Fat 28g (Saturated 13g); Cholesterol 69mg; Sodium 390mg; Carbohydrate 62g (Dietary Fiber 5g); Protein 9g.

Broiled Veggie Tortillas

Prep time: 15 min • **Cook time:** 7 min • **Yield:** 4 servings

Ingredients	Directions
1 tablespoon olive oil	*1* Preheat the broiler.
¼ teaspoon minced garlic	*2* In a large skillet, sauté the garlic and vegetables in olive oil on high heat until they're tender crisp, about 3 minutes.
¼ green bell pepper, cut into thin strips	
½ small zucchini, sliced	
¼ medium onion, sliced thin	*3* Stir in the parsley, oregano, Italian seasoning, salt, and pepper.
½ small portobella mushroom, cut in half and sliced thin	
½ teaspoon dried parsley	*4* Reassemble the tortilla wedges together to form a circle on a baking sheet.
¼ teaspoon dried oregano	
¼ teaspoon Italian seasoning	*5* Spoon the veggies evenly over the tortilla wedges and then sprinkle with feta cheese.
Dash of salt	
⅛ teaspoon pepper	*6* Broil for 7 minutes or until the tortillas are crisp.
10-inch rice flour tortilla, cut into 4 wedges	
¼ cup crumbled feta cheese	

Per serving: Calories 100; Fat 7g (Saturated 2g); Cholesterol 8mg; Sodium 192mg; Carbohydrate 8g (Dietary Fiber 1g); Protein 3g.

Vary It! You can easily adapt this recipe for a wrap. Instead of cutting the tortilla into wedges, spoon the vegetables onto two whole tortillas and then roll each one up. After baking, cut each tortilla wrap in half.

Roasted Vegetable Pizza

Prep time: 35 min • **Cook time:** 11–28 min • **Yield:** 6 servings

Ingredients	*Directions*
1 recipe Basic Pizza Dough (see Book V, Chapter 6)	**1** Preheat the oven to 450 degrees. Prepare the Basic Pizza Dough. Put the dough on a cold cookie sheet, stretching and patting so it fits the pan. Let it rise while you prepare the vegetables.
2 large ripe tomatoes	
1 zucchini, thinly sliced	
2 large portobello mushrooms, thinly sliced	**2** Remove the core from the tomatoes and slice them ¼-inch thick. Prepare all the vegetables.
1 large bell pepper, sliced ¼-inch thick	**3** Place the vegetables on a cookie sheet and coat with 2 tablespoons of the oil. Roast for 5 to 10 minutes, or until the edges start to brown. Remove them from the oven and set them aside.
2 tablespoons plus 2 tablespoons extra-virgin olive oil or kalamata olive oil	
3 ounces fresh basil leaves	**4** Gently rub the remaining 2 tablespoons oil into the dough.
8 ounces (2 cups) grated mozzarella cheese (optional)	**5** Place the basil leaves on the dough in a single layer and arrange the vegetables on top. Top with the cheese (if desired).
Salt and pepper to taste	
	6 Bake for 6 minutes for a no-cheese pizza. Bake for 15 to 18 minutes for a pizza with cheese, until the cheese melts and browns.
	7 Let the pizza cool for 3 minutes before cutting to serve.

Per serving: Calories 343 (From Fat 116); Fat 13g (Saturated 2g); Cholesterol 0mg; Sodium 496mg; Carbohydrate 54g (Dietary Fiber 5g); Protein 7g.

Book V

Losing the Gluten, Keeping the Baked Goods

Top 5 Gluten-Free Baking Mixes to Have on Hand

- **All-purpose baking mix:** Several companies make various types of all-purpose baking mixes, and most are excellent. Some companies use the garbanzo/fava bean mixture, and some use mixtures of other gluten-free flours. Use these mixes for baking or as a coating for fried or baked foods.

- **Bread mixes:** Many different kinds of bread mixes are available today, most of which you can fix in a bread machine or mix by hand and cook in the oven.

- **Brownies:** The brownie mixes today are absolutely amazing. Some come with chunks of chocolate, but if they don't, you can add your own. You can also personalize them with nuts or even frosting.

- **Cakes:** Gluten-free cake mixes come in just about any flavor you want, and these days, they're all incredibly moist, light, and tasty. With slight modifications that are almost always on the package, you can make your cakes into cupcakes.

- **Pizza dough:** Mixes to help you whip up a quick pizza crust are available. You just top the crust with your favorite toppings. The pizza is as good as or better than anything other people deliver. Keep in mind that many gluten-free foods, even some of those you buy commercially, don't have preservatives in them. So unlike a store-bought pastry that has a shelf life of seven millennia, your gluten-free foods should usually be refrigerated or even frozen.

Find out how to adjust your gluten-free baking to high altitudes by visiting www.dummies.com/extras/glutenfreeaio.

Contents at a Glance

Chapter 1

Unique Issues of Gluten-Free Baking

Gluten-free baking has special issues that are distinct from the issues and rules of baking with wheat products. How do you build structure yet keep baked goods tender without the helping hand of gluten? Are there special methods that can "trick" a bread or cake into acting like gluten is part of the structure? And what about taste?

You can build structure and flavor without gluten. Special methods do exist, and they aren't difficult; they just take a bit of extra time and skills that are easy to learn. In this chapter, you look at the tricks of gluten-free baking for each category of recipe, because each type of baked good has its own characteristics that you want to emphasize.

Tricks and Traps

Gluten is the stretchy protein that forms when wheat flour is exposed to water and is manipulated, either through beating or kneading. This protein forms a literal web that traps air, creating the *crumb,* or texture, of breads, cookies, cakes, and pastries.

In this section, you discover how to build structure, keep baked goods tender, and create the distinctively nutty taste of wheat flour without using the gluten found in wheat flour. It is possible!

Measuring, proportion, and mixing

When gluten-free products were first developed decades ago, they had many problems. Breads tended to be dense and tough and usually were crumbly and flavorless. Cakes weren't tender or fluffy but had a tough crumb and were heavy. Cookies crumbled or were sticky and dense. Things have changed in the past few years, as intrepid bakers became determined to buck these disasters and make gluten-free baked goods that are just as good as those made with wheat.

Two of the essential steps in baking are key to delicious, gluten-free baked goods: measuring and mixing. Because gluten-free flours are heavier than wheat flours, weighing them (grams) instead of measuring by volume (cups and tablespoons) was a breakthrough. Here are some other points to keep in mind regarding measuring, proportion, and mixing:

- Use a scale set to gram weights and measure each flour you use. Be sure to zero out the scale after each measurement. (By the way, measuring in ounces is called *imperial weights* while measuring in grams is called *metric weights*. Just another cocktail party tidbit for you!)

- The proportion of flours to liquid is different in gluten-free baked goods. Doughs are rare; most of the recipes, even for yeast breads, are batters. Gluten-free flours are heavier and absorb more moisture than wheat flours, so they need a bit more liquid for the baked goods to be tender and moist.

- If you do measure by volume, be especially careful with flour and mixes. To measure flour with cups, tablespoons, and teaspoons, always spoon the flour into the measuring cup or spoon and then level off with the back of a knife. Never pack the flour, shake the cup, or press on the flour. Don't scoop the flour out of its container or bag with the measuring cup or you'll end up with too much flour and your products will be heavy and dry.

- You usually chill batters and doughs before baking. This gives the flour proteins and starches time to absorb the liquid in the recipe, which helps develop structure and flavor.

- When substituting flours in gluten-free breads, *always* substitute by weight. Don't substitute cup for cup or you'll end up with a disaster. If a recipe calls for 1 cup of potato starch, which weighs 190 grams, and you want to use tapioca starch, you need to add 190 grams of tapioca starch, not 1 cup — because a cup of tapioca starch (also called tapioca flour) weighs 125 grams! Substituting cup for cup just doesn't work. Use that scale and substitute gram for gram! Try to get within 4 grams of the total amount.

✔ Mixing, especially for yeast breads, is very different when you use gluten-free flours. First of all, you must mix together the different flours thoroughly before you add them to batters. Gluten-free flours are all different colors. The best way to make sure the flours are well-mixed is to stir them together with a wire whisk until the mixture is one color. Then, you use a stand or hand mixer to thoroughly mix the dry ingredients with the wet ingredients. You really can't overmix gluten-free batters or doughs because they have no gluten to overdevelop, so beat to your heart's content!

Fixing the lack of structure

Gluten-free baking has evolved over the past few years, ever since dedicated bakers discovered new tricks. Because gluten plays such a critical role in the structure of baked goods, replacing it is difficult. But bakers have discovered many ingredients for gluten-free recipes that help replicate gluten's function in baked goods:

✔ **Agar-agar:** Commonly used in processed foods, this vegan alternative to gelatin is made from seaweed. Agar-agar is very high in fiber. Using too much of this ingredient can make baked goods soggy, so measure carefully. Use about a teaspoon of agar-agar powder for each cup of liquid in a recipe.

✔ **Chia seeds:** These are the same seeds from that cheesy commercial that usually runs the day before Christmas (this may be the world's most perfect ear worm: "chi-chi-chi-chia!"). Like flaxseeds, chia seeds form a gel when mixed with boiling water. They're a good substitute for xanthan and guar gums.

✔ **Eggs:** The protein in eggs forms a web that traps air and water when beaten. Eggs are an easy way to add structure to any gluten-free baked product. However, if you're allergic to eggs, you can substitute a gel made from flaxseeds or chia seeds in many recipes.

✔ **Expandex:** This product, which is uncommon in retail markets, is modified tapioca starch. It forms a web with water, so it really mimics gluten's structure with no added taste because it's flavorless. You add from ¼ to ¾ cup of Expandex to bread recipes in place of some of the flour.

✔ **Gelatin:** This ingredient is used to make doughs more pliable. When mixed with water, gelatin forms, well, a gel that helps trap water and makes doughs stretchier. Use the unflavored variety only; your breads don't need to be strawberry-flavored!

✔ **Ground flaxseed:** Flaxseed, when ground, absorbs water and becomes a gel. You grind the seeds first and then combine them with boiling water to form a thick mixture. Flaxseed is very high in fiber and omega-3 fatty acids, so it's good for you. Do yourself a favor and use only golden flax-seeds. The brown ones contain a bit of chlorophyll, and you may end up with green-tinged bread.

- **Guar gum:** This gum is made from a legume plant. It's less expensive than xanthan gum but has incredible thickening power. It makes breads that are less "gummy" than breads made with xanthan gum. Both xanthan gum and guar gum have laxative properties, which can cause digestive distress in some people.

- **Pectin:** Pectin is a complex carbohydrate used to thicken jams and jellies. Dried pectin, which can be difficult to find, helps provide structure for breads and cakes. It absorbs moisture, which helps keep baked goods from drying out and keeps them soft.

- **Xanthan gum:** Older gluten-free recipes relied heavily on gums. Xanthan gum is made from corn. You use only a tiny bit in recipes — usually a teaspoon. If you use too much, the product can become heavy or slimy.

Gums form a stretchy web when mixed with water, which replicates gluten's structure. But xanthan gum is expensive, and some people who are sensitive to gluten are also sensitive to xanthan gum. Some people can taste the gum in baked goods.

The latest incarnations of gluten-free breads, cakes, and cookies use no gums, gelatin, or artificial structure-makers at all. How is this possible? Gluten-free bakers have found that using a combination of high-protein, high-starch, gluten-free flours helps mimic the structure provided by wheat flours. This knowledge, combined with new weighing and mixing methods, has revolutionized the gluten-free baking world.

Some of these new recipes do use a little bit of gums, especially for yeast breads with little fat, such as French bread. Yeast breads generally need some type of addition to re-create the classic wheat-bread texture. Chia seeds or flaxseeds are preferred over gums, gelatin, or artificial ingredients.

If you want to avoid gums or other artificial add-ins, you need to combine gluten-free flours and starches. No single gluten-free flour has the characteristics, protein content, and starch content to singlehandedly replicate wheat flour.

Getting the ratios right

The newest thing in the gluten-free baking world is called the *ratio*. Recipes for everything from scones to cakes to breads are based on a ratio of gluten-free flours to sugar, liquids, eggs, and fat. If you follow these ratios, you have a better chance of getting the result you want with gluten-free flours. Ratios of ingredients are what make a cookie different from a cake and a scone different from a pancake.

Ratios aren't new in the baking world. For example, people have been making pound cakes for centuries using 1 pound each of butter, flour, eggs, and sugar. Most commercial bakers use ratios for measuring, and if you go to the Culinary Institute of America or the Cordon Bleu School in France to take baking classes, you're taught to measure by weight and to create recipes with ratios.

When you bake using ratios, you can double or triple a recipe with ease. Remember, you still need to weigh the dry ingredients! You may want to weigh the other ingredients, such as milk and sugar, just to make sure you're following the ratio as closely as possible. After all, the biggest variable in every single recipe is the cook. Standardizing how you measure by using grams instead of cups is one way to take one variable out of the baking equation.

When you make a recipe using ratios, you need to establish the base ingredient. This can be any of the ingredients. Most bakers use eggs as the base because eggs are the least variable of all the ingredients. A large egg weighs 2 ounces, or 56 grams. If your recipe calls for 3 parts flour to 3 parts liquid to 1 part egg, you need 168 grams (3 × 56) of flour and liquid.

Of course, you can use the liquid for the base ingredient and simply crack, beat, and measure the eggs. Just keep the ratios consistent and weigh every ingredient and your gluten-free baked goods will be delicious.

With these ratios, you can substitute teff flour for sorghum flour and almond milk for buttermilk without worry. You can change the flavor of a recipe from sweet to savory and vice versa with the confidence of knowing that scones will be flaky and crumbly, cakes will be tender, and breads will have a lovely, airy crumb.

You can find many formulas for baked goods, depending on the result you want. For instance, the ratio for angel food cake is different from the ratio for a shortening cake. Try to keep your ratios within 5 to 10 percent of the recommended numbers for each particular baked good and you should have success.

Table 1-1 lists some of the basic ratios for common baked goods. Remember that these ratios are measured by weight, not by volume.

Of course, the formulas in Table 1-1 are used for developing recipes, but you can use them to check whether a recipe should work. If the ratios in the suspect recipe are way off of these numbers, you may want to try another recipe.

Table 1-1	Basic Ratios for Common Baked Goods				
Product	*Flour*	*Liquid*	*Egg*	*Fat*	*Sugar*
Angel food cake	1 part		3 parts		3 parts
Biscotti	5 parts	3 parts	2 parts	2 parts	
Brownies	1 part (½ part for fudgy)		1 part	1 part	2 parts
Drop cookies	3 parts		1 part	2 parts	1 part
Muffins	2 parts	2 parts	1 part	1 part	
Pancakes	4 parts	4 parts	2 parts	1 part	
Pie crust	3 parts	1 part		2 parts	
Pound cake	1 part		1 part	1 part	1 part
Quick breads	2 parts	2 parts	1 part	1 part	
Roll-out cookies	2 parts		½ part	1 part	1 part
Scones	3 parts	1 part	1 part	1 part	
Shortening cakes	2 parts	2 parts	1 part	1 part	2 parts
Yeast breads	5 parts	3 parts			

Not all ratios for all baked goods are the same; the numbers in Table 1-1 are general, not specific. You may find that for the scones you like, you prefer more flour and more egg, or that for muffins, you want a bit less flour and more egg. If you choose to bake with ratios, be sure to measure carefully by weight and keep track of the ratios that work for you by writing them down in a notebook.

Tools of the Trade

You can find the tools you need to bake yummy, gluten-free recipes in most kitchens. These products and tools aren't specialty products and aren't hard to find, but using them helps make the gluten-free baking process easier.

This section covers the kitchen tools and products that bring you the most success in gluten-free baking. You can find these products in most large supermarkets and at all baking supply stores. The Internet is also a great source for these tools.

Parchment paper and plastic wrap

Book V

Losing the
Gluten,
Keeping
the Baked
Goods

Parchment paper may sound like something from ancient times, but it's made by treating paper pulp with an acid. This process makes the paper fibers cross-link, which makes the paper nonstick! Some parchment papers are coated with silicone or other ingredients, but basic parchment paper works well in gluten-free baking.

When baking with gluten-free batters and doughs, use parchment paper to form doughs and stiff batters, which tend to be sticky and difficult to handle. Using parchment paper, you can form calzones (stuffed pizzas), cinnamon rolls, and French bread.

You can also use parchment paper to line baking sheets so you don't have to grease the pan. Cookies release easily from parchment paper, whereas some cookies stick to a baking sheet no matter how much grease you use. You may need to peel the parchment paper away from the cookie; just go slowly and work gently and you'll have success.

Plastic wrap, also known as cling wrap or cling film, is also used to form doughs and stiff batters. It's made of polyvinyl chloride (PVC), which may sound threatening. In fact, some PVC does transfer plasticizers into foods. You can find some plastic wraps made from low-density polyethylene (LDPE), which doesn't have the same toxic additives that PVC contains. The problem with LDPE plastic wrap is that it doesn't stretch or cling as well as PVC plastic wrap. But because you want plastic wrap *not* to cling to foods, LDPE plastic wrap is the better choice for gluten-free baking!

You can't use plastic wrap for baking (or in the microwave oven); it melts right into the food. Use it only to shape doughs and batters. You can't use waxed paper for baking either; the wax coating melts into the food. Both plastic wrap and parchment paper are single-use products. Don't try to reuse them or flavors may transfer to other doughs and batters. These products also break down with repeated use.

Ice-cream scoops

Ice-cream scoops (also known as dishers) aren't just for scooping ice cream anymore! These handy tools make getting cupcakes, muffins, and cookies the same size as easy as pie. Be sure that you buy a scoop that has a release lever that sweeps along the bowl so that every bit drops out onto the pan or into the muffin cup.

These scoops are handy for gluten-free baking in several ways. First, because the batter or dough tends to be sticky, you can quickly form cookies, cupcakes, and muffins without getting your hands dirty. The release lever also helps you make sure that each cookie or cupcake is the same size because it releases all the batter or dough into the cup or onto the pan. And your cupcakes and cookies will all bake through at the same time because they're all exactly the same size. For muffins, the scoop shapes the muffins perfectly.

Buy the best ice-cream scoops you can afford, and they'll last a lifetime. Stainless steel ice-cream scoops are affordable and clean well in the dishwasher. To prevent sticking, dip the scoop into hot water occasionally or spray it with nonstick cooking spray.

Ice-cream scoops come in several different sizes. Check out the list in Table 1-2. The smaller the number, the bigger the scoop! Traditionally, the size is equivalent to the number of scoops in one quart of ice cream (that's another cocktail party tidbit!).

To use these measurements, follow the recipe directions. For instance, because a standard 12-cup muffin tin holds 3½ ounces in each cup, use a number 24 or a number 20 ice-cream scoop to fill that cup ½ to ¾ full. For large cookies, use a number 70 scoop; for regular-size cookies, use a number 100 scoop.

Table 1-2	Ice-Cream Scoop Sizes		
Scoop Size	*Fluid Ounces*	*Grams of Batter*	*Approx. Volume*
Number 100	⅓	9½	2 teaspoons
Number 70	½	14	1 tablespoon
Number 40	⅞	24	A bit less than 2 tablespoons
Number 30	1¼	35	7½ teaspoons
Number 24	1½	43	3 tablespoons
Number 20	1¾	50	10½ teaspoons
Number 16	2	57	¼ cup
Number 10	3½	99	6 tablespoons (about ⅓ cup)
Number 8	4	113	½ cup
Number 6	5¼	149	⅔ cup
Number 4	8	227	1 cup

Piping bags

You use *piping bags* to form cookies, biscuits, and rolls. Most piping bags are made of coated cloth to prevent sticking. You can find them in most large supermarkets and at kitchen supply stores. You can also find single-use piping bags at these stores.

To use a piping bag, drop a *coupler* (a plastic ring with threads that holds the piping top) into the bag, screw a tip onto the outside of the coupler that pokes through the bottom hole, and then fold back the bag top. Add batter or dough to the bag, fold the top back, and shake the bag lightly to settle the batter at the bottom. Twist the open top of the bag to close it and then squeeze the bag with your dominant hand while you guide it with your nondominant hand.

You can make your own piping bag by using a heavy-duty zip-lock disposable plastic bag. Just fill the bag ½ to ⅔ full and then snip off a tiny piece of the corner. Force the batter or dough through the bag out the opening. You can also use parchment paper to make a piping bag. Simply roll a large piece of parchment paper into a cone, fold down the large end once to hold the cone in place, fill it, and squeeze the batter through the small end.

Scales

A scale is the most important tool in gluten-free baking. Gluten-free flours are all different weights, so if you substitute one for another by volume (cup for cup), you're going to run into trouble. A cup of wheat all-purpose flour weighs 125 grams. If you substitute a cup of sweet rice flour, which weighs 155 grams, your baked good will be dry and heavy. *Always* try to substitute by weight. The correct substitution for 1 cup of wheat all-purpose flour is 125 grams of sweet rice flour.

Scales are common and easy to find. Get one with a digital readout for best accuracy. To use a scale, follow these steps:

1. **Turn on the scale.**

2. **Place the container you're using for the ingredient on the scale.**

   The scale will register a weight.

3. **Zero out the scale (this is also called *taring*) by pressing the "Tare" or "Zero out" button.**

   The scale will read "0."

4. **Add the ingredient you're measuring until the scale reads the correct number.**

5. **Remove the ingredient to a separate bowl, place the container on the scale, zero out the scale, and measure another ingredient.**

   Or you can continue adding ingredients, adding up the total number. This takes some math skills! Or to keep it simple, keep the container on the scale, zero it out again, and add another ingredient until it reaches the number you want.

Weighing ingredients may feel a bit awkward at first, but you'll get the hang of it quickly. It makes cleanup easier, too, because you use only one bowl. And after you see how good your gluten-free baked goods are, you'll never go back to measuring flours by volume! And remember to check if your scale turns off if you haven't added ingredients after a minute or two. Stir the mixture in the bowl if this happens, to keep the scale "awake"!

Thermometers

Two kinds of thermometers are crucial to gluten-free baking: an oven thermometer and an instant-read thermometer. You use the first to make sure that your oven temperature is accurate so that baking times are accurate. You use the second to measure the baked good's doneness.

Oven thermometers

You need to monitor your oven's temperature no matter how new, expensive, or sophisticated the oven is. Over time, temperature sensors can get a little wonky, and if you're baking something that requires a temperature of 350 degrees but your oven is 360 degrees, you'll overbake the food.

Get the best oven thermometer you can buy. Most supermarkets carry thermometers but they aren't very accurate. Buy a good one and keep it in your oven. Thermometers that hang off the bottom of a rack, so they're in the middle of the oven, are the best choice. That's where the temperature should be measured, and in that location the thermometer won't get in the way of pans in the oven.

If your oven is off, check the owner's manual to see whether you can manually adjust the thermometer or temperature. If you can, fiddle with it until the temperature is correct. If not, call a qualified technician and have him or her regulate the temperature.

Instant-read thermometers

When baked goods are done, most of the liquid has evaporated from the batter or dough, and the temperature rises to a certain point. You can use instant-read thermometers to take the temperature of your food. They measure the temperature within 3 to 5 seconds (hence the "instant" moniker) and are quite accurate. Baked goods all have different temperature doneness points.

Book V

Losing the Gluten, Keeping the Baked Goods

Quick Bread Issues

Quick breads are breads that are leavened with baking powder or baking soda. These breads don't need to take time to rise; in fact, the faster you can get the batter into the oven, the better! You don't use yeast in quick breads. Quick breads are usually made of batters, not doughs. Muffins are included in the quick bread category.

Find out in this section about the issues behind some quick bread failures and ways you can make the most tender and moist quick breads, even with gluten-free flours and starches.

Keeping it tender when you convert

The main issue with wheat-based quick breads is that you have to mix them as little as possible so a lot of gluten doesn't form. So you're automatically one step ahead, because gluten-free flours don't have gluten! Many gluten-free quick breads tend to crumble when you slice them, and grittiness is a problem. Some people miss the flavor that wheat flours provide, but you can solve those issues! Remember that for the recipes in this book, don't make these changes. These tips are to help you convert wheat-based recipes into gluten-free treats.

To keep gluten-free quick breads tender and moist, follow a few rules. Use these tips when you're altering a wheat flour quick bread recipe to the gluten-free standard.

- ✔ Combine flours for best results. No gluten-free quick bread recipe is made using just one flour.
- ✔ Consider grinding flours in a food processor to make them finer, or look for extra-fine gluten-free flours.
- ✔ Measure flours by weight, not by volume.
- ✔ Make sure you mix the flours together really well before combining them with any of the other ingredients.

✔ Use a larger amount of oil and liquid than you would with most standard quick breads. Remember, these flours soak up more liquid than wheat flours.

✔ Add yogurt or sour cream to the batter in place of water or juices to help make the structure more tender.

✔ Add nutrition and flavor to gluten-free quick breads using fruit purees.

✔ Soak dried fruit in some of the liquid used in the recipe before adding it to the batter.

✔ Toast nuts before adding them to quick breads. This adds flavor and also helps a bit with the structure.

✔ Increase the amount of baking soda or baking powder by ½ teaspoon. Gluten-free flours are heavier than wheat flours, so a little bit more leavening helps create a good texture.

✔ When you combine the flours, make a hollow in the center. Combine all the wet ingredients and beat well. Add the wet ingredients to the flours and mix until combined.

✔ Use the correct size pan and grease it well according to the recipe. You may want to use a smaller pan size. Pans that are 8-x-4 inches or 6-x-3 inches may work better than the standard 9-x-5-inch loaf pan. Fill the loaf pan about ⅔ full for best results. You may have some batter left over; use it to make two or three muffins.

✔ Bake at the correct temperature for the right amount of time. Be sure that your oven is properly calibrated.

✔ Understand doneness tests. Quick bread doneness tests include observing a brown crust with a crack down the center, an internal temperature of about 200 degrees, and a firm texture. You can also check doneness with a toothpick; it should come out moist, with just a few crumbs sticking to it.

✔ Let the bread cool completely before cutting it. Cutting warm bread is just asking for trouble; it will crumble and fall apart.

✔ Gluten-free quick breads may become dry and taste stale more quickly than wheat-based quick breads. So eat them within a day or two, or freeze them when they've cooled completely.

Building structure in quick breads

Quick breads should have an even crumb, but more open, with larger air holes than yeast breads. The top should be bumpy. The crust should be moist and rich, not hard or dry. You can experiment with lots of different types of flours in your quick breads or you can add other ingredients to help keep the structure firm but tender.

To build structure in quick breads, follow these tips:

- ✔ Use flours with high protein and flours with low protein. A good mix of different flours helps compensate for lack of gluten.

- ✔ Flours that are high in fiber, like coconut flour and brown rice flour, help add strength to the structure without making the bread tough or dry.

- ✔ Mix flours and starches. A combination of flours, like coconut or sweet rice flour, mixed with starches like cornstarch or potato starch give the bread good structure.

- ✔ Add gums. Use xanthan gum or guar gum in small quantities to add structure to quick breads. Use a little less than ½ teaspoon per cup of flour in quick bread recipes.

- ✔ You may want to add another egg to a quick bread recipe you're converting to gluten-free. Egg proteins help provide structure in any baked good and especially in quick breads. Be sure to reduce the liquid in the recipe by 2 tablespoons if you add another egg.

- ✔ Get the quick breads into the oven as soon as possible. Gluten-free bread structure is more fragile than wheat bread structure, and you want to hold on to all those bubbles you worked so hard to create.

- ✔ Make sure that your oven temperature is accurate. If the oven temperature is too high, the outside of the bread will brown and set before the inside is done.

Yeast Bread Issues

Ah, yeast bread. There's nothing like the aroma of baking bread wafting through your home. And the tender but crunchy crust, the soft crumb, the wonderful chewiness; will you ever be able to taste that again?

Of course! Would we tease you like that and not solve the problem of making gluten-free yeast breads? In this section, we tackle the flavor and texture issues in gluten-free yeast breads, including why gluten-free batters are different from wheat batters and doughs and how to get the perfect crust.

Understanding the basics of gluten-free yeast breads

Making gluten-free yeast breads is very different from making wheat-based yeast breads, although the goal is to achieve the same texture and flavor. Because ordinary yeast breads use gluten for structure, you have to come up with another way to build that structure without gluten.

Here are some basic rules and methods for making the best gluten-free bread with the texture you find in wheat breads:

- You make gluten-free yeast breads with thick batters. You may find some gluten-free doughs floating around (or thudding around), but generally they produce very heavy, dense breads. Because gluten-free flours are heavier than wheat flour, without proper structure they can't hold the air that the yeast produces, and you end up with something resembling a doorstop. And because gluten-free flours are drier than wheat flour, they need more liquid. Making gluten-free yeast breads out of batters instead of doughs makes them more tender.

- Mix the flours together very well before you add any liquid ingredients. The combination of flours, with their different protein and starch contents, is what provides the structure in these breads.

- Choose gluten-free flours that are high in protein for better structure and more stability. These proteins may not have exactly the same characteristics as gluten, but they can come pretty close.

- Beat the doughs with a stand mixer for five to ten minutes. This helps work air into the dough and ensures that all the ingredients are well-mixed. It also gives the flour time to absorb liquid and helps the eggs form the structure. You can't knead the batters, so this step helps to form the structure with the proteins and starches in the flour as they hydrate.

- Gluten-free breads only rise once. If you stir or punch down the dough for a second rise, you'll destroy the delicate structure. You just mix these breads and pour them into a pan, and then they rise and bake. Enjoy the freedom of less work for great breads!

- You need to use pans to form gluten-free breads. Use muffin tins for rolls and loaf pans for breads. You can find specialty loaf pans, such as pans for French bread loaves, that you can use to shape gluten-free yeast breads.

- Don't let the batter rise too long! Because the structure of gluten-free yeast breads is more delicate than that of wheat yeast breads, if the yeast overdevelops it forms acid, which can ruin the structure. And too much carbon dioxide produced by the yeast can overwhelm the structure, and the bread will collapse.

Here are several ingredients you can use to get a tender, even crumb in gluten-free yeast breads:

- **Carbonated water:** Use this to add more air to gluten-free yeast breads. Anything you can do to add bubbles is good!

- **Chia and flaxseed slurries:** These are wonderful ways to add structure to these bread recipes. They add fiber and nutrition, too.

- **Dry milk or whey:** These also improve the structure of gluten-free yeast breads. They add protein and nutrition, too.

- **Eggs:** Use eggs to add texture and structure to these breads. If you're sensitive to eggs, use a flaxseed slurry instead. Combine 1 tablespoon ground golden flaxseeds with 2 tablespoons water. Heat until thickened. Use this amount to replace one egg.

- **Xanthan gum and guar gum:** Use these in gluten-free yeast breads to provide structure. This addition also helps keep the bread from crumbling and makes it less grainy.

Building flavor in gluten-free yeast breads

The nutty flavor of wheat flour is hard to replicate. But by using the right types of gluten-free flours, you can get pretty close. Obviously, the flavor of the yeast is paramount in any yeast bread. But flavors and textures of flours play an important part.

Gluten-free flours all have different flavors and characteristics. For making yeast breads, these are the flours that add a wheaty, nutty flavor. Be sure to always substitute by weight, not by volume.

- **Almond and nut flours:** Well, nut flours have a nutty flavor! Almond meal or flour adds delicious flavor to yeast breads. Chestnut flour has a strong nutty flavor, too.

- **Amaranth flour:** This flour is nutty and sweet. It makes a thick and chewy crust on yeast breads. Don't use it as the main flour in bread recipes, but you can use it for about ¼ of the total flour amount.

- **Buckwheat flour:** Despite its name, this grain doesn't contain gluten. It has a very strong, earthy flavor when roasted.

- **Garfava flour:** This combination of fava bean and garbanzo bean flours has a bean flavor and lots of protein. It also adds fiber to bread recipes.

✔ **Rice flour:** Brown rice flour adds a nutty and sweet flavor to breads. If you can find wild rice flour, add it for a nutty flavor. Sweet rice flour is more neutral.

✔ **Sorghum flour:** This flour has a wheat taste and doesn't have a gritty texture. It's also very high in protein, so it helps with the bread's structure.

✔ **Soy flour:** This flour has a strong flavor, so use it sparingly. It helps bread brown quickly and is high in protein.

✔ **White bean flour:** This is a high-protein flour with a mild taste. If you don't like the taste of soy or garfava, this light-colored flour is a good substitute.

One way to build flavor in gluten-free yeast breads is to add other ingredients. Here are some options:

✔ **Finely grated cheese:** This is a wonderful flavor addition to many yeast breads. Cheeses also add protein and more nutrition.

✔ **Fruit juices or vegetable juices:** You can use these for part of the liquid in bread recipes. They add a sweet or a savory flavor to many breads.

✔ **Gluten-free beer:** Gluten-free yeast breads rise only once, so the yeast flavor may be less pronounced. Beer can add a yeasty flavor to any bread recipe; use it in place of some of the liquid.

✔ **Herbs and spices:** These are good ingredients to add more flavor. You can use fresh or dried herbs. Use three times the amount of fresh herbs, simply because they're less potent.

✔ **Seeds and nuts:** These can add great flavor, along with texture, to gluten-free yeast breads. Toast the seeds and nuts before adding them to the batter to help bring out the flavor.

✔ **Sourdough:** This is the ultimate yeast bread flavor. See Chapter 6 of Book V for info about sourdough starters and how to make your own.

Pie Crust Issues

Pie crust is all about the fat and the flour. Pie crust doesn't need much leavening; what you want is tender flakiness. You create that characteristic by the way in which you combine the ingredients and by the ratios of fat to flour to liquid.

In this section, you find out how to make a perfect gluten-free pie crust that has all the texture and flavor of a wheat pie crust. With a few tips and tricks, you can make delicious gluten-free pie crusts with ease.

Building a tasty pie crust structure

When bakers make wheat pie crusts, they battle gluten. When pie crust has too much of that stretchy and pliable protein, it becomes tough and doughy, not flaky and tender. So, just as with quick breads, you're ahead of the game when making pie crust with gluten-free flours.

A combination of flours is the best way to get a tender and flaky pie crust that holds together when you cut it and that doesn't crumble or taste gritty. Here are the ingredients to use when making a gluten-free pie crust:

- **Cold butter or fat:** For best results, make sure that the fat you use is very cold. The fat has to keep its shape as you blend it with the flour. Then, when the crust bakes, the layers of fat melt, creating the flaky layers you want in your pie crust.

- **Cold liquid:** Because the fat needs to be cold, the liquid should be cold, too! Most pie crust recipes use cold water. To make sure it stays cold, fill a small bowl with cold water and add ice. Then measure the water for the crust directly from the bowl of ice water.

- **Cream cheese:** This ingredient used to be very popular in pie crust recipes. It helps make the crust very tender. To use it, blend together the cream cheese and butter or other fat and then add the flours. With a cream cheese pie crust, you don't need any added liquid.

- **Eggs:** Eggs can help keep the flour moist and hold the pie crust structure together. If you're avoiding eggs, try using a vegan egg replacer.

- **Leaf lard:** Leaf lard is pork fat, but it's a special type that's more expensive (and more difficult to find) than ordinary lard. Leaf lard really makes your pie crusts flaky because it resists blending with the flour. The lard stays in nice layers, creating beautiful flaky layers in the finished crust.

- **Superfine flours:** Ordinary gluten-free flours, such as rice flour, tend to be gritty. You want a very fine flour so it blends well with the fat. If you can't find superfine flours, grind any type of gluten-free flour in a coffee grinder until it's powdery.

- **Xanthan or guar gum:** Some pie crust dough recipes do add these gums to help build structure and prevent the crumblies. But if you're sensitive to these ingredients, use flaxseed or chia seed slurries instead.

When you're making a gluten-free pie crust, follow these tips for making and handling the dough for best results:

- Try using a food processor instead of making the dough by hand. This machine mixes the ingredients very quickly, which is the best way to keep the ingredients cold.

- Combine the flour and fat until the fat is the size of small peas. The fat should be visible in the flour. This keeps the pie crust tender and helps build the layers.

- Check the dough consistency several times while you mix it. Remember, these flours need a lot of liquid. You may need to add more water to make a dough that holds together. But don't add too much water! The dough should be crumbly but hold together when pressed.

- Handle the dough as little as possible. You're not concerned about the overdevelopment of gluten in these recipes; you just want to keep the dough cold!

- Let the dough rest before you roll it out. This gives the flour time to absorb the liquid so the pie crust won't be crumbly or gritty.

- Use waxed paper or parchment paper to roll out the dough. Gluten-free doughs are usually stickier than wheat doughs. These papers make it easier to handle the dough.

- Bake the pie crust at a high temperature. You want the crust to bake really quickly so the fat melts and the structure sets at about the same time. This preserves those flaky layers you've worked so hard to build.

Getting a flaky or mealy texture

People use lots of words to describe pie crust. The most common are "flaky" and "mealy." But what do they mean? Do you sometimes want a flaky crust or a mealy crust? Here's how:

- You make flaky pie crusts with larger pieces of fat. These larger pieces leave larger holes when the fat melts, creating more layers. When your fork hits those layers as you eat the pie, they break apart, creating the flaky sensation.

- You make mealy pie crusts with smaller pieces of fat. For a mealy crust, cut the fat into the flour until the pieces of fat are small. This makes a dough that's denser, with fewer layers.

So would you ever want a mealy pie crust? Surprisingly, yes! If you're making a fruit pie or a pie with a wet filling, a mealy bottom crust is the way to go. It absorbs less moisture from the filling as the pie bakes and won't crumble or fall apart.

Cake Issues

Everyone wants a light and fluffy cake with a soft and tiny crumb. For gluten-free cakes, you're in luck! This is another product where you want to minimize gluten and its effects. Most cakes are built on egg protein. The flour is just there to stabilize the batter and add some starch for tenderness.

This section shows you how to build tender and even cake structure, adding moistness to the gluten-free cakes you bake, and adding flavor to any cake recipe.

Keeping tenderness and moistness

Think about the best cake you ever ate. Chances are it was very tender and moist, with an even, almost velvety texture. In cakes, you want a fine crumb, which means very tiny air holes. And the cake should be moist, not dry. You want to add ingredients that attract moisture and hold it in the structure.

Here are several ways of getting a tender, fine crumb in cakes:

- Add a little extra leavening. Gluten-free flours are heavier and grab more moisture than wheat flours. Adding a little bit more baking soda and baking powder can give the cake batter the extra lift it needs for a fine and tender crumb.

- Beat well. You need to aerate these batters. And because you don't have to worry about gluten, you can beat the batters for a fairly long period of time — usually three to five minutes. This adds air to the batter. The protein and starch in the flour and eggs will form around the air bubbles.

- Use flours with a low protein content. A 50:50 split of flours and starches gives the cake enough structure but keeps the texture fine.

- Substitute sparkling water or soda pop for some of the liquid. This adds more air to the batter, which helps get the lift you want in any cake.

- Add some *finely divided solids,* such as ground chocolate or cocoa powder. That's a food science term for ingredients that are chopped very finely.

✔ Use brown sugar. Brown sugar has more moisture than white sugar (which is why you have to pack it into the cup to measure it), so it makes the cake crumb more tender and moist.

✔ Use more sugar. Sugar adds tenderness to cakes, and it's *hygroscopic,* which just means that it attracts water. So more sugar means a more tender cake with a finer crumb.

Adding more flavor

Most cake recipes are designed to be full of flavor. Chocolate cakes should taste rich and full of, well, chocolate. Fruit cakes should taste of the fruit and be very moist. Vanilla cakes should have a strong vanilla flavor. You get the idea!

If you find a recipe that has a wonderful texture but the flavor isn't quite there, try these tricks:

✔ Add fruit purees in place of some of the liquid. Applesauce, pear purees, or any other pureed fruit really helps cakes stay moist and tender.

✔ For cake recipes that use cocoa powder, bloom the powder in some hot water first. *Bloom* just means to enhance the flavor in some way. When you mix cocoa with hot water, the flavor is accentuated.

✔ Use another type of liquid instead of milk or water. Coffee adds great depth of flavor to chocolate cakes.

✔ Add more spices. Cinnamon, nutmeg, and cloves are classic cake spices. A tiny bit adds flavor and interest to just about any cake recipe.

✔ Use real extracts. Real vanilla or real almond extract adds more flavor than imitation extracts. And you can add a bit more than the recipe calls for. In fact, double the vanilla extract in any cake recipe for fabulous flavor.

Cookie Issues

Cookies are easy to make and mouth-watering. Because they're so small, building structure in them is easier than in other baked goods. Cookies are a balance among flour, fat, egg, and sugar, with flour the largest amount, fat the second, and sugar the third.

The only issue with gluten-free cookies is choosing the type of texture you want. Do you want a crisp cookie or a chewy one? And how do you make cookies that are tender and moist? In this section, you find the methods for making the kind of cookie you want and ways to use gluten-free flours for the best results.

Making the best gluten-free cookies

A combination of gluten-free flours and starches is the best way to make the best cookies. In fact, an even proportion of flours to starches is the best way to make tender cookies. Gluten-free cookie batters and doughs are softer than wheat-based cookie doughs because more liquid is needed to hydrate the flour.

To make the best gluten-free cookies, use these tips:

- Let the dough rest. Resting time, preferably in the refrigerator, gives the flour enough time to absorb the liquid and set the cookie's structure. Chilling also solidifies the fat so that the cookies hold their shape in the oven.

- Reduce the oven temperature. Overbaking cookies makes them hard and tough. A longer bake at a lower temperature lets the cookies bake through before the edges get hard or overbrown.

- Try freezing the dough before you bake it. Then let the dough thaw in the fridge until you can handle it and form and bake the cookies. This helps the cookies keep their shape.

- If your cookies are thin and flat and you want thicker cookies, substitute solid shortening for some of the butter.

- Use finely ground flours. Cookies don't have a lot of ingredients, and using a fine flour helps prevent grittiness.

- Use parchment paper, plastic wrap, or waxed paper to roll out the dough. Gluten-free doughs are stickier than wheat-based doughs, so these products help you shape cookies with less fuss and mess.

- Make sure the cookie sheet is completely cool before you add another batch of cookie dough. Warm cookie sheets make the dough spread before it even gets into the oven, which weakens the structure.

Deciding between crisp and chewy

Cookies come in two basic types: crisp and chewy. Everyone has a favorite type, and each type of cookie should have a certain texture. How do you make a chewy cookie? And what ingredients make a cookie crisp?

Chewy

To make a chewy cookie, your dough needs more moisture. More high-protein flour, eggs, and sugar help keep a cookie chewy. For chewy cookies, follow these rules:

- ✔ Solid shortening makes a chewier, thicker cookie. This type of fat doesn't spread as much as the cookie bakes.

- ✔ Chewy cookies have more moisture in the batter or dough.

- ✔ More eggs typically means the cookie will be chewy. Add an egg yolk to add more fat to the dough; this helps make the cookies chewy.

- ✔ Use brown sugar. This sugar has more moisture than granulated sugar, so the cookies will be chewier.

- ✔ Use flour with a high protein content. Because you don't have to worry about gluten developing in these cookies, more protein makes the cookie structure stronger.

- ✔ Underbake the cookies a little bit. They should still be done, but less baking makes a chewier cookie.

Crisp

Crisp cookies have less liquid and more fat. To make a crisp cookie, follow these rules:

- ✔ Use butter or margarine. These fats spread more in the oven, allowing more moisture evaporation, which makes the cookies crisper.

- ✔ Choose low-protein flours. They make the cookies spread out more as they bake, which makes them crisper.

- ✔ Use less liquid. Crisp cookies shouldn't have much, if any, liquid.

- ✔ Use granulated sugar rather than brown sugar for crisp cookies.

- ✔ For crisp roll-out cookies, refrigerate the cookies right on the cookie sheet before you bake them.

Chapter 2

Gluten-Free Baking Mixes and Sweet Yeast Breads

In This Chapter

▶ Using baking mixes

▶ Getting familiar with several mix recipes

▶ Making sweet breads with yeast

*O*ne of the best and most efficient ways to bake gluten-free is to make some mixes with a combination of gluten-free flours and starches. Then all you need to do is add some water, milk, and sometimes an egg or some oil; stir; and bake cakes, cookies, brownies, or breads.

With mixes in your pantry, you don't need to feel stymied by a recipe that requests five different flours, four starches, and a gum or two. You can use these mix recipes on their own and in many recipes in this book. The basic instructions for using each mix, along with how much mix and additional ingredients you need, are in each recipe. This chapter shows you mixes for cakes, cookies, quick breads, and a couple of different mixes for yeast breads and general baking.

This chapter also offers recipes for everything from Monkey Bread to Honey Oat Bread to Cinnamon Rolls to Bismarck Doughnuts. These recipes are usually reserved for special occasions, such as a birthday breakfast or a holiday brunch. But you may want to make a Wednesday morning special and serve some sticky buns to your family! Because one of the great pleasures of life is coming into a kitchen where cinnamon rolls have just finished baking.

Getting Started with Easy Baking Mix Recipes

Baking mixes, like baking recipes, are scientific formulas. You must measure carefully and accurately for best results. You measure many baking recipes using weights, and mixes are no exception. In fact, in nonmix recipes in this book, you need to weigh the flours and starches, but with mixes, you really should weigh every ingredient.

You've no doubt used mixes in the past, so you're familiar with the process; you just dump the mix into a bowl, add other ingredients, stir, pour the batter or dough into a pan, and bake.

Here are a few rules to follow when you're creating your own mixes.

- ✔ **Measure using a scale.** Be sure that you weigh each flour ingredient separately for the most accurate results. Always zero out the scale after the bowl is on the scale, before you add each ingredient. If you don't use a scale, always measure by spooning the flour or flour mix lightly into a measuring cup and leveling off the top with the back of a knife.

- ✔ **Be sure all your ingredients are fresh.** Baking powder, baking soda, and yeast all have expiration dates, beyond which they just don't work as well. There's no point in making all this effort and spending all this money on a mix, only to have it fail because your ingredients are too old.

- ✔ **Try to use the exact ingredients the mix calls for.** You can make some substitutions for food allergy reasons or if you can't find a certain flour. For instance, you can substitute a flour with a similar protein content for another. When you make a substitute, be sure to do so by weight, not by volume. Try to weigh all flours, always!

- ✔ **Always label the mixes.** After mixes are mixed and stored in your pantry, you won't be able to differentiate between the Cookie Mix and the High-Protein Bread Flour Mix. Mark the name of the mix, the date you made it, and instructions for use directly on the bag or container.

- ✔ **Store the mixes in airtight containers in a cool, dry place.** Flours are very absorbent and absorb excess moisture from the air when it's very humid. And heat may affect the leavening properties of the baking soda or baking powder. Finally, some high-fat flours can become rancid in the presence of high heat and moisture.

Working with Yeast

Yeast can be a tricky creature. And it is a creature: a one-celled organism that uses sugar and water to multiply fruitfully. As it grows, yeast gives off carbon dioxide, which makes yeast breads rise. The yeast also ferments the sugar in the batter or dough, imparting the distinctive and characteristic flavor that only comes from these types of recipes.

Here are a few rules to follow when working with yeast.

- ✔ Before you even start mixing the dough, make sure your yeast is fresh. Active dry yeast packets have expiration dates stamped clearly on them. Abide by these dates, as the yeast isn't as lively after the dates have passed.

- ✔ You can depend on those expiration dates, but if you want to make sure, proof the yeast before you start. To *proof* — or reactivate — yeast, mix it with a bit of water or milk from the recipe, along with a pinch of sugar. After about 10 minutes, if the mixture is puffy, then your yeast is active and can be used.

- ✔ Be careful about temperatures when working with yeast. You shouldn't expose active dry yeast to temperatures over 110 degrees. Fresh compressed yeast, which is more difficult to find, must stay below 110 degrees also. When dry yeast is mixed with flour, the temperature of the liquid in the recipe can get to 120 degrees before you run into problems.

- ✔ Because most gluten-free bread doughs aren't kneaded, one rise is all they get. Make sure the breads rise in a warm, draft-free place. If your house is cool, you can put the breads into an oven with a pilot light on. Or turn on the oven for a few minutes, turn it off (be sure to turn it off!), and add the proofing bread dough.

- ✔ Any ingredient in the bread dough or batter other than flour slows down the yeast fermentation. Sugar speeds the process, up to a point. Lots of sugar actually slows yeast growth. Salt is added even to sweet yeast breads to temper the yeast growth. Doughs and batters made with eggs, fat, dairy products, and other ingredients take longer to rise.

Enjoying Easy Sweet Yeast Bread Recipes

Enjoy the process when you're making these breads. There's something very contemplative about working with yeast. Baking yeast breads is an ancient art. And get your family involved in the process, too. Nothing's cozier than baking a sweet yeast bread on a snowy morning. You're teaching your kids a life skill and making their childhood wonderful, too.

Make sure that you measure all the ingredients carefully when making yeast breads. Weighing the flour when working with yeast doughs and batters is particularly important. In most wheat flour–based yeast bread recipes, you knead the dough, which gives you the ability to adjust the flour amounts to the correct point. With these recipes, measuring the flours by weighing is crucial. If you don't use a scale to measure flours and mixes, always measure by spooning the flour lightly into a measuring cup and leveling off the top with the back of a knife.

White Flour Mix

Prep time: 10 min • **Yield:** 18⅓ cups

Ingredients	Directions
5½ cups (685 grams) tapioca flour (also known as tapioca starch)	**1** In a very large bowl, combine all ingredients and blend using a wire whisk until they're a single color.
8⅓ cups (1,370 grams) potato starch	**2** Store in an airtight container and use in recipes.
4½ cups minus 1 tablespoon (685 grams) sweet rice flour (glutinous rice flour)	

Note: For accuracy and best results, weigh out the flours for this mix and weigh the mix when you use it in recipes. One cup of this mix weighs 148 grams.

Note: This mix is used as a flour substitute in many recipes in the book, especially cake, bar cookie, and cookie recipes. It's a good substitute for all-purpose white flour in any recipe that you want to convert to a gluten-free recipe. For tips on converting recipes, see Book II, Chapter 4.

Tip: You can find glutinous rice flour at local Asian markets.

Whole-Grain Flour Mix

Prep time: 10 min • **Yield:** 14 cups

Ingredients	Directions
4½ cups minus 1 tablespoon (600 grams) brown rice flour 4¾ cups plus 2 tablespoons (600 grams) sorghum flour 3¼ cups minus 1 tablespoon (400 grams) millet flour 1¾ cups (275 grams) sweet rice flour	*1* In a large bowl, combine all ingredients until the mixture is one color. Use a wire whisk to stir for best results. *2* Store in an airtight container and use in baking recipes in place of flour.

Note: Weigh these flours instead of measuring them by volume. You end up with much better results, and you find that with a little experience, weighing is faster than measuring by cups. One cup of this mix weighs 135 grams.

Note: This flour mix is used in a lot of bread recipes in this book. It's a good substitute for whole-wheat flour in many recipes.

Cookie Mix without Gums

Prep time: 20 min • **Yield:** 11 cups

Ingredients	Directions
4 cups sugar 2 tablespoons baking soda 3 tablespoons baking powder 1 tablespoon sea salt 2 cups minus 2 tablespoons minus 1 teaspoon (250 grams) regular grind brown rice flour 1 cup (160 grams) regular grind white rice flour 1 cup minus 1 teaspoon (160 grams) potato starch 2 cups (246 grams) sorghum flour 1 cup minus 1 tablespoon (116 grams) tapioca flour	*1* Combine the sugar, baking soda, baking powder, and salt in a large, sealed, plastic bag or container, stirring until the sugar is well coated in the baking soda, powder, and salt. This step is essential to eliminate tiny pockets of bitterness in your cookies. *2* Add all the remaining ingredients and mix well to combine completely and thoroughly. *3* Store in an airtight container at room temperature. Use this mix in any recipe as a substitute for a cookie mix, or use it in the recipes in Book V, Chapter 3. Spoon this mix into a measuring cup and level off the top before adding it to the recipe.

Note: This is a good base for making lots of cookies. It's easier to stir up a big batch of this mix than to drag out and measure all the different flours many times. Recipes using this mix need an overnight rest in the refrigerator to let the flours rehydrate and the sugars dissolve. And if you prefer a sweeter cookie, you can add up to 1 more cup of sugar to the mix.

Vary It! You can use a fine grind of flour for these cookies. Substitute the fine grind for the regular grind by weight. In other words, if you want to use fine grind brown rice flour, use 250 grams of it, not 2 cups minus 2 tablespoons minus 1 teaspoon. The texture of cookies made with fine grind flour changes. As a bonus of using fine grind flours, you can mix the cookie dough and bake it immediately rather than waiting while the batter rests overnight.

Cake Mix

Prep time: 20 min • **Yield:** Six 9-inch round cake layers, or 48 servings

Ingredients	Directions
6 cups sugar	*1* In a large bowl, combine the sugar, White Flour Mix, Whole-Grain Flour Mix, baking powder, and salt; mix until they're a single color.
5¾ cups (852 grams) White Flour Mix (earlier in this chapter)	
2⅓ cups plus 1 tablespoon (324 grams) Whole-Grain Flour Mix (earlier in this chapter)	*2* Using a mixer or a pastry blender, blend the butter into the flour mixture until the mixture looks like sand.
2 tablespoons baking powder	*3* Divide the mixture into six portions and place each portion in a glass storage container or a heavy-duty Ziploc plastic bag.
1 teaspoon salt	
3 cups unsalted butter	

Note: Everyone deserves a homemade birthday cake! Keep this simple mix in the fridge or freezer and you're ready to prepare a cake at a moment's notice. You can store this mix in the fridge for three weeks or freeze it for up to three months.

Cake Mix Cake

Prep time: 10 min • **Cook time:** 48–50 min • **Yield:** 6–8 servings

Ingredients	Directions
1 portion (2 cups) Cake Mix (earlier in this chapter)	*1* Allow the Cake Mix to come to room temperature. Preheat the oven to 350 degrees, and grease a 9-inch cake pan with unsalted butter.
2 eggs, separated	
½ cup milk	*2* In a large bowl, beat the Cake Mix, egg yolks, milk, and vanilla for 3 minutes.
1 teaspoon vanilla	
⅛ teaspoon salt	*3* In a small bowl, beat the egg whites until soft peaks form. Add the salt and beat until stiff peaks form.
	4 Fold the egg whites into the batter gently. Pour into the prepared pan. Bake for 48 to 50 minutes, or until the cake is golden-brown and starts pulling away from the sides of the pan.
	5 Cool the cake in the pan for 5 minutes and then move it to a wire rack to cool completely.

Per serving: Calories 250 (From Fat 107); Fat 12g (Saturated 7g); Cholesterol 99mg; Sodium 149mg; Carbohydrate 34g (Dietary Fiber 0g); Protein 4g.

Quick Bread Mix

Prep time: 20 min • **Yield:** 3 standard loaf pans; 18 servings

Ingredients	Directions
4½ cups minus 1 tablespoon (600 grams) Whole-Grain Flour Mix (earlier in this chapter)	**1** Combine all ingredients in a large bowl and mix until they're one color.
2½ cups minus 1 tablespoon (360 grams) White Flour Mix (earlier in this chapter)	**2** Divide the mixture into three batches. Store the batches in airtight, heavy-duty plastic bags or plastic containers.
1 cup plus 3 tablespoons packed brown sugar	
1 cup granulated sugar	
3 tablespoons baking powder	
4½ teaspoons baking soda	
1½ teaspoons salt	

Note: You can store Quick Bread Mix at room temperature for about a month. For longer storage, freeze it for up to three months.

Tip: Weighing the flours will give you the best results. But if you need to measure this mix by volume, just be sure to stir the flour first and then spoon it into the measuring cup and level off with the back of a knife. Just a little extra flour in each cup makes the overall mix heavier and creates denser baked goods.

Vegan Applesauce Quick Bread

Prep time: 10 min • **Cook time:** 45–48 min • **Yield:** 8 servings

Ingredients	Directions
Unsalted butter or solid shortening	*1* Preheat the oven to 350 degrees. Grease an 8-x-4-inch loaf pan with unsalted butter or solid shortening.
1 portion Quick Bread Mix (earlier in this chapter)	*2* In a medium bowl, combine the Quick Bread Mix, applesauce, vanilla, and oil and beat until well mixed. Pour into the prepared pan.
1 cup applesauce	
1 teaspoon vanilla	*3* Bake for 45 to 48 minutes, or until a toothpick inserted in the center comes out clean. The internal temperature should be 190 to 200 degrees.
¼ cup vegetable oil	
	4 Cool the bread in the pan for 10 minutes and then move it to a wire rack to cool completely.

Per serving: Calories 277 (From Fat 69); Fat 8g (Saturated 1g); Cholesterol 0mg; Sodium 573mg; Carbohydrate 52g (Dietary Fiber 2g); Protein 2g.

Brownie Mix

Prep time: 15 min • **Yield:** 8 cups

Ingredients	Directions
1 cup minus 2 teaspoons (142 grams) White Flour Mix (earlier in this chapter)	**1** In a large bowl, combine all ingredients and mix until they're one color.
1¼ cups minus 1 teaspoon (165 grams) Whole-Grain Flour Mix (earlier in this chapter)	**2** Divide the mixture into four containers and store at room temperature.
5 cups sugar	
1 cup cocoa powder	
2 teaspoons baking powder	
1 teaspoon salt	

Tip: This mix works well as a basic chocolate brownie, somewhere between cakey and chewy. You can easily bend the results toward your favorite texture by varying the amount of butter and cooking time. More butter and a shorter cooking time make a chewier brownie. Less butter and a longer cooking time make a more cake-like brownie.

Brownies

Prep time: 15 min • **Cook time:** 48 min • **Yield:** 16 servings

Ingredients	Directions
Unsalted butter or shortening	*1* Preheat the oven to 350 degrees. Grease a 9-inch square cake pan with unsalted butter or solid shortening.
1 portion Brownie Mix (earlier in this chapter)	
6 ounces dark chocolate, melted and cooled	*2* For chewy brownies, combine Brownie Mix, chocolate, butter, vanilla, and eggs and beat until combined. For cakey brownies, reduce the chocolate amount to 3 ounces. Mix and bake both types of brownies as directed.
½ cup softened butter	
2 teaspoons vanilla	
3 eggs	*3* Pour the batter into the prepared pan and bake for 48 to 50 minutes, or until the brownies are set and have a shiny crust. Cool completely before cutting.

Per serving: Calories 203 (From Fat 90); Fat 10g (Saturated 6g); Cholesterol 55mg; Sodium 87mg; Carbohydrate 29g (Dietary Fiber 2g); Protein 3g.

Note: If you like fudgy or chewy brownies, more chocolate makes the brownies moister. For cake-like, lighter brownies, use less chocolate.

Vary It! You can embellish this basic brownie easily by adding chocolate chips, melted chocolate, or dried fruits to the batter; by layering with different frostings; or by stirring in ¾ cup chopped walnuts per batch.

Light Cakey Corn Bread Mix

Prep time: 10 min • **Yield:** 6–7 cups

Ingredients	Directions
3 cups yellow or white cornmeal	*1* Combine the cornmeal, White Flour Mix, Whole-Grain Flour Mix, sugar (if desired), baking powder, baking soda, and salt in a large bowl and stir well with a wire whisk until the mixture is all one color.
1¾ cups plus 3 tablespoons (284 grams) White Flour Mix (earlier in this chapter)	
1¼ cups minus 1 teaspoon (165 grams) Whole-Grain Flour Mix (earlier in this chapter)	*2* Add butter, buttery sticks, or coconut oil (if you're going to use the mix just for corn bread and not for cornmeal pancakes) and cut the fat into the flour until the mixture resembles sand.
½ cup sugar (optional)	
5 teaspoons baking powder	*3* Divide into four equal portions, about 1½ cups each, and place in glass jars or plastic freezer bags.
1 teaspoon baking soda	
1½ teaspoons salt	
¾ cup butter, buttery sticks, or coconut oil (optional)	

Note: People from the southern United States are usually horrified at the thought of sugar in corn bread, while those from the North like sugar in this quick bread. So to keep the peace, the sugar in this recipe is optional. This recipe makes light and cake-like muffins and corn bread.

Note: Store Light Cakey Corn Bread Mix in the refrigerator for three months or in the freezer for six months.

Light Cakey Corn Bread

Prep time: 15 min • **Cook time:** 25 min • **Yield:** 9 servings

Ingredients	*Directions*
Unsalted butter or solid shortening	*1* Preheat the oven to 350 degrees. Grease a 9-inch square pan with unsalted butter or solid shortening.
2 eggs	
1 portion Light Cakey Corn Bread Mix (earlier in this chapter)	*2* In a medium bowl, beat the eggs until fluffy. Add Light Cakey Corn Bread Mix, milk or buttermilk, and oil; mix well.
1½ cups milk or buttermilk	
¼ cup vegetable oil	*3* Pour into the prepared pan. Bake for 25 to 28 minutes, or until the bread sets and turns light golden-brown. Serve warm. If you'd rather bake muffins, reduce the baking time to 20 to 22 minutes.

Per serving: Calories 187 (From Fat 108); Fat 12g (Saturated 4g); Cholesterol 61mg; Sodium 169mg; Carbohydrate 17g (Dietary Fiber 1g); Protein 4g.

Hearty Corn Bread Mix

Prep time: 15 min • **Yield:** 6–7 cups

Ingredients	*Directions*
4 cups yellow or white cornmeal	**1** In a large bowl, combine the cornmeal, Whole-Grain Flour Mix, White Flour Mix, sugar (if desired), baking powder, baking soda, and salt and mix well with a wire whisk until the ingredients are well-blended and all one color.
1¼ cups minus 1 teaspoon (165 grams) Whole-Grain Flour Mix (earlier in this chapter)	
1 cup minus 2 teaspoons (142 grams) White Flour Mix (earlier in this chapter)	**2** Add the unsalted butter, buttery sticks, or coconut oil (if desired) and blend the fat into the flour until the mixture resembles sand.
½ cup sugar (optional)	
5 teaspoons baking powder	**3** Divide the mix into four equal portions and place them in glass jars or plastic freezer bags.
1 teaspoon baking soda	
1½ teaspoons salt	
¾ cup unsalted butter, buttery sticks, or coconut oil (optional)	

Note: Store Hearty Corn Bread Mix in the refrigerator for three months or in the freezer for six months.

Hearty Corn Bread

Prep time: 15 min • **Cook time:** 25 min • **Yield:** 9 servings

Ingredients	Directions
Unsalted butter or solid shortening	*1* Preheat the oven to 350 degrees. Grease a 9-inch square pan with unsalted butter or solid shortening.
2 eggs	
1 portion Hearty Corn Bread Mix (earlier in this chapter)	*2* In a medium bowl, beat the eggs until fluffy. Add Hearty Corn Bread Mix, milk or buttermilk, and oil; mix well.
1½ cups milk or buttermilk	
¼ cup vegetable oil	*3* Pour into the prepared pan. Bake for 25 to 28 minutes, or until the bread is set and turns light golden-brown. Serve warm.

Per serving: Calories 282 (From Fat 96); Fat 11g (Saturated 2g); Cholesterol 53mg; Sodium 37mg; Carbohydrate 41g (Dietary Fiber 5g); Protein 8g.

Note: This corn bread is grainier and heavier than the Light Cakey Corn Bread. Use it when you want a dense and well-textured corn bread to serve with chili in the fall and winter.

High-Protein Bread Flour Mix

Prep time: 20 min • **Yield:** 15 cups

Ingredients	Directions
4⅓ cups (583 grams) brown rice flour	**1** In a large bowl, combine all ingredients and mix until they're one color.
4¾ cups (583 grams) sorghum flour	
4½ cups plus 2 tablespoons plus 2 teaspoons (583 grams) millet flour	**2** Store in a large container at room temperature for no longer than one month.
1¼ cups minus 2 teaspoons (155 grams) white bean flour	
½ cup plus 2 tablespoons (74 grams) garfava flour	

Note: Gluten-free folk have a true problem re-creating the structure and function of the protein gluten. Some people use lots of xanthan and guar gum to mimic the stickiness and stretchiness of gluten molecules. But breads made with these ingredients can be a bit, well, gummy. This mixture mimics the high-protein content of bread flour.

Bread flour contains 14 percent protein as well as fat and fiber. This mixture creates a lovely loaf of bread that rises high and stays tender. If you're sensitive to bean flours or one of the other flours, substitute another flour (by weight only!) that has a similar protein content.

Note: This mix will keep in the freezer for six months.

Lemon Cardamom Coffeecake

Prep time: 45 min • **Cook time:** 25 min • **Yield:** 9 servings

Ingredients	Directions
¾ cup plus 2 tablespoons milk	*1* In a medium saucepan, warm all the milk over low heat. Pour 2 tablespoons into a small bowl and add the yeast; let stand 10 minutes.
1¼ teaspoons active dry yeast	
2 tablespoons plus 2 tablespoons unsalted butter	*2* Add 2 tablespoons butter, granulated sugar, and salt to the remaining milk in the pan and heat until the butter melts. Pour into a medium bowl and let cool; stir in the lemon peel.
3 tablespoons granulated sugar	
¼ teaspoon salt	
½ teaspoon grated lemon peel	*3* Add the egg yolk to the yeast and milk mixture and beat until smooth.
1 egg yolk	
¼ teaspoon lemon extract	*4* Stir in the lemon extract, ¼ teaspoon cardamom, White Flour Mix, and High-Protein Bread Flour Mix; beat for 1 minute.
¼ teaspoon plus ⅛ teaspoon cardamom	
¾ cup plus 1 tablespoon plus 1 teaspoon (124 grams) White Flour Mix (earlier in this chapter)	*5* Grease a 9-inch square cake pan with unsalted butter.
	6 Place the batter into the prepared pan.
½ cup minus 1 teaspoon (62 grams) High-Protein Bread Flour Mix (earlier in this chapter)	*7* In a small bowl, combine the brown sugar, 2 tablespoons butter, and ⅛ teaspoon cardamom; mix well. Sprinkle over the batter in the pan.
¼ cup packed brown sugar	*8* Let rise for 30 to 40 minutes.
	9 Preheat the oven to 350 degrees. Bake the coffeecake for 24 to 27 minutes, or until golden-brown, and set. Cool in the pan until warm; cut into squares to serve.

Per serving: Calories 177 (From Fat 60); Fat 7g (Saturated 4g); Cholesterol 41mg; Sodium 81mg; Carbohydrate 29g (Dietary Fiber 1g); Protein 2g.

Vary It! Cardamom is a Scandinavian spice that's like nutmeg but milder. You can substitute ground nutmeg for the cardamom in this recipe if you'd like.

Cinnamon Rolls

Prep time: 1 hr • **Cook time:** 35 min • **Yield:** 8 servings

Ingredients	*Directions*

Dough:

1½ cups plus 2 tablespoons (240 grams) White Flour Mix (earlier in this chapter)

1½ cups plus 1 teaspoon (200 grams) High-Protein Bread Flour Mix (earlier in this chapter)

¼ cup plus 2 teaspoons (40 grams) Whole-Grain Flour Mix (earlier in this chapter)

¼ cup organic cane sugar

1 tablespoon active dry yeast

½ teaspoon salt

½ cup dry milk

1 teaspoon xanthan gum

1 egg

2 egg yolks

½ cup unsalted butter, softened

¾ cup plus 1 tablespoon plus 1 teaspoon water

½ teaspoon vanilla

Filling:

¼ cup unsalted butter

⅔ cup packed brown sugar

2½ teaspoons ground cinnamon

½ cup powdered sugar in a sifter or sieve

1 For the dough, combine the White Flour Mix, High-Protein Bread Flour Mix, Whole-Grain Flour Mix, cane sugar, yeast, salt, dry milk, and xanthan gum in a large bowl; mix until the mixture is one color.

2 Beat in the egg, egg yolks, and butter. Add the water and vanilla; beat for 3 minutes. Cover and let rest while you make the filling.

3 For the filling, melt ¼ cup butter. In a medium bowl, combine the brown sugar and cinnamon.

4 Grease a 9-x-12-inch pan well with unsalted butter or solid shortening.

5 Place a 16-inch-long piece of plastic wrap on your work surface. Sprinkle heavily with powdered sugar.

6 Place the dough in the center of the powdered sugar and sprinkle the top heavily with more powdered sugar. Cover with another 16-inch piece of plastic wrap.

7 Roll the dough out to a rectangle ½-inch thick that completely fills the plastic. Peel off the top layer of plastic wrap.

8 Spread the dough with ¼ cup melted butter. Then sprinkle the dough with the brown sugar and cinnamon mixture, leaving 1 inch at one long end of the dough uncovered.

9 Lift the plastic wrap from the long side completely covered with filling. Let the dough fold toward itself, pulling it tightly into the center. Lift the plastic wrap off as you work and roll toward the other long edge.

10 Cut the dough into 2-inch rounds. Place each roll in a greased pan, cut-side down so the spiral of filling shows, leaving space between each roll for rising.

11 Cover the pan with plastic wrap and let rise until doubled, about 30 to 40 minutes.

12 Preheat the oven to 450 degrees. Remove the plastic and place the rolls in the oven. Immediately reduce the heat to 400 degrees and bake the rolls for 20 minutes.

13 Reduce the heat to 350 degrees and bake the rolls for 15 minutes longer, until the rolls are brown and set. The internal temperature of the rolls should be 190 to 200 degrees.

14 Cool the rolls in the pan for 5 minutes and then carefully move them to wire racks to cool completely.

15 Frost the rolls with Cream Cheese Frosting (see Book V, Chapter 4) when they've cooled. Store in an airtight container at room temperature for up to two days. If they're frosted, keep them in the fridge.

Per serving: *Calories 600 (From Fat 251); Fat 28g (Saturated 16g); Cholesterol 149mg; Sodium 198mg; Carbohydrate 85g (Dietary Fiber 2g); Protein 8g.*

Note: Living gluten-free doesn't mean you lose a desire for gooey good cinnamon rolls. Make these rolls for your family on Christmas mornings or for other celebrations that deserve that warm sweet smell coming from the kitchen.

Hot Cross Buns

Prep time: 40 min • **Cook time:** 30–40 min • **Yield:** 9 servings

Ingredients	Directions
Buns:	**1** For the buns, warm the milk to 110 degrees in a small saucepan. Stir in the yeast and set aside.
½ cup whole milk	
1 tablespoon active dry yeast	**2** In a large bowl, combine the White Flour Mix, Whole-Grain Flour Mix, xanthan gum, nutmeg, cinnamon, salt, and granulated sugar; mix until the mixture is one color.
1¼ cups plus 1 tablespoon (196 grams) White Flour Mix (earlier in this chapter)	
1¼ cups minus 1 teaspoon (165 grams) Whole-Grain Flour Mix (earlier in this chapter)	**3** Beat in the eggs, egg yolk, and vanilla and then add the milk mixture; beat for 2 minutes.
½ teaspoon xanthan gum	**4** Add the butter and beat 1 minute longer. Stir in the dried currants or raisins and orange peel.
Pinch nutmeg	
Pinch cinnamon	**5** Cover the bowl with plastic wrap and let rise for 15 minutes.
½ teaspoon salt	
½ cup granulated sugar	**6** Grease nine muffin cups with unsalted butter or solid shortening.
2 eggs	
1 egg yolk	**7** Use a large ice-cream scoop to fill the muffin cups. Cover with plastic wrap and let rise for 30 minutes.
1 teaspoon vanilla	
6 tablespoons unsalted butter	**8** Preheat the oven to 450 degrees. Uncover the pan and place the buns on the middle rack of the oven.
¼ cup dried currants or raisins	
¼ cup minced candied orange peel	**9** Immediately reduce the heat to 350 degrees and bake for 30 to 32 minutes, or until the buns are browned. Internal temperature should be 190 to 200 degrees.
Icing:	
¼ cup powdered sugar	
1 drop almond extract	
1 tablespoon milk	

10 Cool the buns in the pan for 5 minutes and then turn the buns onto a wire rack to cool.

11 For the icing, combine the powdered sugar, almond extract, and milk. Use this mixture to make a cross on top of the cooled buns.

Per serving: Calories 321 (From Fat 93); Fat 10g (Saturated 6g); Cholesterol 93mg; Sodium 159mg; Carbohydrate 55g (Dietary Fiber 2g); Protein 5g.

Gooey Orange Rolls

Prep time: 45 min • **Cook time:** 35 min • **Yield:** 8 servings

Ingredients	Directions
Cinnamon Roll dough (earlier in this chapter)	**1** Make the Cinnamon Roll dough through Step 2.
¼ cup unsalted butter	**2** Melt the butter. In a small bowl, combine the granulated sugar, 2 teaspoons orange peel, and 2 tablespoons orange juice; mix well.
1 cup granulated sugar	
2 teaspoons plus 2 teaspoons grated orange peel	**3** In another small bowl, combine the powdered sugar, 2 teaspoons orange peel, and 3 tablespoons orange juice; set aside. This is the final glaze for the rolls.
2 tablespoons plus 3 tablespoons orange juice	
⅔ cup powdered sugar	**4** Roll out the dough on powdered sugar–covered plastic wrap, as directed in Steps 4 through 7 of the Cinnamon Roll recipe.
	5 Brush the dough with melted butter and sprinkle with the sugar-and-orange mixture.
	6 Continue with the Cinnamon Roll recipe through Step 13.
	7 When the rolls are done, immediately pour the powdered sugar mixture over them. Let the rolls cool completely in the pan before eating them.

Per serving: Calories 591 (From Fat 200); Fat 22g (Saturated 13g); Cholesterol 134mg; Sodium 190mg; Carbohydrate 95g (Dietary Fiber 2g); Protein 8g.

Note: These rolls should cool completely before you eat them, but if you just can't resist, at least let them get down to "warm" before you devour them.

Sticky Buns

Prep time: 1 hr • **Cook time:** 35 min • **Yield:** 8 servings

Ingredients	*Directions*
Cinnamon Roll dough (earlier in this chapter)	*1* Make the Cinnamon Roll dough through Step 2.
½ cup unsalted butter **1 cup sugar**	*2* Melt the butter and spread it evenly into a 9-x-12-inch pan, completely covering the bottom of the pan.
2 cups pecan halves or raisins or a combination	*3* Sprinkle evenly with the sugar. Then add the nuts or raisins or both, pressing them down into the sugar and butter.
	4 Continue with the Cinnamon Roll recipe from Steps 3 through 13. When the buns are done, immediately invert them onto a serving plate. If any nuts or raisins stick to the pan or if any of the glaze is still in the pan, carefully scoop them/it out with a spoon (it's hot!) and put on top of the rolls. Serve warm.

Per serving: Calories 763 (From Fat 406); Fat 45g (Saturated 18g); Cholesterol 149mg; Sodium 192mg; Carbohydrate 87g (Dietary Fiber 4g); Protein 10g.

Note: If you're from the Jersey shore, Sticky Buns are another name for Cinnamon Rolls but with one special twist: The rolls are layered with more butter, more sugar, and nuts or raisins, or maybe even both. As the rolls bake, the sugar and butter create a lovely sticky glaze. You turn the buns out hot from the oven so that the glaze trickles down the sides. One bite and you'll be back at Beach Haven! Just skip the Cream Cheese Frosting; no one needs that much sugar at one time.

Bismarck Doughnuts

Prep time: 50 min, plus rising time • **Cook time:** 4–6 min • **Yield:** 9 servings

Ingredients	Directions
5 eggs	*1* In a large bowl, beat the eggs until they're light, fluffy, and pale yellow, about 5 to 6 minutes.
1 cup plus 3 tablespoons (155 grams) High-Protein Bread Flour Mix (earlier in this chapter)	
1 cup minus 2 tablespoons (110 grams) tapioca flour	*2* Add the High-Protein Bread Flour Mix, tapioca flour, buckwheat flour, sugar, salt, butter, and yeast and beat for 1 minute longer.
2 tablespoons (20 grams) raw or regular buckwheat flour	*3* Tear off parchment paper into twelve 4-inch squares. Using an ice-cream scoop, scoop the batter onto the center of each parchment paper square. The dough will look very thin and liquid; don't worry about this.
2 tablespoons sugar	
½ teaspoon salt	*4* Let the dough rise for 2 hours. It will still be very thin. When the dough hits the fat, it will puff and become firm.
2 tablespoons unsalted butter, melted	
1 tablespoon active dry yeast	*5* Prepare the Bavarian Cream Filling while the batter rises.
Bavarian Cream Filling (next in this chapter)	*6* Cover a cooking sheet with several pages of newspaper and then cover that with paper towels; set aside.
4 cups safflower oil	
6 ounces dark chocolate, melted	*7* In a large, deep, heavy frying pan, heat the oil to 365 degrees.
	8 Carefully lift up two of the doughnuts, one at a time, still on the parchment paper, and place them into the oil, paper-side down. Work quickly but carefully. Don't slide them into the oil or the dough may come off the paper and the doughnuts will be misshapen.
	9 Let them fry for 2 to 3 seconds and then flip the dough-nuts. Remove the parchment paper using tongs.

10 Let the doughnuts fry for 1 to 2 minutes. Flip the doughnuts again and fry for 1 minute longer. Place them on the prepared cookie sheet to drain. Repeat with the remaining doughnuts.

11 Cool completely. To fill, put the Bavarian Cream Filling in a pastry bag or plastic bag. Cut a slit into the side of each doughnut and pipe the filling inside.

12 Spread the doughnuts with the melted chocolate. Store in the refrigerator up to two days.

Per serving: Calories 546 (From Fat 322); Fat 36g (Saturated 14g); Cholesterol 210mg; Sodium 202mg; Carbohydrate 53g (Dietary Fiber 3g); Protein 9g.

Bavarian Cream Filling

Prep time: 15 min, plus chilling time • **Cook time:** 10 min • **Yield:** 2 cups

Ingredients	Directions
¾ cup heavy cream	**1** In a large, heavy saucepan, combine the heavy cream, milk, and sugar. Cook over medium heat until the mixture simmers, stirring occasionally so the sugar dissolves.
⅔ cup whole milk	
¼ cup plus 2 tablespoons sugar	
1 egg	**2** Meanwhile, in a mixing bowl with the whisk attachment, beat the egg and the egg yolks until they're pale yellow and fluffy.
2 egg yolks	
2 tablespoons cornstarch	**3** Beat in the cornstarch.
2 tablespoons unsalted butter	**4** When the milk mixture has come just to a simmer with consistent bubbles, pour 2 tablespoons of the milk mixture into the egg mixture and beat.
1 teaspoon vanilla	
	5 Continue to add all the milk mixture gradually, beating constantly.
	6 Turn the egg mixture back into the pan and cook over medium heat until the mixture begins to steam and thicken. This should take less than a minute.

7 Remove from the heat and whisk in the butter and vanilla.

8 If you love perfectly smooth centers to your doughnut, feel free to strain the mixture through a sieve.

9 Cover the Bavarian Cream Filling with plastic wrap directly on the surface and chill until cold, about 2 hours.

Per ¼-cup serving: Calories 175 (From Fat 118); Fat 13g (Saturated 8g); Cholesterol 94mg; Sodium 38mg; Carbohydrate 13g (Dietary Fiber 0g); Protein 2g.

Note: Because of the eggs, you must refrigerate this mixture. And make sure it's completely cold before you fill the doughnuts. You can use this mixture to fill cakes, too. You should refrigerate any cake filled with this cream as well.

Note: If you have trouble filling the doughnuts with the cream filling, just cut the doughnuts in half, add the cream, and then put the tops back on and frost. You won't have any complaints!

Monkey Bread

Prep time: 45 min, plus rising time • **Cook time:** 30 min • **Yield:** 12 servings

Ingredients	Directions
½ cup milk	**1** In a small saucepan, heat the milk to 110 degrees. Stir in the yeast and set aside.
1 tablespoon yeast	
1¼ cups plus 1 tablespoon plus 1 teaspoon (196 grams) White Flour Mix (earlier in this chapter)	**2** In a large bowl, combine the White Flour Mix, Whole-Grain Flour mix, xanthan gum, ½ cup cane sugar, nutmeg, cinnamon, and salt and mix until the mixture is one color.
1¼ cups minus 1 teaspoon (165 grams) Whole-Grain Flour Mix (earlier in this chapter)	**3** Beat in the eggs, egg yolk, and vanilla. Stir in the yeast mixture and beat for 2 minutes.
½ teaspoon xanthan gum	
½ cup plus ¼ cup organic cane sugar	**4** Add 6 tablespoons butter and beat 1 minute longer.
¼ teaspoon nutmeg	**5** Cover the bowl with plastic wrap and let rise for 15 minutes.
½ teaspoon cinnamon	
½ teaspoon salt	**6** Melt ½ cup butter and coat a 12-cup Bundt pan completely, making sure to coat the center stem as well. Reserve the remaining butter.
2 eggs	
1 egg yolk	**7** In a food processor, combine ¼ cup cane sugar, brown sugar, and lemon peel. Start the machine running and add the nuts through the feed tube; process until the nuts are finely ground but not oily.
1 teaspoon vanilla	
6 tablespoons plus ½ cup unsalted butter, melted	
¼ cup brown sugar	**8** Sprinkle the inside of the cake pan with 3 tablespoons of the nut mixture. Place the remaining nut mixture in a shallow bowl.
1 teaspoon grated lemon peel	
1 cup almonds, walnuts, or pecans	**9** Use a small ice-cream scoop to scoop the dough out of the bowl and into the nut mixture. Roll each ball in the nut mixture to coat and place them into the prepared pan. When the pan has one layer of balls, drizzle with 1 tablespoon melted butter.

10 Repeat with the remaining dough, nut mixture, and butter. You should have three layers of dough balls in the pan when you're done.

11 Cover the pan with plastic wrap and let rise for 2 hours, or until doubled in size.

12 Preheat the oven to 450 degrees.

13 Remove the plastic wrap and place the pan on the middle rack of the oven.

14 Immediately reduce the temperature to 350 degrees. Bake the rolls for 30 to 32 minutes, until deep golden-brown. The temperature on an instant-read thermometer should be 190 to 200 degrees.

15 Cool the bread in the pan for 5 minutes and then turn out onto a wire rack to cool completely.

16 Serve this bread with tongs so people can pull off one piece at a time.

Per serving: *Calories 333 (From Fat 202); Fat 22g (Saturated 10g); Cholesterol 90mg; Sodium 68mg; Carbohydrate 31g (Dietary Fiber 2g); Protein 5g.*

Vary It!: If you can't eat nuts, just grind up some orange peel with the sugars for a nice variation.

Honey Oat Bread

Prep time: 20 min, plus rising time • **Cook time:** 60–70 min • **Yield:** 16 slices

Ingredients	Directions
Unsalted butter	**1** Grease a 9-x-5-inch loaf pan with unsalted butter.
2 cups plus 2 tablespoons (290 grams) Whole-Grain Flour Mix (earlier in this chapter)	**2** In the bowl for a stand mixer, combine all ingredients. Beat on medium speed for 2 minutes.
1 cup minus 2 tablespoons (105 grams) oat flour	**3** Pour the mixture into the prepared bread pan. Cover and let rise for 1 to 2 hours, or until the batter has doubled in size and almost reaches the rim of the pan.
⅔ cup rolled oats	
2 eggs	
2 tablespoons honey	**4** Preheat the oven to 350 degrees. Using a razor blade, make a cut down the center of the loaf for even more oven spring.
¼ teaspoon sea salt	
1 teaspoon active dry yeast	
½ teaspoon xanthan gum	**5** Bake for 60 to 70 minutes, or until the temperature on an instant-read thermometer reads 190 to 200 degrees. The bread will be golden-brown, pull away from the pan sides, and sound hollow when tapped.
1⅓ cups warm water (102 to 103 degrees)	
	6 Cool the bread in the pan for 3 minutes and then move it to a wire rack to cool completely. Cool the bread completely before slicing.

Per serving: Calories 130 (From Fat 17); Fat 2g (Saturated 0g); Cholesterol 27mg; Sodium 45mg; Carbohydrate 25g (Dietary Fiber 2g); Protein 4g.

Note: This bread makes the most amazing toast. The eggs provide a bit more protein to help the structure develop and add great flavor.

Chapter 3

Cookies, Brownies, and Bars

In This Chapter

▶ Knowing the keys to making cookies, brownies, and bars
▶ Finding a collection of scrumptious cookie recipes
▶ Checking out tasty recipes for brownies and bars

Cookies just out of the oven are a real treat. Cookies can celebrate an occasion or soothe a hurt. And just because you have to avoid wheat flour doesn't mean you have to skip cookies! Brownies and bar cookies are some of the easiest treats to make. You just put batter or dough into a pan and bake. And they're perfect for any occasion.

In this chapter, you find recipes for everything from classic Chocolate Chip Cookies to madeleines and even a variation on a popular Girl Scout cookie. This chapter is also chock-full of delicious brownies and bar cookies, like decadent Lemon Truffle Bars and simple, snack-tastic Granola Bars.

How to Make the Best Cookies

Baking cookies isn't very different from any other type of baking, but gluten-free cookies are a bit different. Here are some tips for making the best cookies:

✓ Measure flour carefully. Yes, this book says that every time, but unless you want dense or tough cookies, measure by weight. If you don't use a scale to measure flours and mixes, always measure by spooning the flour or mix lightly into a measuring cup and leveling off the top with the back of a knife.

✔ Most gluten-free cookie doughs are chilled before baking. The chilling lets the flour hydrate completely so the structure of the cookies is strong enough to hold their shape but tender enough to be delicious. Always chill the dough as the recipe directs.

✔ Doneness tests are different for cookies than for most other baked goods. You don't need to check the internal temperature or do a toothpick test. Most people simply use the observation test — when a cookie looks done, it's done! You may even want to take cookies out of the oven a few minutes before they're actually browned because they continue to cook on the baking sheet.

✔ Always cool cookies on a wire rack. If you leave the cookies on the cookie sheet, they may stick or overbake. If you cool cookies on a solid surface, their bottoms may become damp, which defeats the purpose of a crisp cookie like Crisp Chocolate Roll Out Cookies.

You can make most cookie doughs well ahead of time and chill or even freeze them until you're ready to bake them. That's a huge time savings in the kitchen. And you impress people who drop by unexpectedly when you whip some just-baked cookies out of the oven.

The Keys to Delicious Brownies and Bar Cookies

The most important part of making brownies and bar cookies is doneness. Overbaked brownies are tough and dry, no matter how perfectly you measure the ingredients. And underbaked bar cookies don't hold together, so you can't cut and serve them.

To make the best brownies and bar cookies:

✔ Always grease the pan well, using unsalted butter, solid shortening, or nonstick cooking spray. (But do check the label before using nonstick cooking spray; many versions contain gluten as a stabilizer.) Salted butter makes the cookies stick to the pan, and oil doesn't work very well for greasing.

✔ If you don't use a scale to measure flours and mixes, always measure by spooning the flour or mix lightly into a measuring cup and leveling off the top with the back of a knife.

✔ You may want to line the cake pan or baking pan with foil or parchment paper and then grease the foil if the recipe calls for it. Use enough foil to extend past the pan's edges. Smooth the foil down so it fits closely inside the pan. When you bake the brownies or bar cookies, cool them completely in the pan and then lift them out of the pan using the foil edges. Peel off the foil and cut into bars.

✔ If a recipe calls for baking a crust before adding a filling, be sure to bake it until it's done. Crusts get soggy and fall apart if you don't thoroughly bake them before you add a soft or creamy filling.

✔ To cut brownies and bar cookies, use a sharp knife. Dip the knife in hot water and wipe it off before each cut for smooth edges and well-defined squares.

✔ Store brownies and bar cookies well covered at room temperature unless the recipes specify otherwise. The cut edges of these foods can dry out if they aren't well covered.

✔ If you need to serve a crowd or make goodies for a bake sale, brownies and bar cookies are the way to go. A 13-x-9-inch pan of treats serves 24 to 36 people, depending on how small you cut the bars. You should cut some bar cookies, like Double Chocolate Caramel Bars, small simply because they're so rich. You can cut Granola Bars larger because they're a healthier treat.

Chocolate Chip Cookies

Prep time: 20 min, plus chilling time • **Cook time:** 15 min • **Yield:** 48 servings

Ingredients	Directions
1¾ cups plus 3 tablespoons (284 grams) White Flour Mix (see Book V, Chapter 2)	*1* In a large bowl, combine the White Flour Mix, Whole-Grain Flour Mix, baking powder, salt, brown sugar, and granulated sugar; mix until the mixture is one color.
⅓ cup minus 1 teaspoon (42 grams) Whole-Grain Flour Mix (see Book V, Chapter 2)	*2* Add the softened butter and beat until sandy crumbs form.
1 teaspoon baking powder	
½ teaspoon salt	*3* Add the eggs and vanilla and beat until well combined. The batter will be quite soft.
1 cup packed brown sugar	
¾ cup granulated sugar	*4* Add the chips and nuts and stir until well mixed.
1 cup butter, softened	
2 eggs	*5* Cover the dough and chill at least 2 hours or overnight. If you can, chill the dough up to 2 days. This rest lets the flours absorb the moisture in the dough and lets the brown sugar create a true caramel undertone in the cookie.
1 teaspoon vanilla	
2 cups chocolate chips	
1 cup chopped walnuts or pecans	
	6 When you're ready to bake, preheat the oven to 350 degrees. Line cookie sheets with parchment paper or grease them lightly.
	7 Drop the dough by teaspoons, 2 inches apart, onto the prepared cookie sheets.

8 Bake for 15 to 16 minutes, rotating the cookie sheets in the oven halfway through the baking time.

9 Remove the cookies from the oven, let them cool on the sheets for 2 minutes, and then remove them to wire racks to cool completely.

Per serving: Calories 139 (From Fat 70); Fat 8g (Saturated 4g); Cholesterol 19mg; Sodium 38mg; Carbohydrate 18g (Dietary Fiber 1g); Protein 1g.

Vary It! You can use dark chocolate chunks, dried tart cherries, or any other type of candy in these delicious cookies. Just keep the total weight of the ingredients you add to 510 to 525 grams and you'll have success.

Coconut Macaroons

Prep time: 15 min • **Cook time:** 12–15 min • **Yield:** 30 cookies

Ingredients	Directions
½ cup (55 grams) coconut flour	**1** Preheat the oven to 350 degrees. Line a cookie sheet with parchment paper or foil; set aside.
3 cups flaked coconut	
⅓ cup sugar	**2** In a large bowl, combine the coconut flour, flaked coconut, and sugar and mix well. Add the light cream, egg white, vanilla, coconut extract, and salt and mix until combined. You may need to add more light cream to make a workable soft dough, depending on how much moisture the coconut flour soaks up.
¾ cup light cream	
1 egg white	
1½ teaspoons vanilla	
½ teaspoon coconut extract	**3** Using a small (1½ inch) ice-cream scoop, scoop out the dough onto the prepared cookie sheet. You can spray the scoop with nonstick cooking spray or dip it into cold water before scooping to prevent sticking.
Pinch salt	
	4 Bake the macaroons for 12 to 15 minutes, or until lightly browned and set. Let them cool 10 minutes on the baking sheet and then move them to wire racks to cool completely.

Per serving: Calories 64 (From Fat 34); Fat 4g (Saturated 3g); Cholesterol 4mg; Sodium 32mg; Carbohydrate 7g (Dietary Fiber 1g); Protein 1g.

Crisp Chocolate Roll Out Cookies

Prep time: 20 min, plus chilling time • **Cook time:** 10–12 min • **Yield:** 48 cookies

Ingredients	*Directions*
½ **cup unsalted organic butter, softened**	*1* Place the butter in a large bowl and beat until light and fluffy. Gradually add the Cookie Mix and cocoa and continue to beat until well blended.
2½ **cups Cookie Mix without Gums (see Book V, Chapter 2)**	*2* Beat in the egg, milk, and vanilla and continue to beat for 1 minute. The batter will be pliable and thick.
½ **cup cocoa powder**	
1 **egg**	*3* Cut off a 15-inch piece of plastic wrap and place it on the work surface. Place the dough in a long, even log down one side of the wrap and roll the dough into the plastic. Refrigerate for 3 to 4 hours before baking.
1 **tablespoon milk**	
1 **teaspoon vanilla**	
	4 To make the cookies, preheat the oven to 350 degrees. Place a large sheet of parchment paper on the work surface. Add the dough and top with another sheet of parchment paper. If the dough is hard or stiff, let stand at room temperature for 30 minutes.
	5 Roll out the dough to ½-inch thickness and cut with cookie cutters. Place it on Silpat-lined cookie sheets. (Silpat liner is a reusable sheet made from silicone that prevents baked goods from sticking. If you don't have one or can't find one, use parchment paper.)
	6 Bake for 10 to 12 minutes, until the cookies puff slightly and feel slightly firm to the touch. Let them cool on the cookie sheets for 2 minutes and then move them to wire racks to cool completely.

Per serving: Calories 54 (From Fat 20); Fat 2g (Saturated 1g); Cholesterol 10mg; Sodium 145mg; Carbohydrate 8g (Dietary Fiber 1g); Protein 1g.

Note: You can freeze this dough for up to three months. Let it thaw in the refrigerator overnight before using. And always use the parchment paper to roll out the cookies because the dough is difficult to handle. These cookies are crisp and tender. For a more cake-like cut-out chocolate cookie, simply add 2 tablespoons of water to the recipe along with the egg and vanilla.

Oatmeal Raisin Cookies

Prep time: 30 min, plus chilling time • **Cook time:** 15 min • **Yield:** 24 servings

Ingredients	Directions

Ingredients

¼ cup granulated sugar

1 cup packed brown sugar

1 cup minus 2 teaspoons (142 grams) White Flour Mix (see Book V, Chapter 2)

½ cup plus 1 tablespoon plus 2 teaspoons (83 grams) Whole-Grain Flour Mix (see Book V, Chapter 2)

2 teaspoons baking powder

½ teaspoon salt

2 teaspoons cinnamon

¼ teaspoon nutmeg

½ teaspoon ginger

½ cup unsalted butter, softened

¼ cup vegetable oil

1 egg

2 teaspoons honey

1 teaspoon vanilla

⅓ cup milk

1¾ cups gluten-free rolled oats

½ cup chopped walnuts

¾ cup raisins

Directions

1 In a large bowl, combine the granulated sugar, brown sugar, White Flour Mix, Whole-Grain Flour Mix, baking powder, salt, cinnamon, nutmeg, and ginger and mix until the mixture is one color.

2 Add the butter and vegetable oil and beat until the mixture is the texture of wet sand.

3 Add the egg, honey, vanilla, and milk and beat for 1 minute.

4 Stir in the oats, nuts, and raisins. Cover and refrigerate the dough for at least 2 hours to let the oats absorb the liquid.

5 When you're ready to bake, preheat the oven to 350 degrees. Line two cookie sheets with Silpat liners or parchment paper.

6 Drop the dough by spoonfuls onto the prepared cookie sheets, making 24 cookies in all.

7 Bake for 13 to 15 minutes, or until the cookies are lightly browned. Let them cool on cookie sheets for 3 minutes and then move them to a wire rack to cool completely.

Per serving: Calories 126 (From Fat 22); Fat 3g (Saturated 0g); Cholesterol 9mg; Sodium 90mg; Carbohydrate 25g (Dietary Fiber 1g); Protein 2g.

Chocolate Crackle Cookies

Prep time: 20 min, plus chilling time • **Cook time:** 10–12 min • **Yield:** 36 cookies

Ingredients	*Directions*
1 batch Crisp Chocolate Roll Out Cookies (see recipe earlier in this chapter)	*1* Prepare the Crisp Chocolate Roll Out Cookie dough as directed, using 2 tablespoons water in place of the milk, and chill for 3 to 4 hours.
2 tablespoons water	
1 cup powdered sugar	*2* Preheat the oven to 350 degrees. Line cookie sheets with Silpat liners or parchment paper.
	3 Break off tablespoons of the dough or use a small cookie scoop to make small balls. Roll the dough between your palms until smooth.
	4 Drop each ball of dough into the powdered sugar, making sure it's well coated. Place the balls at least 2 inches apart on the prepared cookie sheets.
	5 Bake for 10 to 12 minutes, or until the cookies puff slightly and are firm to the touch. Let them cool on the cookie sheets for 2 minutes and then move them to a wire rack to cool. Store them in an airtight container.

Per serving: Calories 85 (From Fat 27); Fat 3g (Saturated 2g); Cholesterol 13mg; Sodium 194mg; Carbohydrate 14g (Dietary Fiber 1g); Protein 1g.

Note: These little cookies have a crunchy, sweet shell and a tender, dark heart. They make a perfect afternoon snack with a glass of milk. The shaping is so simple that any child can help.

Vary It! You can use a different extract or flavoring for the cookies if you'd like. A drop of orange oil adds a rich taste. Or use ¼ or ½ teaspoon of peppermint extract. You can also roll the dough in finely ground nuts or baking sprinkles for a fun change of pace.

Vanilla Roll Out Cookies

Prep time: 20 min, plus chilling time • **Cook time:** 10–12 min • **Yield:** 48 cookies

Ingredients	Directions
½ cup organic unsalted butter, softened 3 cups Cookie Mix without Gums (see Book V, Chapter 2) 1 egg 1 tablespoon vanilla 2 tablespoons water	**1** In a large bowl, beat the butter until it's light and fluffy. Add the Cookie Mix and continue to beat until well blended.
	2 Stir in the egg, vanilla, and water and beat for 1 minute. The dough will be soft and thick.
	3 Cut a 15-inch-long piece of plastic wrap and place it on your work surface. Place the dough in a long log down one side of the wrap. Roll the dough into the plastic and refrigerate for 3 to 4 hours. The dough can be frozen at this point for slice-and-bake cookies.
	4 When you want to bake the cookies, preheat the oven to 350 degrees.
	5 Place a sheet of parchment paper on the work surface and add the dough. Top with another sheet of parchment paper. If the dough is hard or stiff, let stand at room temperature for 30 minutes.
	6 Roll out the dough to ½-inch thickness. Cut out using cookie cutters.
	7 Place the cookies on ungreased cookie sheets about 2 inches apart. Bake for 10 to 12 minutes, until the cookies puff slightly, the edges are golden-brown, and the cookies feel slightly firm to the touch. Let them cool on the cookie sheets for 1 minute and then move them to wire racks to cool completely.

Per serving: *Calories 56 (From Fat 19); Fat 2g (Saturated 1g); Cholesterol 10mg; Sodium 161mg; Carbohydrate 9g (Dietary Fiber 0g); Protein 1g.*

Note: To bake the cookie dough when it's frozen, remove the dough from the freezer and slice it ½-inch thick. Place it on ungreased cookie sheets and bake it at 350 degrees for 15 to 20 minutes.

Note: Have fun frosting these cookies during the holidays. Use the Buttercream Frosting recipe in Book V, Chapter 4. Divide the frosting into several smaller bowls and tint it using gluten-free food coloring.

Madeleines

Prep time: 20 min • **Cook time:** 15 min • **Yield:** 12 cookies

Ingredients	Directions
½ cup butter, softened	**1** Preheat the oven to 375 degrees. Spray a Madeleine pan with nonstick cooking spray or vegetable oil spray.
⅔ cup sugar	
2 eggs	**2** In a medium bowl, combine the butter and sugar and beat together until fluffy.
1 teaspoon vanilla	
½ teaspoon grated lemon peel	**3** Add the eggs, vanilla, lemon peel, and salt and blend well.
Pinch salt	
½ cup plus 1 tablespoon plus 2 teaspoons (83 grams) Whole-Grain Flour Mix (see Book V, Chapter 2)	**4** Stir in the Whole-Grain Flour Mix and White Flour Mix.
	5 Place the batter into the molds, filling just to the top of the pan. Don't overfill the molds or the Madeleines will run together as they bake.
½ cup minus 1 teaspoon (71 grams) White Flour Mix (see Book V, Chapter 2)	
	6 Bake for 15 to 16 minutes, until the Madeleines start to pull away from the pan at the edges. The upper side will be a soft golden color; the pan side will be golden-brown.
	7 Remove the cookies from the pans immediately and cool them on a wire rack.
	8 Before baking the next batch, wipe out the pans to remove the crumbs.

Per serving: Calories 138 (From Fat 77); Fat 9g (Saturated 5g); Cholesterol 56mg; Sodium 23mg; Carbohydrate 14g (Dietary Fiber 0g); Protein 2g.

Note: Proustian references about these cookies abound, so people think they must be hard to make. Actually, these are one of the simplest cookies imaginable. You need the correct specialized pan — called, obviously, a Madeleine pan — if you want to make the classic shell-shaped cookie, but you can use the same batter to make round cookies. Just use a muffin tin and fill with an inch of the batter. Bake as directed.

Six Vegan Cookie Fillings

Prep time: 10 min • **Cook time:** 3 min • **Yield:** 1 cup

Ingredients	Directions
2 tablespoons boiling water	*1* In a medium, heat-proof bowl, combine the boiling water and shortening. Let the shortening melt.
2 tablespoons organic palm oil shortening	
2 cups powdered sugar	*2* Stir in the powdered sugar and vanilla. Beat with a mixer until the mixture is light. The consistency will be plastic and spreadable.
1 drop vanilla	
	3 Use the filling to make sandwich cookies. Roll the filling into a ball and place it between two cookies, flat sides together. Gently press down to spread the filling.
	4 Cover the bowl with plastic wrap to prevent drying if you make this filling before the cookies are ready.

Per 1 tablespoon serving: Calories 72 (From Fat 15); Fat 2g (Saturated 1g); Cholesterol 0mg; Sodium 0mg; Carbohydrate 15g (Dietary Fiber 0g); Protein 0g.

Vary It! You can vary this filling in many ways:

(1) For **Coconut Cream Filling:** Substitute 2 tablespoons coconut oil for the shortening and coconut extract for the vanilla.

(2) For **Fudge Crème Filling:** Reduce the shortening to 1 tablespoon and melt 1 ounce chopped bittersweet or unsweetened chocolate into the shortening and then add the sugar and water.

(3) For **Peanut Crème Filling:** Reduce the shortening to 1 tablespoon and add ¼ cup natural peanut butter to the shortening and water mixture.

(4) For **Grasshopper Crème Filling:** Substitute 2 tablespoons boiling peppermint tea for the boiling water and mint or peppermint extract for the vanilla. You can tint this green with a drop of food coloring.

(5) For **Almond Crème Filling:** Substitute almond extract for the vanilla.

Thin Mints

Prep time: 25 min • **Cook time:** 10–20 min • **Yield:** 48 cookies

Ingredients	Directions
1 recipe Crisp Chocolate Roll Out Cookies (see recipe earlier in this chapter)	*1* Prepare the cookie dough as directed. Roll the dough into plastic wrap but don't roll it out between parchment paper. Just slice the dough ¼-inch thick and place it on parchment-lined cookie sheets.
1 recipe Grasshopper Crème Filling (see previous recipe, variation 4)	*2* Bake the dough at 350 degrees for 10 to 12 minutes, or until the cookies puff slightly and feel firm to the touch.
1 pound dark chocolate bar, chopped	*3* Remove the cookies from the cookie sheets and let them cool completely.
3 tablespoons organic palm oil shortening	*4* Break off 1 teaspoon of the Grasshopper Crème Filling and roll it into a ball. Place the ball on one cookie and use a glass bottom to flatten it. The filling shouldn't reach the edge of the cookie. Repeat with the remaining cookies.
2 teaspoons mint extract	*5* In a medium, heat-proof bowl, combine the chopped chocolate and shortening. Melt over simmering water just until melted. Stir in the mint extract.
	6 Place each cookie on a fork and gently dip it into the melted chocolate mixture, turning it to coat the other side. Then turn it right-side up, scoop it out with a fork, tap it on the side of the bowl gently to remove excess chocolate, and place it on waxed paper until firm. Store in an airtight container at room temperature.

Per serving Calories 136 (From Fat 60); Fat 7g (Saturated 4g); Cholesterol 10mg; Sodium 146mg; Carbohydrate 19g (Dietary Fiber 1g); Protein 1g.

Vary It! You can omit the Grasshopper Crème Filling and just coat the plain chocolate cookies for a more authentic version of the classic Girl Scout cookie.

Note: These cookies taste even better than the original and are especially tasty frozen.

Incredibly Easy Peanut Butter Cookies

Prep time: 5 min • **Cook time:** 20 min • **Yield:** 24 cookies

Ingredients	Directions
2 eggs	*1* Preheat the oven to 350 degrees.
1 cup chunky peanut butter	*2* Beat the eggs in a medium-sized bowl. Stir the peanut butter and sugar into the eggs.
1 cup sugar	*3* Drop dollops of dough from a spoon onto the cookie sheet, about 2 inches apart. Use the back side of a fork to press them flat.
	4 Bake the cookies for 10 to 12 minutes, or until the cookies spring back a little when you poke them.

Per serving: Calories 203 (From Fat 106); Fat 12g (Saturated 3g); Cholesterol 35mg; Sodium 110mg; Carbohydrate 21g (Dietary Fiber 1g); Protein 6g.

Quadruple Chocolate Cookies

Prep time: 30 min • **Cook time:** 11 min • **Yield:** 48 cookies

Ingredients	Directions
4 ounces unsweetened chocolate, chopped	*1* In a heavy, medium saucepan over low heat, melt together the unsweetened chocolate, semisweet chocolate, milk chocolate, and butter. Stir until smooth and then remove from heat.
4 ounces semisweet chocolate, chopped	
4 ounces milk chocolate, chopped	*2* In a large mixing bowl, beat the eggs until they're combined. Gradually add granulated sugar and brown sugar, beating on high speed until the mixture is thick, light, and lemon-colored. This should take about 5 minutes.
½ cup butter	
4 eggs	
¾ cup granulated sugar	*3* Beat in the melted chocolate mixture.
⅔ cup brown sugar	
¼ cup (30 grams) sorghum flour	*4* In a small bowl, combine the sorghum flour, potato starch, tapioca flour, salt, and baking powder and stir with a wire whisk to combine. Add to the batter and mix well, and then stir in the chocolate chips.
1 tablespoon (10 grams) potato starch	
1 tablespoon (7 grams) tapioca flour	*5* Let the batter stand for 25 minutes at room temperature. Preheat the oven to 350 degrees.
¼ teaspoon salt	
¼ teaspoon baking powder	*6* Line cookie sheets with Silpat liners or parchment paper. Drop the batter by spoonfuls onto the prepared sheets, about 3 inches apart.
½ cup mini semisweet chocolate chips	
	7 Bake for 9 to 11 minutes, or until the cookies are just set. Let them cool on the cookie sheets for 2 minutes and then pull the parchment paper with the cookies onto a wire rack to cool completely.

Per serving: Calories 94 (From Fat 51); Fat 6g (Saturated 3g); Cholesterol 23mg; Sodium 21mg; Carbohydrate 11g (Dietary Fiber 1g); Protein 1g.

Peanut Butter Chocolate Bars

Prep time: 15 min • **Cook time:** 25 min • **Yield:** 36 bar cookies

Ingredients	*Directions*
2 cups plus ½ cup creamy peanut butter	*1* Preheat the oven to 350 degrees. Line a 13-x-9-inch pan with foil and set aside.
½ cup packed brown sugar	
½ cup powdered sugar	*2* In a large bowl for a stand mixer, combine 2 cups peanut butter, brown sugar, powdered sugar, granulated sugar, honey, eggs, and vanilla. Beat well until combined.
⅓ cup granulated sugar	
¼ cup honey	
2 eggs	*3* Spoon and spread the mixture into the prepared pan. Bake for 15 to 25 minutes, or until the bars are set and light golden-brown around the edges. Remove them from the oven and place them on a cooling rack.
1 teaspoon vanilla	
One 12-ounce package (2 cups) semisweet chocolate chips	*4* In a medium, microwave-safe bowl, combine the chocolate chips with ½ cup peanut butter. Microwave on high for 1 minute; remove and stir. Continue microwaving the mixture on high for 1-minute intervals, stirring after each interval, until the mixture is melted and smooth.
1 cup chopped peanuts	
	5 Pour the chocolate mixture over the warm bars and spread to cover. Sprinkle with chopped peanuts and let stand until cool. Cut into bars to serve.

Per serving: Calories 209 (From Fat 126); Fat 14g (Saturated 4g); Cholesterol 12mg; Sodium 89mg; Carbohydrate 19g (Dietary Fiber 2g); Protein 6g.

Vary It! You can vary these bars in many ways. Swirl some of your favorite jam into the bars just before baking them or top the finished bars with a thin layer of jam and some ground peanuts. You can also top the bars with chocolate chips, peanut butter chips, or white chocolate chips before baking them instead of frosting them. Enjoy these delicious bars with a big glass of cold milk!

Tangy Lime Bars

Prep time: 30 min • **Cook time:** 35–45 min • **Yield:** 16 servings

Ingredients	Directions
3 tablespoons unsalted butter, softened	**1** Place the oven rack in the lower third of the oven. Preheat the oven to 350 degrees. Spray a 13-x-9-inch baking pan with nonstick cooking spray and set aside.
⅓ cup plus ⅔ cup sugar	
2 egg yolks	
1 tablespoon yogurt or ¼ teaspoon vinegar	**2** In a large bowl, beat the butter until it's light and fluffy. Add ⅓ cup sugar and beat until creamy. Add the egg yolks, yogurt or vinegar, and vanilla, beating well.
¼ teaspoon vanilla	
1 cup plus 2 tablespoons (165 grams) White Flour Mix (see Book V, Chapter 2)	**3** Add the White Flour Mix, Whole-Grain Flour Mix, salt, and baking soda and beat well.
½ cup plus 1 tablespoon plus 2 teaspoons (83 grams) Whole-Grain Flour Mix (see Book V, Chapter 2)	**4** Press the dough into the prepared pan and prick all over with a fork.
Pinch salt	**5** Bake 20 to 25 minutes, until the crust is golden-brown.
⅛ teaspoon baking soda	
2 eggs	**6** Meanwhile, make the topping. In a medium bowl, combine the eggs and egg whites and beat well.
2 egg whites	
½ cup strained fresh lime juice	**7** Add ⅔ cup sugar, lime juice, lime zest, and tapioca flour and mix well.
1 teaspoon grated lime zest	
2 tablespoons (16 grams) tapioca flour	**8** Remove the crust from the oven and pour the topping over.

9   Return the crust to the oven and bake for 15 to 20 minutes longer, until the topping is set.

10   Cool completely and then cover and chill the bars for 2 to 3 hours before serving.

Per serving: *Calories 145 (From Fat 32); Fat 4g (Saturated 2g); Cholesterol 59mg; Sodium 36mg; Carbohydrate 27g (Dietary Fiber 0g); Protein 2g.*

Note: Either yogurt or vinegar works to create the tang in the crust and add some acidity. Use whichever one you have on hand.

Butterscotch Brownies

Prep time: 15 min • **Cook time:** 35 min • **Yield:** 16 bars

Ingredients	Directions
¼ cup unsalted butter	**1** Preheat the oven to 325 degrees. Lightly grease an 8-x-8-inch square baking pan with unsalted butter and set aside.
1 cup packed brown sugar	
1 egg	
1 teaspoon vanilla	**2** In a medium saucepan, melt the butter. Add the brown sugar and heat, stirring, until the sugar is dissolved. Set aside to cool for 10 minutes.
½ cup minus 2 teaspoons (63 grams) brown rice flour	
1 teaspoon baking powder	**3** Beat in the egg and vanilla.
¼ teaspoon salt	
½ cup finely chopped walnuts	**4** In a small bowl, combine the flour, baking powder, and salt. Stir the flour mixture into the butter mixture. Add the nuts, mixing gently.
	5 Pour the batter into a prepared pan and bake for 25 to 33 minutes, until brownies are set and light golden-brown. Cool and cut into bars.

Per serving: Calories 121 (From Fat 51); Fat 6g (Saturated 2g); Cholesterol 21mg; Sodium 70mg; Carbohydrate 17g (Dietary Fiber 0g); Protein 1g.

Vary It! These delicious brownies pack and ship well. You can frost them with a chocolate or caramel frosting. They're also delicious with some butterscotch or chocolate chips (gluten-free, of course) stirred in along with the walnuts.

Rocky Road Bar Cookies

Prep time: 25 min • **Cook time:** 15–20 min • **Yield:** 16 bar cookies

Ingredients	Directions
½ batch Crisp Chocolate Roll Out Cookies (see recipe earlier in chapter)	*1* Prepare the Crisp Chocolate Roll Out Cookie dough, adding water along with the egg and vanilla in that recipe. Divide the batch in half; refrigerate or freeze half for later use.
2 tablespoons water	
½ cup coarsely chopped walnuts	*2* Preheat the oven to 350 degrees. Grease a 9-inch square baking pan with unsalted butter or nonstick cooking spray.
⅔ cup mini marshmallows	
⅓ cup semisweet or milk chocolate chips	*3* Press the cookie dough evenly into the pan. Sprinkle the walnuts, marshmallows, and chocolate chips on the dough and press in lightly.
	4 Bake for 15 to 20 minutes, or until the marshmallows are toasted and the chips are melted. Let the cookies cool completely on a wire rack before cutting into squares.

Per serving: Calories 137 (From Fat 69); Fat 8g (Saturated 3g); Cholesterol 14mg; Sodium 220mg; Carbohydrate 17g (Dietary Fiber 1g); Protein 2g.

Vary It! You can vary the topping according to your taste. Some people want some coconut on their Rocky Road. You can use different types of chocolate chips, too — peanut butter chocolate chips, white chocolate chips, or dark chocolate chips. All are scrumptious on these delightful bar cookies.

Lemon Truffle Bars

Prep time: 45 min, plus chilling time • **Cook time:** 20 min • **Yield:** 16 bar cookies

Ingredients	Directions
½ **recipe Vanilla Roll Out Cookies (see recipe earlier in this chapter)**	*1* Prepare the Vanilla Roll Out Cookie dough. Divide the dough in half and chill both halves as the recipe directs. Reserve one half for later use.
1 cup sugar	
2 tablespoons (16 grams) cornstarch	*2* When you're ready to bake, preheat the oven to 350 degrees. Grease a 9-inch square baking pan with unsalted butter. Press the cookie dough evenly into the pan and prick with a fork. Bake for 15 to 20 minutes, or until the crust is set and light golden-brown.
1 tablespoon (8 grams) tapioca flour	
¼ **teaspoon salt**	
2 egg yolks	*3* Cool the crust completely on a wire rack. When the crust is cool, combine the sugar, cornstarch, tapioca flour, and salt in a medium saucepan and mix with a wire whisk until smooth. In a small bowl, combine the egg yolks and water, beat well, and then beat into the sugar mixture until smooth.
10 tablespoons water	
7 tablespoons lemon juice	
2 tablespoons butter	
½ **teaspoon grated lemon zest**	*4* Cook the egg yolk mixture over medium heat, stirring constantly with a wire whisk, until the mixture thickens and reaches 165 degrees. Remove from the heat and add the lemon juice, butter, and lemon zest, beating well.
1½ cups white chocolate chips	
Three 3-ounce packages cream cheese, softened	*5* Place the white chocolate chips in a medium, microwave-safe bowl. Add 9 tablespoons of the hot lemon mixture. Microwave on low for 2 minutes and then remove and stir. Continue microwaving on low for 1-minute intervals, stirring after each interval.

6 Beat all packages of cream cheese into the white chocolate chip mixture until smooth.

7 Spread the cream cheese mixture over the cooled crust and top with the lemon mixture, spreading to cover. Cover and chill in the fridge for 4 to 5 hours to set. Cut into bars when cool.

Per serving: Calories 301 (From Fat 144); Fat 16g (Saturated 10g); Cholesterol 66mg; Sodium 305mg; Carbohydrate 37g (Dietary Fiber 0g); Protein 3g.

Apricot Crumble Bars

Prep time: 25 min • **Cook time:** 50 min • **Yield:** 24 servings

Ingredients	Directions
2 cups chopped dried apricots 2 cups orange juice ¾ cup butter, softened ⅔ cup packed brown sugar 1 teaspoon vanilla 1¼ cups minus 1 teaspoon (165 grams) Whole-Grain Flour Mix (see Book V, Chapter 2) 1 cup minus 2 teaspoons (142 grams) White Flour Mix (see Book V, Chapter 2) 1½ cups gluten-free rolled oats	**1** In a medium saucepan, boil the apricots and orange juice over medium-high heat for 5 minutes, stirring frequently. **2** Reduce the heat to low and simmer the mixture until all the juice is absorbed but the apricots are still moist, about 15 minutes. Remove from heat. Puree the apricots in a food processor until smooth. **3** Preheat the oven to 350 degrees. Grease a 13-x-9-inch pan with unsalted butter or solid shortening. **4** In a large bowl, beat the butter until it's light and fluffy. Add the brown sugar and vanilla and beat for 3 minutes. **5** Add the Whole-Grain Flour Mix, White Flour Mix, and oats and mix well. The dough will begin to form crumbs; keep mixing until smaller crumbs form. **6** Press half of the oat mixture into the bottom of a prepared pan. Spread with the apricot filling. Top with the remaining oat mixture, pressing down lightly to flatten. **7** Bake until lightly browned, about 30 to 35 minutes. Cool the bars on a wire rack in the pan and then cut into bars to serve.

Per serving: Calories 172 (From Fat 57); Fat 6g (Saturated 4g); Cholesterol 15mg; Sodium 5mg; Carbohydrate 29g (Dietary Fiber 2g); Protein 2g.

Tip: You can substitute a 12-ounce jar of apricot jam for the chopped dried apricots and orange juice mixture to save some time and effort.

Maple Syrup Shortbread

Prep time: 20 min, plus chilling time • **Cook time:** 25 min • **Yield:** 36 servings

Ingredients	Directions
⅔ cup grade B amber maple syrup	*1* In a small saucepan, bring the maple syrup to a boil over medium-high heat and reduce by half. This should take about 10 to 15 minutes. Remove from heat and let stand for 10 minutes.
½ cup unsalted butter, softened	
1¼ cups minus 1 teaspoon (165 grams) Whole-Grain Flour Mix (see Book V, Chapter 2)	*2* Combine the cooled maple syrup, butter, Whole-Grain Flour Mix, White Flour Mix, baking powder, and salt in a mixer. Beat until well blended.
1 cup minus 2 teaspoons (142 grams) White Flour Mix (see Book V, Chapter 2)	*3* Wrap the mixture in plastic wrap and refrigerate it for at least 3 hours, until the dough is chilled.
½ teaspoon baking powder	*4* When the dough is ready to bake, preheat the oven to 350 degrees.
¼ teaspoon salt	*5* Remove the dough from the fridge and roll to ¼-inch thickness between two sheets of plastic wrap.
	6 With cookie cutters, cut the dough into cookies. Place them on an ungreased cookie sheet and bake them until they're light golden-brown, about 10 minutes.
	7 Let the cookies cool on the sheet for 3 minutes and then move them to a wire rack to cool completely.

Per serving: Calories 67 (From Fat 24); Fat 3g (Saturated 2g); Cholesterol 7mg; Sodium 23mg; Carbohydrate 11g (Dietary Fiber 0g); Protein 1g.

Note: Sometimes you want to make a crisp cookie, but you don't want to use sugar. The best syrup to use for this recipe is the grade B amber, which is darker and more flavorful than grade A. And it costs less, too!

Layered Chocolate Fruit Bars

Prep time: 20 min • **Cook time:** 28 min • **Yield:** 24 servings

Ingredients	Directions
16 Graham Crackers (see Book V, Chapter 5), crushed	*1* Prepare the Graham Crackers.
½ cup butter, melted	*2* Preheat the oven to 350 degrees. Spray a 13-x-9-inch baking pan with nonstick cooking spray.
1 cup milk chocolate chips	
1 cup semisweet chocolate chips	*3* Place the Graham Cracker crumbs in the bottom of the prepared pan. Drizzle evenly with melted butter.
1 cup dried cherries	
1 cup unsweetened coconut	*4* Top with both kinds of chocolate chips, cherries, and coconut, layering the ingredients evenly.
One 14-ounce can sweetened condensed milk	
	5 Pour the condensed milk over all.
	6 Bake for 23 to 28 minutes, or until the bars are light golden-brown and set. Cool completely on a wire rack and then cut into bars to serve.

Per serving: Calories 284 (From Fat 128); Fat 14g (Saturated 9g); Cholesterol 23mg; Sodium 66mg; Carbohydrate 38g (Dietary Fiber 2g); Protein 4g.

Vary It! You can substitute any type of dried fruit for the cherries. Use dried blueberries, dried cranberries, or finely chopped dried apricots. You can also use chopped nuts in place of the coconut. But stick with the 2 cups of chocolate chips; they're necessary to hold the bars together.

Double Chocolate Caramel Bars

Prep time: 25 min • **Cook time:** 28 min • **Yield:** 36 bar cookies

Ingredients	Directions

Ingredients

1 cup (123 grams) sorghum flour

½ cup minus 2 teaspoons (62 grams) brown rice flour

⅓ cup plus 1 tablespoon (62 grams) white rice flour

1 teaspoon xanthan gum

⅓ cup cocoa powder

2 cups gluten-free oatmeal

1 cup firmly packed brown sugar

½ cup granulated sugar

1 teaspoon baking soda

¼ teaspoon salt

1¼ cups butter, melted

1 egg, beaten

One 14-ounce package caramels, unwrapped

¼ cup whole milk

2 cups dark chocolate chips

Directions

1 Preheat the oven to 350 degrees. Grease a 13-x-9-inch pan with unsalted butter and set aside.

2 In a large bowl, combine the sorghum flour, brown rice flour, white rice flour, xanthan gum, and cocoa powder. Mix well with a wire whisk until the flours are all one color.

3 Stir in the oatmeal, brown sugar, granulated sugar, baking soda, and salt and mix well.

4 Pour the melted butter and beaten egg over the mixture and mix with your hands until crumbly. Pat half of this mixture into the prepared pan.

5 In a large saucepan, combine the unwrapped caramels and milk. Melt over low heat, stirring frequently, until the caramels are melted and the mixture is smooth. Pour over the crumb mixture in the pan.

6 Sprinkle with dark chocolate chips and top with the remaining crumb mixture; pat down gently with your hands.

7 Bake for 23 to 28 minutes, or until the crust is set and the caramel is bubbling slightly around the edges.

8 Cool on a wire rack and cut into bars when cool.

Per serving: Calories 223 (From Fat 94); Fat 10g (Saturated 7g); Cholesterol 24mg; Sodium 85mg; Carbohydrate 33g (Dietary Fiber 2g); Protein 2g.

Note: You can substitute other flours or starches for the flours called for; just be sure to use the same weight of the alternate flour. For instance, use 62 grams of sweet rice flour in place of the brown rice flour, not ½ cup minus 2 teaspoons of sweet rice flour, which weighs 72 grams.

Peanut Butter Brownies

Prep time: 20 min • **Cook time:** 40 min • **Yield:** 9 servings

Ingredients	Directions
2 tablespoons plus 1 teaspoon cocoa powder	*1* Preheat the oven to 325 degrees. Spray a 9-x-9-inch baking pan with nonstick cooking spray. Sprinkle with 1 teaspoon cocoa powder, shake the pan to distribute the powder evenly, and knock out the excess. Set the pan aside.
½ cup unsalted butter	
1 cup semisweet chocolate chips	
½ cup packed brown sugar	*2* In a large saucepan, melt the butter with 2 tablespoons cocoa powder and the chocolate chips over low heat, stirring frequently, until smooth. Beat in the brown sugar and granulated sugar and then remove from heat.
½ cup granulated sugar	
2 eggs	
½ cup peanut butter	
1½ teaspoons vanilla	*3* Add the eggs, one at a time, beating well after each addition. Beat in the peanut butter and then stir in the vanilla.
⅓ cup plus 1 tablespoon (44 grams) almond flour	
2 tablespoons (18 grams) sweet rice flour	*4* In a small bowl, combine the almond flour, sweet rice flour, xanthan gum, baking powder, and salt; mix with a wire whisk until the mixture is one color. Stir into the batter.
½ teaspoon xanthan gum	
½ teaspoon baking powder	
¼ teaspoon salt	*5* Spread the batter into the prepared pan and top with peanuts.
½ cup chopped peanuts	
	6 Bake for 30 to 40 minutes, or until a toothpick inserted near the center of the pan comes out almost clean, with a few moist crumbs sticking to it. Cool on a wire rack and then cut into squares to serve.

Per serving: Calories 455 (From Fat 273); Fat 30g (Saturated 12g); Cholesterol 75mg; Sodium 175mg; Carbohydrate 43g (Dietary Fiber 3g); Protein 9g.

Vary It! You can serve these brownies plain or top them with any type of chocolate or peanut butter frosting. For a super easy frosting, melt 1 cup semisweet chocolate chips with ⅓ cup peanut butter until smooth; pour over the brownies and let stand until set. Or make any standard butter cream frosting starting with ¼ cup butter and add ⅓ cup peanut butter. Beat until smooth and frost the cooled brownies.

Granola Bars

Prep time: 20 min, plus chilling time • **Cook time:** 45 min • **Yield:** 60 bars

Ingredients	*Directions*
1 cup unsalted butter	*1* In a large saucepan over low heat, melt the butter, brown sugar, honey, and almond butter, stirring until the mixture is smooth with an even texture.
¾ cup packed brown sugar	
½ cup honey	
12 ounces smooth or chunky almond butter	*2* Remove from heat and add the rolled oats. Stir until combined.
5½ cups gluten-free rolled oats	*3* Stir in the eggs, baking soda, salt, and vanilla until well combined.
2 eggs, beaten	
2 teaspoons baking soda	*4* Add the fruits, chopped nuts, coconut, and M&Ms. You can use any combination of any of these ingredients, as long as they add up to 4 cups.
½ teaspoon salt	
1 tablespoon vanilla	
4 cups diced dried fruit, chopped nuts, coconut, and M&M candies	*5* Cover the dough and let it chill overnight to let the oats absorb the eggs, butter, and almond butter.
	6 The next morning, preheat the oven to 300 degrees. Line two cookie sheets with parchment paper. Divide the dough between the cookie sheets and pat into an even layer about ½-inch thick.
	7 Bake for 20 minutes and then rotate the pans and move them around on the racks. Bake 20 minutes longer, until the bars are light golden-brown and set.
	8 Cool completely and cut into bars. Store in an airtight container at room temperature.

Per serving: Calories 155 (From Fat 85); Fat 10g (Saturated 3g); Cholesterol 16mg; Sodium 71mg; Carbohydrate 16g (Dietary Fiber 1g); Protein 3g.

Note: These granola bars are delicious as a quick snack or on a road trip. Keep them on your person at all times for when you get hungry but can't find a gluten-free food. Try to use only unsulfured organic fruits for the best flavor, texture, and nutrition. A nice combination is dried tart cherries, dried apricots, unsweetened flaked coconut, and dark chocolate M&Ms.

Honey Oat Bars

Prep time: 25 min • **Cook time:** 35 min • **Yield:** 32 servings

Ingredients	Directions
½ cup butter, softened	**1** Preheat the oven to 400 degrees. Grease a 13-x-9-inch cake pan with unsalted butter and set aside.
1 cup packed brown sugar, divided in half	
½ cup plus 1 tablespoon plus 1 teaspoon (66 grams) almond flour	**2** In a medium bowl, combine ½ cup softened butter with ½ cup packed brown sugar and mix well.
⅓ cup minus 1 teaspoon (41 grams) brown rice flour	**3** In a small bowl, combine the almond flour, brown rice flour, potato starch, and xanthan gum; mix with a wire whisk until the mixture is one color.
2 tablespoons (20 grams) potato starch	
½ teaspoon xanthan gum	**4** Stir the almond flour mixture into the butter mixture to form a dough. Press the dough into the bottom and ½ inch up the sides of the prepared pan. Prick the crust with a fork and bake for 8 to 10 minutes, until light golden-brown. Remove from the oven and cool on a wire rack.
½ cup butter	
¼ cup granulated sugar	
Pinch salt	
½ cup honey	**5** Meanwhile, make the filling. In a large pan, melt the butter over medium heat. Add the other ½ cup brown sugar, granulated sugar, and salt and mix well.
3 eggs	
1½ teaspoons vanilla	
6 Granola Bars (see previous recipe), crushed	**6** Add the honey, eggs, and vanilla and beat until combined.
⅔ cup semisweet chocolate chips	**7** Stir in the crushed Granola Bars, semisweet chocolate chips, and walnuts.
½ cup chopped walnuts	
	8 Pour over the cooled crust and bake for 20 to 30 minutes, or until the filling is set and light golden-brown. Cool completely on a wire rack before cutting into bars.

Per serving: Calories 158 (From Fat 76); Fat 8g (Saturated 3g); Cholesterol 31mg; Sodium 28mg; Carbohydrate 20g (Dietary Fiber 1g); Protein 2g.

Chapter 4

Pies and Cakes

In This Chapter

▶ Discovering a few tricks for making pies and pastries

▶ Tips for making great cakes and frostings

▶ Baking some sweet pies, pastries, and cakes

Many experienced cooks and bakers fear pies and pastries. Producing a flaky and light pie crust or a tender pastry may seem difficult, but it isn't — it just takes practice! A light hand with pastry, which is essential when making wheat-based pie crusts and pastries, isn't an issue with gluten-free recipes. That fact alone makes these recipes easier.

But cakes are practically a necessity. What would a birthday be without a layer cake, lavishly frosted and brimming with candles? People who must avoid gluten may think that they can only enjoy ice-cream cakes from now on. Not with these recipes!

In this chapter, you find recipes for different types of pie crust, ranging from a Mixed Nut Pie Crust you can use to make ice-cream pies or custard pies to a Meringue Pie Shell that's naturally gluten-free. Tortes, a Pavlova recipe, and a fabulous recipe for Rugelach round out the chapter. And you take a look at how to make the best cakes and frost them beautifully.

So get out your mixer, mixing bowls, and pans and discover how easy fulfilling every cake craving can be with these delicious gluten-free recipes.

Tips for Making Pies and Pastries

When you make wheat flour–based pie crusts and pastries, you must handle them very little to prevent a lot of gluten from developing. Wheat-based pie crusts need to straddle a delicate line between enough gluten development to produce the desirable flaky layers and too much gluten development, which makes the pastry tough. Gluten-free pie crusts and pastries are automatically tender. The trick is to make them flaky.

Here are some tricks for making the best pies and pastries:

- Keep all the ingredients cold. To make a flaky pie or pastry, the butter or other fat should remain as cold and as solid as possible. Then, when the pastry meets the hot oven, the butter melts quickly and creates steam, which puffs up the structure of the pastry, creating those flaky layers.

- If you don't use a scale to measure flours and mixes, always measure by spooning the flour or mix lightly into a measuring cup and leveling off the top with the back of a knife.

- Although you can handle this dough without fear of making it tough, try to keep your hands off as much as possible. You don't want to work the fat into the flour mixture so much that it loses its ability to create layers.

- Xanthan gum and guar gum are usually necessary when making pastries and pie crusts. Gluten provides the critical structure to create flaky layers. Without it, you need something to make the dough pliable. The Rugelach recipe uses gelatin.

- You can use any type of fat you'd like. Butter adds great flavor to pie crusts and pastries. Solid shortening makes for a tender pastry and works well for most recipes. Lard, that long-vilified fat, is actually pretty good for you as far as fats go. Its fat is mostly monounsaturated (the good kind). Leaf lard makes the flakiest pastry you'll ever eat.

- It's easiest to roll out pie crust between two sheets of waxed paper or parchment paper. Just tear off two sheets of the paper and rub your work surface with a damp paper towel so the paper doesn't slip around as you work. Sandwich the dough between the paper and start rolling.

- Roll from the center of the ball of dough out to the edges. Turn the dough around and roll as evenly as you can, making sure there aren't any spots that are thicker or thinner than others. You can get rings to put around your rolling pin that ensure an even thinness.

- Your crusts will have a better final shape if you chill the dough before rolling it out and then chill the shaped pie crust before filling it and baking. Give those fats a chance to solidify so they can create the layers you want. You can chill the crust in the fridge for at least an hour or put it in the freezer for 10 to 15 minutes.

Making the Best Cakes and Frostings

Cake making and frosting is definitely an art and a science. These recipes are carefully calibrated for the best results: light and fluffy cakes (well, except for the Flourless Chocolate Cake) with a tender, even crumb. Follow the directions carefully, measure carefully, and mix and bake the recipes as directed.

Here are some tips for making the best cakes:

- ✔ Always grease the pans well. If you miss a spot, the cake will likely stick to that spot and may tear or break when it comes out of the pan. That's frustrating! Some recipes call for greasing and flouring cake pans. Put a teaspoon of any gluten-free flour in a greased pan and shake and tap the pan until the flour coats the entire surface. Tap out any excess flour into the sink.

- ✔ If you don't use a scale to measure flours and mixes, always measure by spooning the flour or mix lightly into a measuring cup and leveling off the top with the back of a knife.

- ✔ Cake doneness tests are very important. Check doneness by lightly touching the cake surface with your finger. If it springs back, it's done. Another doneness test is observing that the cake is pulling away from the pan sides. Some people think the cake is overbaked when this happens, but really it's done — pulling away from the pan sides indicates that the structure is fully set.

- ✔ Cool sheet cakes in the pan. Layer cakes and Bundt cakes are often cooled in the pan for a few minutes and then turned out onto cooling racks to cool completely. The Angel Food Cake is cooled upside down because its structure is so delicate that it must be "stretched" as it cools so it doesn't collapse.

- ✔ To frost layer cakes, place one layer on the serving plate, rounded side down. Frost with about 1 cup of frosting. Place the second layer on the frosting, rounded side up. Frost the top of the cake and then gently ease the frosting over the cake's sides. Let the cake stand until the frosting sets before storing.

Mixed Nut Pie Crust

Prep time: 15 min, plus chilling time • **Cook time:** 10–15 min • **Yield:** One 9-inch pie crust

Ingredients	Directions
¾ **cup finely ground pecans**	**1** In a medium bowl, combine the pecans, almonds, almond meal, and brown sugar and mix well. Stir in the butter until blended.
½ **cup finely ground almonds**	
2 tablespoons almond meal	
1 tablespoon packed brown sugar	**2** Press firmly into the bottom and up the sides of a 9-inch pie pan. Cover and chill in the refrigerator for 1 hour.
¼ **cup butter, melted**	
	3 Preheat the oven to 350 degrees. Bake the pie crust for 10 to 15 minutes, or until set. Cool completely and then fill with any filling.

Per serving: Calories 177 (From Fat 157); Fat 18g (Saturated 5g); Cholesterol 15mg; Sodium 2mg; Carbohydrate 5g (Dietary Fiber 2g); Protein 3g. Based on 8 servings.

Note: Fill this crust with any prepared pudding or a no-bake cheesecake filling. You can use any combination of ground nuts; just make sure they're finely ground. And don't skip the chilling step; it helps solidify the crust so the oils in the nuts don't separate.

Butter Pie Crust

Prep time: 20 min, plus rest time • **Cook time:** 20 min • **Yield:** 16 servings (2 crusts)

Ingredients	Directions
½ cup plus 3 tablespoons (93 grams) Whole-Grain Flour Mix (see Book V, Chapter 2)	**1** In a large bowl, combine the Whole-Grain Flour Mix, white rice flour, White Flour Mix, sweet rice flour, sugar, salt, and baking powder and mix until the mixture is one color.
½ cup (80 grams) white rice flour	
⅓ cup plus 2 teaspoons (56 grams) White Flour Mix (see Book V, Chapter 2)	**2** Using your hands, rub the butter into the flour, working it between your fingers until the mixture resembles sand with a few chunkier pieces.
⅓ cup plus 2 teaspoons (58 grams) sweet rice flour	**3** Add the vinegar and stir. Add the water, a little bit at a time, stirring with your hands to incorporate the water. The dough should hold together with a gentle squeeze. You may need another tablespoon or so of water to reach this consistency. Every batch of flour has a different moisture content.
1 teaspoon sugar	
½ teaspoon salt	
Pinch baking powder	
½ cup butter	**4** Divide the dough in half and form each half into a disc about an inch thick. Wrap the dough in plastic wrap and chill for at least 30 minutes.
1½ teaspoons apple cider vinegar	
½ cup water	**5** Cover your work surface with a thin layer of tapioca flour. Unwrap one disc of dough and sprinkle it generously with tapioca flour.
1 tablespoon tapioca flour	
	6 Place the dough on the prepared surface. Roll very, very lightly with a floured rolling pin, using almost no downward pressure. The dough is very soft, so it should move gently, becoming flatter. Keep the dough and board sprinkled with tapioca flour.
	7 Ease the crust into a 9-inch pie pan, trim the edges, and flute as desired. Bake according to your pie recipe. Repeat with the remaining dough, use the remaining dough for a top crust, or freeze the remaining dough for another use.

Per serving: Calories 229 (From Fat 107); Fat 12g (Saturated 7g); Cholesterol 31mg; Sodium 159mg; Carbohydrate 29g (Dietary Fiber 1g); Protein 2g.

Cookie Pie Crust

Prep time: 20 min, plus rest time • **Cook time:** 10–14 min • **Yield:** One 9-inch crust

Ingredients	*Directions*
⅓ **cup plus 1 tablespoon unsalted butter, softened** 1½ **cups Cookie Mix (see Book V, Chapter 2)** **1 egg**	*1* In a medium bowl, combine ⅓ cup unsalted butter and the Cookie Mix; stir until combined. Beat in the egg until combined.
	2 Place the dough onto plastic wrap and wrap it, forming it into a ball. Refrigerate the dough for 2 to 3 hours, until firm.
	3 Preheat the oven to 400 degrees. Grease a 9-inch pie pan with 1 tablespoon unsalted butter; set aside.
	4 Place the dough in the prepared pan pie. Press it into the bottom and up the sides of the pan, using plastic wrap as needed to help form the dough. Place the crust in the freezer for 10 minutes.
	5 Remove the crust from the freezer and prick it with a fork in several places. Bake it for 10 to 14 minutes, until the crust is light golden-brown and set. Check the crust halfway through baking time to make sure it's not puffing up too much. If it is puffing, use a fork to gently press down on the crust.
	6 Let the pie crust cool completely on a wire rack and then fill it with fillings.

Per serving: Calories 200 (From Fat 90); Fat 10g (Saturated 6g); Cholesterol 51mg; Sodium 488mg; Carbohydrate 26g (Dietary Fiber 1g); Protein 2g.

Note: This crust is ideal to fill with everything from ice cream to puddings to mousse. You can make any dessert recipe that calls for a baked pie crust with this recipe.

Note: You can use just about any cookie recipe to make a pie crust. Just press it firmly into the pie pan and chill it in the freezer before baking. You may want to weigh the dough down so it doesn't puff up in the oven. To do this, spray a 12-inch sheet of foil with nonstick cooking spray. Place the foil, sprayed side down, over the dough and press gently. Fill the foil with uncooked dried beans or pie weights. Bake for 8 to 10 minutes, until the dough is set. Remove the pie from the oven and gently remove the foil and beans or weights together. Bake the crust until it's light golden-brown. Remember, if you use dried beans, after the beans have been baked they won't soften, so you can't use them in a recipe. Save them to use as pie weights.

Galette Pie Crust

Prep time: 20 min, plus rest time • **Cook time:** 20 min • **Yield:** 6 servings

Ingredients	Directions
1 cup (148 grams) White Flour Mix (see Book V, Chapter 2)	*1* In a large bowl, combine the White Flour Mix, Whole-Grain Flour Mix (or brown rice flour), sweet rice flour, sugar, salt, and xanthan gum. Stir until the mixture is one color.
2 tablespoons (20 grams) Whole-Grain Flour Mix (see Book V, Chapter 2) or brown rice flour	*2* Add the cold butter and blend with a pastry blender or two knives until sandy crumbs form. It's fine if some of the butter is in slightly larger pieces.
1 tablespoon (10 grams) sweet rice flour	*3* Add the egg and citrus juice and beat until the dough forms a soft ball.
1 tablespoon sugar	
½ teaspoon salt	*4* At this point, you can make either one large pie crust or individual tarts. For individual tarts, divide into six balls. For one large tart, leave in one ball. Refrigerate for at least 2 hours.
¼ teaspoon xanthan gum	
6 tablespoons cold butter, cut into cubes	*5* When you're ready to bake, preheat the oven to 375 degrees. Place a ball of dough between plastic wrap. Using a rolling pin with steady pressure, roll the dough to a circle about 4½ inches in diameter for individual tarts. For a large pie, roll out the entire ball of dough into a 12-inch circle.
1 egg	
1 tablespoon lemon or lime juice	
	6 Place the dough onto a cookie sheet. You should be able to fit three individual tarts onto a standard cookie sheet. If you're making a large tart, just place it in the center of the cookie sheet.
	7 Fill, pleat the edges of the crust over the filling, and bake as your pie recipe directs.

Per serving: Calories 213 (From Fat 111); Fat 12g (Saturated 7g); Cholesterol 66mg; Sodium 206mg; Carbohydrate 26g (Dietary Fiber 0g); Protein 2g.

Note: A galette is a free-form pie made without a pie pan. Place the flat circles of dough on a cookie sheet, place about ½ cup filling in the center, and loosely pleat the edges of the dough over the filling, leaving the filling uncovered in the center. This is a classic French recipe.

Meringue Pie Shell

Prep time: 15 min • **Cook time:** 2 hr • **Yield:** One 9-inch pie shell

Ingredients	*Directions*
1 tablespoon unsalted butter	*1* Preheat the oven to 275 degrees. Grease a 9-inch pie plate with unsalted butter and dust it with cornstarch. Shake out the excess cornstarch and set the plate aside.
1 tablespoon (8 grams) cornstarch	
3 egg whites	
Pinch salt	*2* In a medium bowl, beat the egg whites with salt and lemon juice until soft peaks form. Gradually add the sugar, 1 tablespoon at a time, until the meringue forms stiff peaks.
½ teaspoon lemon juice	
11 tablespoons sugar	
1 teaspoon vanilla	*3* Beat in the vanilla. Spread the mixture evenly in the prepared pie plate, building up the edges and creating an impression in the center to form a shell.
	4 Bake the shell for 1 hour and then turn off the oven and let the shell stand in the closed oven for 1 hour longer. Remove the shell from the oven and cool it completely on a wire rack.

Per serving: Calories 74 (From Fat 0); Fat 0g (Saturated 0g); Cholesterol 0mg; Sodium 38mg; Carbohydrate 17g (Dietary Fiber 0g); Protein 1g. Based on 8 servings.

Vary It! You can vary this shell to add more interest to your pies. Add 2 tablespoons of cocoa powder along with the sugar for a chocolate meringue pie shell. Or add a teaspoon of grated lemon or orange peel for a citrus-flavored pie shell. For a mocha pie shell, add the cocoa and ½ teaspoon of instant espresso powder.

Note: Some people may think that this type of recipe in a gluten-free baking book is a "cheat." But meringue pie shells are delicious and easy to make, not to mention fat-free. If you enjoy the texture of light, airy, crisp meringue filled with a smooth and velvety filling, why not enjoy it?

Note: Fill this shell with everything from ice cream to pudding to mousse. It's used in Chocolate Angel Cheesecake Pie (later in this chapter), too. In fact, the three egg yolks left over from making this pie shell are just what's needed in the Chocolate Angel Cheesecake Pie recipe!

Pear Cranberry Tart

Prep time: 30 min, plus chilling time • **Cook time:** 65 min • **Yield:** 8 servings

Ingredients	Directions
½ recipe Butter Pie Crust (see recipe earlier in this chapter)	**1** Prepare the Butter Pie Crust recipe. Press the dough into the bottom and up the sides of a 9-inch tart pan with a removable bottom. Cover and chill for 1 hour or overnight.
1 cup blanched almonds	
⅓ cup superfine sugar	
½ cup organic cane sugar	**2** Preheat the oven to 350 degrees. Place a piece of foil over the crust and top with pie weights or dried beans to keep the crust from puffing while baking. Bake for 20 minutes. Remove the crust from the oven and remove the foil and pie weights.
2 tablespoons water	
1 cup fresh or frozen cranberries (do not thaw)	
2 large ripe pears	**3** In a food processor, combine the almonds and super-fine sugar. Grind until tiny crumbs form. Sprinkle the crumbs into the partially baked crust.
	4 In a small saucepan, combine the cane sugar and water and bring to a boil. Add the cranberries and cook until glazed, about 1 to 2 minutes. Don't cook until the cranberries pop. Set aside while you prepare the pears.
	5 Peel and slice the pears lengthwise into ¼-inch slices.
	6 Place the pears in a pretty pattern onto the almond layer. Drain the cranberries, reserving the glaze. Place the cranberries in the center of the pie and fill in the spaces between the pears. Brush the glaze from the cranberries over the fruit.
	7 Bake for 40 to 45 minutes, or until the pears are tender and the crust is golden-brown. Cool completely on a wire rack. Cut into wedges to serve.

Per serving: Calories 337 (From Fat 138); Fat 15g (Saturated 4g); Cholesterol 15mg; Sodium 85mg; Carbohydrate 48g (Dietary Fiber 4g); Protein 5g.

Lemon Cream Pie

Prep time: 30 min, plus chilling time • **Cook time:** 20 min • **Yield:** 10 servings

Ingredients	Directions
½ cup plus 2 teaspoons (80 grams) White Flour Mix (See Book V, Chapter 2)	**1** Preheat the oven to 400 degrees. Spray a 9-inch pie plate with nonstick cooking spray.
⅓ cup (38 grams) coconut flour	**2** In a medium bowl, combine the White Flour Mix, coconut flour, Whole-Grain Flour Mix, brown sugar, and coconut and mix well.
¼ cup (34 grams) Whole-Grain Flour Mix (see Book V, Chapter 2)	
¼ cup packed brown sugar	**3** Add the softened butter and mix with a fork until crumbs form. Place in the prepared pie pan.
½ cup flaked coconut	
½ cup butter, softened	**4** Bake for 12 to 16 minutes, stirring gently every 4 minutes, until the crumbs are an even light golden-brown. Stir again, then let cool for 15 minutes. Press the crumbs into the bottom and up the sides of the pie pan to form a crust. Cool completely.
3 egg yolks	
¾ cup sugar	
½ cup lemon juice	
⅓ cup water	**5** Meanwhile, combine the egg yolks, sugar, lemon juice, water, and cornstarch in a heavy saucepan. Cook over low heat, beating frequently with a wire whisk until the mixture is thickened and smooth, about 3 to 5 minutes.
3 tablespoons (24 grams) cornstarch	
1 teaspoon finely grated lemon peel	
¾ cup white chocolate chips	**6** Remove the mixture from the heat and stir in the lemon peel and chocolate chips until the chips are melted. Let the mixture cool at room temperature for 1 hour.
Two 8-ounce packages cream cheese, softened	**7** Beat the cream cheese until it's light and fluffy. Gradually add the cooled lemon mixture until smooth, and then spoon into the cooled pie crust.
⅔ cup heavy whipping cream	
2 tablespoons powdered sugar	**8** In a small bowl, beat the cream with powdered sugar and vanilla until stiff peaks form. Spread over the lemon filling. Cover pie and chill for 2 to 3 hours until set.
½ teaspoon vanilla	

Per serving: Calories 550 (From Fat 345); Fat 38g (Saturated 24g); Cholesterol 163mg; Sodium 176mg; Carbohydrate 48g (Dietary Fiber 2g); Protein 7g.

Chocolate Tartlets

Prep time: 30 min, plus chilling time • **Cook time:** 32 min • **Yield:** 24 tartlets

Ingredients	Directions
¼ cup butter, softened	**1** In a large bowl, beat the butter until it's light and fluffy. Add the Cookie Mix without Gums and cocoa powder gradually and beat until combined.
1¼ cups Cookie Mix without Gums (see Book V, Chapter 2)	
¼ cup cocoa powder	**2** Beat in the egg white and vanilla and beat for 1 minute. Scrape the batter onto a large piece of plastic wrap. Wrap up the dough and refrigerate overnight.
1 egg white	
½ teaspoon vanilla	
One 12-ounce package semisweet chocolate chips	**3** When you're ready to bake, preheat the oven to 350 degrees. Lightly spray 24 miniature muffin tins (two pans of 12) with nonstick cooking spray and set aside. Divide the dough into four pieces. Refrigerate the rest of the dough while you work with the first quarter.
1 cup heavy whipping cream	
2 tablespoons butter	**4** Divide the first quarter of the dough into six pieces. Press one of the pieces into the prepared muffin tins, pressing against the sides and bottom to form a shell. Repeat with the second quarter of dough to fill the muffin tin; cover and refrigerate. Repeat with the remaining dough and then prick all the little shells with a fork.
	5 Bake the first pan for 12 to 15 minutes, checking halfway through and pressing down the dough if it puffs, until the shells are set. Let them cool in the pan for 5 minutes and then move them to wire racks to cool completely. Repeat with the remaining pan.

6 In a large, microwave-safe bowl, combine the chocolate chips, cream, and butter. Microwave on 50 percent power for 2 minutes; remove the filling from the microwave and stir. Continue microwaving for 1-minute intervals, stirring after each interval, until the chocolate is melted and the mixture is smooth.

7 Fill each little tartlet shell with the chocolate filling. Cover and refrigerate for 1 to 2 hours before serving.

Per serving: Calories 164 (From Fat 99); Fat 11g (Saturated 7g); Cholesterol 21mg; Sodium 152mg; Carbohydrate 18g (Dietary Fiber 1g); Protein 2g.

Pumpkin Pecan Cheesecake

Prep time: 40 min • **Cook time:** 35–40 min • **Yield:** 12–14 servings

Ingredients	*Directions*
4 ounces Graham Crackers (see Book V, Chapter 5), crushed	*1* Preheat the oven to 325 degrees. Butter a 10-inch springform pan and set aside.
⅓ cup plus ½ cup pecan halves	*2* In a food processor, combine the Graham Cracker crumbs and ⅓ cup pecans; process until crumbly. Add the light brown sugar and melted butter and pulse for a few seconds to blend. Place in a prepared pan. Press the mixture onto the bottom of the pan. Refrigerate for 20 minutes.
2 tablespoons light brown sugar	
1 tablespoon unsalted butter, melted	
½ cup firmly packed dark brown sugar	*3* In a small bowl, combine the dark brown sugar, cinnamon, ginger, cloves, and nutmeg.
2 tablespoons ground cinnamon	*4* Place the cream cheese in a large bowl. Beat with a mixer on medium speed until it's smooth and creamy. Gradually add the brown sugar mixture, beating until smooth.
1 teaspoon ground ginger	
¼ teaspoon ground cloves	
½ teaspoon ground nutmeg	
16 ounces cream cheese, at room temperature	*5* Add the eggs, one at a time, beating well after each addition and scraping down the sides of the bowl with a spatula.
3 eggs	
1 cup pumpkin puree (canned or fresh)	*6* Add the pumpkin puree to the cream cheese mixture, beating until smooth.
2 tablespoons maple syrup	*7* Scrape the batter over the pie crust and smooth the top.

8 Cover the cheesecake with ½ cup pecan halves in a circular pattern. Brush the maple syrup over the pecans.

9 Bake for 35 to 40 minutes, or until just set and a knife inserted near the center comes out clean. Turn off the oven and let the cheesecake stand in the oven until completely cool.

10 Cover the cheesecake and refrigerate it until ready to serve.

Per serving: Calories 309 (From Fat 198); Fat 22g (Saturated 10g); Cholesterol 100mg; Sodium 150mg; Carbohydrate 25g (Dietary Fiber 2g); Protein 6g.

Chocolate Angel Cheesecake Pie

Prep time: 45 min, plus chilling time • **Cook time:** 10 min • **Yield:** 8 servings

Ingredients	Directions
1 recipe Meringue Pie Shell (see recipe earlier in this chapter)	*1* Prepare the Meringue Pie Shell and cool completely.
¼ cup organic cane sugar	*2* In a medium heavy saucepan, combine the cane sugar, brown sugar, and unflavored gelatin and mix with a wire whisk. Stir in the cream, egg yolks, and salt.
⅓ cup packed brown sugar	
1 envelope unflavored gelatin	
½ cup light cream	*3* Place the pan over medium heat and cook, stirring constantly with a wire whisk, until the mixture starts to thicken and the sugar and gelatin completely dissolve, about 6 to 8 minutes. Don't let the mixture boil.
3 egg yolks	
⅛ teaspoon salt	
Two 1-ounce squares bittersweet chocolate, chopped	*4* Remove from the heat and add the chopped chocolate. Beat until the chocolate melts and the mixture is smooth.
Two 8-ounce packages cream cheese, softened	*5* Beat in the cream cheese using an electric mixer until the mixture is smooth and fluffy. Then beat in the vanilla. Chill this mixture in the refrigerator until it's smooth and thick, about 1 hour.
2 teaspoons vanilla	
1 cup heavy whipping cream	
3 tablespoons cocoa powder	*6* In a small bowl, combine the whipping cream, cocoa powder, and powdered sugar. Beat until stiff peaks form.
2 tablespoons powdered sugar	
	7 Using the same beaters, beat the cream cheese mixture until it's light and smooth. Fold in the whipped cream mixture.
	8 Spoon the mixture into the Meringue Pie Shell. Cover and chill for 3 to 4 hours before serving.

Per serving: Calories 537 (From Fat 350); Fat 39g (Saturated 23g); Cholesterol 193mg; Sodium 268mg; Carbohydrate 42g (Dietary Fiber 1g); Protein 9g.

Vary It! You can also serve this filling in graham cracker tartlet shells or in a graham cracker pie shell. It's also delicious layered with cookie crumbs and whipped cream for a parfait.

Posh Pineapple Pie

Prep time: 15 min • **Bake time:** 30 min • **Yield:** 8 servings

Ingredients	Directions
¾ cup plus 2 teaspoons granulated sugar	*1* Preheat the oven to 425 degrees.
1 tablespoon butter	*2* Prepare a double recipe of the Gluten-Free Pie Crust as directed in the recipe later in this chapter.
3 tablespoons cornstarch	
¼ teaspoon cinnamon	*3* In a medium saucepan, stir together ¾ cup of granulated sugar, the butter, cornstarch, cinnamon, pineapple with juice, milk, and lemon juice.
20-ounce can crushed pineapple with juice	
2 tablespoons milk	*4* Cook the mixture over medium heat, stirring constantly, until it thickens, and then continue to stir as the mixture boils for 1 more minute. Remove the pan from the heat and let the mixture cool slightly.
1 teaspoon fresh lemon juice	
Double recipe Double-Crust Gluten-Free Pie Crust (see the recipe later in this chapter)	*5* Pour the mixture into the prepared pie crust, and then cover it with the top crust. Cut slits in the top crust for air vents.
1 egg white	*6* In a small bowl, whisk together the egg white and water. Brush it over the top of the pie.
1 tablespoon water	
2 teaspoons brown sugar	*7* Sprinkle the pie with 2 teaspoons of granulated sugar and the brown sugar.
	8 Bake the pie for 30 minutes, or until the crust is golden.

Per serving: Calories 438; Fat 16g (Saturated 3g); Cholesterol 4mg; Sodium 2mg; Carbohydrate 39g (Dietary Fiber 2g); Protein 1g.

Peanut Butter Custard Pie

Prep time: 25 min • **Bake time:** 10 min, plus refrigeration time • **Yield:** 8 servings

Ingredients	Directions
Nonstick cooking spray	**1** Preheat the oven to 375 degrees. Spray an 8-inch pie plate with cooking spray.
7.2-ounce box shortbread cookies	
¼ cup plus ½ cup creamy peanut butter	**2** Break the cookies in a plastic self-seal bag. Use a rolling pin to crush the cookies until they're finely ground. Transfer the cookies to a medium bowl.
2 tablespoons plus 2¼ teaspoons cornstarch	**3** Add ¼ cup of peanut butter. Using a rubber spatula, mix the cookies and peanut butter until they're thoroughly blended.
1½ cups water	
14-ounce can sweetened condensed milk	**4** Press the mixture onto the bottom and up sides of the prepared pie plate. The mixture will be sticky. Use the back of a wet spoon to help spread the crust, or dip your fingers in confectioners' sugar to spread the crust with your hands.
3 egg yolks, lightly beaten	
2 tablespoons unsalted butter	
1 teaspoon vanilla	**5** Bake the crust at 375 degrees for 10 minutes. Remove the crust from the oven and cool completely.
½ of 11.75-ounce jar hot fudge sauce	
	6 In a large mixing bowl, whisk all the cornstarch into the water until it dissolves.
	7 Stir in the condensed milk and egg yolks.
	8 Add the remaining ½ cup of peanut butter, and use the mixer to whip the ingredients on low speed for 45 seconds.

9 Pour the mixture into a medium saucepan. Bring the mixture to a boil, stirring constantly with a whisk. Lower the heat to medium-high and continue cooking and stirring the mixture until it has thickened. Remove the mixture from the heat.

10 Stir in the butter and vanilla.

11 Cool the filling slightly before pouring it into the pie crust.

12 Warm the jar of hot fudge topping in the microwave (remove the lid first). Pour ½ of the jar onto the top of the pie and smooth it evenly over the top with the back of a spoon.

13 When the pie filling and topping are completely cooled, cover the pie and chill it for at least 4 hours.

Per serving: Calories 605; Fat 33g (Saturated 13g); Cholesterol 48mg; Sodium 214mg; Carbohydrate 97g (Dietary Fiber 3g); Protein 14g.

Gluten-Free Pie Crust

Prep time: 15 min • **Bake time:** 30 min • **Yield:** 8 servings

Ingredients	Directions
2 cups sifted gluten-free flour mixture	**1** In a medium bowl, sift together the flour mixture, sugar, and salt.
¼ cup sugar	
½ teaspoon salt	**2** In a small bowl, combine the oil, water, and vanilla.
½ cup corn oil	**3** Pour the liquid mixture into the center of the flour mixture. With a rubber spatula, stir the dough well until it holds together.
4 tablespoons ice-cold water	
½ teaspoon vanilla	
1 tablespoon confectioners' sugar	**4** With your hands, knead the dough until it forms a smooth ball.
	5 Sprinkle the confectioners' sugar onto a sheet of plastic wrap. Set the ball on the sugar and turn the dough to coat it. Cover it with a second sheet of plastic wrap.
	6 With a rolling pin, roll out the dough into an 11-inch circle.
	7 Place the dough in a greased 9-inch pie plate. Scallop the edges.

Per serving: Calories 287; Fat 14g (Saturated 2g); Cholesterol 0mg; Sodium 146mg; Carbohydrate 39g (Dietary Fiber 2g); Protein 0g.

Tip: When making a double-crust pie, double this recipe and follow the directions for the filling recipe.

Pecan Pie

Prep time: 20 min • **Cook time:** 80 min • **Yield:** 8–10 servings

Ingredients	Directions
½ **recipe Butter Pie Crust (see recipe earlier in this chapter)**	*1* Preheat the oven to 350 degrees.
3 eggs, beaten	*2* Place the Butter Pie Crust into a 9-inch metal pie pan. Line the crust with foil and add pie weights or dried beans to prevent puffing. Prebake the crust for 20 minutes.
¾ **cup dark corn syrup**	
¼ **cup molasses**	
1 cup sugar	*3* Remove the crust from the oven and carefully remove the foil and pie weights.
¼ **cup butter, melted**	
1 teaspoon vanilla	*4* In a large bowl, combine the eggs, corn syrup, molasses, sugar, butter, and vanilla and beat until combined.
2 cups pecan halves	
	5 Stir in the pecans until they're well-coated.
	6 Pour the pecan mixture into the pie crust.
	7 Bake for 55 to 60 minutes, or until a knife inserted 1 inch from the edge of the pie comes out clean.
	8 Cool the pie completely on a wire rack before slicing to serve.

Per serving: Calories 541 (From Fat 245); Fat 27g (Saturated 6g); Cholesterol 95mg; Sodium 155mg; Carbohydrate 74g (Dietary Fiber 3g); Protein 6g.

Note: If you want to take a bit more time and arrange the pecans in pretty concentric circles in the pie crust, reserve a bit of the egg mixture to spoon on the pecans just before the pie goes into the oven. Even the most careful arrangements can get a bit messy.

Decadent Chocolate Torte

Prep time: 20 min, plus chilling time • **Cook time:** 10 min • **Yield:** 16 servings

Ingredients	Directions
1 recipe Chocolate Sheet Cake (see recipe later in this chapter)	*1* Bake and cool the Chocolate Sheet Cake.
8 ounces semisweet chocolate, chopped	*2* Line a 9-inch springform pan with parchment paper and set aside. Cut the cooled cake into 1-inch cubes and place them in a large mixing bowl.
1 ounce unsweetened chocolate, chopped	*3* Place all the chocolate in a large, microwave-safe bowl and melt on 30 percent power for 2 minutes; remove and stir. Continue microwaving at 30 percent power for 2-minute intervals, stirring after each interval, until the chocolate is melted and smooth. Set aside.
8 ounces milk chocolate, chopped	
1¼ cups heavy cream	
¼ cup butter	*4* Combine the cream and butter in a medium, microwave-safe bowl. Microwave on high for 1 minute; remove and stir. Microwave on high for 1 minute longer, watching carefully in case the mixture boils over, until the butter is melted. Whisk the hot cream mixture into the melted chocolate.
	5 Pour 1¼ cups of the chocolate mixture over the cake cubes and mix with an electric mixer until the texture is even and very thick.
	6 Spoon and spread into the prepared springform pan. Press down on the top. Cover the remaining chocolate mixture and set aside at room temperature.

7 Cover and chill the torte for 3 to 4 hours until it's cold and set. Run a knife around the sides of the pan and remove the sides.

8 Pour the remaining chocolate mixture over the cake, spreading evenly to coat. Return the cake to the refrigerator to chill for another 1 to 2 hours before serving. Slice into thin wedges to serve.

Per serving: Calories 498 (From Fat 271); Fat 30g (Saturated 18g); Cholesterol 100mg; Sodium 117mg; Carbohydrate 58g (Dietary Fiber 4g); Protein 6g.

Chocolate Chip Pavlova

Prep time: 35 min • **Cook time:** 2 hr • **Yield:** 8 servings

Ingredients	Directions
7 egg whites	**1** Preheat the oven to 275 degrees. On parchment paper, place a 9-inch round cake pan; draw a circle around the pan with a pencil. Turn the paper over and place it on a large cookie sheet.
⅛ teaspoon cream of tartar	
Pinch salt	
1½ cups organic cane sugar	**2** Place the egg whites in a large bowl and let stand at room temperature for 20 minutes. Then add the cream of tartar and salt.
1 tablespoon cornstarch	
1 tablespoon raspberry vinegar	
1 teaspoon plus 1 teaspoon vanilla	**3** Beat until foamy, about 3 minutes, and then gradually add the cane sugar, beating until stiff peaks form. Fold in the cornstarch, raspberry vinegar, and 1 teaspoon vanilla, and then fold in the miniature chocolate chips.
1 cup miniature chocolate chips	
1¼ cups heavy whipping cream	**4** Place the meringue inside the circle on the parchment paper; spread to form an even layer. Run a spatula around the sides of the meringue to make them straight.
3 tablespoons cocoa powder	
¼ cup powdered sugar	
1 cup raspberries	**5** Bake for 60 to 65 minutes. Then turn the oven off, crack open the door, and let the meringue sit for another hour.
	6 Remove the meringue from the oven and slide it, with the parchment paper, onto a cooling rack; cool completely. Then gently peel the paper off the meringue and place the meringue on a serving plate; cover and store at room temperature.
	7 When ready to serve, in a medium bowl, combine the whipping cream, cocoa powder, powdered sugar, and 1 teaspoon vanilla; beat until stiff peaks form. Pile the cream on top of the meringue and top with raspberries. Cut into wedges to serve.

Per serving: Calories 513 (From Fat 186); Fat 21g (Saturated 13g); Cholesterol 51mg; Sodium 85mg; Carbohydrate 81g (Dietary Fiber 3g); Protein 5g.

Rugelach

Prep time: 35 min, plus chilling time • **Cook time:** 10–15 min • **Yield:** 10 servings

Ingredients	*Directions*
1½ cups plus 3 tablespoons (248 grams) White Flour Mix (see Book V, Chapter 2)	*1* In a food processor bowl, combine the White Flour Mix, Whole-Grain Flour Mix, baking powder, sugar, salt, and gelatin; process until well blended.
½ cup plus 1 tablespoon plus 2 teaspoons (83 grams) Whole-Grain Flour Mix (see Book V, Chapter 2)	*2* With the processor running, drop the butter, cream cheese cubes, and vanilla through the intake chute. Let the dough work until it gathers into a squashy mass.
¼ teaspoon baking powder	
3 tablespoons sugar	*3* Turn off the processor, turn the dough over, and work it for another couple of minutes to ensure that the fat is incorporated into the flour mixture.
¼ teaspoon salt	
1 teaspoon gelatin powder	
4 tablespoons butter, cut into pieces	*4* Shape the dough into three equal balls. Wrap them in plastic wrap and chill them in the refrigerator for 30 minutes. While the dough chills, make the Rugelach Filling by combining all ingredients in a small bowl.
8 ounces cream cheese, cut into 1-inch cubes	
1 teaspoon vanilla	*5* Take the dough out of the fridge and let it stand for 15 minutes. Preheat the oven to 425 degrees.
Rugelach Filling:	
½ cup finely chopped walnuts	*6* Roll out each ball into a 10-inch circle. Cut each into 8 to 12 pie-shaped pieces. Place 1 teaspoon of the filling in a circle ½ inch from the outer round edge of each pie-shaped piece of dough.
1 tablespoon sugar	
1 teaspoon cinnamon	
1 pinch nutmeg	*7* Roll the dough over the filling, rolling to the narrow tip. The filling may spill out a tiny bit, but those crispy parts are delicious.
	8 Place each Rugelach on a cookie sheet and bake for 10 to 15 minutes, until golden-brown. Cool them on the cookie sheet for 3 minutes and then move them to a wire rack to cool completely.

Per serving: Calories 292 (From Fat 150); Fat 17g (Saturated 8g); Cholesterol 37mg; Sodium 137mg; Carbohydrate 35g (Dietary Fiber 1g); Protein 4g.

Sour Cream Almond Bundt Cake

Prep time: 30 min • **Cook time:** 60 min • **Yield:** 16 servings

Ingredients	Directions
2 tablespoons plus 4 teaspoons plus ¼ cup unsalted butter, melted	*1* Preheat the oven to 350 degrees. Generously grease a 12-inch Bundt pan with 2 tablespoons melted unsalted butter and sprinkle with the granulated sugar; set aside.
¼ cup granulated sugar	
¼ cup finely ground almonds	*2* In a small bowl, combine the ground almonds, sweet rice flour, ¼ cup packed brown sugar, and cinnamon. Mix in 4 teaspoons melted butter until crumbly; set aside.
¼ cup (37 grams) sweet rice flour	
¼ cup plus ½ cup packed brown sugar	*3* In a medium bowl, combine the White Flour Mix, Whole-Grain Flour Mix, ½ cup brown sugar, baking powder, baking soda, and salt and mix until the mixture is one color.
½ teaspoon ground cinnamon	
2 cups plus 1 tablespoon (307 grams) White Flour Mix (see Book V, Chapter 2)	*4* In a large bowl, beat the eggs, sour cream, ¼ cup melted butter, and almond extract until light and fluffy.
1¼ cups minus 1 teaspoon (165 grams) Whole-Grain Flour Mix (see Book V, Chapter 2)	*5* Add the flour mixture and beat for 1 minute.
1 tablespoon baking powder	
1 teaspoon baking soda	*6* Pour the batter into the prepared Bundt pan. Sprinkle with the ground almond mixture and sliced almonds (if desired).
½ teaspoon salt	
4 eggs	*7* Place on the bottom rack of the oven and bake for 30 minutes. Then turn the pan 180 degrees to even out the baking and bake for 25 to 35 minutes longer, until the cake is golden-brown and the top springs back when lightly touched.
1 cup organic sour cream	
2 teaspoons almond extract	
⅓ cup sliced almonds (optional)	*8* Let the cake cool in the pan for 5 minutes and then gently remove it from the pan and cool it completely on a wire rack.

Per serving: Calories 249 (From Fat 87); Fat 10g (Saturated 5g); Cholesterol 71mg; Sodium 251mg; Carbohydrate 39g (Dietary Fiber 1g); Protein 4g.

Yellow Butter Cake

Prep time: 20 min • **Cook time:** 35–38 min • **Yield:** One 9-inch layer cake

Ingredients	Directions
1 cup unsalted butter, softened	**1** Preheat the oven to 350 degrees. Line two 9-inch cake pans with a circle of parchment paper and set aside.
2¼ cups sugar	
4 egg yolks	**2** In a large bowl, combine the butter and sugar and beat until fluffy. Add the egg yolks and vanilla and beat again.
1½ teaspoons vanilla	
4 egg whites	**3** In a medium bowl, beat the egg whites with ⅛ teaspoon salt until they're light and fluffy but not dry; set aside.
½ teaspoon plus ⅛ teaspoon salt	
1¾ cups plus 3 tablespoons (284 grams) White Flour Mix (see Book V, Chapter 2)	**4** In a large bowl, combine the White Flour Mix, Whole-Grain Flour Mix, baking powder, and ⅛ teaspoon salt. Mix until the mixture is a single color.
¾ cup plus 1 tablespoon (108 grams) Whole-Grain Flour Mix (see Book V, Chapter 2)	**5** Add half the flour mixture to the butter mixture and beat until combined. Add half the milk to the butter mixture and beat until combined. Repeat with the remaining flour mixture and milk.
2 teaspoons baking powder	
1 cup milk	**6** Stir ⅓ of the egg white mixture into the batter to lighten it. Then gently fold in the remaining beaten egg whites.
	7 Divide the batter into the prepared pans. Tap the pans gently on a counter to remove larger air bubbles.
	8 Bake for 35 to 38 minutes, or until the cake springs back when lightly touched in the center and has started to pull away from the pan's edges.
	9 Let the cakes cool in the pan for 5 minutes and then turn them out onto a wire rack to finish cooling.

Per serving: Calories 398 (From Fat 193); Fat 21g (Saturated 13g); Cholesterol 137mg; Sodium 174mg; Carbohydrate 49g (Dietary Fiber 1g); Protein 5g.

Mocha Fudge Cake

Prep time: 40 min • **Cook time:** 55 min • **Yield:** 8 servings

Ingredients	Directions
1 large baking potato, peeled and chopped	*1* Preheat the oven to 350 degrees. Spray a 9-inch cake pan with nonstick cooking spray and set aside.
4 ounces dark chocolate, chopped	*2* Place the chopped potato into a large saucepan and cover it with cold water. Bring to a boil over high heat. Reduce the heat to low and cook until the potato is soft, about 18 to 22 minutes. Reserve 3 tablespoons of the cooking water; drain off the remaining water.
2 teaspoons instant coffee granules	
1 egg	
¾ cup sugar	
⅓ cup unsweetened applesauce	*3* Mash the potato in the saucepan until it's smooth and then add the chopped chocolate and instant coffee granules. Cover the pan and let the chocolate melt. Stir gently to blend and let cool.
1 teaspoon vanilla	
⅓ cup minus 1 teaspoon (42 grams) Whole-Grain Flour Mix (see Book V, Chapter 2)	*4* Beat in the egg, sugar, applesauce, and vanilla until smooth.
¼ cup (36 grams) White Flour Mix (see Book V, Chapter 2)	*5* In a small bowl, combine the Whole-Grain Flour Mix, White Flour mix, baking soda, and salt. Stir with a wire whisk until the mixture is all one color. Stir into the potato mixture.
½ teaspoon baking soda	
¼ teaspoon salt	
	6 Pour the batter into a prepared pan. Bake for 33 to 35 minutes, or until a wooden toothpick inserted into the center of the cake comes out clean.
	7 Cool in the pan for 10 minutes and then invert the cake onto a cooling rack. Remove from the pan and let the cake cool completely.

Per serving: Calories 162 (From Fat 49); Fat 6g (Saturated 3g); Cholesterol 28mg; Sodium 161mg; Carbohydrate 27g (Dietary Fiber 2g); Protein 2g.

Note: When you want a moist, fudgy cake and don't want to settle for something dry and unsatisfying, try this surprising cake. The mashed potato keeps the cake fresh and moist for days — if it lasts that long! You can frost this cake with any of the frostings from this chapter.

Vegan Carrot Cupcakes

Prep time: 15 min • **Cook time:** 25–28 min • **Yield:** 12 cupcakes

Ingredients	Directions
2 large carrots, grated	***1*** Preheat the oven to 350 degrees. Grease 12 muffin tins or line them with paper liners.
1-inch piece fresh ginger root, grated	
¼ cup light olive oil	***2*** In a medium bowl, combine the carrots, ginger root, olive oil, vanilla, applesauce, and raisins and mix well.
2 teaspoons vanilla	
1⅓ cups applesauce	***3*** In a large bowl, combine the Whole-Grain Flour Mix, White Flour Mix, brown sugar, granulated sugar, baking powder, baking soda, salt, and cinnamon. Stir with a wire whisk until the mixture is one color.
½ cup raisins	
1½ cups minus 1 teaspoon (200 grams) Whole-Grain Flour Mix (see Book V, Chapter 2)	
¾ cup plus 1 tablespoon (120 grams) White Flour Mix (see Book V, Chapter 2)	***4*** Add the wet ingredients to the dry ingredients and stir for 1 minute. Stir in the coconut.
⅓ cup packed brown sugar	***5*** Fill the prepared muffin tins ½ full of batter.
⅓ cup granulated sugar	
1 tablespoon baking powder	***6*** Bake for 25 to 28 minutes, or until the cupcakes begin to pull away from the sides of the pan. Let them cool completely in the muffin tins.
1 teaspoon baking soda	
½ teaspoon salt	
2 tablespoons ground cinnamon	
¾ cup unsweetened shredded coconut	

Per serving: Calories 254 (From Fat 79); Fat 9g (Saturated 4g); Cholesterol 0mg; Sodium 308mg; Carbohydrate 44g (Dietary Fiber 3g); Protein 2g.

Note: These cupcakes are tasty as is, but for a truly decadent treat, frost them with a vegan cream cheese frosting. Just substitute vegan cream cheese and margarine for the cream cheese and butter in any cream cheese frosting recipe, and don't beat the mixture more than 30 seconds.

Flourless Chocolate Cake

Prep time: 25 min • **Cook time:** 60 min • **Yield:** 16 servings

Ingredients	*Directions*
Two 1-ounce squares unsweetened chocolate, chopped Two 1-ounce squares semisweet chocolate, chopped One 12-ounce bag dark chocolate chips ½ cup water 1 cup butter, cut into pieces 1 teaspoon espresso powder ½ cup packed brown sugar ¼ cup granulated sugar ¼ cup cocoa powder 6 eggs 1 tablespoon vanilla ½ cup white chocolate chips, finely ground *Glaze:* 1 cup milk chocolate chips 3 tablespoons butter 2 tablespoons honey 1 teaspoon vanilla	*1* Preheat the oven to 325 degrees. Grease a 10-inch springform pan with unsalted butter and line the bottom with parchment paper. Grease the parchment paper with unsalted butter. Wrap the outside of the pan with a large single sheet of heavy-duty foil (to prevent leaks) and set aside. *2* Place the chocolate in a medium, microwave-safe bowl. Add the water, butter, and espresso powder. Microwave on high for 1 minute and then remove and stir. Continue microwaving for 1-minute intervals, stirring after each interval, until the mixture is melted and smooth, about 2 to 3 minutes. *3* Beat in the sugars and cocoa powder and then let cool for 15 minutes. *4* Beat in the eggs, one at a time, beating well after each addition. Stir in the vanilla and ground white chocolate chips. *5* Pour into the prepared pan. Bake for 50 to 60 minutes, or until a thin crust forms on the top and the cake is just barely firm in the center. *6* Remove the cake from the oven and let it cool on a wire rack for 15 minutes. Run a knife around the sides and invert onto a serving plate. Remove pan sides and pan bottom. Cool completely. *7* To glaze, combine the milk chocolate chips, butter, and honey in a small saucepan over low heat. Cook and stir until smooth. Remove from the heat and stir in the vanilla; let cool for 15 minutes. Stir and pour carefully over the cake.

Per serving: Calories 417 (From Fat 264); Fat 29g (Saturated 18g); Cholesterol 120mg; Sodium 44mg; Carbohydrate 40g (Dietary Fiber 2g); Protein 4g.

Pear Almond Yogurt Cake

Prep time: 20 min • **Cook time:** 40 min • **Yield:** 10 servings

Ingredients	Directions
3 eggs	**1** Preheat the oven to 350 degrees. Spray a round, 10-inch, springform pan with nonstick cooking spray and set aside.
One 6-ounce container plain Greek yogurt	
⅓ cup light olive oil	**2** In a large bowl, combine the eggs, yogurt, oil, sugar, almond extract, lemon juice, and lemon peel and whisk until combined. Add the chopped pears and stir to combine.
⅔ cup sugar	
1 teaspoon almond extract	
1 tablespoon fresh lemon juice	**3** In a small bowl, sift the Whole-Grain Flour Mix, White Flour Mix, baking powder, baking soda, cardamom, and salt. Stir in the sliced almonds.
1 teaspoon grated lemon peel	
1 large pear, peeled, cored, and finely chopped	**4** Add the dry ingredients to the wet ingredients and stir with a large spoon just until well blended.
1¼ cups minus 1 teaspoon (165 grams) Whole-Grain Flour Mix (see Book V, Chapter 2)	**5** Pour the batter into the prepared pan and sprinkle with the raw sugar crystals. Bake for 35 to 48 minutes, until a toothpick inserted into the center comes out clean.
⅓ cup plus 1 tablespoon plus 1 teaspoon (61 grams) White Flour Mix (see Book V, Chapter 2)	
1½ teaspoons baking powder	**6** Let the cake cool on a wire rack for 10 minutes and then run a knife around the edge of the pan. Carefully remove the pan sides; cool the cake completely before serving.
½ teaspoon baking soda	
½ teaspoon ground cardamom	
¼ teaspoon salt	
½ cup sliced almonds	
2 teaspoons coarse raw sugar crystals	

Per serving: Calories 270 (From Fat 106); Fat 12g (Saturated 2g); Cholesterol 65mg; Sodium 146mg; Carbohydrate 37g (Dietary Fiber 2g); Protein 6g.

Note: This cake is wonderful served with a side of frozen yogurt or softly whipped cream. You can also drizzle it with a thin icing by mixing ½ cup powdered sugar with 2 tablespoons almond milk. Drizzle over the cooled cake.

Vanilla Cupcakes

Prep time: 25 min • **Cook time:** 35–50 min • **Yield:** 6 servings

Ingredients	Directions
1 batch Cake Mix (see Book V, Chapter 2)	*1* Let the Cake Mix come to room temperature if it was frozen.
2 eggs, separated	*2* Preheat the oven to 350 degrees. Grease a 9-inch round cake pan with 1 tablespoon unsalted butter or line six muffin cups with paper liners; set aside.
½ cup milk	
1 teaspoon vanilla	
Pinch salt	*3* In a large mixer bowl, place the egg yolks, milk, vanilla, and Cake Mix. Beat for 3 minutes.
	4 In a small bowl, beat the egg whites until soft peaks form. Add the salt and beat until stiff peaks form.
	5 Fold the egg white mixture into the batter gently. Pour the batter into the prepared pan or muffin cups.
	6 Bake the cupcakes for 35 to 40 minutes, until they're golden-brown and set. Bake the cake layer for 48 to 50 minutes, or until the edges pull away from the sides of the pan and a toothpick inserted in the center comes out clean.
	7 Cool the cake in the pan for 5 minutes and then turn it out onto a wire rack to cool completely. Cool the cupcakes in the pan for 5 minutes and then remove them to a wire rack to cool completely. Store the cake in the fridge for up to four days.

Per serving: Calories 250 (From Fat 107); Fat 12g (Saturated 7g); Cholesterol 99mg; Sodium 101mg; Carbohydrate 34g (Dietary Fiber 0g); Protein 4g.

Tip: If you're going to store the cupcakes for a few days, add a spoonful of cherry or raspberry jam to each cupcake before you bake it. This helps keep the cupcakes moist a bit longer. The jam will drop down to the bottom, but that's okay.

Note: You can frost these cupcakes any way you'd like. For transferring them to school, individual cupcake holders are great.

Note: You can double this recipe to make a 9-inch layer cake or 12 cupcakes.

Chocolate Sheet Cake

Prep time: 28 min • **Cook time:** 45 min • **Yield:** 16 servings

Ingredients	Directions
8 ounces 74% dark chocolate, chopped	**1** Preheat the oven to 350 degrees. Grease a 9-x-13-inch cake pan and set aside.
¾ cup cocoa powder	**2** In the top of a double boiler, melt the dark chocolate, stirring frequently, until smooth, about 4 to 6 minutes. Remove from the heat and cool to room temperature.
1 cup minus 2 teaspoons (142 grams) White Flour Mix (see Book V, Chapter 2)	
⅓ cup minus 1 teaspoon (42 grams) Whole-Grain Flour Mix (see Book V, Chapter 2)	**3** In a medium bowl, combine the cocoa powder, White Flour Mix, Whole-Grain Flour Mix, baking soda, baking powder, and salt. Stir until the mixture is one color and set aside.
½ teaspoon baking soda	
¼ teaspoon baking powder	**4** In a large mixer bowl, beat the butter until it's light and fluffy. Add the sugar gradually, beating constantly.
¼ teaspoon salt	
12 tablespoons unsalted butter, softened	**5** Add the eggs, one at a time, beating well after each addition until the egg is completely incorporated, about 2 to 3 minutes.
1½ cups sugar	
4 eggs	
1 teaspoon vanilla	**6** Add the vanilla.
1¼ cups sour cream	**7** Add half the sour cream and beat well; then add half the flour mixture and beat well. Repeat.
	8 Fold in the melted and cooled chocolate.
	9 Pour the batter into the prepared pan, spreading evenly into the corners.
	10 Bake for 34 to 40 minutes, or until the center of the cake springs back when lightly touched. Cool completely on a wire rack.

Per serving: Calories 329 (From Fat 169); Fat 19g (Saturated 11g); Cholesterol 85mg; Sodium 110mg; Carbohydrate 40g (Dietary Fiber 2g); Protein 4g.

Clementine Cake

Prep time: 40 min • **Cook time:** 1 hr • **Yield:** 8 servings

Ingredients	Directions
3 clementines, cut into pieces	*1* Place the clementines, peel and all, in a saucepan and add water to cover them. Cook them over medium heat until they're tender, about 25 to 30 minutes. They're done when the peel is all the same color with no area of white. Let the water evaporate.
½ cup butter, softened	
4 eggs	
1 cup sugar	*2* Remove all the seeds from the clementines. Place the fruit in a food processor and process until very smooth and uniform.
1 cup minus 2 teaspoons (142 grams) White Flour Mix (see Book V, Chapter 2)	
½ cup blanched almond meal	*3* Measure out 1 cup of the clementine puree. Add the butter to the clementine mixture and let melt for 5 minutes.
1½ teaspoons baking powder	*4* Preheat the oven to 350 degrees. Grease and flour a 10-inch springform pan.
¼ teaspoon salt	
	5 In a large bowl, beat the eggs at medium-high speed until they're thick and lemon-colored. Add the sugar, 2 tablespoons at a time, beating constantly. Beat for 5 minutes.
	6 Blend in half the White Flour Mix and the almond meal; beat for 1 minute.
	7 Add half the clementine and butter mixture and beat for 1 minute.

8 Repeat Steps 6 and 7, adding the baking powder and salt with the second addition of White Flour Mix.

9 Pour the cake mix into the prepared pan. Bake for 35 to 38 minutes, until the cake is set and a knife inserted just off center comes out clean.

10 Cool the cake completely on a wire rack and then run a knife around the edges. Remove the sides and serve.

Per serving: Calories 305 (From Fat 126); Fat 14g (Saturated 8g); Cholesterol 137mg; Sodium 178mg; Carbohydrate 44g (Dietary Fiber 1g); Protein 4g.

Note: Top this cake with whipped cream sweetened with a bit of powdered sugar, or frost it with a butter cream icing made with tangerine juice instead of milk.

Angel Food Cake

Prep time: 30 min • **Cook time:** 55 min • **Yield:** 10 servings

Ingredients	Directions
¼ cup (29 grams) tapioca flour	**1** Preheat the oven to 325 degrees.
¼ cup (40 grams) potato starch	**2** In a medium bowl, combine the tapioca starch, potato starch, sweet rice flour, cornstarch, xanthan gum, ⅓ cup granulated sugar, and powdered sugar. Mix well and set aside.
3 tablespoons (29 grams) sweet rice flour	
2 tablespoons (16 grams) cornstarch	
½ teaspoon xanthan gum	**3** In a large mixer bowl, combine the egg whites, cream of tartar, and salt. Start beating at low speed until foamy and then turn the mixer to high speed.
1 cup plus ⅓ cup granulated sugar	
3 tablespoons powdered sugar	**4** Gradually beat in 1 cup granulated sugar, 2 tablespoons at a time, beating until stiff peaks form.
13 egg whites, room temperature	**5** Beat in the vanilla and lemon rind.
¼ teaspoon cream of tartar	**6** Carefully fold in half the flour mixture, trying to keep as much volume as possible. Then fold in the remaining flour mixture.
⅛ teaspoon salt	
2 teaspoons vanilla	
2 teaspoons grated lemon rind	**7** Spoon the batter onto an ungreased 10-inch tube pan with a removable bottom.
	8 Bake for 50 to 60 minutes, or until the cake is golden-brown and it springs back when lightly touched with a finger.

9 Cool the cake upside down on a wire rack.

10 To serve, run a sharp knife around the sides of the pan, both the outside and around the inner tube. Remove the outside ring of the pan. Then cut along the bottom of the pan, underneath the cake, and remove the cake. Store covered at room temperature.

Per serving: Calories 158 (From Fat 0); Fat 0g (Saturated 0g); Cholesterol 0mg; Sodium 30mg; Carbohydrate 39g (Dietary Fiber 0g); Protein 0g.

Note: Eggs separate more easily when they're cold, so separate the eggs right out of the fridge. Then let the eggs stand at room temperature for 30 to 45 minutes so they warm up before you start beating.

Cream Cheese Frosting

Prep time: 15 min • **Yield:** 8 servings

Ingredients	Directions
¼ cup unsalted butter, softened	**1** In a medium bowl, beat the butter until it's light and fluffy.
1¾ cups powdered sugar	
4 ounces cream cheese, softened	**2** Add the powdered sugar in three parts, beating well after each addition until fluffy.
2 tablespoons milk	
½ teaspoon vanilla	**3** Beat in the cream cheese until smooth and combined.
	4 Add the milk and vanilla; beat well until smooth and creamy. Use immediately or cover and refrigerate up to two days.

Per serving: Calories 205 (From Fat 97); Fat 11g (Saturated 7g); Cholesterol 31mg; Sodium 45mg; Carbohydrate 27g (Dietary Fiber 0g); Protein 1g.

Note: You can easily double this recipe to fill and frost an 8-inch layer cake or a 13-x-9-inch sheet cake. You may need to add more powdered sugar to reach the desired spreading consistency.

Note: Most food experts say that you should refrigerate any cakes or cookies that have cream cheese frosting because it's a perishable product.

Vegan Cream Cheese Frosting

Prep time: 10 min • **Yield:** 6 servings

Ingredients	Directions
8 tablespoons Tofutti cream cheese 8 tablespoons Earth Balance Buttery Spread ½ cup powdered sugar ¼ teaspoon almond extract	*1* Place all the ingredients in a medium bowl. Using a spoon, beat until combined. Don't use a mixer or the frosting will break apart and become oily.

Per 1 tablespoon serving: Calories 170 (From Fat 135); Fat 15g (Saturated 6g); Cholesterol 0mg; Sodium 188mg; Carbohydrate 8g (Dietary Fiber 0g); Protein 1g.

Maple Frosting

Prep time: 10 min • **Yield:** 4 servings

Ingredients	Directions
½ cup maple syrup	**1** Combine all the ingredients in a medium bowl.
2 tablespoons meringue powder	
¼ teaspoon vanilla	**2** Beat with a mixer for 7 to 8 minutes, or until the frosting is fluffy and has the texture of marshmallow crème. Spread immediately on cake or cupcakes.

Per 1 tablespoon serving: Calories 30 (From Fat 0); Fat 0g (Saturated 0g); Cholesterol 0mg; Sodium 8mg; Carbohydrate 7g (Dietary Fiber 0g); Protein 0g.

Note: This is a wholesome variation on the classic seven-minute cooked frosting. Using prepared meringue powder means that you don't have to worry about raw eggs.

Note: This recipe is gluten-free, casein-free, and refined sugar–free. Wilton's Meringue Powder is gluten-free.

Mocha Frosting

Prep time: 10 min • **Yield:** 9 servings

Ingredients	Directions
1 tablespoon hot water 2 teaspoons instant espresso powder ½ cup (1 stick) unsalted butter, softened 1 pound (3¾ cups) powdered sugar ¼ cup cocoa powder 4 to 5 tablespoons milk	*1* In a small bowl, combine the hot water and instant espresso powder and mix until dissolved. *2* In a large bowl, beat the butter until it's light and fluffy. Gradually add the powdered sugar, beating well after each addition. *3* Beat in the cocoa powder and espresso. The mixture will be very thick at this point. *4* Gradually add the milk, beating until the frosting is of desired consistency. Use to fill and frost one 9-inch layer cake.

Per 1 tablespoon serving: Calories 55 (From Fat 18); Fat 2g (Saturated 1g); Cholesterol 5mg; Sodium 1mg; Carbohydrate 10g (Dietary Fiber 0g); Protein 0g.

Note: The flavor of this frosting develops after it stands for a while. Make the frosting just after you put the cake in the oven, and let the frosting stand at room temperature, covered, while the cake bakes and cools. Beat it again just before spreading; you may need to add a little more milk, too.

Note: If you have leftover frosting, place dollops on a cookie sheet and freeze them until firm. Roll them into balls for truffles. They can be refrozen and then dipped into melted chocolate.

Vary It! You can use brewed espresso in this frosting recipe. Just substitute ¼ cup brewed espresso for the hot water, espresso powder, and milk. But the espresso powder does provide a stronger coffee flavor. A good brand is Medaglia D'Oro, available on Amazon.com.

Creamy Chocolate Frosting

Prep time: 20 min • **Cook time:** 3–5 min • **Yield:** 8 servings

Ingredients	Directions
2 tablespoons coconut oil	*1* In a large saucepan, combine the coconut oil, butter, and chocolate chips. Melt over low heat until smooth, stirring frequently, about 3 to 5 minutes.
½ cup butter	
1 cup semisweet chocolate chips	
6 tablespoons cocoa powder	*2* Remove from the heat and beat in the cocoa powder and salt. Transfer the mixture to a large bowl.
Pinch salt	
¼ cup heavy cream	*3* In a small bowl, combine the heavy cream, sour cream, and vanilla; whisk to combine.
⅓ cup sour cream	
2 teaspoons vanilla	*4* Alternately add the powdered sugar and cream mixture to the melted chocolate mixture, beating well after each addition. You may need to add more heavy cream or more powdered sugar for desired spreading consistency. This recipe fills and frosts one 9-inch layer cake.
3½ cups sifted powdered sugar	

Per 1 tablespoon serving: Calories 82 (From Fat 40); Fat 4g (Saturated 3g); Cholesterol 8mg; Sodium 5mg; Carbohydrate 11g (Dietary Fiber 0g); Protein 0g.

Note: Coconut oil is solid at room temperature; in fact, it's so solid that it's difficult to combine with the butter unless both are melted together. It gives this frosting a satiny texture. You can add more cocoa powder if you like a deeper chocolate taste.

Buttercream Frosting

Prep time: 10 min • **Yield:** 8 servings

Ingredients	Directions
1 cup butter, softened	**1** In a large bowl, beat the butter until it's creamy. Gradually add 2 cups of the powdered sugar and the meringue powder, beating until fluffy.
3½ cups powdered sugar	
2 tablespoons meringue powder	**2** Add the vanilla and salt and beat well.
2 teaspoons vanilla	
⅛ teaspoon salt	**3** Alternately add the remaining powdered sugar and the light cream. You may need to add more powdered sugar or more light cream for desired spreading consistency.
4 to 6 tablespoons light cream	
	4 Beat the frosting at high speed until light and fluffy. This recipe will fill and frost a 9-inch layer cake or 24 cupcakes.

Per 1 tablespoon serving: Calories 107 (From Fat 55); Fat 6g (Saturated 4g); Cholesterol 17mg; Sodium 15mg; Carbohydrate 13g (Dietary Fiber 0g); Protein 0g.

Note: The meringue powder adds some body to this frosting recipe and makes it fluffier.

Vary It! To make this chocolate frosting, add ⅓ cup sifted cocoa powder. Increase the light cream to 5 to 7 tablespoons. For a mint frosting, add ½ teaspoon mint extract, omit the vanilla, and add 2 to 3 drops green food coloring. For an orange frosting, add 2 teaspoons grated orange peel and substitute 2 tablespoons of orange juice for 2 tablespoons of the cream.

Chapter 5

Batters, Doughs, Biscuits, and Crackers

In This Chapter

▶ Whipping up great batters and doughs

▶ Working with biscuits and crackers

▶ Enjoying recipes for muffins, pretzels, and more

*Y*ou can use basic batters and doughs in so many ways. For example, after you figure out how to make the best type of dough for gluten-free calzones, you can fill them with hundreds of different combinations of ingredients. You can also vary the flours you use in these doughs and batters, as long as you substitute other gluten-free flours by weight, not by volume.

Biscuits and crackers are all made from doughs. Biscuits are usually made from soft doughs, and crackers are made from firm dough. The difference between the types of dough is in the amount of liquid in the recipe and how the dough is formed and shaped.

In this chapter, you look at the basics of gluten-free batters and doughs. From a great pizza dough that's just like the pizzas you find in New York City to ethereal dumplings and flaky pie crusts, these recipes are what you've been craving.

Most of these recipes freeze well. Make sure that the breads are completely cooled before you wrap them for the freezer, and be sure to mark the package with the recipe name and date to avoid those unidentified mystery packages that float around in every freezer. Thaw these goodies by leaving them unwrapped on the countertop. You can rewarm them briefly in the microwave for a few seconds or in the oven for a few minutes. Serve with nut butters or regular butter for a wonderful treat.

Making the Best Batters and Doughs

Gluten-free batters and doughs are different from wheat batters and doughs. Because the flours don't contain gluten, you need to build structure in other ways. Combining flours and starches is the easiest and, really, the best way to make good doughs and batters.

Some doughs need gums or other additives simply because, even with high-protein gluten-free flours, you still need more structure. Adding whey, dry milk powder, or eggs can also help build structure.

To make the best gluten-free doughs and batters, follow these tips:

- Always mix the additives, such as xanthan gum or guar gum, into the dry ingredients before you add the wet ingredients.

- If you don't use a scale to measure flours and mixes, always measure by spooning the flour or mix lightly into a measuring cup and leveling off the top with the back of a knife.

- Mix the dry ingredients very thoroughly using a wire whisk. Mix until the dry ingredients are well blended and the mixture is one color. Different gluten-free doughs have different colors, so mixing until the colors are blended is a good way to tell that they've been thoroughly combined.

- Be sure to beat the doughs and batters for the specified time period. Most gluten-free doughs and batters must be more aerated than wheat-based doughs. Beating works air into the structure of the dough so it can rise in the oven.

- If a recipe calls for a dough to be refrigerated, follow those instructions to the letter. Resting time lets the flours absorb more of the liquid in the recipe so the protein structure can develop.

- Use pans to shape most gluten-free doughs and batters. Most of these recipes are softer than wheat-based doughs. In fact, a kneadable gluten-free dough is very rare! Use loaf pans, jellyroll pans with sides, muffin tins, and cake and springform pans to shape doughs and batters.

Basic Rules for Biscuits and Crackers

Measure flour and other ingredients carefully, by weight if possible, and mix the dough as directed. Measuring, building structure, and doneness tests are crucial to the success of these recipes. And if you can't use xanthan gum, raw buckwheat flour is a good substitute: Use 1 tablespoon of raw buckwheat flour and 2 tablespoons of water for ½ teaspoon of xanthan gum. As mentioned in Chapter 4 of Book II, you must grind your own raw buckwheat flour because the store-bought variety is toasted. Buy raw buckwheat kernels and grind them to a powder.

If you don't use a scale to measure flours and mixes, always measure by spooning the flour or mix lightly into a measuring cup and leveling off the top with the back of a knife.

Be sure the flours you use are the grind or texture the recipe specifies. If a recipe calls for super-fine flour and you can't find it, use fine flour or regular flour and grind it in the blender or food processor. Fine flours produce smoother dough with no grittiness. Sometimes you want more texture in a recipe, but sometimes, for a tender product, less texture is desirable.

Biscuits

Biscuits are quick breads, leavened by baking powder and/or baking soda. You make them by cutting a fat into flour and adding liquid until a soft dough forms. You can form biscuits in several ways. You can simply drop soft dough onto a cookie sheet and bake it; you can make these "drop biscuits" quickly and easily. Biscuits that you roll and cut with a cookie cutter require a little more finesse and the correct dough texture.

Crackers

Cracker dough is firm enough to roll out or shape into balls to flatten with a fork or the bottom of a water glass. For crisp crackers, some fat is necessary. The fat in crackers is what makes them crisp and flaky. Be sure that you mix the fat well with the flour before you add the liquid. And don't be afraid to handle this type of dough. Cut it into shapes with cookie cutters or make free-form crackers with a sharp knife.

Calzone Dough

Prep time: 15 min, plus rest time • **Cook time:** 20–23 min • **Yield:** 4 servings

Ingredients	Directions
1 cup minus 2 teaspoons (142 grams) White Flour Mix (see Book V, Chapter 2)	*1* Combine all ingredients in a large mixing bowl and beat for 2 minutes.
½ cup plus 1 tablespoon plus 2 teaspoons (83 grams) Whole-Grain Flour Mix (see Book V, Chapter 2)	*2* Cut a piece of parchment paper as long as your cookie sheet and place it on the cookie sheet.
⅓ cup (38 grams) corn flour	*3* Spread the batter over the parchment paper in a large rectangle. You can also spread the batter into a large circle.
2 tablespoons (20 grams) raw buckwheat flour	
2 teaspoons olive oil	*4* Let the dough rise for 1 hour. Make the fillings during this time. You can use any combination of foods for the fillings, like olives, cooked sausages, mozzarella cheese, cooked chicken cubes, feta cheese, and cooked chopped onions. Don't use runny or liquid filling ingredients because the batter won't set if the filling is too wet.
2¼ teaspoons (1 packet) active dry yeast	
¼ teaspoon salt	
1 cup warm water (102 to 103 degrees)	
Filling ingredients: cheese; cooked chicken, sausage, ham, and vegetables; olives; and so on	*5* Preheat the oven to 500 degrees.
	6 Place the filling in ½ cup amounts on one side of the rectangle, lining up the filling evenly in four mounds with space in between.
	7 Lift the parchment paper up and over the filing. Press down around the filling to seal the edges. Leave the parchment in place.
	8 Bake the calzones for 15 minutes and then remove the parchment paper so the calzones can set. Bake the calzones for another 5 to 8 minutes, or until golden-brown.

Per serving: Calories 270 (From Fat 31); Fat 4g (Saturated 0g); Cholesterol 0mg; Sodium 147mg; Carbohydrate 59g (Dietary Fiber 3g); Protein 5g.

Note: Don't use any sauces in the filling because the dough is a batter. Sauces make the dough too wet, and it won't set and bake.

Crepe Batter

Prep time: 15 min, plus rest time • **Cook time:** 3 min • **Yield:** 10–12 servings

Ingredients	Directions
⅓ cup (41 grams) sorghum flour	**1** In a medium bowl, combine the sorghum flour, potato starch, sweet rice flour, cornstarch, salt, and xanthan gum. Mix until the mixture is one color.
¼ cup (40 grams) potato starch	
¼ cup (37 grams) sweet rice flour	**2** In a small bowl, beat the eggs with the butter, milk, and water. Add to the flour mixture and beat with a mixer for 1 minute.
¼ cup (35 grams) cornstarch	
¼ teaspoon salt	**3** Let the batter sit, uncovered, at room temperature for 20 to 30 minutes, until it thickens slightly. If you need to, you can refrigerate this batter, covered, overnight.
¼ teaspoon xanthan gum	
3 eggs	
3 tablespoons butter, melted	**4** When you're ready to cook, place an 8-inch nonstick skillet over medium heat. Coat the pan with butter.
1 cup milk	
¼ cup water	**5** Add ¼ cup batter to the skillet. Twist and turn the skillet so the batter evenly covers the bottom of the skillet in a thin layer.
	6 Cook the crepe until it sets, about 1 to 2 minutes. Carefully flip the crepe and cook for 30 seconds to 1 minute on the second side. Place the crepe on waxed paper to cool. Don't stack the crepes or they'll stick together.

Per serving: Calories 123 (From Fat 53); Fat 6g (Saturated 3g); Cholesterol 76mg; Sodium 90mg; Carbohydrate 14g (Dietary Fiber 0g); Protein 3g.

Vary It! You can use almond or soymilk instead of the cow's milk to make this batter casein-free. For dessert crepes, add 3 tablespoons sugar to the batter.

Note: You may need to add more milk or water after the batter has rested. The batter should be the consistency of thick cream. It must spread easily, because it starts cooking as soon as it hits the hot pan.

Note: Crepes freeze really well. Wrap each crepe in waxed paper or plastic wrap and place them in a freezer bag. Freeze up to three months. Thaw at room temperature and use as directed in your recipe.

Muffin Batter

Prep time: 20 min • **Cook time:** 30–33 min • **Yield:** 12 servings

Ingredients	Directions
1¾ cups plus 1 tablespoon plus 1 teaspoon (248 grams) Whole-Grain Flour Mix (see Book V, Chapter 2)	*1* Preheat the oven to 350 degrees. Grease muffin tins with cooking spray and set aside.
1 cup plus 3 tablespoons (177 grams) White Flour Mix (see Book V, Chapter 2)	*2* In a large bowl, combine the Whole-Grain Flour Mix, White Flour Mix, brown sugar, salt, baking powder, baking soda, cinnamon, and nutmeg and stir until the mixture is one color.
½ cup brown sugar	
½ teaspoon salt	*3* In a medium bowl, combine the eggs, sour cream, oil, vanilla, and milk and beat well.
2 teaspoons baking powder	
1 teaspoon baking soda	*4* Add the wet ingredients to the dry ingredients and mix well. At this point, you can add fruits or nuts as desired (see the note after the recipe).
1 teaspoon cinnamon	
¼ teaspoon nutmeg	
3 eggs	*5* Spoon the batter into the muffin tins.
½ cup sour cream	
½ cup vegetable oil	*6* Bake for 15 minutes, rotate the pan, and then bake 15 to 18 minutes longer, or until the muffins are golden-brown and a toothpick inserted into the center comes out clean.
1 tablespoon vanilla	
¾ cup milk	
	7 Cool the muffins in the pans for 5 minutes and then move them to wire racks to cool completely.

Per serving: Calories 292 (From Fat 124); Fat 14g (Saturated 3g); Cholesterol 59mg; Sodium 298mg; Carbohydrate 39g (Dietary Fiber 1g); Protein 4g.

Vary It! In Step 4 of the recipe, you can add 2 cups diced fruit, such as apples or pears, or ½ cup diced dried fruits like apricots, currants, or pineapple. Along with the fruit, you can add ½ cup chopped nuts, such as walnuts or pecans.

Vary It! For a vegan version, substitute 2 teaspoons ground golden flaxseeds and 3 tablespoons water for the 3 eggs. Substitute coconut or soy yogurt for the sour cream. Substitute rice, soy, almond, or hemp milk for the dairy milk.

Dumpling Batter

Prep time: 20 min, plus rest time • **Cook time:** 10 min • **Yield:** 8 servings

Ingredients	Directions
⅓ cup minus 2 teaspoons (46 grams) superfine brown rice flour	*1* In a medium bowl, combine the brown rice flour, tapioca flour, sorghum flour, millet flour, xanthan gum, baking powder, baking soda, and salt. Mix until the mixture is one color.
¼ cup (29 grams) tapioca flour	
¼ cup (32 grams) sorghum flour	*2* Work in the butter with your fingers or a pastry blender until the mixture looks like sand.
2 tablespoons (18 grams) millet flour	
1 teaspoon xanthan gum	*3* In a small bowl, combine the egg and buttermilk; beat well. Add to the flour mixture and stir until a dough forms. Let the dough stand for 20 minutes while you simmer some soup to use for the dumplings, or bring 4 cups of chicken broth or water to a simmer in a large saucepan.
½ teaspoon baking powder	
½ teaspoon baking soda	
½ teaspoon salt	
3 tablespoons butter	*4* Use a Number 70 ice-cream scoop or a tablespoon measure to make the dumplings. Dip the scoop into the simmering liquid and then into the dough. Drop the dough carefully into the liquid. Repeat until you use all the dough.
1 egg, beaten	
⅓ cup buttermilk	
	5 Cover the pot and simmer for 9 to 12 minutes. Don't lift the lid until 9 minutes has passed. The dumplings are done when they've puffed and a toothpick inserted in the center comes out clean.

Per serving: Calories 110 (From Fat 48); Fat 5g (Saturated 3g); Cholesterol 39mg; Sodium 268mg; Carbohydrate 14g (Dietary Fiber 1g); Protein 2g.

Vary It! This recipe is easy to vary. Add any kind of chopped fresh or dried herbs to the batter for more flavor. Use chicken broth, soymilk, or vegetable broth instead of the buttermilk; in that case, add ¼ teaspoon apple cider vinegar to the liquid.

Basic Buttermilk Biscuits

Prep time: 15 min • **Cook time:** 25–30 min • **Yield:** 12 biscuits

Ingredients	Directions
½ cup (78 grams) sweet rice flour	*1* Preheat the oven to 400 degrees. In a food processor or blender, combine the sweet rice flour and brown rice flour and process or blend until very fine. Pour into a large mixing bowl and add the potato starch, tapioca flour, sugar, xanthan gum, baking soda, baking powder, and salt.
½ cup (80 grams) superfine brown rice flour	
½ cup minus 1 teaspoon (80 grams) potato starch	
½ cup minus 1 teaspoon (58 grams) tapioca flour	*2* Using two knives or a pastry blender, cut in the butter until it's the size of tiny peas.
3 tablespoons sugar	
1 teaspoon xanthan gum	*3* Measure the buttermilk into a glass measuring cup and add the egg; beat until combined. Add all at once to the flour mixture and stir just until the liquid is absorbed. Let stand 5 minutes.
1½ teaspoons baking soda	
½ teaspoon baking powder	
½ teaspoon sea salt	*4* Using a spoon rinsed in cold water to prevent sticking, drop the biscuits the size of a golf ball onto ungreased cookie sheets, leaving about 4 inches between each biscuit. Bake for 25 to 30 minutes, or until the biscuits are light golden-brown. Cool on a wire rack.
6 tablespoons cold butter, cut into pieces	
1 cup cold buttermilk	
1 egg, beaten	

Per serving: Calories 153 (From Fat 60); Fat 7g (Saturated 4g); Cholesterol 34mg; Sodium 298mg; Carbohydrate 22g (Dietary Fiber 0g); Protein 2g.

Note: You can make your own buttermilk by putting 1 tablespoon of lemon juice or vinegar in a measuring cup. Add enough sweet milk to make ½ cup and let stand for 5 minutes. Use as directed in the recipe.

Spicy Cheese Biscuits

Prep time: 20 min • **Cook time:** 15 min • **Yield:** 8 servings

Ingredients	Directions
²/₃ cup heavy cream	**1** Preheat the oven to 425 degrees. Line a cookie sheet with a Silpat (silicone) liner or parchment paper.
½ cup plus 1 tablespoon plus 2 teaspoons (83 grams) Whole-Grain Flour Mix (see Book V, Chapter 2)	**2** Place the cream in a large mixing bowl. Zero out the scale and measure each ingredient into the bowl.
⅓ cup plus 2 teaspoons (54 grams) White Flour Mix (see Book V, Chapter 2)	**3** Blend all ingredients together well. When the dough starts to come together, start kneading the dough.
2 tablespoons (20 grams) raw buckwheat flour	**4** Knead for 1 minute and then pat the dough on the Silpat liner into a circle ¾-inch thick.
½ teaspoon chili powder	
¼ teaspoon ground cumin	**5** Cut the dough into eight wedges with a sharp knife or bench knife. For soft edges, leave the wedges touching each other. For crisp edges, separate the wedges slightly.
1½ teaspoons baking powder	
½ cup shredded Mexican cheese blend	
	6 Bake for 12 to 15 minutes, until deep golden-brown. Move to a wire rack to cool completely.

Per serving: Calories 166 (From Fat 96); Fat 11g (Saturated 7g); Cholesterol 36mg; Sodium 132mg; Carbohydrate 16g (Dietary Fiber 1g); Protein 3g.

Vary It! You can make these biscuits with any kind of cheese and any seasoning. Use Cheddar cheese and ½ teaspoon dried thyme leaves for a different flavor, or try grated Gouda cheese with dried marjoram.

Note: Be sure you use raw buckwheat flour that you grind yourself from raw buckwheat groats. Store-bought buckwheat flour doesn't have the same thickening properties.

Herbed Cream Biscuits

Prep time: 15 min • **Cook time:** 15 min • **Yield:** 8 servings

Ingredients	Directions
1 cup plus 3 tablespoons (175 grams) White Flour Mix (see Book V, Chapter 2)	**1** Preheat the oven to 425 degrees. Line a cookie sheet with parchment paper.
¾ cup plus 1 tablespoon (110 grams) Whole-Grain Flour Mix (see Book V, Chapter 2)	**2** In a large bowl, combine the White Flour Mix, Whole-Grain Flour Mix, sugar, baking powder, and salt; stir until the mix is one color. Mix in the herbs.
2 teaspoons sugar	
2 teaspoons baking powder	**3** Add the cream and mix well. The dough should be soft but pliable.
½ teaspoon salt	
2 tablespoons minced fresh rosemary, tarragon, or other herbs	**4** On a board dusted with some more White Flour Mix, pat the dough out to ¾-inch thickness.
1½ cups heavy cream	**5** Cut out biscuits using a sharp-edged cutter. If you don't want scraps, cut the dough into 2½-inch squares.
	6 Place the biscuits on a prepared cookie sheet. Bake for 12 to 15 minutes, or until the biscuits are light golden-brown. Move to a wire rack to cool; serve warm.

Per serving: Calories 281 (From Fat 153); Fat 17g (Saturated 10g); Cholesterol 61mg; Sodium 258mg; Carbohydrate 32g (Dietary Fiber 1g); Protein 3g.

Ham and Cheese Muffins

Prep time: 20 min • **Cook time:** 23–25 min • **Yield:** 12 muffins

Ingredients	Directions
1¼ cups minus 1 teaspoon (165 grams) Whole-Grain Flour Mix (see Book V, Chapter 2)	*1* Preheat the oven to 350 degrees. Line 12 muffin cups with paper liners or grease them with nonstick cooking spray.
¼ cup plus 1 tablespoon (45 grams) White Flour Mix (see Book V, Chapter 2)	*2* In a large bowl, combine the Whole-Grain Flour Mix, White Flour Mix, baking powder, baking soda, and salt. Mix with a wire whisk until the mixture is one color.
1 teaspoon baking powder	
½ teaspoon baking soda	
½ teaspoon salt	*3* In a small bowl, combine the eggs, oil, yogurt, milk, and Dijon mustard and beat until all the ingredients are combined.
3 eggs	
⅓ cup vegetable oil	
⅓ cup whole milk plain yogurt	*4* Add the egg mixture to the flour mixture until well combined. Gently fold in the ham and cheese cubes.
⅓ cup milk	
2 teaspoons Dijon mustard	*5* Fill the prepared muffin cups, filling each ⅔ full.
½ cup diced ham	
½ cup diced Colby or Cheddar cheese	*6* Bake for 23 to 25 minutes, or until the muffins are golden-brown and spring back when lightly touched in the center. Cool them in the pan for 3 minutes and then move them to a wire rack to cool completely.
	7 Store leftovers in the refrigerator. You can rewarm them in the microwave on high for 10 seconds per muffin.

Per serving: Calories 174 (From Fat 96); Fat 11g (Saturated 2g); Cholesterol 64mg; Sodium 254mg; Carbohydrate 15g (Dietary Fiber 1g); Protein 6g.

Note: These muffins are delicious with a bowl of hot soup. They can even replace a meal. The Dijon mustard adds a nice kick, but you can omit it if you like.

Note: Because these muffins contain ham, you must store them in the refrigerator.

Sesame Seed Crackers

Prep time: 20 min • **Cook time:** 10 min • **Yield:** 48 crackers

Ingredients	*Directions*
1 cup plus 3 tablespoons (132 grams) almond flour	*1* Preheat the oven to 375 degrees. Line two cookie sheets with parchment paper and set aside.
½ cup minus 2 teaspoons (62 grams) brown rice flour	
¼ cup (29 grams) tapioca flour	*2* In a large mixing bowl, combine the almond flour, brown rice flour, and tapioca flour; whisk until blended. Stir in the sesame seeds and sea salt.
½ cup sesame seeds	
½ teaspoon sea salt	*3* Using a pastry blender or two knives, cut in the butter until the particles are fine.
¼ cup cold butter, cut into pieces	
1 egg white	*4* In a small bowl, combine the egg white with 2 tablespoons almond milk. Whisk until foamy and then stir it into the flour mixture. Add more milk, tossing with a fork, a tablespoon at a time until you can form a dough by pressing it together. The dough should be moist but firm.
⅓ cup almond milk	
More sesame seeds and sea salt	
	5 Divide the dough in half and place each half on a prepared cookie sheet. Top with another sheet of parchment paper and roll out until the dough is ⅛-inch thick. Remove the top sheet of parchment paper. Repeat with the second half of dough on a second cookie sheet.
	6 Cut into squares or other shapes using a sharp knife, cookie cutter, or pizza cutter. Sprinkle with more sesame seeds and a bit of sea salt.
	7 Bake for 9 to 12 minutes, or until the crackers are light golden-brown. Cool the crackers on the cookie sheets for 3 minutes and then carefully move them to a wire rack to cool completely.

Per serving: Calories 42 (From Fat 28); Fat 3g (Saturated 1g); Cholesterol 3mg; Sodium 26mg; Carbohydrate 3g (Dietary Fiber 0g); Protein 1g.

Olive Oil Crackers

Prep time: 15 min • **Cook time:** 12–14 min • **Yield:** 48 crackers

Ingredients	*Directions*
2 cups (270 grams) Whole-Grain Flour Mix (see Book V, Chapter 2)	*1* Preheat the oven to 400 degrees. Line two cookie sheets with parchment paper or silicone sheets. Set aside.
3 tablespoons quinoa grains, rinsed if not pre-rinsed	*2* In a mixer bowl, using a dough hook, combine the Whole-Grain Flour Mix, quinoa grains, pepper, and onion powder; blend well with a wire whisk.
¼ teaspoon black pepper	
½ teaspoon onion powder	
5 tablespoons olive oil	*3* Add the olive oil and water. Mix, adding more water if the dough seems dry, until a firm dough forms. Cover and let stand for 10 minutes.
½ cup warm water	
½ teaspoon sea salt	
	4 Wet your hands with cold water and divide the dough in half. Press each half of dough onto each cooking sheet, making a thin layer. Prick the dough with a fork and cut it into pieces using a pizza cutter. Sprinkle with sea salt.
	5 Bake the crackers for 12 to 14 minutes, or until firm and light golden-brown. Carefully move the crackers to a wire rack to cool completely. Store in an airtight container at room temperature.

Per serving: Calories 36 (From Fat 14); Fat 2g (Saturated 0g); Cholesterol 0mg; Sodium 24mg; Carbohydrate 5g (Dietary Fiber 0g); Protein 1g.

Note: You may have to visit a health food store to find quinoa seeds. They're available online, too.

Graham Crackers

Prep time: 40 min, plus chilling time • **Cook time:** 14 min • **Yield:** 44 servings

Ingredients	Directions
3¾ cups minus 1 tablespoon (495 grams) Whole-Grain Flour Mix (see Book V, Chapter 2)	**1** Line a 9-x-5-inch bread pan with plastic wrap. Make sure the wrap fits into the corners so that the crackers will have rectangular edges.
3 cups minus 2 tablespoons (426 grams) White Flour Mix (see Book V, Chapter 2)	**2** In a large bowl, combine the Whole-Grain Flour Mix, White Flour Mix, sweet rice flour, cinnamon, baking powder, salt, and brown sugar. Mix until the mixture is one color.
½ cup plus 1 teaspoon (81 grams) sweet rice flour	
1 tablespoon cinnamon	
1 tablespoon baking powder	**3** Add the butter and let the mixer run until the mixture looks like sand, about 2 to 3 minutes. Add the honey, vanilla, and water; beat for 1 minute.
½ teaspoon salt	
6 tablespoons packed brown sugar	**4** Pat the mixture into the prepared pan. Cover with plastic wrap. Pat down the dough to make sure it doesn't have any air bubbles.
12 tablespoons unsalted butter	
⅓ cup honey	**5** Refrigerate overnight, or at least 2 hours, before slicing.
3 teaspoons vanilla	
¾ cup water	**6** When ready to bake, preheat the oven to 400 degrees and line cookie sheets with parchment paper.

7 Remove the top layer of plastic wrap and slice the dough into ⅛-inch slices. Place the slices on the prepared cookie sheets, leaving ½-inch space between each cracker. Dock the crackers by poking holes in the dough with a fork.

8 Bake, two cookie sheets at a time, for 8 minutes. Then rotate the pans and bake 5 to 6 minutes longer, until the crackers are golden-brown.

9 Remove from the oven and let stand on cookie sheets for 2 to 3 minutes; then move the graham crackers to wire racks to cool completely.

Per serving: Calories 122 (From Fat 31); Fat 3g (Saturated 2g); Cholesterol 8mg; Sodium 54mg; Carbohydrate 23g (Dietary Fiber 1g); Protein 1g.

Toasted Onion Buckwheat Crackers

Prep time: 20 min • **Cook time:** 60 min • **Yield:** 60 servings

Ingredients	Directions
1 cup raw buckwheat	*1* Preheat the oven to 350 degrees. Line two large cookie sheets with parchment paper and set aside.
1½ cups boiling water	
1 medium onion, finely chopped	*2* In a medium saucepan, stir the buckwheat into boiling water. Bring back to a boil and then turn the heat to low and simmer for 15 minutes, until the buckwheat kernels are very soft. Drain off the excess water, letting the buckwheat sit in the strainer for a few minutes. The drier the buckwheat, the crispier the cracker.
¼ cup golden flaxseeds	
¼ cup plus 1 tablespoon (49 grams) sweet rice flour	
1 teaspoon smoked paprika	*3* In a dry frying pan, cook the onion until it's well browned and the liquid evaporates, stirring frequently. Don't let the onions burn.
½ teaspoon salt	
2 tablespoons olive oil	*4* When the onions are completely browned, reduce the heat and add the cooked buckwheat. Cook for 1 minute; the mixture will begin to form a ball. Remove from heat.
	5 Grind the flaxseeds in a spice grinder or coffee mill until they're a fine powder.
	6 In a medium bowl, combine the flaxseeds, sweet rice flour, smoked paprika, and salt.
	7 Add the flaxseed mixture and olive oil to the buckwheat mixture in the pan. Beat for 1 minute. The groats may get a bit mushy; that's fine.
	8 Divide the dough in half. Spread out each half onto a prepared cookie sheet until the sheet is completely covered with dough. Score the dough into 2-inch squares.

9 Bake for 15 minutes and then rotate pans. Bake 15 minutes longer.

10 Remove the cookie sheets from the oven. Slide the crackers, with the parchment paper, directly onto the oven racks.

11 Bake 10 to 15 minutes longer, until the crackers are well browned and crisp. Move them to a wire rack to cool completely.

Per serving: Calories 20 (From Fat 7); Fat 1g (Saturated 0g); Cholesterol 0mg; Sodium 20mg; Carbohydrate 3g (Dietary Fiber 1g); Protein 1g.

Note: The baking time varies depending on the size of your cookie sheets and how thin you make the crackers.

Note: You may have to visit a health food store or co-op to find flaxseeds, although they're becoming more available in regular grocery stores. You can also find them online.

Soft Pretzels

Prep time: 30 min, plus rising time   •   **Cook time:** 10–12 min   •   **Yield:** 8 servings

Ingredients	Directions
1½ cups (199 grams) High-Protein Bread Flour Mix (see Book V, Chapter 2)	**1** In a large bowl, combine the Bread Flour Mix, White Flour Mix, and buckwheat flour; stir until the mixture is one color.
½ cup plus 2 tablespoons (93 grams) White Flour Mix (see Book V, Chapter 2)	**2** Add the remaining ingredients except the baking soda and coarse salt and beat for 2 minutes.
2 tablespoons (20 grams) raw buckwheat flour	**3** Form the dough into ropes by rolling on the counter to 14 inches long, about the diameter of a thick pencil.
1 tablespoon honey	
1 tablespoon vegetable oil	**4** Place each rope in the shape of a "U," and then cross the ends over the center to form a classic pretzel shape. Or, for simplicity's sake, just leave the pretzels in rods.
1 tablespoon active dry yeast	
1 teaspoon salt	
½ cup plus 2 tablespoons water	**5** Place each pretzel on a square of parchment paper. Cover with plastic wrap and let rise 1½ hours. While the dough is rising, place 6 cups of water in a shallow pan. Add the baking soda. When 1¼ hours has passed, place the pan on the stove and bring the water to a boil.
6 tablespoons baking soda	
3 tablespoons coarse salt	
	6 Preheat the oven to 425 degrees. Place one pretzel at a time in the boiling water, parchment paper side down.

7 Let cook for 1 minute and then flip the pretzel over in the water; remove the paper. Cook for 1 minute longer. Remove the pretzel from the water with a slotted spatula. Let drain for a few seconds. Discard the parchment paper square.

8 Place the boiled pretzel on a greased cookie sheet and immediately sprinkle with some of the coarse salt. Repeat with remaining pretzels.

9 After you finish boiling and salting all the pretzels, bake for 8 to 10 minutes, or until well browned.

Per serving: Calories 123 (From Fat 24); Fat 3g (Saturated 0g); Cholesterol 0mg; Sodium 1,553mg; Carbohydrate 23g (Dietary Fiber 2g); Protein 4g.

Crisp Pretzels

Prep time: 30 min • **Cook time:** 25 min • **Yield:** 8 servings

Ingredients	Directions
Recipe for Soft Pretzels (see previous recipe)	*1* Make the Soft Pretzels, except roll the dough a bit thinner. Form into 16 logs.
	2 Let the pretzels rise as directed and prepare water bath.
	3 Simmer each pretzel as directed in the Soft Pretzel directions.
	4 Preheat the oven to 375 degrees.
	5 When you finish boiling all the pretzels and sprinkling them with salt as directed, bake for 22 to 25 minutes, until the pretzels are deep golden-brown. Cool on a wire rack.

Per serving: Calories 123 (From Fat 24); Fat 3g (Saturated 0g); Cholesterol 0mg; Sodium 1,553mg; Carbohydrate 23g (Dietary Fiber 2g); Protein 4g.

Chapter 6

Savory Breads and Pizzas

In This Chapter

▶ Using some tips for making yeast and quick savory breads
▶ Working with pizza dough
▶ Baking delectable savory breads and pizzas

*W*hen most people are diagnosed with celiac disease or gluten intolerance, the first thing that usually comes to mind is, "What about bread?" There's nothing like biting into warm bread, fresh from the oven, with a crisp crust and a melting interior. With these delicious recipes, you can still enjoy that wonderful treat.

In this chapter, you find recipes for all kinds of savory breads, both yeast and quick breads. Chewy bagels, flavorful sourdough bread, crisp and light popovers, satisfying sandwich bread, and light and fluffy rolls can be part of your every-day menus.

After you master the basics, use these recipes to create your own treats. For instance, you can use the recipe for Parmesan Lemon Thyme Baguettes and make plain baguettes, or flavor the bread with chopped chives and grated Cotija cheese.

Basic Rules for Yeast and Quick Savory Breads

Gluten-free yeast breads are a bit different from wheat yeast breads. When substituting flours in these recipes, choose flours with a high protein content for the best structure. Nut flours, such as almond flour or hazelnut flour, are a good choice, and they mimic the nutty taste of wheat flour. As always, when substituting ingredients, use weight measurements instead of volume measurements.

To make the best gluten-free yeast and other savory breads:

- Remember that you don't knead these breads. The "dough" is actually a soft or stiff batter.

- If you don't use a scale to measure flours and mixes, always measure by spooning the flour or mix lightly into a measuring cup and leveling off the top with the back of a knife.

- Let the dough rise only once. Because the structure is more delicate than wheat-based yeast breads, more than one rise weakens the web of protein and starch, which makes the structure too fragile to hold the air that gives yeast bread its texture.

- Always beat the batter for the time specified in the recipe. During this time, the flour absorbs moisture to develop the proteins, and the yeast is fully distributed throughout the bread.

- Always check the expiration date on yeast and baking powder before you start a recipe. Expired yeast won't rise, and expired baking powder won't give your breads the height you want.

- Check for doneness of savory gluten-free breads with an instant-read thermometer and doneness tests. When breads are done, their internal temperature is 190 to 200 degrees, and the crust is deep golden-brown. The bread should pull away from the sides of the pan and sound hollow when lightly tapped.

- A few recipes in this chapter call for raw buckwheat flour, which isn't the same as the buckwheat flour you buy in packages. That buckwheat flour has been toasted. For these recipes, you must grind raw green buckwheat groats to a powder.

Tips for Making Pizzas

Just as with savory yeast and quick breads, gluten-free pizza are a bit different from yeast crusts. Pizza crust is a stiff batter, similar to yeast bread doughs, but the preparation method is different.

You've probably heard of pizza stones. This product is literally made of stone. It heats up quickly and holds heat so the pizza crust has a wonderful crackly bottom. For best results, get one! You can find them at kitchen supply stores, big box stores, and even some large supermarkets.

Here are some tips for making pizzas:

- ✔ Gluten-free pizza doughs use more yeast than wheat-based pizza doughs, and the dough rises just once on parchment paper.

- ✔ If you don't use a scale to measure flours and mixes, always measure by spooning the flour or mix lightly into a measuring cup and leveling off the top with the back of a knife.

- ✔ Make sure the pizza stone is very hot. An oven takes only 10 minutes to heat, but the racks and oven walls aren't at the correct temperature until at least 20 minutes have passed. Pizza stones take at least 20 minutes to heat up to the correct temperature.

- ✔ You must bake the crust before adding the toppings. And don't overload the crust with lots of sauce and toppings. This pizza is New York style, which means the crust is crisp but bendable. If you add tons of sauce, meats, and cheeses, you can't pick up a piece and bend it in half to eat it in the classic manner!

Book V

Losing the Gluten, Keeping the Baked Goods

Vegan Rolled Oat Bread

Prep time: 20 min, plus rise time • **Cook time:** 60–70 min • **Yield:** 16 slices

Ingredients	Directions
1¼ cups plus 3 tablespoons (190 grams) High-Protein Bread Flour Mix (see Book V, Chapter 2)	**1** Grease a 9-x-5-inch loaf pan with unsalted butter or solid shortening.
1 cup minus 2 tablespoons (105 grams) rolled oat flour	**2** In a bowl for a stand mixer, combine all ingredients. Beat on medium speed for 2 minutes.
⅔ cup rolled oats	**3** Pour the batter into the prepared loaf pan.
¾ cup (100 grams) Whole-Grain Flour Mix (see Book V, Chapter 2)	**4** Let the batter rise in a warm, draft-free place for 1 to 2 hours, until the batter has doubled in size and is almost to the rim of the pan.
1 tablespoon sugar	
¼ teaspoon sea salt	
1 tablespoon golden flaxseeds, finely ground	**5** Preheat the oven to 350 degrees. Bake the bread for 60 to 70 minutes, or until the temperature registers 190 to 200 degrees. Cool the bread in a pan for 5 minutes and then turn it out onto a wire rack to cool completely.
1 teaspoon yeast	
1⅔ cups warm water (102 to 103 degrees)	**6** Let the bread cool completely before slicing.

Per serving: Calories 117 (From Fat 14); Fat 2g (Saturated 0g); Cholesterol 0mg; Sodium 37mg; Carbohydrate 23g (Dietary Fiber 3g); Protein 4g.

Note: Be sure to grind the flaxseeds to a fine powder. You use them to replace the eggs and the gums in this recipe. Keep a coffee grinder dedicated to this task in your kitchen, because nobody wants flaxseed-flavored coffee!

Note: Use golden flaxseeds in all your baking. The brown flaxseeds contain more chlorophyll and can turn your baked goods green. This may be festive for St. Patrick's Day but is otherwise off-putting.

Sandwich Bread

Prep time: 15 min, plus rise time • **Cook time:** 40 min • **Yield:** 8 servings

Ingredients	Directions
½ cup water	**1** Grease an 8-x-4-inch baking pan using nonstick cooking spray or unsalted butter and set aside.
½ cup milk	
2 tablespoons honey	**2** In a large mixing bowl, combine all ingredients. Beat at medium speed for 2 minutes.
2 tablespoons oil	
2 teaspoons salt	**3** Pour the mixture into the prepared pan, cover, and let it rise in a warm place until doubled, about 1 to 1½ hours.
2¼ cups minus 1 teaspoon (300 grams) Whole-Grain Flour Mix (see Book V, Chapter 2)	
1¼ cups plus 1 tablespoon (196 grams) White Flour Mix (see Book V, Chapter 2)	**4** Preheat the oven to 350 degrees.
	5 Place the bread in the center of the oven. Bake for 35 to 40 minutes, or until the bread is golden-brown and the temperature is 190 to 200 degrees.
1 egg	
	6 Remove the bread from the pan and place on a wire rack to cool completely before slicing.

Per serving: Calories 281 (From Fat 51); Fat 6g (Saturated 1g); Cholesterol 29mg; Sodium 598mg; Carbohydrate 56g (Dietary Fiber 2g); Protein 5g.

Note: When you want a soft, simple sandwich bread, this is it. It slices perfectly and has a wonderful texture. This bread stays nice and soft for several days after baking because it's enriched with egg and milk.

Popovers

Prep time: 15 min • **Cook time:** 20–25 min • **Yield:** 12 servings

Ingredients	Directions
½ cup minus 1 teaspoon (58 grams) tapioca flour	**1** Preheat the oven to 450 degrees. You need a cast-iron popover pan, glass custard cups, or really sturdy muffin tins for these popovers to work. If you're using a cast-iron pan, heat it in the oven for at least 10 minutes and then grease it. Grease each cup very well because the batter needs to move easily in the pans to rise. Don't preheat the glass custard cups or the muffin tins.
½ cup (80 grams) white rice flour	
¼ cup (37 grams) sweet rice flour	
2 tablespoons (16 grams) sorghum flour	
¼ teaspoon xanthan gum	**2** In a large bowl, combine the tapioca flour, white rice flour, sweet rice flour, sorghum flour, xanthan gum, salt, and sugar and mix until the mixture is one color.
⅛ teaspoon salt	
1 tablespoon sugar	
1 cup milk	**3** Add the milk, melted butter, and eggs and beat for at least 2 minutes.
2 tablespoons butter, melted	**4** Pour the batter into the oiled pans (remember, the cast-iron pans should be hot).
3 eggs	
	5 Bake for 20 to 25 minutes, until the popovers pop and are deep golden-brown.
	6 Remove the popovers from the pans immediately; eat them while they're hot with butter and jam.

Per serving: Calories 108 (From Fat 36); Fat 4g (Saturated 2g); Cholesterol 61mg; Sodium 50mg; Carbohydrate 16g (Dietary Fiber 0g); Protein 3g.

Vary It! For cheese popovers, add ¼ cup grated Parmesan cheese; omit the salt. Bake for the same time.

Egg-Free Yeast Bread

Prep time: 15 min, plus rise time • **Cook time:** 65–70 min • **Yield:** 32 slices

Ingredients	Directions
3½ cups plus ⅓ cup (500 grams) High-Protein Bread Flour Mix (see Book V, Chapter 2	*1* Grease two 8½-x-4½-inch bread pans with solid shortening or unsalted butter.
3¼ cups plus 2 tablespoons (455 grams) Whole-Grain Flour Mix (see Book V, Chapter 2)	*2* In a large bowl, combine the High-Protein Bread Flour Mix, Whole-Grain Flour Mix, sugar, salt, xanthan gum, guar gum, and active dry yeast. Mix well with a wire whisk until completely combined.
2 tablespoons sugar	*3* Add the water and stir until combined; then beat for 3 minutes.
1 teaspoon salt	
2 teaspoons xanthan gum	*4* Pour the dough into the prepared pans and cover them with plastic wrap.
1 teaspoon guar gum	
1 tablespoon active dried yeast	*5* Let the dough rise in a warm, draft-free place for 2 to 3 hours, or until doubled in size.
4 cups water	*6* Arrange the oven rack in the bottom third of your oven. Preheat the oven to 350 degrees.
	7 As soon as the loaves have doubled in size, bake for 30 minutes, and then rotate pans to ensure even baking. Bake 35 to 40 minutes longer, or until the temperature on an instant-read thermometer reads 190 to 200 degrees.
	8 Cool the loaves in the pans for 5 minutes and then move them to a wire rack to cool completely. Store them in an airtight container at room temperature. Use a serrated knife for slicing.

Per serving: Calories 110 (From Fat 8); Fat 1g (Saturated 0g); Cholesterol 0mg; Sodium 74mg; Carbohydrate 24g (Dietary Fiber 2g); Protein 3g.

Note: Simple, wonderful, plain bread is the one food most newly diagnosed celiacs covet. It can be so hard to find a tender loaf! This lovely, yeasty loaf slices like a dream, and you can slice it and freeze it for travel or to make delicious sandwiches for the school lunchbox.

Parmesan Lemon Thyme Baguettes

Prep time: 20 min, plus rise time • **Cook time:** 15–20 min • **Yield:** 8 servings

Ingredients	Directions
½ batch Egg-Free Yeast Bread (see previous recipe)	*1* Make the Yeast Bread dough as directed but stir in the thyme and Parmesan cheese.
1 tablespoon minced fresh lemon thyme	*2* Cut a piece of parchment paper the length of your baguette pan. Most baguette pans have two indentations to make two loaves at once. You'll fill both indentations with the batter.
¼ cup grated Parmesan cheese	
Sweet rice flour (about ½ cup; exact measurement doesn't matter)	*3* Sprinkle the parchment paper heavily with sweet rice flour. Place ½ of the dough onto the floured paper by spoonfuls, letting the balls of dough touch each other.
	4 Grab the long side of the paper and gently roll the bread away from you. The dough balls will begin to connect, to form the long narrow baguette shape. If this doesn't occur easily, press them together gently with your fingers.
	5 Continue to roll the baguette across the paper until it's completely covered with flour. Lift the paper to the baguette pan and gently roll the dough onto the pan. Repeat with the second half of the dough, rolling it into the second baguette pan.
	6 Cover the pan securely with plastic wrap to hold in the moisture as the bread rises. Let the bread rise in a warm, draft-free place until it doubles in size. Unwrap the pan and cut slashes across the baguette to allow for oven spring.
	7 Preheat the oven to 450 degrees. Place the baguettes gently into the oven and bake for 15 to 20 minutes, or until they're golden-brown and crunchy. The bread's temperature should be 190 to 200 degrees.

Per serving: Calories 252 (From Fat 27); Fat 3g (Saturated 1g); Cholesterol 3mg; Sodium 223mg; Carbohydrate 51g (Dietary Fiber 4g); Protein 8g.

English Muffins

Prep time: 20 min, plus rise time • **Cook time:** 20 min • **Yield:** 8 servings

Ingredients	Directions
2 teaspoons cornmeal	*1* Place eight 4-inch English muffin rings on a Silpat-covered (silicone) baking sheet. Sprinkle ¼ teaspoon cornmeal into the rings; reserve the rest for later.
1 cup (131 grams) High-Protein Bread Flour Mix (see Book V, Chapter 2)	
½ cup plus 1 tablespoon plus 2 teaspoons (89 grams) White Flour Mix (see Book V, Chapter 2)	*2* In a large bowl, combine the High-Protein Bread Flour Mix, White Flour Mix, Whole-Grain Flour Mix, buckwheat flour, sugar, salt, and yeast until the mixture is one color.
¼ cup plus 2 teaspoons (41 grams) Whole-Grain Flour Mix (see Book V, Chapter 2)	*3* Add the water and beat well by hand.
3 tablespoons (30 grams) raw buckwheat flour	*4* Divide the dough evenly among the rings, smoothing the tops to level the batter. Sprinkle the tops with the remaining cornmeal.
1 tablespoon plus 1 teaspoon sugar	
½ teaspoon salt	*5* Cover the dough with plastic wrap and let it rise for ½ hour.
2 teaspoons active dry yeast	*6* Preheat the oven to 375 degrees. Bake the muffins for 20 minutes, or until the internal temperature registers 190 to 200 degrees. They won't brown; that happens in the toaster!
¾ cup water	
	7 Remove the muffins from the oven; let them stand for 2 minutes on the cookie sheet and then remove.

Per serving: Calories 139 (From Fat 8); Fat 1g (Saturated 0g); Cholesterol 0mg; Sodium 147mg; Carbohydrate 31g (Dietary Fiber 2g); Protein 3g.

Note: These are lovely to have on hand in the freezer. If you split them before freezing you can just drop them into the toaster and toast. They're delicious topped with a fried egg, a piece of Canadian bacon, and some Cheddar cheese. Broil until the cheese melts.

Bagels

Prep time: 30 min, plus rise time • **Cook time:** 15 min • **Yield:** 8 servings

Ingredients	Directions
1½ cups (199 grams) High-Protein Bread Flour Mix (see Book V, Chapter 2)	*1* In a large bowl, combine the High-Protein Bread Flour Mix, White Flour Mix, and raw buckwheat flour and mix until the mixture is one color.
½ cup plus 2 teaspoons (81 grams) White Flour Mix (see Book V, Chapter 2)	*2* Add the honey, oil, yeast, and ½ cup plus 2 tablespoons water and beat for 2 minutes.
2 tablespoons (20 grams) raw buckwheat flour	*3* Form the mixture into eight balls. Poke a hole at least 1 inch in diameter into the center of each ball.
1 tablespoon honey	
1 tablespoon vegetable oil	*4* Place each bagel on a 4-inch square of parchment paper. Place the squares on a cookie sheet. Cover the bagels with plastic wrap and let them rise for 1½ hours.
1 tablespoon active dry yeast	
½ cup plus 2 tablespoons plus 8 cups water	*5* While the bagels rise, prepare the water bath. Place 8 cups of water in a large pot; add the sugar. Bring to a boil over high heat.
2 tablespoons sugar	
Toppings: sesame seeds, poppy seeds, coarse salt	*6* Preheat the oven to 425 degrees.
	7 After the bagels have doubled in size, place them, one at a time, into the boiling water, paper-side down. Boil for 1 minute and then turn, remove the paper, and boil 1 minute longer.
	8 Remove the bagels from the water with a slotted spoon; let them drain and place them onto a Silpat-covered cookie sheet. Sprinkle them with the toppings of your choice.
	9 Bake for 13 to 15 minutes, or until the bagels are deep golden-brown. Move the bagels to a wire rack to cool completely.

Per serving: Calories 157 (From Fat 25); Fat 3g (Saturated 0g); Cholesterol 0mg; Sodium 2mg; Carbohydrate 32g (Dietary Fiber 2g); Protein 4g.

Sourdough Starter

Prep time: 10 min, plus rest time • **Yield:** 2 cups

Ingredients	Directions
583 grams brown rice flour	**1** For Starter Mix, combine all the ingredients and mix them together until the mixture is one color. Store this mixture in an airtight container and use it to make the Sourdough Starter.
583 grams sorghum flour	
583 grams millet flour	
290 grams sweet rice flour	**2** For the Starter, combine equal weights of the Starter Mix and water, such as 1 cup Starter and 1 cup water.
74 grams garfava flour	
155 grams white bean flour	
	3 Let sit, uncovered, in a warm spot in the kitchen for three days, stirring the mixture once a day. You're trying to capture yeast spores that are naturally occurring in the air in your kitchen. You'll have more success with this process if you bake some yeast breads in the days before you create a Starter. The Starter is ready when it bubbles and it smells like bread baking.
	4 When the Starter starts bubbling, hopefully by the third day, feed it with 1 cup Sourdough Starter and 1 cup water. Let it grow for a day and then feed it again. Repeat once more and the Starter is ready to use.

Note: Some experienced cooks use unwashed organic grapes in the Starter to give it a boost, but this can add chlorophyll to your Starter. Try capturing wild yeast first by using just this flour mixture and water.

Sourdough Bread

Prep time: 30 min, plus rise time • **Cook time:** 35 min • **Yield:** 24 servings

Ingredients	Directions
150 grams potato starch 150 grams tapioca starch 140 grams sorghum flour 35 grams sweet rice flour 30 grams sugar 10 grams salt 20 grams xanthan gum 10 grams guar gum 1500 grams Sourdough Starter (see earlier recipe) ½ cup water Coarse sea salt (optional)	*1* Using a scale to measure the ingredients, combine the potato starch, tapioca starch, sorghum flour, sweet rice flour, sugar, salt, xanthan gum, and guar gum in a large mixing bowl for a stand mixer. Mix until the mixture is one color. *2* Stir the Sourdough Starter to mix in any liquid that may be floating on the top. Add the starter and water to the flour mixture. *3* Beat on high for 5 minutes. The bread will change from a mass of soft dough to one with some bounce. The dough will look like strands on the sides of the bowl and will gather on the beater. *4* To form a boule, place half the dough on a parchment paper square. Use a spatula to smooth and shape the dough into a ball. Repeat with the second half of dough. *5* Lift the paper holding the balls and place them into a bowl a little bit smaller than the pot you'll use for baking. Cover with plastic wrap and place in a warm spot to rise. *6* Let the dough rise for 4 hours, or until it doubles in size. You can refrigerate the dough instead; it will rise there for 12 hours. If you refrigerate the dough, bring it to room temperature before baking. *7* Remove the dough balls from the bowl using the paper. Using a sharp knife or razor blade, cut slashes into each loaf. Create two parallel lines on either side of the balls, turn them 90 degrees, and slash two more lines to form a square on top. These slashes allow for oven spring. *8* Place an 8-cup ovenproof pot into the oven and preheat both to 450 degrees.

9 When the oven is preheated, carefully remove the pot from the oven with oven mitts.

10 Remove the lid and place the bread dough into the pot, keeping it attached to the paper. Sprinkle with coarse sea salt, if desired, and replace the lid. Put the pot in the oven and set the timer for 35 minutes.

11 When the timer goes off, check the bread's temperature. It should be 190 to 200 degrees and look deep golden-brown. If the bread isn't brown enough, remove it from the pot, place it on the oven rack, and bake it for 5 minutes longer. Let the bread cool on a wire rack.

12 For baguettes, sprinkle a piece of parchment paper or Silpat with sweet rice flour for a crisp crust or millet flour for a softer crust.

13 Divide each half of dough into a long log and sprinkle them with a bit more sweet rice or millet flour.

14 Using the paper, extend and roll the dough into a long baguette shape. Roll onto a baguette pan. Repeat with the other half of the dough.

15 Let the dough rise as directed for the boule, wrapping the pan in plastic wrap.

16 Preheat the oven to 450 degrees. Remove the plastic wrap. Add the bread and bake for 15 minutes.

17 Reduce the heat to 400 degrees, rotate the pan, and bake for 15 minutes more.

18 Test the bread; it should be 190 to 200 degrees and look deep golden-brown. Bake 5 minutes longer if the bread tests done but isn't brown.

19 Move the bread to a wire rack to cool completely.

Per serving: Calories 254 (From Fat 16); Fat 2g (Saturated 0g); Cholesterol 0mg; Sodium 165mg; Carbohydrate 56g (Dietary Fiber 4g); Protein 6g.

Rosemary Parmesan Pull-Apart Rolls

Prep time: 30 min, plus rise time • **Cook time:** 40 min • **Yield:** 12 servings

Ingredients	Directions
One batch Sourdough Bread (see earlier recipe)	**1** Make the Sourdough Bread but don't let it rise yet.
1 cup grated Parmesan cheese	**2** On a large plate, combine the Parmesan cheese and pepper.
½ teaspoon black pepper	
3 tablespoons fresh minced rosemary	**3** Stir the rosemary into the Bread dough.
Extra-virgin olive oil or melted butter	**4** Prepare a 12-cup Bundt pan by spraying with nonstick cooking spray.
	5 Scoop the balls of dough using a Number 70 (⅓ cup or DP-12) ice-cream scoop. Drop each ball into the cheese mixture and roll to coat.
	6 Place each ball into the prepared pan in one layer. Drizzle with a bit of extra-virgin olive oil or melted butter.
	7 Repeat with the next layer of dough, placing each ball of dough on the junction of two rolls below. Drizzle with more oil or butter. Repeat until all the dough is used.
	8 Cover the dough with plastic wrap and let it rise for 8 to 10 hours, until doubled.
	9 Preheat the oven to 425 degrees. Cover the pan with foil and bake for 35 to 40 minutes, or until the internal temperature is 190 to 200 degrees.
	10 If the rolls aren't brown enough, remove the foil and bake 5 minutes longer.

Per serving: Calories 540 (From Fat 50); Fat 6g (Saturated 2g); Cholesterol 5mg; Sodium 455mg; Carbohydrate 112g (Dietary Fiber 7g); Protein 15g.

Fluffy Hamburger Buns

Prep time: 30 min, plus rise time • **Cook time:** 20 min • **Yield:** 6 servings

Ingredients	*Directions*
2½ teaspoons active dry yeast	*1* In a small bowl, combine the yeast and water and mix. Let stand until foamy, about 5 minutes.
¾ cup lukewarm water	
1 cup minus 2 teaspoons (142 grams) White Flour Mix (see Book V, Chapter 2)	*2* Meanwhile, combine the White Flour Mix, Whole-Grain Flour Mix, raw buckwheat flour, dry milk powder, sugar, and salt and mix until one color.
1 cup minus 1 tablespoon (125 grams) Whole-Grain Flour Mix (see Book V, Chapter 2)	*3* Add the yeast mixture and butter and beat together until the dough forms a soft ball.
5 tablespoons (50 grams) raw buckwheat flour	*4* Divide the dough into six portions. Form each portion into a ball.
3 tablespoons dry milk powder	
2 tablespoons sugar	*5* Place the portions into a greased support ring. (See note below for making support rings.)
1 teaspoon salt	
2 tablespoons butter, melted	*6* Let the dough rise in a warm place for 45 minutes. Brush it with oil or melted butter for a soft crust.
	7 Preheat the oven to 350 degrees. Remove the rings and place the pan in the oven.
	8 Bake for 20 minutes, rotating the pan once during baking time.
	9 Move to a wire rack to cool completely before slicing.

Per serving: Calories 247 (From Fat 48); Fat 5g (Saturated 3g); Cholesterol 13mg; Sodium 398mg; Carbohydrate 48g (Dietary Fiber 2g); Protein 5g.

Note: To make support rings, tear off a piece of foil 16 inches long. Fold it in half lengthwise and cut along this line. Fold the foil toward the center from one long edge about 1 inch at a time to form a long, 1-inch wide strip. Form a circle into hamburger bun size, or form an oval shape to make hot dog buns. Alternately, for hot dog buns, form the dough into rods and place in a greased 9-x-13-inch pan, not touching.

Soft Egg Bread

Prep time: 30 min, plus rise time • **Cook time:** 50 min • **Yield:** 8 servings

Ingredients	Directions
2 ¼ cups minus 1 teaspoon (292 grams) High-Protein Bread Flour Mix (see Book V, Chapter 2)	*1* Grease an 8-x-4-inch bread pan with unsalted butter and set aside.
1 ⅓ cups minus 1 teaspoon (177 grams) Whole-Grain Flour Mix (see Book V, Chapter 2)	*2* In a large bowl, combine the High-Protein Bread Flour Mix, Whole-Grain Flour Mix, sugar, yeast, and salt and stir until the mixture is one color.
¼ cup sugar	*3* Add the eggs, butter, and water and beat well until combined.
1 tablespoon active dry yeast	
1 ¼ teaspoons salt	*4* Pour the mixture into the prepared pan. Cover with plastic wrap and let rise for 1 hour.
3 eggs	
¼ cup butter, melted	*5* Preheat the oven to 350 degrees. Bake for 45 to 50 minutes, or until the internal temperature registers 190 to 200 degrees.
½ cup water	
	6 Remove from the pan and cool completely on a wire rack before slicing.

Per serving: Calories 297 (From Fat 84); Fat 9g (Saturated 4g); Cholesterol 95mg; Sodium 391mg; Carbohydrate 47g (Dietary Fiber 4g); Protein 9g.

Note: This tender bread is like challah. For a nice change of pace, incorporate ¼ cup dried currants into the dough before rising.

Basic Pizza Dough

Prep time: 10 min, plus rest time • **Cook time:** 22–25 min • **Yield:** 6–8 servings

Ingredients	Directions
2 ¼ cups minus 1 teaspoon (300 grams) Whole-Grain Flour Mix (see Book V, Chapter 2)	**1** In a large bowl, combine the Whole-Grain Flour Mix, White Flour Mix, yeast, salt, and sugar. Mix until the mixture is all one color.
1 ¼ cups plus 1 tablespoon (196 grams) White Flour Mix (see Book V, Chapter 2)	**2** Add the olive oil and water and beat for at least 1 minute.
1 tablespoon active dry yeast	**3** Immediately press the dough on a greased cookie sheet or a greased deep-dish pizza pan.
1 teaspoon salt	
½ teaspoon sugar	**4** Let the dough rise for 45 minutes. Preheat the oven to 425 degrees.
1 tablespoon olive oil	
1 ¼ cups plus 1 tablespoon warm water	**5** Place the dough in the oven for 10 minutes to partially bake it, remove, and add toppings to make a pizza.
	6 Return to the oven and bake 12 to 15 minutes more, until the toppings are hot, the cheese is melted and beginning to brown, and the crust is golden-brown.

Per serving: Calories 226 (From Fat 31); Fat 4g (Saturated 1g); Cholesterol 0mg; Sodium 390mg; Carbohydrate 46g (Dietary Fiber 2g); Protein 5g.

Note: To make individual pizzas, divide the dough into fourths. Partially bake each for 5 minutes and then bake for 10 to 12 minutes more after topping.

Note: This dough freezes well after partial baking. Shape the dough, let it rise, bake it for 10 minutes, cool it, and then freeze it. To use it, let it thaw at room temperature and then top and bake again.

Vegan Focaccia Bread with Kalamata Olives

Prep time: 30 min, plus rise time • **Cook time:** 30 min • **Yield:** 12 servings

Ingredients	Directions
¼ **cup golden flaxseeds, finely ground**	*1* Combine the ground flaxseeds and buckwheat flour in a large mixing bowl with warm water. Beat for 1 minute to develop the structure because these ingredients act as gums in this recipe.
½ **cup (80 grams) raw buckwheat flour**	
1¼ **cups warm water**	
1 cup minus 2 teaspoons (142 grams) White Flour Mix (see Book V, Chapter 2)	*2* Stir in the White Flour Mix, High-Protein Bread Flour Mix, salt, sugar, and yeast and beat for 1 minute.
1 cup plus 1 teaspoon (133 grams) High-Protein Bread Flour Mix (see Book V, Chapter 2)	*3* Use 1 tablespoon of oil to grease a 9-x-13-inch baking pan. Use another tablespoon of oil to grease your hands.
¼ **teaspoon salt**	
2 tablespoons sugar	*4* Gather the soft dough and press it into an even layer in the pan. It should fill the pan completely.
1 tablespoon active dry yeast	
4 tablespoons olive oil	*5* Sprinkle the dough with rosemary and olives, pushing gently into the dough. Drizzle with the remaining 2 tablespoons of olive oil.
1 tablespoon chopped fresh rosemary	
⅓ **cup pitted kalamata olives**	*6* Cover the pan with plastic wrap and let the dough rise 1 hour.
Coarse sea salt (optional)	

7 Preheat the oven to 400 degrees. Remove the plastic wrap and sprinkle the dough with coarse sea salt (if desired).

8 Bake on the lower oven rack for 15 minutes and then rotate the pan and bake 15 minutes longer, until the temperature is 190 to 200 degrees. Remove the bread from the pan to cool completely before cutting it into squares.

Per serving: Calories 176 (From Fat 73); Fat 8g (Saturated 1g); Cholesterol 0mg; Sodium 166mg; Carbohydrate 25g (Dietary Fiber 2g); Protein 3g.

Vary It! You can use chopped reconstituted or oil-packed sun-dried tomatoes, any grated cheese, or finely chopped cooked meats in place of the olives. Use other herbs, too.

Vegan Pizza Crust without Gums

Prep time: 20 min, plus rising time • **Cook time:** 20 min • **Yield:** 8 servings

Ingredients

½ cup plus 1 tablespoon plus 1 teaspoon (81 grams) Whole-Grain Flour Mix (see Book V, Chapter 2)

1 cup minus 2 teaspoons (142 grams) White Flour Mix (see Book V, Chapter 2)

½ teaspoon salt

⅓ cup (38 grams) corn flour

2 tablespoons (20 grams) raw buckwheat flour

2 tablespoons extra-virgin olive oil

2 ¼ teaspoons dried yeast (1 packet)

1 cup warm water

Toppings of your choice

Directions

1 In a large bowl of a stand mixer, combine all ingredients. Beat with the paddle attachment for 2 minutes. The dough will be soft and spreadable, like frosting in texture.

2 Cut a piece of parchment paper to fit a 10-inch pizza stone for a thick crust. Spread the dough onto the parchment paper. If you don't have a stone, just line a cookie sheet with parchment paper and spread the dough to its edges for a thin crust.

3 Let the dough rise in a warm place for 1 hour. You can reduce the rising time to 30 minutes, but the dough won't be as puffy.

4 Preheat the oven and pizza stone together to 500 degrees. This may take as long as 20 minutes; make sure the stone is very hot.

5 Slide the parchment paper with the dough onto the hot stone. If you're using a cookie sheet, just place it in the oven.

6 Bake for 10 minutes, until lightly browned. If any areas get very puffy, poke them with a fork.

7 Top with tomato sauce or pesto and other pizza toppings.

8 Bake for 10 minutes longer. Cool for 2 to 3 minutes before cutting.

Per serving: Calories 148 (From Fat 35); Fat 4g (Saturated 1g); Cholesterol 0mg; Sodium 147mg; Carbohydrate 28g (Dietary Fiber 1g); Protein 2g.

Cornmeal Pizza Crust

Prep time: 20 min • **Cook time:** 25–30 min • **Yield:** 8 servings

Ingredients	Directions
¾ cup yellow cornmeal	**1** Preheat the oven to 425 degrees. Put the pizza stone in the oven to heat while you make the dough.
⅓ cup minus 1 teaspoon (49 grams) sweet rice flour	
⅓ cup plus 1 teaspoon (46 grams) millet flour	**2** In a large bowl of a stand mixer, combine the cornmeal, sweet rice flour, millet flour, corn flour, and raw buckwheat flour; mix until the mixture is one color.
⅓ cup (38 grams) corn flour	
3 tablespoons (28 grams) raw buckwheat flour	**3** Add the remaining ingredients and beat with the paddle attachment for 2 minutes.
2 tablespoons extra-virgin olive oil	**4** Cut a piece of parchment paper to fit a 10-inch pizza stone for a thick crust. Spread the dough onto the parchment paper. If you don't have a stone, just line a cookie sheet with parchment paper and spread the dough to its edges for a thin crust.
1½ teaspoons baking powder	
½ teaspoon baking soda	
½ teaspoon salt	
1 cup water	**5** Slide the parchment paper onto the hot pizza stone or put the cookie sheet in the oven.
Toppings of your choice	
	6 Bake for 15 minutes, remove, and top with toppings.
	7 Return to the oven and bake for 10 to 15 minutes longer, until the crust is browned and the toppings are hot and melted. Cool for a few minutes before cutting.

Per serving: Calories 146 (From Fat 37); Fat 4g (Saturated 1g); Cholesterol 0mg; Sodium 296mg; Carbohydrate 25g (Dietary Fiber 2g); Protein 3g.

Note: Cornmeal adds great crunch to this simple pizza crust. This crust is a good choice for dinner in a hurry because you don't have to wait for the dough to rise. Top it with anything you like!

Index

• C •

• H •

• Q •

• T •

About the Authors

Ian Blumer, MD, FRCPC: Dr. Blumer is a specialist in internal medicine in the Greater Toronto Area of Ontario, Canada. He has a teaching appointment with the University of Toronto, is the medical advisor to the adult program of the Charles H. Best Diabetes Centre in Whitby, Ontario, and is a member of the Clinical and Scientific Section of the Canadian Diabetes Association (CDA), where he currently serves as Chair of the Dissemination and Implementation Committee for the 2008 CDA Clinical Practice Guidelines. Dr. Blumer is the coauthor of *Diabetes For Canadians For Dummies* and *Understanding Prescription Drugs For Canadians For Dummies* (with Dr. Heather McDonald-Blumer). He can be found on the web at www.ourdiabetes.com. Dr. Blumer would love to get your comments about this book; please e-mail him at celiacdisease@ianblumer.com. celiacdisease@ianblumer.com.

Sheila Crowe, MD, FRCPC, FACP, FACG, AGAF: Sheila is a professor of medicine at the University of Virginia in Charlottesville, Virginia. She is a gastroenterologist with special interests in immune, infectious, and food-mediated gastrointestinal disorders, including celiac disease and food allergies. Dr. Crowe is named in "Best Doctors in America" and is nationally known as an educator, clinician, and researcher. She has served on various committees and panels of the American Gastroenterological Association and many other organizations. Dr. Crowe is the medical advisor to the local "Charlottesvilli" Celiac Support Group. She especially enjoys the opportunity to educate gastroenterologists, other physicians, and patients and their families about celiac disease, whether in Charlottesville, elsewhere in the United States, or overseas.

Danna Korn: Danna is also the author of *Living Gluten-Free For Dummies* (Wiley). Often referred to as "The Gluten-Free Guru" and respected as one of the leading authorities on the gluten-free diet and the medical conditions that benefit from it, she speaks around the world to healthcare professionals, celiacs, parents of celiacs, parents of autistic kids involved in a gluten-free/casein-free dietary intervention program, and others on or considering a gluten-free lifestyle. She has been invited twice to be a presenter at the International Symposium on Celiac Disease and is frequently featured in the media. In 1991, Danna founded Raising Our Celiac Kids (ROCK), a support group for families of children on a gluten-free diet. Today, Danna leads more than 100 chapters of ROCK worldwide. She is a partner with General Mills on its gluten-free initiatives and acts as a consultant to retailers, food manufacturers, testing companies, dietitians, nutritionists, and people newly diagnosed with gluten intolerance and celiac disease.

Linda Larsen: Linda is an author and journalist who has written 26 books, many about food and nutrition. She earned a BA degree in biology from St. Olaf College and a BS with high distinction in food science and nutrition from the University of Minnesota. Linda worked for the Pillsbury Company for many years, creating and testing recipes. She was a member of the Pillsbury Bake-Off staff five times, acting as manager of the search team and working in the test kitchens. Linda is the Busy Cooks Guide for About.com and writes about food, recipes, and nutrition. She has written articles for *Woman's Day, Quick & Simple,* and *First* magazines. Her books include *Eating Clean For Dummies, Medical Ethics For Dummies,* and *Detox Diets For Dummies* (all published by Wiley).

Dr. Jean McFadden Layton: Dr. Layton specializes in celiac disease and gluten intolerance, attracting patients from around Washington State and the lower mainland of Canada. She serves on the board of directors for the Bellingham Gluten Intolerance Group and facilitates the local Healthy Gluten-Free Kids group. Building on the medical oath she swore to uphold, which includes the concept of *docere* (doctor as teacher), Dr. Layton teaches gluten-free baking and cooking classes with the Community Food Co-op and Whatcom Community College. Conveying the ease and breadth of healthy gluten-free food, Dr. Layton has written her well-known blog, *GFDoctorRecipes,* since 2006. As @GFDoctor, Dr. Layton is active in the social media world with thousands of international Twitter followers. Her website, www.gfdoctor.com, and her Facebook sites, GFDoctor and Healthy Gluten-Free Kids, convey even more information to the general public about up-to-the-minute changes in foods and products.

Nancy McEachern: Nancy is a business owner, consultant, author, speaker, champion of gluten-free issues, and mom to a child who had to go gluten-free in high school As the founder of Gluten Freeville (http://glutenfreeville.com), Nancy runs a popular website and writes about all aspects of gluten-free living, including new products, restaurants offering gluten-free menus, gluten-free medical news, travel options for families, practical tips for moms and students, and how to make great-tasting food. Nancy also runs the companion health and wellness Facebook fan page Gluten Freeville. With more than 50,000 members from throughout the world, this large and active online community discusses the everyday struggles and victories of living gluten-free and shares information and advice. Thousands also follow Gluten Freeville on Twitter and Pinterest as a way to connect with the gluten-free community and stay up-to-date on gluten-free news, food, and advice.

Connie Sarros: Connie is a pioneer in writing gluten-free cookbooks for celiacs, beginning at a time when few people had even heard of the disease. She has written six cookbooks, a "Newly Diagnosed Survival Kit," and made a DVD that covers all you need to know about gluten-free cooking. She writes weekly menus for people with additional dietary restrictions and distributes two monthly newsletters. Connie is also a staff writer for other celiac news-letters, and she frequently contributes to celiac magazines. In addition to being a featured speaker at national celiac conferences, Connie travels the country, speaking to celiac and autistic support groups and often meets with dietitians to explain the gluten-free diet.

Publisher's Acknowledgments

Acquisitions Editor: Tracy Boggier

Editorial Project Manager: Carmen Krikorian

Development Editor: Elizabeth Kuball

Copy Editor: Christine Meloy Beck

Technical Editor: Elizabeth Tapp MS, RD, CLT

Art Coordinator: Alicia B. South

Cover Photos: ©iStock.com/george tsartsianidis